Also by Nancy Frederick

Love and Sex Under the Stars, 2014

Dawn Any Minute
Hungry for Love
Touring the Afterlife
A Change of Heart
Starstruck
The Sportin' Life

Love and Sex Under the Stars, 1989
The Lover's Dream
Love Games: Psychic Paths to Love
Palmistry: All Lines Lead to Love
Tarot: Love is in the Cards

Need in-depth information about your love life?
Want to know what really makes your lover happy?

Check out the newly updated and re-released version of Nancy's first, best-selling astrology book, *Love and Sex Under the Stars*, now available for kindle and print.

This is your chance to understand your own heart, and the needs and desires of those you love best. The planets Venus and Mars are the source of everything romantic and sexy about you. In this newly updated and expanded version of her first, best-selling astrology book, internationally acclaimed astrologer Nancy Frederick concentrates on Venus and Mars, the planets of love and sex, and gives detailed information about both planets in every sign. In addition, there are in-depth delineations of all the 144 Venus-Mars combinations. You need to have no prior knowledge of astrology to understand and benefit from the information in this book. Nancy Frederick shows you how to locate the exact position of Venus and Mars at your birth in the easy-to-navigate charts right here in this book. If you know your birthday, you can instantly look up your Venus and Mars—right here. Then she tells you what the planets reveal. To know the secrets of your lovestyle, all you need to know is your birthday! And the same goes for that special someone who's caught your eye. In this fascinating guide to the planets that rule the heart and the sensual passions, Nancy Frederick shows you how to discover your own romantic and sexual requirements: Find out if the lover who turns you on today is the one who will bring you happiness tomorrow and "forever after"; Look into the heart of a potential partner; Please your partner--and yourself; Liberate your sensual self. Love and Sex Under the Stars is an in-depth guide to your personal lovestyle and the key to the romantic needs and desires of everyone you meet.

The Astro Tutor

Nancy Frederick

Copyright 2007 and 2014 by Nancy Frederick
Heart and Soul Press

ISBN-13: 978-0692281284
ISBN-10: 0692281282

All rights reserved. No part of this book may be reproduced or transmitted in any form or by any means, electronic or mechanical, including photocopying, recording, or by any information storage and retrieval system, without permission in writing from the copyright owner.

Portions of this book previously published in Dell *Horoscope* Magazine; reprinted with permission by Dell *Horoscope*.

To Ronnie, Ed, and Jack—thanks for so many great years of collaboration and camaraderie.

Introduction

New Age enthusiasts rely upon astrology for several main purposes: psychological understanding of one's self and others, comprehension of the inner dynamics of relationships, planning events, and predicting the future. As a professional astrologer, I counsel clients all over the world. Being able to help people live happier lives is one of the most rewarding aspects of my career.

Astrology is a complicated subject and a very fascinating one. It's been my pleasure to teach what I've learned, and during the last two decades, I've developed easy to understand techniques to help students learn deep information quickly and without confusion. Astrology magazine readers and people in the online community frequently contact me for advice about how to interpret their horoscopes and indicate that my techniques provide the insight they're seeking in the study of astrology.

For over twenty years, I've been quite fortunate to enjoy a warm and productive working relationship with the editors of Dell Horoscope Magazine. During this period, I've published many articles about astrology and other New Age topics. This book represents a collection of some of my most popular and instructive pieces.

If you're a complete beginner, seeking an understanding of astrology, here's the perfect place for you to start. This book covers the basics clearly and comprehensively and leads you forward toward a greater depth of knowledge. You can open to chapter one, with absolutely no prior knowledge of astrology, and with a little concentration, learn everything you need to know to begin unraveling even the most complicated of horoscopes.

More advanced students can benefit from the chapters in which charts are delineated precisely in an organized fashion which you can duplicate with horoscopes in your own collection. Once you've learned this technique, no chart will be too difficult for you to unravel.

Many people study astrology as a means of gaining better understanding of human interaction, and there are clear explanations and techniques described here to help you become a master at relationship astrology.

Everyone wants to know what the future holds, and this book will give you the necessary tools to look at a horoscope and unravel potential events. In addition, there are insights about how to plan events using astrology.

As a spiritualist, I've spent decades working with spirit in séances, learning to channel guides' messages, and deriving specialized information about the nature of Karma. My single most popular article shows how a horoscope can reveal deep Karmic details of this lifetime and the ones which preceded it. Many horoscopes do reveal shadings from other lives and this is fascinating information, available in the final chapter of this book.

Astrology is all about life lessons and maximizing on your potentials, and in this book, I've offered you easily comprehensible techniques which will help you master the ancient and rewarding discipline of astrology. Good luck!

Table of Contents

Chapter One: Learning the Basics

Here's where you gain the information you need to make sense of astrology. You may have to memorize at first, but soon enough it will all make sense to you and you'll go on instinct.

    The Signs of the Zodiac..11
    The Planets..26
    The Houses...41
    The Major Aspects...57

Chapter Two: The Details

Let's look at each planet in every sign and every house so you see how each placement works.

    Sun 68
    Moon...77
    Mercury..86
    Venus..96
    Mars...105
    Jupiter..114
    Saturn..121
    Uranus...128
    Neptune...134
    Pluto...140

Chapter Three: Speaking Astrology More Fluently

Now that you have a good grounding in astrology, take some time to delve a little more deeply, to ponder the symbols involved and the essential meanings involved.

    Astrology in Action..145
    Combining Astrological Symbols 155

Chapter Four: Delineating A Horoscope
Nothing is more helpful when learning to unravel the meaning in any horoscope than to see how it's done, bit by bit. Here are some eye-opening examples.

    Delineating A Horoscope..165
    Harrison Ford and Clark Gable—The Male Icon...................181
    Martha Stewart..190

Chapter Five: Relationship Astrology

This is why most people study astrology — and you're probably no exception. Once you know what makes someone tick, you want to know what makes him or her a good partner, true love, or best pal..

    Relationship Astrology—Jane Fonda's Three Marriages...........200
    Matt Damon and Ben Affleck—An Enduring Friendship.........221
    Obsessive Love..232

Chapter Six: Predicting and Planning Events

Astrology is as much art as science, as much intuition as supposition, but it's a great tool for planning events and predicting the future.

    Using Astrology to Plan Events..244
    Predicting the Future with Astrology..................................256
    The Predictive Tools of Astrology.......................................265
    The Outer Planets Transiting the Houses............................278
    The Outer Planets Transiting Themselves...........................292

Chapter Seven: Astrology and Spirituality

Astrology provides information that is strongly psychological, but it goes deeper than that and helps us see what life lessons we must learn in this incarnation. It can also point toward former lifetimes and the journeys we're completing.

    Karmic Astrology...303

About the Author..316

Chapter One: Learning the Basics— Signs, Planets, Houses and Major Aspects

Here's where you gain the information you need to make sense of astrology. You may have to memorize at first, but soon enough it will all make sense to you and you'll go on instinct.

Part One: The Signs of the Zodiac

Everybody knows Sun sign astrology. I remember back to somewhere a little after the Big Bang when I was in college and had just met my future husband. It was inevitable, and sure enough I asked, "What sign are you?" He replied Cancer and I nodded, thinking, yes that was a good match for me. Where exactly did I get that information? I have no idea! It was probably something I distilled from an article in a fashion magazine, but it seemed reasonable, and it made sense to me at the time. I didn't study astrology for real for more than another decade, and then I learned how little I'd really known.

Astrology is more than just Sun sign information. It's more than just yes if you're an Aries, you get along better with a Gemini than a Capricorn. To me, astrology is a system of encodement for every particle of energy in the entire universe. To decode astrological symbolism is to speak the very language of God, to have at your fingertips all the mysteries of the universe, there to be unraveled and understood.

The beginning of astrological studies is a little daunting, because there is so much to learn and understand. I've often said it's the hardest, and most rewarding, thing I've ever studied, and even after several decades, I still feel that way. There's nothing more rewarding than immersing yourself in something challenging and emerging with an excellent grasp of the subject, a knowledge deep enough to look at a horoscope and feel in your gut the essence of who that person is. It allows you to cast aside the superstition, to eschew being one of those people who spouts clichés as though they are somehow relevant. "Mercury is retrograde," the hobbyist will say, assuming that means something very profound. It means something, but there's much more to astrology than that omnipresent cliché.

When we think of Sun sign astrology, its like little personal cartoons. Aries are self-centered. Virgos are picky. Scorpios are sexy. And on and on! We use it as a shorthand to describe people without really getting to know them. And, amazingly, these clichés are more often on the money than out of left field. Perhaps that's why so many people who know no astrology know Sun signs.

A better way to learn astrology is to de-personalize it. Think of the energy of each sign as a vibration, a buzz, a harmony. And taken all together they form the symphony that is life itself. The Zodiac tells a story, and there is always a sense of progression, a spiral that moves upward, rather than a collection of different but equal qualities. Each sign builds upon the ones that follow it, relates to the ones that precede it, and interacts with every other sign. They are all building blocks of energy, vibrations that harmonize, one with the other.

Let's begin at the beginning, and go through the Zodiac sign by sign. And at the end of this chapter, you'll find several charts summarizing what's covered so you can refer to them for a quickie refresher.

Aries
Cardinal Fire, ruled by Mars, planet of action.
Keywords: Action, haste, impetuous, self, beginnings, creative.

The Zodiac begins in spring, just as does life in nature. Baby animals are born, sprouts burst from the earth, and life renews itself in spring, so perhaps that's why Aries is the first sign, rather than Capricorn, even though the latter lies at the beginning of the calendar year. More than any other sign, Aries is about beginnings and it does represent the spark of life, not just in the sex act, but in the essential "I," the existence of a self. Just as a baby is completely self-involved, a creature whose needs must come first, the energy of Aries is about that essential "I."

Self is a huge dimension of the Aries energy. There are so many aspects to the nature of self, huge disciplines have been created to explore the philosophy involved. If a tree falls in the woods and nobody is witness to it, does it make a sound? There are so many answers to that question, but as a Virgo, I can think of three: 1) who cares; 2) existence without witness is still existence, so of course it does; 3) the self that is the tree is there and certainly would know of its own demise, both in feeling and in sound. At the bottom of this question, is the essence of "I." It's all about what it takes for life to be real, and that is an essential Aries issue.

Aries is pure force, and it's all about that sense of energy — action, movement, doing. That's what a true beginning is all about. Something that never was before now is, action has occurred and a beginning has begun. That is the vibration of Aries. Its energy is not so much force motivated by thought, but something more raw, more elemental, unthinking and primal. If you decide to go clean out your garage, that is not the energy of Aries. Turning the key in your car's engine and hearing it roar is closer to Aries, but still not quite. Even having raw, animal sex isn't really Aries energy, although planets in Aries do tend to be very sexual. Instead Aries is the energy of your heartbeat, the hum of your blood flowing through your veins, it's the sperm speeding toward the egg, the thud of a jogger's sneakers on the road. Take a match and light it — that's the energy of Aries.

Planets in Aries behave in a way that is very direct. There is always action, force, and self-involvement. Aries is meant to serve the self, and planets there serve the person who has them. Self-sacrifice is not a dimension of Aries; it is the opposite of that energy. Just as an infant will not cease crying and say "No, no, take care of big brother first," Aries is about the "I." Who am I and what do I need are the questions asked by planets there, and before an answer is even intellectualized, action is taken. To feel hunger and grab food is Aries. To desire anything and grab — also Aries.

Taurus
Fixed Earth, ruled by Venus, planet of love and beauty.
Keywords: Practical, sensual, financial, determined, steady, earthy.

Once we move into the concept of grabbing, we come to Taurus. If life is created in a Petrie dish — well okay the actual creation of life is more about Scorpio — but at the moment of creation, when the cells have merged, and divided, or whatever they do, and a new cell has been given life, then we have Aries. As it begins to live and survive, we have Taurus. The Petrie dish too is Taurus, as it provides the physical sustenance.

Taurus is about the earth, and many people feel that the sign's true ruler is not Venus, but our home planet, and that makes a great deal of sense to me. Taurus is about taking from the earth all forms of sustenance and building a life. If you envision a seed dropped into the ground, the sprout bursting from it is Aries, but the earth is what nurtures it over time and allows it to grow and thrive. That energy belongs to Taurus and explains why there's such an affinity for gardening within the sign.

Just as Aries is immediacy, haste, and speed, Taurus mimics the earth itself in its stability, longevity, and constancy. You could drop a seed into a cluster of dirt embedded in a tire tread, and it might sprout, but for it to thrive, that would not be a good source of life. Thus what follows Aries must be stable, reliable, and unwavering, or life would be simply an impulse that would spark then die.

The material world is a very important thing, and although it does come down to a simple metaphor about seed sprouting, it's also more complex than that. Our modern world revolves on a financial foundation as much as an agrarian one, but either way, it's still the energy of Taurus that sustains us.

Planets in Taurus are practical, stable, and down to earth. Sometimes that energy seems a bit plodding, and often life moves too slowly when Taurus is involved. The Taurus energy is about sticking with something for as long as necessary — in stark contrast to the Aries energy, which is about beginning then racing off to something new. Together they form a sort of couplet, and pairs are a very big theme in astrology.

Gemini
Mutable Air, ruled by Mercury, planet of communication.
Keywords: Intellect, communication, movement, changeable.

Although life for a single-cell organism in a Petrie dish is relatively simple, for the rest of the universe it's more complex. Even that microbe in the dish requires air, and that's where we come to Gemini. Gemini is not just air — oxygen — but the breath of life itself. It's the world around us, the vast environment in which we each play such a small part. Once life begins and is physically nurtured, there is a need to look around and ask, gee what's this all about? That is the vibration of Gemini.

The third sign describes thought and communication. What did the philosopher say? I think therefore I am. Thought is the natural result of life, and sometimes I wonder, does a tree think? I know animals do. Sensation is part of everything in the universe and although the plant world probably doesn't have the sort of thoughts we find among animals, there is still a need for air. It is the air that carries the seeds which fall on the ground and bring new life to different places, and air that promotes life. Ideas are shared through verbalization — the essence of Gemini — but in the breeze that carries seeds to distant places, isn't that the same as an idea—the idea of a certain type of life, shared with a new environment through air current rather than words. Plant life generates oxygen, and we might concede that's their form of communication. But it is through ideas and words that we humans make sense of the universe—and all these processes are the vibration of Gemini.

Look at our most primitive ancestors, determinedly recording moments of their existence through cave paintings. Okay, they lacked the diversion of television, but something within their tiny brains compelled them to document life as they knew it—as a way of sharing their truths, proving the validity of their existence, or perhaps as a way of gaining a tighter grasp on the only reality they knew. That is the Gemini impulse.

Planets in Gemini focus on thought and communication. They're speedy, and changeable, and seem often to act upon whim. Gemini's energy is fleeting and can't be tied down for very long. It is quite different than the rather plodding Taurus vibration, and although its speed is more akin to Aries, it's not so raw and self-directed. It's like a child, racing around, seeking stimulation, and moving distractedly to the next interesting diversion.

Cancer
Cardinal Water, ruled by the Moon, planet of emotions.
Keywords: emotional, sensitive, nurturing, family-oriented.

Scientists have done studies and they've discovered that babies will die if they're not held, despite having adequate physical nutrition. Emotion, while invisible, is a necessary dimension of nurturing, and we all require a mother's touch. Baby animals who've lost their mother can be given to another animal to suckle, and they survive, like a chipmunk, whose picture was in the paper recently, as it nursed on an adopted Chihuahua mom, alongside puppy siblings. This is the energy of Cancer, the loving breast that suckles life, the mother's arms that cradle the child, the family that welcomes new life.

We see the natural progression here, life beginning in Aries, supported by the earth in Taurus, given breath in Gemini, and placed at mother's breast in Cancer. If the universe has a heart, it is described by Cancer, which embodies the need to nurture and sustain life, no matter what. In Cancer is the respect for life of all sorts, which is why nursing mothers will embrace a child not their own—sometimes not even their own species. There is the sense that life itself has such value, such importance, that it must be respected, sustained, and nurtured, and that is the vibration of Cancer.

Parenting is one of the most essential impulses throughout all of life, and in each person's heart is the ability to feel that mother urge, and whether man or woman, there's the Cancer-driven sense that life should be given a chance to thrive. It's easy to translate the love in our hearts for our own children to appreciation and affection for any living creature, particularly the young. That's why people adopt pets, nurse fallen baby birds and release them, and so on. We all have the capacity to have a mother's heart—and that is Cancer.

Within that maternal well spring is a sense of empathy—the emotional bond that ties all of us to each other. You are like me...we relate to each other...your needs are no different than mine. We all need love, a hug, some tenderness. This is the beautiful energy of Cancer.

Planets in Cancer behave emotionally—they function on instinct, on impulse, based on the gut far more than the head. They're passionate, and determined, and quite strong. Never assume that something emotionally driven is weak; the truth is just the opposite.

In Cancer, we come to the end of the first third of the Zodiac, and complete the idea of life beginning and being nurtured. In the next grouping of signs, we move beyond survival into actual living.

Leo
Fixed Fire, ruled by the Sun, planet of self-definition.
Keywords: self-expression, creative, sunny, generous.

We all have some inner sense of destiny, the sense of what we were meant to do with our lives, based on an inner reality. When you ask someone what he does for a living, the answer is I am.... People don't usually say I work as a bus driver, a doctor, an astrologer. They say I am a teacher, a pilot, an architect, a homemaker. Perhaps it's because of modern society that we define ourselves according to profession, but I feel it's more that through a sense of who we are, we choose what we do, and together that is our self-expression. Animals do this too. My cat feels it's his job to protect the house—on the level he is capable of doing—and that means he must alert me when a bug has invaded our home. He takes this work very seriously and does it diligently—he sees himself not as a pampered freeloader, but rather someone with responsibilities—and skills.

Obviously there are other ways to express one's identity than a career. We are parents, movie lovers, amateur actors, cooking enthusiasts, hang gliders, golfers, and so on. But by the very act of creating adjectives, we say I am.... And this is Leo energy. Within Leo is the impulse not just to express who we are, but to do a good job at it. Golfers keep trying to improve their score. I read cookbooks avidly and by now know as much as a pro chef. It's not just my avocation, but part of my identity, and I love cooking something spectacular to share with those I love. It's a Leo process, involving passion, and generosity! And perhaps that's why showmanship is part of the Leo vibration, because once we get good at something, it's a lot sweeter to share it than to keep it just for ourselves.

Through Leo, we express the self we've developed in Aries. As fire signs, Aries and Leo share an affinity, the need to be and to express that energy of being. Planets in Leo are passionate, just as they are in Aries, but they're steady, strong-willed, and imbued with stamina. The act of creation—the cell splitting and coming into being—takes a nanosecond, but life takes a whole lifetime, thus the Leo energy is radiant and long-lasting—like the Sun—compared to the spark of a match that is Aries. Of course that doesn't mean that Aries people are inconsequential and Leos are in any way better. We're talking here about energy as a vibration, not the Sun signs!

Virgo
Mutable Earth, ruled by Mercury, planet of communication.
Keywords: analytical, organized, particular, helpful, work.

In Leo we see the child scampering out into the world, ready to cultivate and express his talents. In Virgo, the world must be analyzed, quantified, and organized for optimum survival. School isn't just about playtime and fun; there is work involved. The student must organize his little cubby, help playmates put away blocks, diligently attend classes, being sure to bring the materials needed, and persevere until growth is attained. This is the Virgo energy! While reading and writing come under the province of Gemini, the labor itself is Virgo.

Life is complicated, and with Virgo, we try to manage all the details that are relevant to us. In the most primitive worlds, survival depends on developing keen skills, staying acutely aware, and attending to life's needs. This is the energy of Virgo—doing what must and should be done—very carefully. During the process of working to make life function smoothly, it's very easy to look around and see other people in need of some help, a detail that needs attending, and perhaps that is the source of the Virgo tradition of service.

In Leo, we share who we are, but in Virgo, we notice other people and their needs—apart from our own. That's another aspect of tradition of service, but it's also emblematic of developing complexity as the Zodiac progresses. In the first earth sign, Taurus, the material world is a source of sustenance. In the second, Virgo, the urges are still material, practical, and they represent a more intricate approach to survival. Where Taurus is steady, Virgo is more flexible, allowing for change, so that if need be, different avenues to the same goal can be found.

Planets in Virgo behave in an orderly, analytical fashion. They think before they act, and that explains the connection to ruler Mercury, planet of the intellect. Planets in Virgo are relatively unselfish and they usually are willing to consider the needs of other people. Despite being one of the flexible, mutable signs, Virgo tends to insist on completion before moving on, so planets here feel obliged to finish what's begun. Virgo is the sixth sign of the Zodiac, and here we see the beginnings of the person being oriented toward others. In the second half of the Zodiac, we look beyond ourselves and see who and what we are in relation to the rest of our species, and the universe itself.

Libra
Cardinal Air, ruled by Venus, planet of love and pleasure.
Keywords: relationships, courtly, social, interactive, seeking balance.

The poet e.e.cummings wrote, "I am through you so I." This is the essence of the Libra energy. We all seek a mirror of who and what we are, reflected in the eyes of other people. In Virgo, we see adulthood, and the capabilities of surviving in the world independently. But in Libra we realize that we all need someone else to survive happily. Life is about more than food and shelter, more than mother's love, it's about interpersonal dynamics. We all seek a significant other. That philosopher who posed the question about the sound a tree does or doesn't make falling in an uninhabited woods might more properly have posed this question instead: Does a heart which beats alone make a sound?

We all need love, and a desire for mother's love, and the successful realization of it, leads to an adult desire for the love of a mate. And of course, there is the biological need to renew the species, and in Libra that first step is taken, gazing into the eyes of someone else. We see an interesting progression here relating to the Cardinal signs. In Aries, the life begins; in Cancer it is nurtured by mother; in Libra it reaches out for a mate. There's always assertiveness, always a goal.

When you ask friends why they love a certain mate, the replies are, "he understands me;" "she listens;" "we feel comfortable together;" "he makes me feel special." And so on. Love is a function of recognition, and that is the essence of Libra, and of the e.e.cummings line. There is much validation in knowing that another person can see in us what we think is there. Remember Tom Cruise in *Jerry Maguire* saying, "You complete me." That describes the Libra impulse, as well as the Libra desire for balance. You can't ride a see-saw by yourself!

Libra is the second air sign, and like Gemini, its urge is to connect. Although we leap into lust with our eyes, we fall in love through conversation. A shared word here or there is usually the turning point for lovers, and that means that love grows from what probably began as innocuous conversation. In Gemini, the urge is to explore all ideas, but in Libra it's about sharing the thought most relevant to who we are. Gemini is more scattered — any stimulus will do, but in Libra there is a goal — the mating dance!

Planets in Libra are assertive, yet genteel. It's always possible to get what you want without steamrollering anyone else, and that's the Libra urge — in contrast to the way planets operate in opposite sign Aries. The self is served, but others are also considered.

Scorpio
Fixed Water, ruled by Pluto, planet of birth, death, and extreme transformation.
Keywords: incisive, secretive, sexual, healing, transformational.

Everybody knows that Scorpio is the sexy sign, and in following the path of the Zodiac, it makes perfect sense. What do you do after you've fallen in love and given your heart away? You propagate the species! Merging is a very important Scorpio concept. In Libra we share hearts and flowers, but in Scorpio, we merge, heart, soul, and loins. In the spirit world, where there is nothing physical to form a barrier, entities merge in love — they flow into and out of each other, like streams of steam fused in the air. Reproduction is an act of merging — the sperm with the egg, you and I together forming a new life that is part of each of us. But more than that, in sex we merge with God. Really great sex leads to mind-blowing orgasms, and a merging of the two souls involved, just as they might merge in the spirit world, and in the act of surrendering completely to orgasm and merging with a lover, we lose ourselves and gain the infinite.

Surrender is wonderful, yet also very scary. There are risks involved and courage is needed to give in to that state of complete vulnerability. Perhaps that's why the Scorpio energy must be fierce, yet also private. And when we mate so completely that our souls merge, we come away with some part of the other person, and are transformed. With a soulmate, this is a beautiful act that enriches and heals, but with the wrong partner, negative vibrations—and diseases—can be absorbed. That's why sex was meant to be a special—and holy—thing.

Scorpio is a vibration of pure energy, and that's where the healing dynamic comes in. A healer can see murky energy swamping a sick person, and can draw it out and reflect it up to the universe, where it can be cleaned and transformed. The ability to do this takes skill, and a need to cloak oneself so as not to absorb the murkiness.

Scorpio is the second Water sign, and is just as emotional as Cancer, but its sentiment is less obvious. Where Cancer is Cardinal, and seeks a goal, namely survival and love, Scorpio is Fixed, and its vibration is steadier, more constant, and in this sign there is the need to persevere and endure—even if times get difficult. Scorpio is the third Fixed sign, and along with Taurus and Leo, it describes the soul's need to survive, express itself, and merge with a partner. These are daunting tasks that require commitment—and longevity, thus the Fixed signs are the steadiest—so that the race doesn't give up and wash out!

Planets in Scorpio are determined, and they can withstand calamities and endure. There is a strong desire here to get one's own way, by sheer force of endurance—or by emotional manipulation. In Scorpio there is a sense of divine right—it should be done—and thus it seems acceptable sometimes to exploit others. Just as in opposite sign Taurus, in Scorpio there is a good deal of selfishness, but there can also be great self-sacrifice and healing of others. The higher vibration of Scorpio—and all the signs, for that matter, is to be a tool of God.

With Scorpio we come to the end of the second third of the Zodiac which is about connecting and merging beyond the self. We move into the final grouping of signs and look out beyond ourselves into life as a whole.

Sagittarius
Mutable Fire, ruled by Jupiter, planet of expansion and personal growth.
Keywords: philosophy, culture, society, religion, law.

It seems as though there is no greater gulf between two signs than exists between Scorpio and Sagittarius. Scorpio is so fierce and personal, so passionate and intense, and Sagittarius seems so mellow, so outwardly focused. There is a bridge, however. How many times have you heard idealists say, "I can't bring a child into a world like this." It's quite natural after the sex act is complete and a child is on the way to begin worrying about the world that infant will inhabit. Will the world be safe, can the child grow and survive without threat of annihilation, and how can we make the world a better place for children and grandchildren? The impulse to ask those questions is how we move from Scorpio into Sagittarius.

The Sagittarian vibration is very intellectual, like its opposite sign Gemini. It seeks knowledge, but more than just information, Sagittarius seeks truth. What is the meaning of life? How do we fit into the greater scheme of things? In Scorpio, through sex, comes the awareness of God, but in Sagittarius, spirit is pondered more intellectually, rather than viscerally. Religion and law have often merged within primitive societies, and God is frequently used as a justification for seizing political power. We've witnessed this recently ourselves through terrorist and middle east power mongers, but in other equally primitive societies this mentality flourishes as well. A sense of God inspires a desire for law and order—for right, which sometimes unfortunately translates into might. That would be a perversion of the Sagittarian ideals. The Sagittarian vibration is to see that we are one with God and therefore with each other. It is to seek good, to do good, and to expect good to be done. Violence in the name of God is not Godly—nor is it Sagittarian.

Sagittarius is the third Mutable sign, and its energy is flexible, and changeable. In Gemini, there is a need to assimilate information; in Virgo, the desire to analyze it, and in Sagittarius comes the search for the deeper truth that evolves out of the study of reality. It is the final Fire sign, and is just as passionate as Aries and Leo. The Fire progression is existence, self-expression, meaning of self within all of existence.

Planets in Sagittarius are outgoing, friendly, and they seek a connection to the world around them. They are changeable, and often flow from one course of action to another without hesitation.

Capricorn
Cardinal Earth, ruled by Saturn, planet of structure, Karma, and earthly life lessons.
Keywords: achievement, practical, financial, building.

Do you know anybody who doesn't care about success? I don't. However we define success, it matters, and we all want to feel we've made something worthwhile of ourselves. Strictly speaking, success isn't always defined by money and achievement, but in Capricorn, those qualities are very important. The Capricorn vibration is about building something of substance in the outside world. In Capricorn, we see how we're defined by those around us, how we measure up, how much we've achieved compared to everyone else.

Capricorn's energy is traditional, and it values home and family just as much as does its opposite number, Cancer. Although Capricorn is about achievement, it's seldom about solitary wealth; Capricorn believes in building success—professionally and personally. If you could write your own obit, how would it look? That's the Capricorn question, because within that sign is the idea of the entirety of a life, of summing up, of leaving something behind. That's why it's the builder of the universe and the sign of the architect. The structure of things comes under the Capricorn umbrella.

Capricorn is the final Cardinal sign, and like the others it is goal-oriented, perhaps more so than any other sign. We see the progression from Aries' creation of the self, to the Cancer nurturing, to Libra reaching out to a mate, to Capricorn, building a life to sustain it all. As the final earth sign, Capricorn is very much about building wealth and maintaining property. It is the culmination of the Taurus need to derive sustenance from the earth and the Virgo desire to organize the material realm.

Planets in Capricorn are assertive, financially motivated, and determined to build something of value. There is always a sense of work and evaluation of progress within Capricorn.

Aquarius
Fixed Air, ruled by Uranus, planet of innovation and sudden change.
Keywords: innovative, society, intellect, pioneer, friendship.

In Capricorn, we see the need to succeed as a member of society so that a solid life and family can be sustained. In Aquarius, we turn our attention to society itself. What is necessary to make this world a better place? That's the Aquarian question. A philosopher said that society is only as strong as its weakest member, and perhaps that's where the Aquarian need to do positive social work derives. We can't just take care of ourselves if we're to survive as a people; the stronger ones must offer a helping hand to the weak.

Aquarius is the sign of the dreamer, of thought unbounded by limitation, and within that sign is limitless potential for positive change. It certainly stands for doing unto others as you'd have them do unto you, but it's also about allowing people to have their personal freedoms. In the ideal world, everyone would do just as he pleased, yet would always want to make the good choice, the positive decision, the right thing. That is Aquarius, and it is a very appealing notion. When you combine anarchy with a social consciousness, you get the perfect world! The essential Aquarius question is, "What if...."

Friendship is another dimension of this idea. Offering a helping hand to someone in need doesn't imply a paternalistic mindset but rather a desire to lift up someone who's faltering, to make him equal, to build a stronger society, person by person. It's easy to see how Communism could have derived from the Aquarian vibration, one comrade in step with another. Of course the ideal and the reality are often incongruent because human beings are seldom as perfect as the ideals they create.

Aquarius is the energy of the future, of innovations our forebears could never have dreamed. Could a cave man have thought of the telephone? No, but he managed to build a hammer. It's the same thing—it's the urge to do better, to change things, to use the power of intellect to create a better future.

Aquarius is the final Fixed sign and it's very stable, and even stubborn. Its great flaw is in assuming it always knows best. The brave new world it envisions may be perfect for only one person—the architect of the dream, but Aquarius seldom sees it that way. It assumes it knows what's best for itself—and for everyone else. Despite this flaw, Aquarius has heart, and a relatively selfless desire to make things better. In Taurus we saw the stability of life, clinging to the earth; in Leo self expression; in Scorpio reproduction, and in Aquarius, the desire to make society a good place for the future. Aquarius is also the final Air sign, and as such it's all about ideas and communication. Gemini is about unrestricted access to information, Libra about communicating one's essence, and Aquarius is about using the power of the mind to build a better world for tomorrow.

Planets in Aquarius function with determination. They are strong and often quite unwavering, just as they are in opposite sign Leo. There is always a sense of sharing, also something in common with Leo. But planets here are often the most impersonal in the Zodiac as they're driven by ideas rather than any form of emotional desire.

Pisces

Mutable Water, ruled by Neptune, planet of illusion, delusion and spirituality.

Keywords: emotional, sensitive, creative, psychic, endings.

In Aquarius we deal with powerful, abstract, intellectual urges. In Pisces, we transcend the intellect altogether and connect more viscerally to the source of all ideas, all creativity. God is the well of inspiration for all of life, and Pisces is the lightning rod for that inspiration. Creativity is a force in the ether, and people absorb its energy, then manifest it in creations of their own. That's why we often see two similar but previously unwritten movies (books, recipes, whatever) come out at the same time — the idea was in the ether and two writers internalized it and made it their own.

Pisces is the energy of divine emotion, the force of unselfish universal love, of the self liberated from its individuality so it can merge with the infinite. The negative vibrations of Pisces can be very harmful — drugs, alcohol, delusions, and they lead to lies and self-deception. Thus it's not a good thing to use drugs as a tool to feel a oneness with God. Do it the hard way — learn to meditate because that will enhance your vibration rather than sullying it. Pisces says, I release my personal needs, let me be a vehicle to serve the universe. That is a beautiful thing, when done honestly, but it is hard to do here on the earth plane where we have obligations, responsibilities, and personal stresses. It's a goal to think about, however.

Pisces is the final water sign, and as such is deeply emotional. Cancer is about nurturing, Scorpio about merging, and in Pisces we relinquish the self and merge permanently with the infinite. Is the spirit world a Pisces dimension? I think so! Pisces is also the final Mutable sign, and it is the most changeable, most flexible vibration in the Zodiac. Gemini flits from one idea to the next, Virgo seeks perfection through trying different possibilities, Sagittarius tries on systems of belief in search of ultimate truth, and in Pisces is the ultimate reality — the purity of God's love.

Planets in Pisces are often unselfish to the point of dysfunction, changeable, wavering, and very creative. They are driven by emotion, and can thus lack the stability of energy motivated by thought.

The charts below summarize what we've discussed in this section. Next we'll discuss the energies of the planets and help you see how they combine.

Sign	Mode	Element	Ruler	Keywords
Aries	Cardinal	Fire	Mars	Action, haste, impetuous, self, beginnings, creative
Taurus	Fixed	Earth	Venus	Practical, sensual, financial, determined, steady, earthy
Gemini	Mutable	Air	Mercury	Intellect, communication, movement, changeable
Cancer	Cardinal	Water	Moon	Emotional, sensitive, nurturing, family-oriented
Leo	Fixed	Fire	Sun	Self-expression, sunny, creative, generous
Virgo	Mutable	Earth	Mercury	Analytical, organized, particular, helpful, work
Libra	Cardinal	Air	Venus	Relationships, courtly, social, interactive, seeking balance
Scorpio	Fixed	Water	Pluto	Incisive, secretive, sexual, healing, transformational
Sagittarius	Mutable	Fire	Jupiter	Philosophy, culture, society, religion, law
Capricorn	Cardinal	Earth	Saturn	Achievement, practical, financial, building
Aquarius	Fixed	Air	Uranus	Innovation, society, intellect, pioneering, friendship
Pisces	Mutable	Water	Neptune	Emotional, sensitive, creative, psychic, endings

Elements	Are always	Signs Represented have these traits in common
Fire	Passionate, active, creative	Aries, Leo, Sagittarius
Earth	Practical, earthy, material	Taurus, Virgo, Capricorn
Air	Intellectual, social, communicative	Gemini, Libra, Aquarius
Water	Emotional, sensitive, deep	Cancer, Scorpio, Pisces

Modes	Are always	Signs Represented have these traits in common
Cardinal	Pro-active, leaders, energetic	Aries, Cancer, Libra, Capricorn
Fixed	Steady, completion-oriented	Taurus, Leo, Scorpio, Aquarius
Mutable	Flexible, changeable	Gemini, Virgo, Sagittarius, Pisces

Part Two: The Planets

How many times have you heard a disbeliever grouse that the planets—including the nearby Moon—are like a zillion miles away and thus how could they possibly affect us mere mortals grounded way down here on earth? I've had this discussion numerous times and you know what—I agree. The Moon may be sending little moonbeams at us, but that's not what defines our world. Venus doesn't send little cupid arrows and make us fall in love. It's more complicated than that! And simpler!

When I had this argument with a physician friend some years back, he asserted that it was absurd to think that the planets affect us. And I said, guilelessly, sure, it's like cloning—how could they take a snippet of skin and produce a whole animal? No way! Can't be done! His voice got patient, and he endeavored to explain to me, the biological uninitiate, that the blueprint for the whole is encoded in each and every cell. Well, gotcha! The same is true of the universe.

Astrology is a system of encodement for the sum and total of universal energies. The universe is a living, breathing thing, made up of spirit, matter, and energy. Like some spectacular whirligig, each infinitesimal element clicks together with each other and is part of a much greater, constantly changing, whole. And although the movement of the planets doesn't exactly cause things to happen (unless a meteor comes crashing down into your satellite dish), it is all part of the life breath of the universe. So when we notice the planets whirling along, and we describe human life, future events, and personality traits according to the rules of astrology, it works, because we are deciphering the symbols that encode the energy patterns describing the whole universe. There is no bit of energy, no personality trait, no event, that can't be described by astrological symbolism. That's why it's such a fascinating discipline to study.

Now let's go through the planets one by one to see how they function and interrelate. At the end of this section is a chart summarizing what we've covered here so that you can use it for speedy reference.

Sun, planet of Identity, ruler of Leo
Keywords: Identity, task in this lifetime, personality.

The Sun is a star, not a planet, and of course neither is the

Moon, but for astrological purposes we include both heavenly bodies in the roster of planets. The Sun is the planet which defines basic identity, personality, and more important, the Karmic form of self-expression the soul incarnating under that sign wishes to express. We are all more like our Sun sign than different from it, and we all have many traits in common with those born under our own Sun sign. We all have a task in this lifetime, and of course that task goes beyond Sun sign astrology and encompasses the whole of any individual horoscope. But there are, shall we say, categories of self-expression, and the Sun signs define those very well indeed.

The Sun is about who we are in the outside world, how we thrust ourselves into life, the person we are when among other people. Some people say it also represents the father, paternal figures in general, and of course men, particularly in a woman's chart. This makes sense because any individual's sense of identity is formed not just at birth, but by refinements made over time based on individual performance, social interaction, and role models surrounding that person. What we can do, expect to do, and want to do is molded to a great extent by the guidance and expectations—whether positive or negative—of Daddy.

A college professor of my mother's generation, once told me that when she discussed her future with her father, she was told that if she wanted to be a professor, she could marry one. Another older woman wanted to play the cello, but her father felt that sitting with legs akimbo to do so was unseemly. Apparently the only instrument he felt appropriately ladylike was the waffle iron! Thus society too— and the times in which we live—impede who and what we can be. People in restrictive societies must deal with caste, sexism, social classes and other limitations and those things are very important, yet still the horoscope will apply. A horoscope could show scientific abilities, manual dexterity, and courage, and the person could end up a neurosurgeon—or a butcher. The horoscope is the same but its expression depends on the level that person can reach based on individual expectations and starting points in life.

The Sun functions differently in each sign and the basic purposes of life through the Zodiac are as follows. With Sun in Aries, development of the self; in Taurus, to derive sustenance from the material realm; in Gemini, to make sense of and communicate about the world around one; in Cancer to build a loving family and home; in Leo, sharing with others through self-expression; in Virgo, to analyze one's world and help others; in Libra, to find the mate who completes one's destiny; in Scorpio, to merge body, mind, and soul; in Sagittarius, to discover the truth and meaning of life; in Capricorn, to build a successful life; in Aquarius, to create a better world; in Pisces, to be one with all that is.

Obviously these are the foundations upon which personality will rest, not the tiny details that actually describe an individual. For example, if you're a Pisces, and your basic task is to be one with all that is, you're not going to sit around 24/7 meditating and releasing yourself into the void. But you do feel a kinship with people, animals, spirit, and so on, and you have a better developed sense of empathy than many others, and you are psychically attuned to vibrations that others can't feel. Those are the details of how your energy functions, but it all flows from the basic essence that is you, being one with all that is. And every other sign functions similarly.

But just because it's the Taurus task to derive sustenance from the material realm, that does not mean Taurus is incapable of being one with all that is. It just means that in choosing to incarnate as a Taurus, a person is building a life based upon that foundation. I'm a Virgo and in my life path I analyze and organize, yet here I am a metaphysical counselor and I constantly release myself to channel Spirit and to share that information with other people. That's what you might call a Pisces profession, being one with all that is, but when the information comes in via psychic means, my approach then is to analyze and make sense of it all, so I'm doing Pisces work but in a Virgo way. That's the way that Sun signs function. We are what we are—like Popeye!

Moon, planet of emotion, ruler of Cancer
Keywords: emotions, childhood, domesticity, mother.

The Moon describes your inner world, your emotions and the way you feel about yourself, life, and the world. The Moon shows your childhood, the way your mother treated you, the nurturing you need, and how you share yourself with other people. The Moon is not just emotional, but also domestic. It shows the sort of home you need and how you organize your cupboards! Compatible lunar pictures help a lot when combining households with someone because it means that you will agree on which way to point the spoons. Taken together, the Sun and Moon deliver a complete picture of the self that is you—inside and out, and they form one of the couplets that are so prevalent in astrology, like pairs of animals boarding Noah's Zodiacal Ark.

A positive emotional picture is very important in every aspect of life. If you feel good about yourself, life's challenges can be met and vanquished. If you don't, even the littlest problems feel monumental.

Roseanne Barr tried for a long time to have another child in her middle years, because she had finally come to the realization of how to mother and she said the key was simply to "tell you you're wonderful." She's not wrong, is she? Even mischievous children deserve a mother's love and with that sort of unwavering support, someone can grow up and do great things.

The Moon in a horoscope will always show what to expect from a person, how well you can count on someone, and how that person feels about everything. In a man's chart it often describes the sort of woman who appeals to him.

The Sun is essential, but without a strong Moon, there will be problems in that life. There is a single imperative describing the Sun through the signs, but there always seems more to say about the Moon.

With Moon in Aries, you act, based upon emotion, usually without thinking, and seldom with empathy or any long-standing focus on other people. The emphasis is on YOU. In Taurus, material things have an emotional dimension, and you require a comfortable home, filled with possessions. You often show or feel love through the exchange of money or things. In Gemini, the emotions are fleeting and transitory, lack depth, and are less emphasized than experience and knowledge. It's easy for you to feel comfortable with any number of people and your attachments change with your moods. In Cancer, your feelings are deep and you require the love and security of a home and family. You mother everyone! In Leo, you enjoy sharing your beautiful home with people whose affection warms your heart. You love children and keep your own inner child alive. In Virgo, you need an orderly world and have a strong sense of what's appropriate as a life path. You seem a bit austere because you save deep feelings for private moments when it's seemly to be vulnerable.

With Moon in Libra, you need a significant other to function harmoniously and love sweet, romantic gestures. In Scorpio, your emotions are intense, and sometimes scary, and you shield them from prying eyes until you feel safe with that person. You yearn for a mate whom you can trust, heart and soul. In Sagittarius, you feel one with just about everyone and you are comfortable in a tent or a palace, because all lifestyles have something appealing. You share your ideas and your feelings equally, but are seldom awash in emotion. In Capricorn, you restrain your emotions in order to accomplish something in the world. You have traditional values and your home is very important as a bastion of security. In Aquarius, you want to adopt the world. You feel a kinship with everyone and will share anything you have with someone in need. In Pisces, you are deeply emotional in ways you seldom can express. You trust your heart and your gut, and even if they lead you in difficult directions, you feel confident it's the right choice. You connect with everyone and can absorb feelings from people, plants, and objects.

Mercury, planet of communication, ruler of Gemini and Virgo
Keywords: thought, intellect, communication, movement.

With the Sun and Moon, we see who a person is, but once a self is formed, we need to be able to express that energy to other people. That's the province of Mercury. Ask ten people to explain the identical thing to you and you'll get that many different explanations, different approaches to the idea, different styles of speaking, and different emphasis. Mercury is how we make sense of the world around us and how we share that vision with other people.

The energy of Mercury is sparkling, like those twinkling Christmas lights. It functions best in air, which allows the purity of its ideas to float through the ether. The pairing of Mercury with Gemini is a perfect fit. Gemini appreciates ideas and doesn't require limitations to discern which are worth bothering with. Gemini will discuss anything quite happily, then when boredom intervenes, move on to the next topic. Libra, the next air sign, understands Mercury too, and in Libra, the planet of communication tends to flirt, and change its mind. But then it's at least as changeable in Gemini. Mercury doesn't object, because it's content when minds are changed! In Aquarius, Mercury also works well, though it's more controlled, more bent toward science, technology, and outrageous ideas. But in all air signs there is flair of communication, an ease with words.

Mercury also rules Virgo, an earth sign, and that's not as good a fit. Virgo is analytical, and that is a Mercury process, but Virgo demand thoroughness, completion, and that saddles Mercury with restrictions—but also produces concrete results. In Taurus, Mercury moves more slowly, and is attuned to methodical processes, detailed work. In Capricorn, Mercury focuses on what's relevant, and useful.

In water signs, Mercury tends to move slowly and rather uncomfortably, because in water sensation happens below ideas and seems more meaningful than mere thought. Not everything can be quantified by words, and that's pretty much the position of all those whose Mercury lies in water signs. In Cancer, the tendency is to enjoy conversation because of the connection with the person, but not to listen to specific things being said. In Scorpio, deep ideas are interesting, and there's an urge to unravel some secrets, but not always to share them. In Pisces, the truth of life is complex and far beyond words, and in general Mercury here either spins its wheels, or prefers to be succinct and to rely on impressions rather than the stated word.

Mercury is rather comfortable in fire signs, and it shares ideas with passion and volubility. In Aries, there is lots of talk, and Mercury here often dominates the conversation. In Leo, Mercury likes artistic expression and takes pride in its own intelligence. In Sagittarius, Mercury wants to explore the meaning of life and vibrates with intellectual curiosity.

Venus, planet of affection and beauty, ruler of Taurus and Libra
Keywords: love, affection, pleasure, romance.

When I first began studying astrology, I knew both the Moon and Venus had to do with love, and because of that I was bewildered. If they both were about love, what was the difference? One day I had an epiphany. Venus is about the love you give to other people! If there's a planet that best describes the good life, it is Venus. Love, beauty, romance, pleasure, art, jewelry, and so on! That's Venus!

With Venus, we reach out, wanting to share ourselves, wanting to give our hearts, and to receive the same in return. Venus is about inter-personal connection, based on affection and appreciation of the other person. Venus does not require the object of affection to be deserving—there is no system of ratings involved. It is simply one heart reaching out to another, one person seeing something happy and simpatico in another, a hand wanting to be held.

Venus is the second Yin planet, and taken together with the Moon (and sometimes also Neptune), we see the emotional dynamics in any individual. The Sun may be the identity in a horoscope, but Venus and the Moon are its heart and soul. Venus is the way a woman expresses her femininity, the way a man shows tenderness, and what he seeks in return from a woman.

Venus describes taste as well, and that makes perfect sense. Whether it's a person, a place, a thing, it's all about what we "like," what feels harmonious—and pretty to us.

As the ruler of Libra, Venus makes perfect sense. Its airy, courtly, artistic, affectionate nature is perfectly expressed in the sign of one-to-one relationships. Life is better when walking arm in arm with a compatible significant other. In Taurus, Venus also works well, although here is it more earthy, more sensual. There are more physical pleasures rather than ethereal ones, more of an emphasis on food than on dancing, more touch and less talk. Either way, Venus is quite delightful.

Venus is generally considered to work better in some signs than in others, and certainly there are levels of compatibility. In the very nature of Venus is the desire is to reach out, to connect with someone else, and that implies a willingness to put someone else first, at least some of the time. Thus signs which are comfortable with that concept make a better home for Venus.

In Aries, Venus is rather self-centered and the desire is to receive love more than to give it, and Aries has no problem dragging a desirable object of affection back to its cave. In Gemini, Venus changes its mind a lot—and has few problems overcoming rejection because of this blessedly short attention span. It seeks an intellectual connection first and can best be wooed with words. In Cancer, Venus seeks a companion of the bosom, someone to nurture and be nurtured by. In Leo, Venus seeks a partner who is desirable and attractive, sometimes a showpiece, but also a worthy mate. In Virgo, Venus wants to serve and shows affection by doing favors, often asking little in return. It's earthy though, and sensual too. In Scorpio, Venus is passionate and desires to possess the object of its affection, to transcend together in a holy fire of love. In Sagittarius, Venus seeks inspiration and can be satisfied by serial relationships that are filled with cultural diversity. In Capricorn, Venus seeks security, and wants to share a solid life. In Aquarius, Venus seeks a best friend, and sometimes doesn't even care about mating if the pal factor is pleasant enough. In Pisces, Venus seeks to give and receive unconditional love.

Mars, planet of action, ruler of Aries
Keywords: action, sex.

Venus is Yin—receptive, rather than active, and it uses a sort of personal magnetism to draw to it what is desired rather than going out and grabbing. Venus embodies the concept of attraction and together with Mars, it forms another couplet, the one describing love and sex in the Zodiac.

Mars is easy to understand. It's about action—and grabbing. You want it? Go get it! That's Mars, baby! The energy of Mars is hot, fast, and unapologetically selfish. Mars is about aggression, assertiveness, the way you thrust yourself into the world, what you consider yours for the taking, and how you go about that process of grabbing. Mars is confidence too, courage, and on some level self-esteem. Of course the Sun is identity, and a good Sun will reflect positive self-esteem, but with a strong Mars, there's a sense of being able to do what must be done, the confidence that attempts can be made and they will succeed.

Tony Danza gets up at daybreak, even when he's filming, because he refuses to miss a daily workout. He says that way he can run faster than any bus ...and "feels invincible." Mars is exercise and physical vitality, and that feeling of invincibility certainly helps achieve whatever is desired out in the world. Mars is a Yang planet, and it works in service to the Sun. What the person wants and needs can be procured through Mars. Wherever there is physical activity, there is sex, and Mars describes the sex drive. It's how a man sees his masculinity, the sort of man a woman desires.

As the planet of energy, Mars is responsible for many of the events we experience. Other planets set up the possibilities, and Mars rolls along and delivers the action, thus it's very important to consider when reviewing transits to a horoscope.

Mars in Aries is perfectly matched. They are both self-focused, assertive without apology, and action-oriented. In Taurus, Mars moves so slowly as to be rather uncomfortable. It has stamina, but maintains too long courses of action that might better be abandoned. In Gemini, Mars is speedy and flexible, has excellent reflexes, but often changes its mind half way through any action. In Cancer, Mars is driven by emotions, acts on gut feelings, but is nevertheless quite assertive, as this is a Cardinal, goal-oriented sign. In Leo, Mars has stamina, and enjoys receiving kudos for a job well done. In Virgo, Mars is restrained and tends to over think action before taking it. In Libra, Mars is so focused on others that it's hard for it to be assertive enough in its own behalf. Libra is Cardinal, however, and ultimately Mars does take action, though often in ways that are subtle rather than direct. In Scorpio, Mars is intense and passionate, and very sexual, and often it manipulates to get its own way. In Sagittarius, Mars is active and energetic and loves to travel across the globe. In Capricorn, Mars is harnessed toward achievement of goals and can be a very effective leader in this Cardinal, focused sign. In Aquarius, Mars is determined and can sustain its desired course despite many obstacles. In Pisces, Mars is rather uncomfortable, because its energy tends to drown in the watery emotion and it feels ashamed about putting itself ahead of others.

Mars is the final personal planet. After this, we move forward into the next couplet of energy, Jupiter and Saturn, planets that describe vibrations generations have in common.

Jupiter, planet of expansion, ruler of Sagittarius
Keywords: expansion, personal growth, luck.

Jupiter affects all the babies born during the twelve months it remains in a sign, which probably explains why teachers say some years of students are more simpatico than others. The energy of this, the largest planet in the Zodiac, is warm and expansive, like a balloon being filled with Helium. Jupiter shows the things that are naturally easy for us, the qualities we've mastered and have little difficulty using, and it shows areas upon which we can happily expand. The lore of Jupiter is that it's the planet of luck, but in reality, it's simply about positive expectations leading to hoped-for results.

As one famous psychic told me years ago, Jupiter is Santa Claus. It certainly represents the sense that there are infinite possibilities in the universe and that we all can get what we need. Jupiter is also positive role models, fathers and grandfathers, teachers, the male energy that nurtures and supports growth, but not the stern taskmaster or drill sergeant. That would be Saturn. Jupiter also represents religion and law, in a positive, philosophical way. These are the systems of belief and order upon which society rests. Where Jupiter lies, we think of more than just ourself or our individual needs. We reach out, do good, try to help, share, and be part of something greater, and that is why its energy is so expansive.

Jupiter and Sagittarius are a perfect fit. Both have verve and passion and feel a kinship with diverse forms of life. The Sagittarian imperative toward justice and religious freedom comes from Jupiter. It also bestows the love of travel to explore distant realms and experience distant cultures. Sagittarius is one of the most expansive signs, is always reaching for connections to others, and wishes good things on just about everyone.

Jupiter in Aries is more restrictive, because it functions to expand the self, but it can be a good thing because it encourages the person to become his or her best self. That's the Jupiter by word—the good thing. In Taurus, Jupiter seeks expansion in the material realm and can bestow wealth. In Gemini, breadth of scholarly exploration is emphasized. In Cancer, there is the desire to nurture the world, and perhaps to adopt. In Leo, showmanship and creativity are accentuated. Jupiter in Virgo is somewhat restricted because of the Virgo need to get everything in perfect order, but it can lead to better systems of organization—like the development of the card catalog at the library and so on. It's also beneficial for health systems. In Libra, it brings a solicitous mate—or perhaps a surfeit of applicants for the position! In Scorpio it brings religious passion, the desire to heal and convert, or maybe an excess of sex. In Capricorn, it's rather restricted in the pursuit of success, but can lead to achievement that benefits others as well as the person in whose chart it lies. In Aquarius, there is a desire to make a better world, and Jupiter is quite happy inspiring innovation, but feels a bit uncomfortable when too much eccentricity is expressed because after all, Jupiter is very traditional. In Pisces, it encourages spiritual growth, universal love, and a do-good mentality that can heal the world.

Saturn, planet of Karma, ruler of Capricorn
Keywords: timing, Karma, limitations, restrictions, life lessons.

Ancient astrologers, and some misguided current ones, felt that Saturn described everything bad that could happen to us. As Jupiter was the planet of expansion and good things, Saturn represented limitations and calamities. Saturn's energy is dry and restrictive, like a belt being tightly cinched at the waist.

There is no question that Saturn does describe what is difficult for us, because it represents the Karma that we've incarnated to discharge. We all know the feeling of being not terribly adept at something and working hard to improve. The need to master a difficult task is the essence of Saturn. While Jupiter endeavors to hand life to us on the proverbial silver platter, Saturn demands we work for it.

Thus Saturn represents the stern taskmaster, the parent who has the ability to punish, the demands placed upon us that feel burdensome, but which must be met in order to feel good about ourselves. Saturn provides a series of checks and balances so that we may review, revamp, and move forward again. When sewing, sometimes it's necessary to pull out the stitches, make adjustments, and resew. That's Saturn at work, stopping to correct mistakes before moving onward.

Saturn has a strong affinity with the earth, with timing, and it describes the rules in this realm of life. It's the last planet visible to the naked eye and represented the end of Zodiac to ancient astrologers. Saturn describes the lifespan—the time allotted to accomplish our Karmic goals. And it relates to the structure—of just about everything, from the inner structures of personal expectations, the way a person has organized his external life, to the outer foundations of the physical things that support life.

Saturn as the ruler of Capricorn makes perfect sense. The Saturnine ideal of achievement built through consistent effort over time is the Capricorn credo. Saturn works best in signs that are comfortable with discipline and have the stamina to invest effort for the long-term. But in every sign placement of Saturn, there is a Karmic message. In Capricorn it indicates a person who's had success and squandered it and now must build it slowly with concerted effort. In Aries, there's a Karmic need to develop a strong personal identity, not to be a contentedly bleating sheep in the herd. In Taurus, you must follow your heart, not sell out for money. In Gemini, the need is to emphasize intellect, but often as a result there's little money. In Cancer, there's a Karmic history of intertwining your life with the wrong people and the task now is to find those who will love and support your efforts—and to let those who will not leave your life. In Leo, you must find the courage to express yourself and to develop your talents rather than squandering them.

Saturn in Virgo is very comfortable and it counsels a healthy mind in a healthy body. The tendency to concentrate on only the intellect or only the physical must be released. In Libra, Saturn is supposedly exalted, and supposedly works very well, but the Karmic message here is that in other lifetimes you've abandoned mates and now will realize what that feels like when lovers leave you. Reverence for commitment must be learned. In Scorpio, Saturn demands responsibility in choosing sex partners, and other people with whom you allow your energies to merge. In Sagittarius, Saturn asks you to trust your heart in choosing what beliefs must create the foundation for your world. In Aquarius, you must learn to be more selfless, to reach out and help those around you without expecting anything in return. And in Pisces, Saturn demands more grounding, not to give your life away to drug use and mind-bending substances or pursuits, but to maintain a grasp on the self while merging with the universe.

After Saturn we move out into the void, to the planets that have been discovered only since the telescope gave us the power to look farther than mere eyeballs can take us. These are the planets that describe the more complex, universal energies.

Uranus, planet of sudden change, ruler of Aquarius
Keywords: sudden change, high technology, innovation, eccentricity.

Uranus forms the first bridge beyond the personal and out into the universe, and it's a higher octave of Mercury, planet of communication. Uranus' energy is bright and crackling, the electricity that we use to power our telephones. It represents the great new idea, and in cartoons, how is an idea represented? A light bulb comes on above the head. That is classic Uranus. All inspiration, all creativity, and all ideas come from God, and are out there crackling with energy, waiting for a human lightning rod to channel them down into our earthly realm.

That's where the idea of sudden change comes in. A fabulous new idea changes the world completely, and life is never the same afterwards. And similarly, an insight can change your personal life as well. You can be sailing along contentedly in your rut when suddenly everything changes and you're on a new path, the direction that best suits you now. It feels like a disruption, but the Uranus quantum leap merely represents the manifestation of an idea whose time has come, the change that was building all along.

Uranus remains in a sign for about six years, and that means a whole cluster of people born during that time are affected by a need to seek changes in the area defined by that particular sign. All of society is affected and pretty much an entire generation is defined by this energy. Life is a constant process of evolution and that means challenging the accepted norms and moving away—and up—toward something better. That's where Uranus comes in. It's always healthier to remain relatively detached from the status quo and willing for the next phase to begin. That way the effects of Uranus come as a pleasant change rather than a hideous shock.

In your horoscope, Uranus shows ways in which your generation will become unburdened of the past and will reach for a brave new world. In my Baby Boomer generation, we had Uranus in Cancer and we saw the breakdown of the traditional family unit and all sorts of new groupings of people who nevertheless define themselves as families, changing roles among men and women, children being conceived in-vitro, and so on. We went from Donna Reed to Kate & Allie while growing up. This is the way Uranus work—it takes what we're accustomed to and provides a new set of standards that usher in a more modern age, and as such, its rulership of Aquarius makes perfect sense.

Neptune, planet of illusion, ruler of Pisces
Keywords: spirituality, illusion, delusion, creativity.

Neptune is the energy of spirit, and it is wonderful to behold, but difficult to deal with here in our Saturn-bound earthly reality. Neptune says something doesn't have to make sense to be true, that the facts and the truth are often incongruent, that the truth lies beyond reason, deep in your soul—and perhaps, over the rainbow! Neptune's vibration is misty; it's the fog, damp and mysterious. The spirit world is quite magical. There are no physical barriers and entities flow into and out of each other, merging at will. They are part of all that is. And so are we, but it's more difficult for us to feel those sensations while alive on earth, trapped as we are in our skins.

The key to Neptune is being willing to open up, willing to let that vibration flow in. The problem is that we can't always tell if what we're receiving is a heavenly benediction or a wacky delusion created in the recesses of our own minds. That's the challenge. But Neptune would say either way, what you're getting has some validity. All that is radiates around us, and we are welcome to absorb whatever we choose. Neptune also rules drugs and alcohol, and people do tend to absorb those things in a mindless, pleasure-seeking, identity-releasing way. It's just not a holy way.

Neptune is a higher vibration of Venus and it offers unconditional love. It also dishes out delusional relationships with sleazy partners who seem wonderful but who in fact are not. But the act of giving love without restraint is a holy one, and even when the relationship falters, the love can still be regarded as a blessing. That's the thing with Neptune — things and their opposites are often equally true and there is no genuine need to draw lines or to quantify. Experience is the key.

Neptune is the mind of God, I often think, vast and limitless, and perhaps that's why universal love — and evil — exist, because in God's world there is a place for everything, yet a desire for all to be beautiful. Could not evil flow over to good, with the right application of unconditional love? That is Neptune! On the earth plane, Uranus functions very well, breaking apart the usual and inserting the unusual. But Neptune is our entrée into realms far beyond our own, into the world beyond earthly life, beyond physical reality, and its our introduction to God.

Neptune remains many years in a sign and truly defines the confusion of a generation. In mine, it was in Libra, and that brought about free love — and Woodstock! Neptune's rulership of Pisces feels right. It helps release the individual and to absorb the universal vibration of spirit, of creativity, of love, no matter what. However Neptune is involved in your horoscope, it will cause you to release the ego, and to put other people first. This can be a good or a bad thing — depending.

Pluto, planet of transformation, ruler of Scorpio
Keywords: birth, death, extreme transformation, sex, healing, manipulation.

Pluto is at the end and the beginning of everything. Like a cosmic garbage disposal, it transforms one thing into the raw materials of another. Pluto is the Big Bang, the orgasm, the violence of birth, the finality of death. We live in the flesh and are accustomed to the idea of death, but the reality of existence is that at the core of our spark of life lies spirit, and once created, spirit does not die, it just transforms. When we die, only the flesh is gone, but the spirit remains.

Pluto is what lies beneath all things, the secrets of reality, the passion and pure force of the universe. If Neptune is the mind of God, Pluto is God's power to create and destroy. Pluto is a higher octave of Mars, planet of action, and together they describe the sex urge. The sort of sex done more for exercise and physical release is Mars, but the sex that grips your heart and soul—and produces a child—that's Pluto! Pluto is the power of creation, and that's why the urge to manipulate is so seductive. Wielding power feels good, and it's tempting, though unhealthy, to play God.

Transformation is at the heart of creation. What do they say you can't make without breaking a few eggs? Lots of things! Pluto represents an exchange of energy and that allies it with both sex and healing—and I guess, cakes and soufflés. Sex can be very healing, of course, because at its best it is a holy exchange of love and the life force. When you remove sex from that process, you have one entity channeling in positive energy to, or removing negative energy from another entity--healing.

Pluto's changes are final, but they lead to rebirth. That's the cycle of life. Something lives, dies, becomes mulch, and from its gases arises new life. Pluto remains in a sign for many years and it signals breakdown across society in those areas. In my Pluto in Leo generation, we saw huge changes in the way we define and express ourselves. Pluto's connection to Scorpio is quite clear and explains why Scorpio people are so sexy and magnetic. That's the power of Pluto—to offer a Svengali to remold you into a new entity, or simply to provide the insights that allow you to change yourself into someone better.

The chart below summarizes some of the ideas we've discussed in this section.

Planet	Rules	Yin/Yang	Keywords
Sun	Leo	Yang	Identity, task in this lifetime, personality
Moon	Cancer	Yin	Emotions, childhood, domesticity, mother
Mercury	Gemini/Virgo	Yang	Thought, intellect, communication,
Venus	Taurus/Libra	Yin	Love, affection, pleasure, romance
Mars	Aries	Yang	Action, sex
Jupiter	Sagittarius	Yang	Expansion, personal growth, luck
Saturn	Capricorn	Yang	Karma, limitations, life lessons
Uranus	Aquarius	Yang	Sudden change, high technology, innovation
Neptune	Pisces	Yin	Spirituality, illusion, delusion, creativity
Pluto	Scorpio	Yang?	Birth, death, transformation, manipulation

Part Three: The Houses of the Horoscope

What is the center of the universe? You are! It makes perfect sense that in astrology, a discipline ruled by Uranus, the planet of individuality, that we are each the center of our own universe. Your horoscope is a map of the heavens at the moment of your birth. The earth — and you — are at the center of this map.

People often talk about their rising signs — or Ascendant — and some folks have an idea what this means. It's how you look, how you seem, and so on. But it has an astronomical designation as well as an astrological one. The rising sign is the constellation of the Zodiac on the horizon — rising — at the moment of your birth.

Imagine your tiny infant self, looking up at the sky, just after your first gasp of air. There lies your horoscope, all the constellations lined up precisely according to the time of year — and time of day — and within them are reflected the planets that will describe your personality, Karmic tasks for this lifetime, and upcoming future events.

In the first section of this chapter, we learned the meaning of the signs, then we explored the planets and their vibrations. Now, we look at the houses, which form the structure of the horoscope. You can certainly know a great deal about anyone simply by looking up that person's planets in the ephemeris. You know where the Sun and Moon lie, where the planets are, and that gives you some sense of who that person is. But you need the houses to construct an actual horoscope, and to see much more information. So let's go through the houses, one by one and discuss their meanings. A chart at the end of this section summarizes what we're learning now.

First House: Image you project

The Ascendant, or rising sign, lies at the center left position on the chart, and that is the beginning of the first house. We move from house to house in a counter-clockwise direction. The first house is how you project yourself into the world, your appearance, your image. Often the Ascendant reflects the Sun or Moon sign of a parent, and perhaps that's why (at least astrologically) we resemble our parents.

The energy of the first house is very immediate, and it's a sort of in-your-face place in the horoscope. Everyone feels this energy about you and it describes the first impression you make. Planets here are very intense, and their vibration colors everything in your life. In fact, I feel that there's something Karmic about first house planets. To me it means that those are energies you haven't fully assimilated in other lifetimes, vibrations that are not totally comfortable to you. So if in this lifetime you come in with first house planets, you say, okay, I'm going to deal with this energy every moment of this lifetime, and when I'm done, it will feel natural to me. It's also possible that you have a weakness for certain planetary vibrations, and that tendency to favor those energies in an unbalanced way can be corrected by having first house planets. When you have a lifetime in which you constantly deal with those vibrations, you learn the need for balance and modulation in all things and in future lifetimes will no longer get sucked into that vibration to the exclusion of others.

With the Sun in the first, you're front and center all the time, and like the many actors who have this placement, you must express yourself! The Moon here is intensely emotional and every encounter seems to radiate with feelings. There's no way you can ignore your emotions — or those of other people. Mercury here makes you a chatterbox, and a bit of a wiggler too. Venus gives beauty and popularity. Mars makes you assertive, but often people who have this placement waver between the desire to take action and the fear of doing so. The lesson is to learn appropriate use of aggression. Jupiter here is outgoing and expansive, often also to the waistline, but is nevertheless popular and cheerful. Saturn implies a need to learn responsibility but can also bring some health issues, but at least overweight isn't usually one of them. Uranus makes you tall, and also quite a bit of a rebel. Neptune can make you a movie star (like Harrison Ford) but it makes you hard for other people to decipher. The lesson is to learn to trust, let go, and be part of all that is, but not so severely that you don't create a sense of individuality. Pluto tends to attract power struggles and can make you a bit fearful. Judicious use of power dynamics is the lesson.

Second House: Money, resources.

The second house is about money and resources. In the ancient days, that's all it was about, but modern astrologers tend to say it's about values. I don't really agree because values are spread all through the horoscope. For example, I love my daughter, so is she now a second house item? I also value free time, daydreams, animals, cookies and the color pink. Can we say that any of those things belong in the second house? I think not. To me it makes the most sense to keep it simple and say the second is the house of earned income, material resources, and money in general.

The second can have a strong tie to the ego, depending on what planets lie there. If you have Sun or Mars here, your identity is often boosted (and conversely deflated) by your earning power (or the lack thereof). Clearly this is not a healthy approach to life—or finances. With the Moon here, emotional decisions are made for financial reasons, as in the case of a woman who marries for money. Mercury here tends to make you talk, write, or think about money. Venus here is similar to the Moon, and the tendency is to overspend on personal pleasure, or to desire a consort who will foot the bill for fun. Jupiter here can bring wealth and Saturn the reverse, and certainly with Saturn here, the desire is to conserve what resources are present, no matter how abundant they may or may not be. Uranus brings financial ups and downs—or perhaps the chance to make a living as an astrologer or in a high-tech field. Neptune would seem to vaporize the resources, but in fact can bestow emotional detachment from money that results in tremendous wealth, perhaps from pharmaceuticals, oil or other similar fields. Pluto imparts the tendency to sell out for money, so watch out for those who will manipulate you because they know you want the cash.

Third House: Communications, siblings, neighborhood.

The third house is about the world around you. It describes your siblings, which would be your immediate world as a small child, but also your neighborhood, which is the world you enter when you're old enough to leave the house. It's local travel too. It's about communications, so learning your first school lessons would come under the umbrella of this house. And the third represents publications, the newspaper, television, and so on. It's how you reach out in the world and how the world communicates with you.

Planets in the third are outgoing and friendly and they seek a connection. With the Sun here, you're a chatterbox who loves to strike up a conversation. You might also be a writer. The Moon gives you many potential contacts and you feel a certain kinship with many people, and an interest in their lives. You might feel a sense of extended family as part of your identity, like Fran Dresher, who hails from Queens and Tony Danza, whose Brooklyn is still so much home to the long-transplanted star. Mercury is right at home here and loves to talk, read, learn, and write. Venus gives you lots of friends and social contacts and might bring you true love while strolling on a street or running for a bus. Mars seeks local mini adventures here and might become a determined scholar. Jupiter brings a love of knowledge and an ability to communicate on many subjects with just about anyone. Saturn requires you to pitch in and make your neighborhood a better place, or to support your siblings in their times of need. Uranus might transport you to an exotic neighborhood, give you unusual siblings, or make you a high-tech expert. Neptune here inclines you toward non-verbal communication, an affection for the cinema, or unusual neighbors—perhaps even alien sightings! Pluto here tends to bring annoying neighbors who want their own way, and the same could be said of siblings, but you do have a fighting chance to overpower them with persuasive verbiage.

Fourth House: Emotional foundation, mother, home.

At the bottom of the chart we have the Imum Coeli, or IC, the cusp of the fourth house, and the point of emotional foundation. The fourth is the house of your childhood, the emotional foundation that gives you inner strength—or inner angst. Just about everyone has a mixture of the two, and most of us have some unresolved childhood issues we must return to and grapple with now and then throughout our lives. The fourth also describes your home, and physical surroundings. It describes Mom, too. So you might say that the experience you had as a child, the mother whose teachings you've internalized, and the home of your youth combine in this house to create the emotional life and home you will build as an adult.

Planets here are very emotional, and tend to be tinged with childhood vibrations. With the Sun here, you are intensely private, often connected very strongly to your childhood, and you yearn for quiet time in a cozy home. The Moon is similar and intensifies these desires. This is the natural home for the Moon, and it is comfortable here, and indicates a deep bond with your mother. Mercury inclines you to talk or write about childhood experiences, like Proust who wrote so passionately about his childhood love of those French dunking cookies, Madeleines. Venus in the fourth gives you a desire for a pretty home and affection for entertaining in it, and describes a loving mother. Mars could make you a home handyman, always redoing. It also could indicate a life in the company of men, perhaps like monks who live in a monastery, and could indicate that a man acted as a maternal figure. Jupiter here brings a large and showy home, with a generous mother. Saturn indicates a cramped dwelling and a mother who was perhaps a bit too stern. Uranus describes an unconventional childhood, like those people who were raised communally in an ashram with hippie moms, and it indicates an open, airy space and love of modern furnishings. Neptune could get you that bungalow by the sea, but Mom might be rather absent, flaky, or too busy in her own world to notice you. Pluto indicates family power struggles and a sense of pressure from your mother that develops into stresses—and plumbing problems—in adult living environments.

Fifth House: Creativity, romance, pleasure, children.

The fifth is the house of pleasure, creativity and self-expression, children being a bit of all three. The fifth is a house of happiness and fun and it's carefree in many ways. This is where you express your joie de vivre, the indefinable qualities that make you special.

Planets in the fifth are inclined toward pleasure and often are rather frothy and lacking in weight or seriousness. With the Sun here you might go on the stage and become an actor, or you could be a celebrated party boy—or girl! Either way you're playful and enjoy sharing your inner lights with others. The Moon here is equally social and you want lots of children. Mercury might want to write or to burn up the phone lines in frivolous, fun chit chat. Venus is a party animal in the fifth, with a tender heart for children. Mars here is very athletic and can signal a career in sports. Jupiter may bring you one too many romances—or children—and Saturn consequences to an excess of partying, or problems with your children. Uranus inclines you to indulge in risqué romance with unusual partners, or to become an avant garde artist. Neptune here seeks true love, but may find as many disappointments as pleasures—and a too-heavy hand on the bottle. Neptune here often signals someone who drinks as a sort of hobby—or romances with equal irresponsibility. Pluto seeks the passion of a lifetime and may indicate flagrantly sexual affairs of the heart.

Sixth House: Work, health, service, pets.

The sixth house is about work and health. This is the day to day labor of going to a job rather than the profession that defines you. The sixth is very much the hum of daily life, and that's how it relates to health, in the way you follow health regimens and adhere to a beneficial diet. This is also the house of service to others, and pets, and of course we could say that pets serve us by subjugating their lives to our world.

Planets in the sixth attempt to behave responsibly. They're serious and conscientious. The Sun here is busy and seems to turn everything into some sort of job. Often people with Sun here go into medical fields. The Moon is a bit of a hypochondriac and tends to develop minor illnesses when there are emotional upsets, but it can help you develop close emotional bonds with coworkers. Mercury concentrates on work and may develop manuals for its efficient completion. There may also be travel on business. Venus in the sixth brings romance with colleagues, and may be used in an art-world career, but it might be a bit subjugated to the work and less romantic than in other houses. Mars here makes you a dynamo at work, and your unstoppable enthusiasm for your job can bring advancement; or you could work in a Mars field—as a butcher, physio therapist and so on. Jupiter can bring you a cushy job. Saturn is right at home in the sixth and will tend to keep you working because one of your life lessons is professional responsibility. Uranus can do just the opposite and make work opportunities erratic, give health issues like irregular body rhythms, or provide a high tech career. Neptune brings health issues that are hard to define, and a need to seek alternative health care. You may also have trouble deciding upon a career or could enter one of the healing professions. Pluto is another healing choice, but it can bring power struggles at work and some digestive issues.

Seventh House: Partners, one-to-one relationships.

The Descendant is the point opposite the Ascendant, and it indicates "You," whereas the Ascendant indicates "I." Once you cross this axis, the energies are directed more to the outer world, to other people and the connections you form with them. The seventh is the house of significant others. It's not just about the partners in your life but the way you relate to them. It's your ability to see yourself through the eyes of intimates. The seventh also rules those with whom you work on a one to one basis, like a therapist, attorney or business partner.

Planets in the seventh are meant to coexist peacefully, if at all possible. This is a house of compromise, of working for the good of the team, although it's a small team usually, just two people. In the seventh, you focus on "We," not "I." The Sun here makes you a partnership person and you desire a significant other. Loneliness is a real issue for you and you'd rather be with someone than all by yourself. You work well with others too and may become a therapist or toil in some other profession where personal interaction is featured. The Moon here is just as partnership oriented, and in fact can sometimes be a bit too co-dependent. Your own emotions are unclear because they're so completely merged with those of a partner. Mercury here is good at intimate discussions and forging partnership agreements. Venus is perfectly at home in this house and seeks a loving marriage. Mars may create an arena of one to one combat and seldom feels comfortable because you feel guilty for doing what you should with Mars—namely looking out for your own interests. Jupiter can bring luck and happiness through devoted partners. Saturn here indicates a Karmic debt to partners, the likelihood that you abandoned a mate in other lives and must now work harder to coexist in a relationship. It can also indicate difficulty in attracting partners but usually will bring you a mate so you can work on your Karma. Uranus may bring sudden, inappropriate, or incompatible marriages (like Elizabeth Taylor, who managed to marry just about everyone she dated). It can bring a partner of vastly different age, social status, or someone with whom you're rebelling. It's hard to maintain stable partnerships with Uranus here. Neptune brings difficult partners too, and a tendency to want to minister to them, as in those who marry drunks or druggies. It's hard to get your needs adequately met with Neptune here, particularly as it inclines you toward self-sacrifice, and that's not a trait best developed through partnership, which should be a marriage of equals. Pluto brings power struggles in intimate relationships; one partner is the master, the other the slave.

Eighth House: Sex, death, partner's assets.

The eighth is the house of sex, death, and other people's money. Of all the houses, it would seem that the eighth has the most divergent areas of rulership. In understanding the sign Scorpio, it's easier to make sense of the eighth house. Sex is a vehicle for spiritual transformation, one which leads to ecstasy, which can lead to God. The French call orgasm le petit mort—little death—because of the way we lose ourselves and merge with another. So that makes sense in terms of the sex-death link. The money relates in part to the fact that the eighth house is opposite the second, which is about your own money; thus the eighth is about other people's money. And also, if the seventh is the house of the partner, and thus your mate's first, then the eighth is partner's second—money.

Planets here are passionate, emotional, and they seek to merge with a mate on all levels. This is where your own identity and assets merge with another person's, and where at the end of your life, you merge with the infinite—and leave all your worldly goods to your mate! The Sun here can make you very sexy, perhaps even a cinema heart throb like John Travolta. It's also good for those who work in finance, like account executives. The Moon here is passionate and intense and desires closeness—and financial security. Mercury likes pillow talk—and the stock exchange. Venus here is similar to the Moon and bestows sizzling sex appeal and charisma—such as we saw in President Kennedy. Mars is intensely sexual, demands frequent gratification, and has no fear of death. Marilyn Monroe had this placement. Jupiter in the eighth could bring you an inheritance—and so can Venus. Saturn here demands fiscal responsibility, can bring difficulty with creditors as well as a less than sizzling sex life. It's also better to focus on positive health regimens with this Saturn placement—and to give up the cigarettes and other negative substances. Uranus here can bring sudden romantic attachments with unusual partners, financial ups and downs, and perhaps death by accident. Neptune urges you to merge right to the soul during sex, but can bring a mate who somehow decimates your assets, or has none of his or her own. You may die peacefully in your sleep. Pluto is intense and passionate here and wants to own a lover, body and soul.

Ninth House: Philosophy, Religion, Law, Higher Education.

The ninth opposes the third house and both relate to the world of ideas. Whereas the third is about communication and learning, the ninth rules higher education, so you might say you graduate from high school in the third and college in the ninth. The third is local travel and the ninth long distance. And the third is ideas in general, but the ninth defines philosophy and law, the tenets by which we live.

Planets in the ninth are rather intellectual and they love reaching for new ideas, new cultures, new locations. With the Sun here you may become a professor, an attorney, or maybe a pilot. You like sharing your thoughts and are a good teacher. The Moon in the ninth could relocate you to a home far from where you grew up and men with this placement often marry women who come from a distance—or another culture. You feel comfortable in foreign places and fit in happily. Mercury here is a natural scholar. Venus loves travel, foreign places and people, and may have a sweetheart in every port. Mars also loves travel and is content assertively exploring the world of ideas—and sharing those ideas with verve. Jupiter here is right at home and can indicate a profession in law or religion. Saturn in the ninth is rather restrictive and may try to rein in ideas, or foist them on people for whom they're ill-suited. Uranus indicates sudden travel or interest in far-out systems of thinking or belief. Neptune can bring a spiritual philosophy or a desire to help those unjustly treated by the law. It too can bring distant travel to unusual lands. Pluto brings a desire to transform the world of ideas, to change people's thinking and bring a new level of consciousness to all.

The ninth is the last of the identity houses. It works in combination with houses one and five. In the first, you give others the impression of who you are. The fifth allows you to express yourself and use your creative abilities. The ninth is where you define yourself intellectually and create your world based upon those beliefs. When looking at a horoscope, it makes sense to examine the planets in all these three houses together to see who a person is and what sort of world he or she wants to inhabit.

Tenth House: Career, father, worldly achievements.

The Midheaven, or MC, lies at the top of the chart and that represents your self in the outer world. Just as the fourth house is your most private self, the tenth is your most public persona. The tenth house relates to the father, as the fourth relates to the mother. In traditional societies, and our own a few generations ago, mom was at home cooking, cleaning and raising the children, and dad was out in the world earning the money. Often, children went into the same profession as their father. Plumber's sons joined the plumber's union, and so on. This is often the same today. Lawyer's sons often become lawyers; children join the family business. That's one way the tenth relates simultaneously to career and to father. But really it's more about what you hope to achieve in the outside world — who you are when you're out there among everyone else and standing up to be counted. Fathers — and mentors — give guidance to their children about what to do and whom to become, and that too relates to the tenth house.

Just as the first is the image you unconsciously project, the tenth is the image you deliberately embody. There is a strong sense of propriety to planets in the tenth house, of what must be done, of the choices you've made for your life. The Sun here gives you a sense of authority. You feel comfortable being in charge and directing other people. Your identity is strongly tied into what you do for a living and if you can't make a living, you feel like less of a person, that somehow you're letting down your destiny, and it's letting you down. You feel close — and similar to — your dad. The Moon here makes you less outwardly emotional, although you often forge personal ties with professional contacts. Men with this Moon sometimes marry a woman they met at work — one whose strengths remind them of a mom who may also have played a dad's role as breadwinner. Mercury here can train other workers or write company manuals. Venus indicates a loving father, gets along harmoniously with colleagues, and may incline you to marry one, but you may also be less romantic and more professionally-focused as mates. It's good for a career in the arts, however, and is very happy when the mate shares the same professional interests. Mars in the tenth makes you a powerhouse who can accomplish so much, although you may work best alone rather than as part of a team. You admire your dad's assertiveness and want to achieve as much as he did. Jupiter can bring huge successes, and people in power rooting for you—as it did to Harrison Ford. Saturn in the tenth is very comfortable, demands long-lasting career efforts, and may indicate a father whose expectations for you are hard to meet. Success isn't easy with this placement—you must earn it because you have Karma that requires you to learn patience and responsibility in building a profession. Uranus can bring high tech work, a career as an astrologer, or an assortment of changing professions each time boredom strikes. It can indicate a father who was very non-traditional. Neptune can bring success in the film business—or with oil wells—but it might also make it hard for you to grasp a career and keep building it. In fact, you may be unclear about whether or not you actually want one and your Dad may be an absentee parent. Pluto can give you great power in the professional area, the ability to be one of the players in your field, but it can also indicate power struggles, and a dad who was far too domineering.

The tenth is the last of the material houses. It works in combination with houses two and six. In the second, you focus on the money and resources you have; in the sixth, on the day to day of working; in the tenth you define yourself in the outside world as a productive citizen who can make his or her own way through life. When looking at a horoscope, it makes sense to examine the planets in all these three houses together to see how well the person will succeed—and at what.

Eleventh House: Friends, long-term goals, group associations.

The eleventh is the house of long-term goals, friendships, and group interaction. This is where you fit in socially among your peers. The eleventh opposes the fifth, and as you express your best qualities in the fifth, the eleventh is where you gain appreciation from pals for the person you are. The fifth is romance with a lover and the eleventh is affection within a group of friends. Your goals are more than career-oriented, but rather how you want your entire life to flow, and as most people yearn for similar lifestyles to those of their friends, it makes sense that these things come under the same house. Do you have a ten-year plan? This is the sort of thing that belongs in the eleventh house.

Planets in the eleventh are chatty, social, and helpful. There is a sense of responsibility not just for yourself but for other people too. If the world is going to continue, you must contribute. You are more than just your individuality — you are part of something greater than just yourself. The Sun here makes you a very friendly person and your relationships are so important to you. To be alone and friendless makes you very sad indeed. You have a strong sense of hope, an image in your mind of where you are in the continuum of your life and what's appropriate for you at which stage. The Moon here brings a nice connection to those around you and a well-developed sense of empathy. You easily feel other people's emotions and give those feelings validity. Mercury gives you the gift of gab and makes you a fun companion for conversation. Venus here brings you many loving friendships and the ability to charm new acquaintances easily. You want a lover to be a friend as well. Mars in the eleventh inspires you to work for social improvements and you may share athletic interests with your pals. Jupiter brings kindly — and possibly prominent — pals. Saturn requires you to put up with friends who are much too needy and to focus more realistically on goals for the future. Uranus bestows kooky pals and perhaps a goal to change the world radically to a less structured place. Neptune brings undependable friends and the desire to sacrifice your personal needs while helping others with their lives. Pluto may bring powerful friends, but more likely will generate power struggles within your peer group.

The eleventh is the last of the social houses. It works in combination with houses three and seven. In the third, you connect intellectually with siblings, people, and places immediately surrounding you. The seventh brings you partners with whom you can relate one to one — intermingling your heart, mind, and soul. The eleventh is where you share your life with compatible people who are your intellectual equals, though usually not your lovers. When looking at a horoscope, it makes sense to examine the planets in all these three houses together to see who a person is and what sort of social interactions he or she will choose.

Twelfth House: the unconscious mind, hidden things.

The twelfth is the house of the unconscious mind, and it's where all your secrets are buried. The parts of your psyche that are a mystery to you, which you have never confronted, lie here. This is the house of dreams, and it's where one period of your life will wind up before a new one can begin. You might say it's your reservoir of emotions.

Planets in the twelfth are sort of hidden and often the energies are shy or work below the surface. There's always an emotional dimension. With the Sun here, you're intensely shy, may be a bit paranoid, and are comfortable toiling behind the scenes. You might become a writer who's very happy to work alone at home, just you and the flickering computer screen. The Moon here is deep and sensitive, and sometimes you feel as though you must retreat from the world because there are just too many emotions out there bombarding you. Mercury can be quite profound and adept at making sense of the psyches of other people. Venus here is shy and is often unexpressed. You might not feel comfortable seeking love, but when you get it, you hug your mate while he or she is sleeping. Mars here has a hard time being assertive enough and you might stoop to plotting revenge or other acts behind people's backs. Jupiter here can bring some blessings, but often you wonder if luck will ever find you. Saturn requires you to work on your subconscious and you may spend much time seeking insights into your own motivations. Uranus brings sudden insights, ideas, or flashes of inspiration. Neptune is perfectly at home in the twelfth and slumbers peacefully, bringing creativity, vivid dreams, and a sense that you can close your eyes and just melt into a pool of loving spirit. Pluto can bring psychological insights, or the desire to overthrow the powers that be.

    The twelfth is the last of the emotional houses. It works in combination with houses four and eight. In the fourth, your emotions are quite conscious and you develop your individuality through childhood experiences. The eighth compels you to merge emotionally, sexually, and spiritually with someone else. The twelfth is the deep reservoir of your unconscious and all those emotions are pooled there. When looking at a horoscope, it makes sense to examine the planets in all these three houses together to see who a person is on an emotional level, and just how solid his or her psyche is.

The chart below summarizes what we've discussed so far.

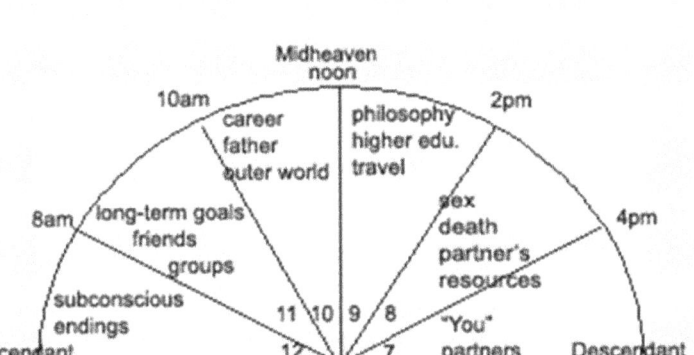

Now that we've considered the houses one by one and have discussed how the planets function in each, let's talk for just a moment about how a horoscope chart is constructed. This is the blessed age of computers and you need know no astrological math at all to create a horoscope chart. You enter the data and the computer does it for you. But it is wise to know a few things, so that if a person is born at, say, 6 a.m., and you notice a chart with a seventh house Sun, you can stop and say, wait, this is a mistake. Computers don't make mistakes in calculations, but people make typos!

If you look at the chart above, you notice times running around the wheel. They indicate the approximate location of the Sun, depending on time of birth. So if you are an Aries, born at 6 a.m., you probably have Aries rising. This isn't exact of course, depending on location and so on, but it gives a good estimation. If you're an Aries and were born at eleven a.m., where is your Sun? The tenth house.

And thus what would your rising sign be? Well, if you put Aries on the tenth house cusp, then Taurus on the eleventh, Gemini on the twelfth, and then you would have Cancer on the Ascendant. And so on. With this system and no computer, you could rough out an approximate chart. I use a computer, although I did learn the math, like a hundred years ago, but I seriously doubt I could remember it today, but at least I can look at a chart and know if a typo has been made.

Now let's think about how the signs work on the house cusps. To start, let's consider the archetype, with Aries rising, and let's look at the house groups as suggested above, the identity, material, social, and emotional houses.

With Aries on the Ascendant, you're assertive and you want to make an immediate—and aggressive impression. That would give you Leo on the fifth house and makes you creative, social, and happily romantic. Sagittarius on the ninth gives you intellectual curiosity. The material houses have Taurus on the second, a natural desire to earn and manage money, Virgo on the sixth, making you a hard worker who tries to remain healthy, and Capricorn on the tenth, giving a desire to achieve a great deal in your profession. The social houses have Gemini on the third, giving you an intellectual interest in siblings and your neighborhood, Libra on the seventh, giving a desire to find a relationship with the partner whose sensibilities match your own, and Aquarius on the eleventh, bringing exciting and intellectually stimulating friends and the desire to make your world a better place. Finally, the emotional houses show Cancer on the fourth, indicating a nurturing childhood and mother, Scorpio on the eighth, making you intensely sexy and willing to merge at all levels with a significant other, and Pisces on the twelfth, making you deep, creative, and very sensitive below the surface.

That's the archetype, but obviously life goes beyond the archetype. You could put any of the fire signs on the Ascendant and the message would be similar because the fire signs coordinate well with the houses of identity, the earth signs with the material houses, and so on.

But what happens, say, when we have earth rising? With Taurus on the Ascendant, you seem stable, sensual and practical. That gives you Virgo on the fifth house, and makes you a bit restrained romantically, and your creativity—and your children—may take a practical turn. Capricorn is on the ninth, and that produces a desire to succeed according to your belief system. The material houses begin with Gemini on the second, and that could indicate earning money through communications—or expending it on books. Libra is on the sixth, and that could mean working in a social field, or the desire to socialize rather than to work. Aquarius is on the tenth and that could lead to a career that benefits society—or life as a rebel. The social houses begin with Cancer on the third and that brings an extended family within the neighborhood—or maybe a mom who's a bus driver. Scorpio is on the seventh and requires a mate who loves and can be loved with your whole heart and soul. Pisces is on the eleventh, and gives you a deep emotional connection with your pals and a psychic seventh sense about where your future lies. The emotional houses begin with Leo on the fourth, and that indicates a glamorous home—and mother. Sagittarius lies on the eighth and you want to connect intellectually as much as emotionally, and may find your best sex partners in distant countries—or after rousing debates. Aries lies on the twelfth and you have active dreams and feel the need to let your unconscious urges emerge.

Just as in the first example, you can place a different earth sign on the Ascendant, and the picture will be similar. But what happens when Air is rising?

Gemini is on the Ascendant, and you are sprightly, changeable, and intellectual. Libra is on the fifth, and you enjoy romantic interludes, your children are well mannered, and your creative output is pretty and well balanced. Aquarius is on the ninth and you seek a system of belief that will heal the world. Cancer begins the material houses on two, and you have an emotional attachment to money and a deep need to build financial security. Scorpio is on your sixth and you are an indefatigable worker, perhaps in a health field. Pisces is on your tenth and you may be an artist, a musician, or other creative type. The social houses begin with Leo on three and you enjoy the cultural aspects of your neighborhood and may have extravagant siblings. Sagittarius is on the seventh, and you need a mate whose outlook stimulates your own, although you may be just as content to enjoy serial romances instead. Aries is on your eleventh, and you seek stimulating friends who agree with your viewpoints and goals. The emotional houses begin with Virgo, and you have a restrained childhood and an organized mom. Capricorn is on your eighth house and you work hand in hand with a mate to increase mutual assets. Taurus is on your twelfth and you are content to let sleeping dogs lie.

Just as in the previous examples, you can swap a different air sign for the Gemini Ascendant and the picture will be similar. And in our final example, what happens when water rises?

Cancer describes the first identity house, on the Ascendant, and you seem shy and tender hearted, and have large, luminous eyes. Scorpio is on your fifth and you are so sexy that everyone wants to date you. Pisces is on your ninth and you feel one with just about everyone on the globe. The material houses begin with Leo on the second and you desire a well-heeled lifestyle and a generous income. Sagittarius is on your sixth and you may travel the globe to heal distant peoples, or work devotedly for an organization in which you believe—or find it hard to give up your free time and work only intermittently! Aries is on your tenth and you need to be self-directed, and possibly self-employed. Your dad is a fireball and so are you! The social houses begin with Virgo on three, and you are a helpful sibling and neighbor. Capricorn is on seven and you seek a mate who is a true life partner so you can achieve a solid life together. Taurus is on eleven and your friends desire wealth and love sharing a good meal. The emotional houses begin with Libra on the fourth. Your childhood was balanced and Mom a gracious hostess. Aquarius is on the eighth and you may believe in free love and divestiture of all personal assets. Gemini is on your twelfth and you like to discuss your deepest feelings and may keep a dream journal.

That's how it works! The houses define the areas of life, and the planets within them function in those areas. The signs on the house cusps describe the ways in which those areas of life are approached.

So far in this chapter, we've discussed the signs, planets, houses, and how they interrelate. Next we look at the geometry of astrology—the aspects among the planets and how they shade planetary meanings.

Part Four: The Major Aspects

Remember that funny scene (okay they were all funny!) in *Down and Out in Beverly Hills* where Bette Midler shared her guru's insights that everything is connected and we all flow into and out of each other constantly? Movie guru jokes are always funny to me because so many people are over the top with that stuff. But in this case, she was right. Everything is connected, and nothing is just itself, alone.

In book we've already discussed the signs, planets, and houses. With just that information, you know quite a bit about the person in question. But there's still more to consider. Now, let's look at the way the planets are interconnected.

Astrology is a vast web of tightly woven geometry, and there are many possible aspects to consider, but if you focus on just the major aspects, you will be quite able to unravel the mysteries of any horoscope. And what is an aspect? It's a geometric relationship, described in degrees within a circle, between two heavenly bodies. There are always shades of precision in astrology, and we allow various orbs for the aspects — the give or take in degrees that indicates an aspect will still function, even if it's not exact. This information is summarized in a chart at the end of this article. Now, let's consider the aspects one by one.

Conjunction: 0 degrees, plus or minus 10 degrees
Keywords: Blended energies.

A conjunction occurs when two planets (or a planet and point of the horoscope) lie next to each other in the sky. For example, if your Sun is 2 degrees Taurus, and your Moon is also 2 degrees Taurus, we'd say you have Sun conjunct Moon. This would also mean you were born during a New Moon, and that who you are on the outside is very similar to your secret, inner self. Say your Moon was at 11 degrees Taurus. The Moon would have moved a bit away from the Sun by the time you were born, but they're still in orb, and still conjunct. Now suppose your Moon were at 23 degrees Aries. What is the distance in degrees between Sun and Moon? Well, if we add 7 degrees, we move into Taurus, then add the two degrees to reach your Sun and find a 9 degree orb, still making the Sun and Moon conjunct. In this case we'd call it an out-of-sign conjunction. You could have Sun and Moon in the same sign, but not conjunct. I have this myself—Sun at 2 degrees Virgo, Moon at 23. They're not conjunct or in the same house, but it still represents a New Moon personality.

Planets in conjunction function together, sort of like a married couple. When one planet is transited, so is the other, and everything happens to both. On the TV show *Frasier*, a hostess complained about the brothers, "When you get one, you get the other one." That's the way it works with a conjunction. And, just as in some marriages, not every planetary pair works harmoniously, but whether or not the two planets' vibrations are compatible, when they lie in conjunction, the energy of each shades the other's. So, if you have Mars (action) conjunct Saturn (limitation), restrained action feels normal to you. You might look at a person with Mars conjunct Jupiter (expansion) and wonder how on earth that person can be so intemperate. You wouldn't say to yourself gee, I should be more carefree. Well you might say that after years of living with yourself, but you'd realize it goes against your nature. It would be more natural for you to say gee, that other guy shouldn't be so spontaneous. That's the thing about conjunctions, when you have them, you can't quite fathom what that planetary energy feels like when it stands alone. I have Sun conjunct Saturn in the tenth house, and it's always felt normal for me to be responsible—and bossy. I rarely even meet people with something like Sun conjunct Venus in the fifth house because that energy would feel very different to me—and mine to them!

It's also possible to have conjunctions among planets and the angles of your horoscope. So, for example, you could have Sun conjunct the Midheaven—making you an achiever. Or conjunct the Ascendant—making you seem very energetic and possibly theatrical. But if your Sun is conjunct the Descendant, you'd say it's opposite the Ascendant, because that's just the way we express that! You could say it's at the IC if it were at the bottom of the chart, but you'd be more likely to say opposite the MC. That's because we tend to designate those two points, Ascendant and MC as benchmarks, so to speak. If it's right at the third house cusp, you might talk about it a lot (what with the third house being about communications) but you wouldn't say it's conjunct because we just don't do that in astrology!

Sextile: 60 degrees, plus or minus 6 degrees
Keywords: Harmony, collaboration, friendship.

You know how Robert Frost said fences make good neighbors? Well that's sort of the idea with sextiles. Take one sign, the next sign is the fence, then the following sign sextiles the first. So, for example,

Aries is sextile Gemini—and Aquarius. And these air signs are very compatible with Aries' fire. Likewise Gemini sextiles Leo, and Aquarius sextiles Sagittarius. Each of these pairs have one sign in-between, creating the good neighbor fence. A sextile is an aspect of ease and harmony, where both energies can express their own vibration, but can also work together. Aries and Gemini feel at home with each other and can collaborate comfortably.

That's the energy of the sextile among signs, but is it as easy when planets are connected? If your Sun is at 5 degrees Aries, and your Moon at 10 degrees Gemini, that is within orb, and thus the two bodies are sextile. You're a fireball whose emotions are changeable and don't weigh you down—and that feels comfortable to you. You'd probably be a bit self-centered and detached emotionally from other people, or inclined toward serial entanglements, but that would bother everyone else more than it would bother you. You'd be comfortable!

Say we combine two incompatible planets like Mars and Saturn. The sextile allows them both to shade each other, but not to overwhelm. It's as though each vibration is learning about the other in a spirit of good will. You'd be orderly and organized, think before you act, but you wouldn't be anal or mired in frustration. You'd just perk along, doing what made sense after some thought.

Sextiles add richness to a horoscope, because they connect energies without too heavy a hand. They're like the herbs and spices that help flavors blend in cooking and turn interesting individual ingredients into a dish that is greater than the sum of its parts.

Square: 90 degrees, plus or minus 10 degrees
Keywords: Disharmony, work, friction.

If you picture two lines going in perpendicular directions, you begin to see the energy of the square. It's two energies at cross purposes. Their goals, vibrations, and directions are different, and when they collide, it creates friction—which releases energy. Effort must be expended to make their vibrations work in harmony.

Signs in square aspect do have one thing in common—similar modes of energy. For example, the Cardinal signs—Aries, Cancer, Libra, and Capricorn, form a big cross in the sky, with each sign in square aspect to the next. They're each assertive, goal-oriented types, but they find each other a little jarring. For example, Aries seems too brash to Cancer, which seems cloyingly emotional to Libra, which seems frivolous to Capricorn, which seems irritatingly materialistic to Aries. Bear in mind what we have here is two sets of pairs, of Aries and Libra, Cancer and Capricorn in opposition, which we will discuss later on.

So, suppose your Sun is 21 degrees Libra and your Moon 12 degrees Cancer. That would be Sun square Moon. You'd be courteous and genteel on the outside, and emotional and security-seeking on the inside. That might not work out too badly because even though the lights are square, you'd want the same things—a relationship. Of course Libra likes to date and Cancer likes security, so you might have a hard time until you felt ready to settle down! Suppose your Moon were at 0 degrees Aquarius. Libra and Aquarius are both Air signs, and would generally be considered a trine aspect, but in fact, that's in orb and you would still have Sun square Moon. In this case, first of all, we'd say gee, that's pretty wide, and out of sign, so it wouldn't be as severe a square as one with more precisely aligned degrees. But it would still exist. Your Libra Sun and Aquarius Moon would make you social, people-oriented, but maybe on the outside you'd be romantic and inside have a social consciousness, inclining you to become romantically involved with people you were always trying to help. Or perhaps the friction would show up in your life via your parents, who could have been compatible but because of different interests in life had a hard time maintaining a stable home. There would be some discord, either way.

If you have a square aspect to one of the angles, that produces energy. If Mars squares the MC, you're a fireball at work and at home. And, in order to produce that square, Mars might likely be in either the first or seventh house, so basically energy would be your major modus operandi in life. Of course if you have a Saturn square, that creates energy, but of a restrictive nature. The Saturn vibration is expressed through the energy of the square, bringing situations into your life that would restrict you getting what you want professionally and at home, and requiring effort (the square) on your part to work through the Karma (Saturn).

Suppose someone says to you that they have Sun square Mercury. What do you answer? Trick question! Mercury and Venus always travel close to the Sun, and the only aspect either of them can make within a horoscope is the conjunction.

Whatever planet or angle is involved with a square, there is always energy. A square is a very dynamic aspect, unlike a sextile, which is all about ease and flow. Squares are important in a chart because they give a person gumption, the sense that things may not work out perfectly at first, but with a little effort, success can be had. Squares provide the awareness that with life comes challenges and without them a person could be too complacent to take advantage—

or make the best of—life's complications. With too many squares, there's a sense of chaos, or of being out of control.

Trine: 120 degrees, plus or minus 10 degrees
Keywords: Compatibility, ease.

Remember the sensation of gliding down the sliding board at the playground? That is the energy of a trine. It's easy, there's no disharmony, and it feels pleasant. Trines exist between the same elements. The fire signs, Aries, Leo, and Sagittarius, lie 120 degrees apart on the circle that is the heavens, and thus they are trine. They have similar qualities and function harmoniously together. Likewise for earth, air, and water.

Planets in trine get along, similar to planets in sextile, although the energy of a trine is stronger, and that's why we use a smaller orb with the sextile. Even planets whose vibrations are basically discordant to each other work acceptably well in trine. Saturn and Neptune are the two most opposite vibrations, in my opinion, but when they trine, there is a desire to balance both energies, to blend the practical with the spiritual, without overemphasizing either.

So if your Sun is at 28 degrees Gemini, and your Moon is at 20 degrees Aquarius, the lights are in trine. You're a people person who feels knowledge can heal the world. But suppose your Moon is at 6 degrees Pisces. Exactly—also trine, although out of sign. Gemini and Pisces are fairly incompatible signs, except that they're both mutable—flexible—and thus with this combination it might be very hard to pin you down. You'd still be a people person and seek company, but you might feel emotionally overwhelmed by all that contact—and chit chat. And such a combo might indicate that your parents were vastly different types of people, making a harmonious family environment difficult. But there is a lesson here—that connecting with other people is a serious thing, that below the surface of even a casual conversation are deep emotional threads that bind us one to the other. So you'd be seeking a lifestyle that combined intellectual stimulation with emotional depth. Each of the signs Gemini and Pisces would need to get along with the other, and you would be a more complex person as a result.

That's the thing about trines, they represent a win-win situation. And when incompatible energies must merge, it's like a little nudge from God to evolve. A universal truth is that there's a place for all things, and that all vibrations must be revered, and all can live in harmony. Trines are the cosmic way we learn these truths.

Trines bring joy—and luck—to a horoscope. Without them, life feels too brusque, too difficult. With trines, we feel that there are many options and that it'll all work out. With too many trines, there's a risk of laziness, or the tendency just to sit back and wait for life to provide everything — without any effort.

Quincunx: 150 degrees, plus or minus 3 degrees
Keywords: Sudden events.

The quincunx used to be classified as a minor aspect, along with the semi-sextile (30 degrees), and together they were called an inconjunct. Nowadays many astrologers consider the quincunx a major aspect, although it's never granted the wide orb given to other aspects.

The quincunx is a peculiar connection, between signs which have no entanglement at all. Aries is quincunx Virgo and Scorpio. They have nothing much in common, not element, mode, etcetera. The energy of the quincunx is a sometimes kind of thing, particularly in transit. It might happen or it might not; you might feel it or might not. Say you have Mars quincunx Saturn. Some of the time you feel compelled to be quite orderly, to do chores, to be efficient and responsible. And some of the time you just go about your business. That's the quincunx!

If your Sun is 12 degrees Virgo and your Moon is 12 degrees Aries, they're in quincunx. Virgo and Aries are a difficult combination. Virgo tends to know it all and be determined to do things correctly and Aries tends to want everything its own way. So with this combination, you'd be pretty supercilious, although you'd want to help people (Virgo) but might come off as insensitive (Aries). With these signs, there's no bridge to work through the energy. Aries and Scorpio fare a bit better, although the tendency is to focus on sex, and on getting sex from other people, whether or not that's a healthy choice to make.

But consider this: the quincunx is near the trine in number of degrees involved. So suppose your Sun is 29 degrees Aries and your Moon is 1 degree Virgo. What's the aspect? They're in trine, not quincunx, although the signs naturally are not trine. So, the question is, how much difference is there between the two Aries Sun, Virgo Moon people when the numbers of the degrees change the aspect? I would say that the person whose lights are trine has a slightly easier time because there is a stronger desire to coordinate that inner energy more compatibly. There's a greater desire for compromise so that the person feels a sense of harmony more often than a sense of discordance.

We could say that like a trine, the Karmic purpose of the quincunx is to create a bridge between energies, but unlike a trine, this merger is neither easy nor harmonious because the energies are mostly incompatible. What it does do is provide a kind of seesaw — sometimes one is on top, sometimes the other. Both vibrations are there, jockeying for position, but they don't really cooperate. You understand this if you have both a cat and a dog. They spend lots of time staring at each other, may grow to love each other, but they know they're completely different animals and never attempt to mate.

Opposition: 180 degrees, plus or minus 10 degrees
Keywords: Conflict, need for compromise with other people.

Remember the movie *Funny Girl*? Barbra Streisand was on a date with Omar Sharif and sang about their differences: she was softer so he could be stronger, and a variety of other differences until she trilled, "I am woman, you are man, let's kiss." That's the energy of the opposition — different vibrations drawn magnetically together.

The signs opposite each other belong to the same mode. Aries and Libra are both Cardinal and they have that in common. They're both assertive and seek certain things. But they have different personalities. Aries is self focused, sometimes too much, and Libra is other-person oriented, also sometimes to an excess. In each other, they see what is lacking, what is missing from their own character. They see the direction they might go in to gain balance. That's the energy of the opposition — an aspect that seeks balance and brings insight into the self through one's polar opposite. This is true of all the pairs of opposite signs. They're significantly different, yet compatible enough to teach each other a lesson. Like the glyphs for yin and yang, things in opposition form each other's missing half and can be nestled together to create a more complete whole.

Think back for a moment to the square. That is an aspect of tremendous energy, a state of friction. Multiply the square's 90 degrees by two and you have the opposition. It contains some of the square's energies, but always seems to affect your life through other people. Whereas the square demands work, the opposition requires compromise.

Suppose your Sun is at 5 degrees Cancer and your Moon is at 12 degrees Capricorn. They're in opposition. You were born during a Full Moon, and you're particularly emotional. With this combo, security would be overemphasized and you might make finance your career — or much too important in your life. But what if your Moon were at 28 degrees Sagittarius? The lights would still be in opposition. In that case, you'd feel an emotional connection with many different types of people, and your natural Cancer nesting urges would be somewhat abated.

The classic opposition is Venus opposite Mars. They are planets which illustrate the magnetic quality of this aspect. If you have Venus in Libra opposite Mars in Aries, that's the archetype. You desire love and share your heart willingly, but you're also able to focus on your own needs — without stepping on anyone's toes!

Oppositions are necessary in a horoscope because they make us see that indeed there are other people in this world and that we don't have complete autonomy. We must consider others. Without any oppositions in a horoscope, we expect always to get our own way. Compromise is nowhere on the agenda. Too many oppositions create a life with too much conflict because it seems as though there is always someone standing in the way, preventing things from happening.

The chart below summarizes what we've discussed so far.

Aspect	degrees	Orb + or -	Keywords
Conjunction	0	10 degrees	Blended energies
Sextile	60	6 degrees	Harmony, collaboration, friendship
Square	90	10 degrees	Disharmony, work, friction
Trine	120	10 degrees	Compatibility, ease
Quincunx	150	3 degrees	Sudden events that may or may not happen
Opposition	180	10 degrees	Conflict with other people

Those are the major aspects connecting one planet to another. But that's not the whole story. The sky is a big circle, surrounding the Earth, and within that circle are many complex and interesting planetary pictures. Very often the planets cluster together in more complicated geometric configurations. And those pictures tell so much about just what sort of person lives inside horoscope. Let's look at just a few of the most common ones.

Suppose you have an opposition — the Sun-Moon opposition mentioned above, Sun in Cancer, Moon in Capricorn. Then if another planet, say Jupiter, is square to both lights, lying at say, 7 degrees Libra, then what you have is a T-Square. If you can picture energy flowing back and forth for a moment, then picture a little applied pressure. The energy erupts out the middle. That's the way a T-square works. The energy of the configuration is blasted out through the planet at square to the other two. So in this case, you'd be cheerful, optimistic, and perhaps might have a few unrealistic expectations. You'd be very emotional (Full Moon) and feel confident (Jupiter) expressing your impulses.

A T-square creates even more dynamic tension than a mere square and produces a life with lots of action and events, although they may not all be pleasant. How well the three planets harmonize depends on the nature and compatibility of the planets in question. If you were to put Saturn at the focal point of the T-Square above, it would block the energy, similar to putting a lid on a pot that's boiling. The steam could erupt and knock off the lid! Or worse, the lid could remain tightly closed, bringing the contents of the pot to a violent boil which roiled in on itself. So that could mean if you had that Sun-opposite-Moon-T-Square Saturn aspect, that you'd often feel frustrated and angry, that your desires were too often unmet, that you felt unsafe in the world. You'd have to learn patience and discipline, and to put a great deal of effort into everything you undertook.

Suppose you had a Sun-Moon trine. That would give you a congenial outlook and pleasant personality. Now what if we place another planet, say Neptune, also at 120 degrees from the Sun and Moon. Your horoscope would have a big triangle of flowing energy, and we call that a Grand Trine. That is a lucky configuration, but also one of laziness. The tendency is just to expect things to work out and not to try any harder than necessary. With that picture, you'd be spiritual, psychic, and musical. Even if Saturn were involved in the Grand Trine, things would work out all right. You'd put effort into things (Saturn), but you'd feel all right about doing so and would still expect your work to be fruitful. I always joke about the Grand Trine that people who have it expect to lie in a hammock until life brings them lemonade — and it usually does!

What if you had a horoscope with many planets in square — two sets of oppositions square to each other? Your horoscope would look like a cross with planets at each end point. We call that a Grand Cross, and it's a very complicated picture. The tendency with that one is to attract a great deal of excitement and to take just about everything but the Apocalypse in stride.

Suppose you had that Sun in Cancer, Moon in Capricorn opposition, crossed with Venus in Libra opposite Mars in Aries. What would you have? A mistake! Remember we said above that Venus can never be that far from the Sun. It's always good to remain steadfast and to notice mistakes so that you don't go off the deep end. But you could have Jupiter in Libra opposite Saturn in Aries making the grand cross. With that picture, you'd feel a bit like a marionette, being jerked up and down on your strings by the powers that be. You'd want something, reach for it and sometimes it would work (Jupiter), sometimes you'd be slammed back to the drawing board (Saturn). In fact that sort of Grand Cross would be very Karmic, because the life lesson would be to take life's reins in your own hands and to build a strong foundation, even if your work kept getting knocked down.

I've found that often with a Grand Cross, the person will have Mars in one of the Fixed signs, and if so, the tendency is to give power away to other people—and sometimes to be a victim. We always think of victim energy as very fluid and malleable, but in fact, often its very fixed—because that way the victim can just stand there—forever—and take the abuse.

Sometimes you'll see two sets of very tight oppositions, not precisely in a cross formation. For example, suppose the Sun is at 14 degrees Aquarius, opposed by Uranus at 14 Leo. The we have Mars at 27 Taurus opposed by Jupiter at 29 Scorpio.

There is a very large orb between these two sets of oppositions. Mars squares the Sun by 13 degrees, and that is too large to be a genuine square. Yet there does seem to be a Grand Cross in that chart. You would need to look carefully at all the energy patterns in any one horoscope to determine just what's going on. Planets tightly in aspect will work more consistently together than those farther apart. But, as we said, everything is connected, and everything does ultimately work together.

There are other clusters of planets, other configurations, but these are the main ones you'll see. In my own chart, I have Mars at 22 Cancer, tightly opposite Jupiter at 23 Capricorn, closely sextile/trine a Moon-Mercury conjunction at 23 and 26 Virgo respectively. That's not a grand trine, but it is a configuration—one for which there's no name. But the aspects are very tight and all those planets work together all the time. My feelings (Moon) are intense (Mars), I write (Mercury) with and about emotion, and often am upbeat and funny (Jupiter). I don't think I can express any of these vibrations without it being shaded by the energy of all the rest.

I think it's a nice thing when there are many planetary connections in a horoscope. It makes the person more complex and the life better integrated. But what happens when there's a planet unconnected to any other? It seems that the energy in question functions separately from that part of life, but it does function. I knew a guy with an unaspected Venus, and he was plenty social and quite a womanizer. He was also successful in business. Some people say the tendency is to go overboard when the energy is expressed. Marlon

Brando had an unaspected Venus too, and some astrologers speculate that his food binges represent an out of control expression of this energy. Brando did say that he overate for emotional reasons, using food as comfort when he was blue. I also knew a guy with an unaspected Capricorn Moon in the 9th house. For him emotions were no big deal and he wasn't terribly involved in the feelings of other people. He wasn't anti-social, just not terribly at home in any sort of emotional realm. To understand the full extent to which this picture affected him and his life you'd need to look at the complete horoscope.

That's what we'll be doing later on in this book. We've discussed signs, planets, houses, and aspects. Even if you were a true beginner when you began reading, you're now fairly familiar with the concepts that form the foundation of astrology. Need to dig a little more deeply? It's time to move on to chapter two! But before we do, here's a little chart showing the astrological glyphs, the symbols that stand for each of the planets and signs. You'll have to learn them so you can read a chart.

PLANETS		**SIGNS**		**ASPECTS**	
Sun	☉	Aries	♈	Conjunction	☌
Moon	☽	Taurus	♉	Sextile	✶
Mercury	☿	Gemini	♊	Square	□
Venus	♀	Cancer	♋	Trine	△
Mars	♂	Leo	♌	Quincunx	⚻
Jupiter	♃	Virgo	♍	Opposition	☍
Saturn	♄	Libra	♎		
Uranus	♅	Scorpio	♏	Points:	
Neptune	♆	Sagittarius	♐	N Node of Moon	☊
Pluto	♇	Capricorn	♑	S Node of Moon	☋
		Aquarius	♒		
		Pisces	♓	Retrograde	℞

Chapter Two:
The Details — The Planets delineated in every Sign and every House

Now that you have a good grounding in astrology, take some time to delve a little more deeply, to ponder the symbols involved and the essential meanings involved.

THE SUN
THE SUN is the planet of identity and describes your task in this lifetime

The Sun is the planet that describes your essential identity and the Karmic path you have chosen to walk in this lifetime. It shows what you want to achieve and who you are. The sign where the Sun lies describes the ways in which you express your identity and the type of person you are.

Sun in Aries requires you to express yourself in this lifetime — once you figure out just who that self is. That's the nature of Aries — it's all about self discovery. Every experience is your teacher and you often say, "I've learned that I'm….." For you that's quite enough. You seldom feel you should be... or should do…. Instead it's fine for you to come to grips with the essential *I*, the person you are deep inside. Your task is learning about who you are so you can just be yourself. And in following your instincts and thrusting yourself un-self-consciously into life and just being, you learn more about who you are! You tend to be impetuous, action-oriented, self-involved, and quite passionate. Your energy is a bit raw and primitive but you don't mind because you accept yourself and enjoy being a fireball of needs and desires.

Sun in Taurus means that you will use and conserve the physical resources entrusted to your care. All the material things that sustain life come under the purview of Taurus, and if that's your Sun sign, you do tend to be a material girl — or guy, like Madonna, who actually is a luxury-loving Leo. Practical matters are strongly represented in your sign, and are a comfortable part of your nature. Life has to make sense to you before you move forward, and the slowness of your sign tends to uphold your tendency to take forever before making a commitment to anything. You like to know that you can continue along any chosen path without interruption, so you realize that it's wise to be absolutely certain you can do so before taking the first step. You are deliberate, determined, famously stubborn, and practical right down to your cashmere socks.

Sun in Gemini makes you a communicator. It's your task to make sense of the world around you and to share your thoughts and ideas—with pretty much any audience you can take captive. You're all about words and often you don't know when to slow down and listen to the silence. You prefer to be in a room with too much stimulation rather than none. You're completely comfortable listening to the radio while watching television while reading a book, and if the phone rings you can chatter to a friend all at the same time. You love reading and find that the more information you ingest, the better. It doesn't matter at all if you're learning something useful; you just like ideas floating across your mind. You're someone who lives to be out in the world, and whether you travel or not, what's going on around you (or out there via TV land) is supremely interesting. You have to know who, what, why, when and where, just like every good journalist.

Sun in Cancer makes you a nurturer and your tender heart is one of your most sentimental—and beloved—characteristics. You live to love and every stray pet that crosses your path deserves to be scooped up and taken home. You need to know that there's a solid foundation in your life—a home and family—and building one is what you're doing in this lifetime. Loving and being loved is the most important thing to you, and by no means does that make you a cream puff. Despite a tender, easily bruised heart, you are a strong person and a survivor. You have a sort of passionate determination to take care of your children, and the need to parent and live within a comforting family unit drives you to achieve success in the world. Your sign forms the bedrock of life on earth as we know it, and you realize that whether you're a breadwinner providing for a family or a homemaker secluded with small children, that your life has tremendous value and importance.

Sun in Leo is all about self-expression. Like fellow fire sign Aries, your theme song is "I gotta be me." You're in touch with who you are, and you enjoy expressing that energy for all to see. Sharing your skills and talents with those who appreciate your inner lights makes you feel good about yourself. That sort of validation is meaningful to you because it means that not only are you doing a good job at whatever you're doing, but that you're being recognized as someone of importance. Your heart is generous and you love sharing what you have with other people, and that includes your famous love of opulence and the good life. It's embarrassing to you to make a fool of yourself and the worst emotion you can experience is humiliation. You need to be yourself, but that means being your best of all possible selves and that's why you try so hard to be good.

Sun in Virgo requires you to serve and heal other people. Like fellow earth sign, Taurus, you need to have a sense of order in your world, and nobody is more analytical than you are. You sit and think about the way things work and devise improvements so that everything can hum a little more smoothly. Forging order from chaos is your personal form of alchemy, and nothing gives you a greater sense of accomplishment to wade into a mess and emerge with everything functioning neatly. That's why you're such a natural helper—you just can't help the urge to set matters to rights. Your nature is a bit austere and you prefer things simple, clean, neat, and sensible. Perhaps that's where your interest in health derives. You recognize that the human body is a machine that runs better on vegetables than potato chips and you enjoy sharing this wisdom with other people.

Sun in Libra is a mirror image of opposite sign Aries—in a way. Aries is all about the self and you're all about the significant other. Your form of self awareness comes through the reflection of you seen in a lover's eyes. You're never more aware of who you are than when a mate shares his or her vision of you. Libra is the partnership sign and you feel rather incomplete without a significant other. That's what you're doing in this lifetime—expressing the value of sharing your life with someone who makes you feel seen and understood. That doesn't mean that you mate at birth, however, and often you're flagrantly single—out there serial dating in search of the perfect mate—night after night! You function best when arm in arm, and as the second air sign, you understand Gemini's urge to chatter. Love to you isn't about being thunderstruck, but about flirting, and sharing lively bon mots—by candlelight of course. Genteel and courtly, you're all about the mating dance as a form of self-expression.

Sun in Scorpio expresses the value of transcendence of the self—via a connection with another person through sex. Scorpio is definitely the sexy sign, and while some Scorpios are absolute satyrs, most recognize that sexual energy is quite holy and a path to the ultimate in spirituality. Through orgasm you lose touch with yourself and merge physically, emotionally, and spiritually with a lover, and in that act of merging, you feel an entrée to all that is—God. Scorpio is the second water sign and you relate strongly to Cancer's need to connect on an emotional level, to know, viscerally, rather than through mere ideas. You rely on instinct, psychic impressions, and your gut feeling, like all water signs. Some things in life are too deep to be described, quantified, or understood intellectually. There is a deeper sense of knowing in the water signs, and you are a force for truth and healing.

Sun in Sagittarius seeks answers about the truths of life. As the third fire sign, Sag believes in self-expression, just as Aries and Leo do, but you want to understand the stage upon which we all stand. What is the meaning of life and how are you a part of the greater scheme of things? That's the question you're working to answer in this lifetime. That sounds like a weighty Karmic task, and indeed it is, but then why are members of your sign so happy-go-lucky? Being a philosopher isn't all grit and grind! You love to ponder reality while lazing on a knoll, your trusty canine panting at your side. After all, nobody is standing over you with a stick waiting for your answers to the mysteries of the universe, and that's how you like it! Being free to contemplate life appeals to you much more than immersing yourself in the day to day details that boggle everyone else. You're interested in philosophy, law, right, justice, and magic, and you like to let everything else just sort of take care of itself. And like opposite sign Gemini, you enjoy sharing your ideas with anyone who will listen.

Sun in Capricorn demands that you achieve something, out in the world. Like the other earth signs Taurus and Virgo, you have a natural affinity for the material realm, and you realize that climbing the path to success means something. Building is your natural element, but that doesn't mean you must become an architect. It means that you strive ever onward and upward, always attempting to best your own achievements. Like opposite number Cancer, you want to build a solid foundation, a home and a family, but you also want a secure neighborhood and you work to be a pillar of your community. Writers often say that you're all work and no play, but you know how to have as much fun as the next person, and your sense of humor can be wild and goofy. But under the surface there is something deeply serious about you, a sense that you absolutely must pull your own weight, must do something of value, must make your life add up to something.

Sun in Aquarius is the sign of friendship, and certainly one of the most important elements in your life is the pals with whom you've bonded. You're reputed to be goofy and eccentric, and whether that's true or not, you know that you can't choose your family or coworkers, but you can certainly choose your friends and they're the people with whom you bond most closely, the ones you feel understand you the best. You have strong ties to society and your task in this lifetime is to function within a group as an enthusiastic participant. You want to forge a brave new world, and despite the fact that like opposite number Leo, you're a strong individual, you always recognize that you're most strongly yourself when you're part of a group with whom you feel a sense of simpatico. You're the third air sign and that makes you a communicator, like Gemini and Libra.

Sun in Pisces is a whirlwind of emotion and sensation. In this lifetime you're blurring the lines between the individual and the infinite and that's why you're sometimes confused about where you end and everyone else begins. As the third water sign, you relate to Cancer and Scorpio's need to experience life through sensation more than thought. You're psychic and intuitive and that way of knowing is far more relevant to you than mere thought and discourse. Pisces is the artist of the Zodiac and you have the ability to channel in inspiration—from God—and to transform that inspiration into art, which is seen and appreciated by people who can then receive from it the universal vibration that first motivated you to create. That makes you a heavenly channel, and it's meaningful and joyous work to do. Of course not every member of your sign is an artist—or even a psychic—but you do sense a sort of universal vibration that binds us all together, and in so doing, we are one with each other and with all that is.

The Sun Through the Houses

The house where your Sun is placed describes the issues that are most important to you in this lifetime; it represents the arena in which all your energy is played out—the stage upon which you live.

The Sun in the first house is immediate, energetic and expressive. Many actors have this placement because they seek the limelight and want to be center stage. The first house is the energy you radiate to others, and planets are here so you can get used to that energy in this lifetime. With the Sun in the first, you are working to allow yourself to be out there in there world where people can see you and interact with you. It's the antidote to shyness, you might say! You have a certain buzz and people notice it the moment you enter a room, which is just fine with you. It's easy for you to concentrate on things that matter to you and to ask for the attention you crave from other people. Because the first is the house of appearance, you take pride in your looks and want to be thought attractive to other people.

The Sun in the second house is financially oriented. Money is very important to you and you might work in some financial area. You tend to define yourself according to how much money you have and while that can be a spur to building a greater level of prosperity, it can also mean that you're not in touch with the real reasons to feel self-esteem. If you were to lose all your money, you could feel worthless, and that would be unjust. There is more to you than your bank account, and that is another important lesson to learn with a second house Sun. The thing to work on is the value of money in your life, and by finding a reasonable balance, you can attract prosperity while at the same time maintaining other positive yardsticks that help you see the other wonderful qualities that make you a worthwhile person.

The Sun in the third house is outgoing, gregarious and communicative. You are a people person who can't help reaching out to those around you. You want to know what's happening, who has something interesting to say, and most of all you want to share what's on your mind. You might be a writer, a teacher or someone who travels for a living. You just enjoy being out in the world and would find life very dull indeed if you were trapped at home in a little room without a television. Yours is a world of ideas and that is what's most important to you. You read, connect with the media and are constantly in search of interesting conversations. Developing and keeping your mind active will always be important to you and it's your natural inner restlessness that keeps you out there in search of intellectual stimulation.

The Sun in the fourth house is sensitive, private and family-oriented. You are very involved in your own inner world and you have your thoughts and feelings to keep you company when you're at home alone. Getting in touch with those deep, inner realities is very important to you and it feels like you're always working on yourself.

Your childhood forms a complex and very significant part of your everyday reality and it seems that every single day has at its core some flash of a memory floating up from your unconscious so you can relive the past and make it a part of the present. Time is like that for you — something in which you float, always merging the past and the present so you can uncover deeper truths about yourself. Having a safe home in which to nest is important to you and you also care about maintaining close family ties.

The Sun in the fifth house is creative, fun-loving and childlike. Expressing yourself is very important to you and like a child at show and tell, you want other people to notice and appreciate what's special about you. There is a strong sense of your inner child and that will stay with you all your life. You can be quite sensitive because that inner child is so close to the surface, and it can mean that your feelings are easily hurt. Although you may not consider yourself an artist, it's important that you find something creative to do as a hobby, because self-expression is a way to balance your energies and to build your self-esteem. Play will always be important to you and no matter what your preferred form of recreation, you will always make time in your schedule for fun. You could be quite athletic, a wonderful teacher or even an actor.

The Sun in the sixth house is hard-working and health oriented. You are one of those busy-busy types who never takes a moment off for frivolity. Even when you have a hobby, you approach it the way other people do work — making it serious and time consuming. You just like to be actively involved in your life and you keep your schedule filled with all the things you want to accomplish. You are a worker bee who does your best, whether you work for someone else or yourself. It's the thrill of a job well done that impresses you more than the compensation you receive. Perhaps it's because you work so much that you're also interested in health. After all, if you don't take care of your body, it won't allow you to maintain that grueling schedule! You might work in the medical field, with small animals or as an assistant to someone else.

The Sun in the seventh house is partnership oriented. You always want to be part of something greater than yourself and you find that the most significant clues to your identity come as a result of your interactions with other people. You feel quite lonely when you don't have some sort of partner and you work well with other people as a result. People who do consulting work, like doctors and lawyers or those in sales often have the Sun here and they find that no matter how much they give to other people, they always get just as much back. Your need is the connection more than the return. You are willing to take care of a loved one unselfishly, because you realize that there is something deep in you that needs this person in your life. Compromise feels quite natural to you and you want to make other people feel safe and happy.

The Sun in the eighth house is magnetic and passionate. Movie stars who become sex symbols often have the Sun here; they radiate so much natural passion and personal magnetism that everyone is drawn to them. With your Sun here, it's easy for you to attract other people into your life to share profound and compelling connections. You get involved in a very deep way in the lives of those around you and may find that everyone you know—and even those you just meet—share all their secrets. You are not a solitary type of person—you seek a connection with other people that can be emotional, sexual or financial. You realize on some level that we are all connected, and even if you're not that involved in those new age principles that teach we are all part of the same fluid mass of energy, on a deep level you feel this. You're very good with money and may work in some financial field. It just feels natural for you to deal with other people's assets.

The Sun in the ninth house is philosophical, intellectual and honest. You care very much about the deep meaning of life as it's lived all around you and it's completely absorbing for you to observe the way other people live. That's why you enjoy foreign travel so much; it gives you a chance to observe other cultures in action and to notice how much we have in common despite all our differences. Justice is very important to you and you will always stand tall on the side of right and honor. If someone you know is dishonest, or worse, dishonorable, you will not want that person in your life. You take these matters so seriously that you may work in a legal field or teach deep truths of some sort or other. You feel connected to the world at large and are never the sort of person who ostrich-like buries your head in the sand. Instead you seek information about what's going on all over the place and lend your support to those good causes that need your help.

The Sun in the tenth house is authoritarian, professional and competent. You are a career person and a natural leader. Your take-charge nature inspires confidence in those around you and you try to maintain their respect and good will by doing the best possible job. Your life is about being out in the world and accomplishing something and because you're so focused on the professional aspects of your life, your personal life may suffer. You don't usually mind though, because you have other things on your mind than casual dinners with a few dear friends. Instead, you spend time with colleagues, work on creating greater success and are absorbed in the day to day of your career. Often you opt to work for yourself because you prefer to have the reins of your life completely in your own hands. Since you're a bit of a workaholic, you might as well be self-employed so you can derive more of the benefits of your obsession with work! You make an excellent mentor for those around you and people naturally seek your counsel and guidance.

Sun in the eleventh house is friendly, social and filled with joie de vivre. You are a people person, and you want to be completely immersed in the world around you. Being in contact with other people is so very important to you and you will go to the ends of the earth to help a friend in need. Being part of something greater than yourself is so important to you and you're just naturally a joiner. You may even keep in touch with the friends you made in grammar school! You care a great deal about your little world and are often involved in do-good works for your community. You just can't help wanting to make the neighborhood a better place, because after all it's your world. You have many goals at any one time in your life and you're always in touch with the thread of your life as you're living it. You enjoy being a child when you're young, yet you can envision yourself as an adult, doing grown up things someday. Time makes sense to you and you live in the moment and look forward to the future with equal enthusiasm.

Sun in the twelfth house is shy, reserved and somewhat private. You enjoy creating a secret little world in which your imagination is given free rein. Writers sometimes have this placement because they are more involved with the world they create than the actual world outside their door. Often you're quite content to stay at home, playing with your computer, reading a book, or watching television. You enjoy the sense of distance between yourself and other people. Sometimes though, you feel a bit neglected when other people don't notice you and your needs, so be sure to speak up and say, "hey, what about me!" when that happens. Likewise, if you work in some capacity behind the scenes, it's all right to blow your own horn now and then and demand that other people sit up and notice you.

THE MOON
The Moon is the planet of emotion and describes your inner reality.

Most of us seem one way externally and feel another way deep inside. That's because the Sun's energy is easily visible to other people, and our inner reality is described by the Moon, which is more private and hidden—and usually in a different sign and house. Thus you can embody a dichotomy of energies. Some people (like me) have Sun and Moon in the same sign. In that case, what you see is what you get!

Moon in Aries is emotionally assertive and self-involved. You're busy dealing with your own needs and feelings and often refuse to allow other people to inflict theirs on you. You can be somewhat childlike in your desire to meet your own needs and you seldom are patient or willing to deal with delayed gratification. Your inner self is just too raw and everything feels too urgent. Yet you have a sensitive and even sentimental side and it upsets you when other people say you're thoughtless. You don't mean to be; you're just so busy living your life and following your own path that you don't always notice other people's feelings. This is the beginning of a new emotional cycle for you and it's important for you to get in touch with your own needs and feelings, so you're doing just what you should.

Moon in Taurus is earthy and you're famous for your green thumb. You have a way with growing things because you relate to the earth and enjoy seeing life blossom all around you. Food is important to you and you might be a very good cook—or at least a passionate one. Stability and security are vital; the life of a wandering gypsy is anathema to you. You need to be in a cozy home, surrounded by your many possessions. Yes, you might be quite a pack rat, but you don't mind because you know where everything is and insist that you need it all. You like shopping and capturing this treasure and that, to add to the comfort of your home. You also care about having financial security and may save obsessively. When your feelings are hurt, you often let the anger simmer and fail to clear the air through a heartfelt conversation. You don't want to risk losing a longstanding relationship, so it feels easier to hold in your anger than to have a confrontation.

Moon in Gemini is not terribly emotional and you enjoy

making new contacts as much as fraternizing with old friends. You seldom sit around whining, recover instantly from any slur and find that your emotional needs can easily be met by a revolving door series of acquaintances. You feel closest to those with whom you can communicate and who have something interesting to say. Sharing ideas is the same as sharing warm feelings to you. In this lifetime, you're experiencing the breadth of human contact rather than needing true depth or singularity of involvement. You're just as content to live on the lam than to build any sort of enduring home. If you can fit everything in a backpack, so much the better, because then you can be on the road in a moment's notice.

Moon in Cancer is the archetype—the Moon in the sign of its rule. It's deep, sensitive, emotional, nurturing, and tender, and you need love and emotional support to feel happy about yourself and your life. Your feelings are so intense that they guide and inform everything you do. You run on instinct, and if your Moon is well-aspected there is nothing you can't accomplish because under the surface it provides that drive to create a happy, secure life. Your parents and your children are the bookends that describe your life and nothing is more important to you than your family. No matter what your life becomes out in the world, deep inside you know that what has mattered most to you is the people whom you love—and who've loved and supported you. You are all about the sanctity of the family and on your heart is an emotional tattoo of the blessed image of parent and child.

Moon in Leo is luxury-loving and generous. You like to live the good life and enjoy being surrounded by the best of everything. Your emotions are steady and long-lasting and your devotion to loved ones equally enduring. Once you love someone, you pretty much always have tender feelings for that person, even if the relationship ends. The people in your life provide a strong emotional foundation, and become the audience which witnesses your every feeling—and triumph. Positive feedback and validation are important to you; as a child you responded strongly to praise—and rebuke. You care what other people think of you and even when you overdo the opulence, you want others to admire your success and largesse. Sometimes you express your feelings with larger than life gestures and over the top emoting.

Moon in Virgo is subtle and sometimes austere. You like everything in its place and being surrounded by clutter or chaos at home makes you feel extremely uncomfortable. You've been known to move the furniture around in loved ones' homes and sometimes they even see that you're right and agree it does look better your way. You feel compelled to offer a helping hand to those you love and admit it's the way you best express your devotion. You can't help worrying and you often worry about people close to you, even if they are blithely indifferent to the disasters that might befall them. You have deep emotions which you resist revealing because you find sloppy displays of feeling intensely embarrassing. Sometimes you have to work to allow yourself to cry when overwhelmed because it's hard to give in to those uncontrolled moments. You need intimacy, but only with a chosen few people. With other people you maintain a sense of privacy and keep your guard up.

Moon in Libra is charming, outgoing, and friendly. You're a people person and you feel happiest when in the company of compatible others. You can't fathom how some people can endure life as a loner when it's so much richer when shared. You like life to be congenial and relationships to be sweet, but not too intense. You don't enjoy sloppy moments of weeping, recriminations, or hysteria. Instead it's much nicer to share happiness and sweep the other stuff aside. There's no point in wallowing! You gain emotional sustenance that way and find that although you crave partnership and marriage, you can also find a great deal of happiness through friendships, both close and casual. You need a multitude of emotional contacts to survive and are glad your personality attracts other people to you.

Moon in Scorpio is intense, passionate, and very private. Although you know that we all are similar and all have deep feelings inside, you prefer to shield yours from all but a few very trusted intimates. In fact, even the person closest to you may not know everything about you. There's a volcano inside you and sometimes it feels a little scary because you sense that you're one step away from completely losing control and being at the mercy of your feelings. You have needs and desires and you recognize that you're pretty much driven by them all the time. You can be content alone, but you prefer to be able to share parts of your life with someone you trust. That way you feel safer because you know that if you go a little out of control, you'll see the reaction in your partner's eyes. You have an uncanny way of understanding how and why other people feel as they do, and it's important to learn not to use that information against them. You have power over others, so use it wisely.

Moon in Sagittarius is friendly and cheerful. You have a strong sense of brotherhood in your heart and no matter where you are, you feel at home. In distant lands you're still quite comfortable and you feel a sense of simpatico with cultures vastly different from your own. That makes you able to bond with just about anyone and no matter where you are, there's someone who can be your friend, someone who can meet your emotional needs. You're not terribly sentimental and you don't give in to emotional displays. Instead you're outgoing and cheerful and feel happy when you have a friend with whom you can share thoughts, ideas, and experiences. You might not opt to be a nester at all because you're completely happy roaming the globe and trying on life in every distant corner you can visit.

Moon in Capricorn is very financially oriented. You need security and seldom choose the frivolous over something more serious and meaningful. You care deeply about conserving resources, and no matter how wealthy you become, you will never opt to toss money away on meaningless pleasure. Although you are sentimental and feel you have deep emotions, many other people are more emotional than you are. They shriek, cry, moan, and wail, and you would almost never allow yourself to behave like that. But you know that you care deeply for the people who matter to you and seeing to their financial security is a responsibility you happily shoulder. You feel pride about the life you're building and want to amount to something so your parents can be proud of you. Having a solid home and loving family of your own matters, but you may delay doing so until your career is secure. As always, financial imperatives regulate emotional decisions in your life.

Moon in Aquarius is friendly, generous, and socially responsible. You have a deep sense of involvement with all around you and your social conscience is strong. You're willing to share and you see financial resources as a communal pool rather than something you'd want to hoard. You love your friends and often turn them into a family, particularly if your birth family is rather distant. You're seldom a loner because you're much happier when in the company of compatible friends. You need companionship to provide emotional fulfillment. People can come and go in your life, and you get what you need, although you prefer to maintain long-lasting friendships all throughout your life. Your home may be a gathering place for all your friends and you enjoy sharing anything you have with pals who need it.

Moon in Pisces is very emotional, sensitive, and psychic. Your feelings are a river of passion that flows through your heart. Nobody is more emotional than you are and you seldom feel embarrassed by expressing even the most intense feelings in front of other people. You're driven by your feelings, whether or not they make sense, and you often act on instinct. You just know what you want and you reach for it, whether it makes sense intellectually or not. Often you are a bit of a sponge and the emotions of other people flow in, merging with your own feelings. That can be a problem when you're out in public around people who are awash in pain or negativity. Suddenly you're depressed and you have no idea why! It helps to learn to shield yourself from other people's vibrations and to allow only intimates to merge their feelings with your own.

The Moon Through the Houses

The house where your Moon is placed describes areas of your life where you function on emotion, where your emotional interactions are more intense. It also shows how you express feelings and how your feelings are shaded by the world around you.

The Moon in the first house is very emotional. Your feelings are right on the surface and everyone sees you as an emotional person. Everything that happens in your life affects you emotionally and it's as though your feelings are a filter through which everything is expressed. In this lifetime you're learning to be more emotional, to get more in touch with your own feelings. You can't hide from them or ignore them because there they are—right in your face! Perhaps you have chubby cheeks or large, luminous eyes, the famous "moon face." You're a sensitive person and it seems as though your feelings color your every reality. You easily absorb the emotions of other people too, so sometimes what you're feeling doesn't start with you, but with the vibrations you absorb from other people.

The Moon in the second house brings financial issues into your most intimate areas. You tend to make emotional decisions for financial reasons. Perhaps you ally yourself with a mate in order to achieve financial security, or could be you hoard what you have. Or maybe you make a living at domestic pursuits—like Martha Stewart, whose domestic talents formed the foundation for her empire. With this placement, domesticity is an important thing and you will always want a nice home to give you a sense of security. Your emotions are most stable when your finances are also solid. You seldom let yourself be emotionally out of control, particularly when it's not in your best financial interest to throw a tantrum. You have strong feelings about money and about your financial security.

The Moon in the third house is friendly, lively, and outgoing. You enjoy emotional interaction and tend to chat freely with strangers as they cross your path. It seems that there's always something to share with new and interesting people and you're seldom guarded about revealing your feelings or hearing about someone else's. Local travel appeals to you and you enjoy roaming around your neighborhood, checking out new attractions. Even if you've lived in the same community all your life, chances are you've had several homes because the idea of relocation appeals to you. Reading provides meaningful insights and you learn about yourself and your own feelings as a result of what you glean from the books you enjoy. You're close to siblings and feel your neighborhood provides sort of an extended family situation.

The Moon in the fourth house is the archetype. This is an emotional, sentimental, very domestic placement. Your home and family provide the foundation that sustains you in the everyday moments of your life—whether happy or sad, and when life grows difficult, you retreat to the bosom of your family for solace. Your childhood seems amazingly real to you all your life, and even when you're quite old, you can speak of those memories as though they happened just yesterday. You have a strong connection to those you love and you know that those are the things that matter most in life—home and family. You enjoy parenting, and even if you have no children, you reach out to the youngsters around you in friendship. Puttering around your home gives you a feeling of security and you're never as happy as when you're home, doing this or that.

The Moon in the fifth house is shimmery and romantic. You live for love and enjoy reminiscing about the dates you shared long after those times have ended. You're fun and outgoing and are never as happy as when attending a party. It's so much fun to share romantic interludes—or to hear about them from someone else. You're an enthusiastic parent and feel your inner child remains alive and well all your life; thus you have a real sense of simpatico with the children in your life. Other people are more tempestuously emotional, yet your feelings are strong and passionate. You love with your whole heart and enjoy knowing that there are people in your life who share your affections. You're often very creative and enjoy filling your home with handmade items you produce or collect from craft shows.

The Moon in the sixth house causes your emotions to be allied with your health, so if you're upset about something, you could feel rather unwell. Sometimes you even go so far as to be a bit of a hypochondriac. Focusing positively on your health is a good way to combat this tendency. You form strong emotional connections with people at work and find that sometimes your colleagues turn into an extended family. You like nurturing them and may always be bringing home made goodies into the office to share with your pals. When you care for someone it feels natural to reach out and offer a helping hand, and the people in your life appreciate you as someone who always can be counted upon to offer support in a crisis. You may end up working in some sort of domestic field, such as a chef, housekeeper, or in the health areas. Your work speaks to your heart and what you do is also who you are.

The Moon in the seventh house requires that you find a partner with whom you can share your life. Your emotional reality is always colored by your attachments to other people. Your feelings are your own, but often you find that you absorb the sentiments—and emotions—from those closest to you. Marriage is an important institution, and you feel happiest when immersed in a life you can share. Being understood is essential to you and that's why sharing your life is so relevant. You have a sensitive side and your feelings are hurt easily if you're overlooked. You are kind and thoughtful because of your sensitivity and make a strong effort not to step on anyone's toes because you know how it feels when someone does it to you.

The Moon in the eighth house is intensely emotional, and very psychic. Your connections with other people are quite profound and it seems that you always have a second sense about the emotions of those around you. What they feel and why they do so is easy for you to understand, thus you can manipulate people if you choose to take that path, but usually you understand about vulnerability and try not to take advantage. You relate strongly to sex and are very passionate and feel most connected to a mate when you're making love. It's as though everything that is you merges with the complete essence of your mate, and that's a very rewarding connection. You have an uncanny second sense about money and are good at intuiting the best approach to take where investments are concerned. But if you get too emotionally distraught, you might make an unwise choice, based on emotional insecurity.

The Moon in the ninth house is adventure-loving. Perhaps you've packed up bag and baggage and have moved to distant lands to live your life, maybe even with someone who doesn't speak your language. You are a member of the world and feel emotionally connected to distant places and people. It's easy for you to feel fulfilled emotionally when sharing your life with all sorts of interesting companions, even if on the surface you have little in common. You have a strong yearning for justice and care very much what happens to the underdog. You relate viscerally to philosophy and law and know that the world depends on responsible action. Perhaps you are deeply religious and feel that it's your faith that sustains you emotionally.

The Moon in the tenth house brings a strong emotional connection to your career. Perhaps you're closest to those in your field, rather than to your family, and certainly you identify yourself emotionally with the work that you do. Your dad was a strong role model and your emotional reaction to how he lived his life helped define the choices you made as an adult in building your own career. This is a relatively unemotional placement for the Moon and you might tend to ignore your feelings in favor of more practical concerns. You do tend to make career decisions based on emotion, however. Perhaps your mother was more of the breadwinner in your family and thus you've developed a positive sense about women in the working world. Your entire experience of men and women in the world is very strongly defined by your childhood view of your parents.

The Moon in the eleventh house allies you strongly with your friends. You need to feel that there's a group of people with whom you're simpatico, who provide you with the support and understanding you need in life. Being a loner is very lonely indeed, and you feel quite unhappy when you lack the validation of your peers. Your goals are very important to you, and from an early age you can envision yourself moving forward in life toward those achievements you view as central to your identity. You have a strong group consciousness and believe that we should all help each other. It's natural for you to offer a helping hand and it feels good to be able to make a difference in the lives of those for whom you care.

The Moon in the twelfth house is intensely emotional and the most psychic of all the placements. Your emotions are a wellspring of life, bubbling up inside you and often they're so deep that not even you are aware of the sum and total of what you're feeling. You live at a visceral level, acting on instinct, going on your gut, and are always immersed in something deep and profound. You connect emotionally and just sort of know about other people. What makes sense matters little to you because your gut is what you trust when dealing with human interactions. Your dreams are intense and often quite wonderful and sometimes they feel more real than your day to day existence. You recognize that your emotions are buried and you know that other people can't quite get what your feelings are. You don't know how to solve this problem, but you offer a warm smile and a hug to those you love, and trust that your affection is clear.

MERCURY
Mercury is the planet of communication and describes how you express yourself.

Mercury is the planet of communication. Like the fabled, winged God Mercury, it's about the rapid transport of ideas. Its energy is crisp and bright and wherever you find Mercury, you find intelligence, speed, intellectual activities and the need to share them. Mercury rules Gemini and Virgo (although it's not nearly such a good match for the earthy Virgo energies as it is for the airy Gemini energies). Mercury is the teacher, the punster, the mailman and even the child pedaling along on a bicycle. Mercury shows the way you think, how you express your ideas and how you learn.

Mercury in Aries is bold, speedy and demanding. With Mercury in Aries, you learn quickly and you have your own ideas about just about everything. Are you opinionated? You bet! You're also a bit impatient. Because knowledge and ideas are so easy for you to grasp, you tend to become irritated with those who require more time than you do for a concept to sink in. Your mind is speedy and even though a person may be just as intelligent as you are, it doesn't feel that way when you're racing through an idea and he or she is lagging behind, mumbling, "Huh?" You prefer to be with people who challenge you intellectually rather than those who always need your help to make sense of life. Sometimes you're so hasty in expressing your ideas that you gloss over needed details and have to go back over them. You think quickly, speak rapidly and love to be out in the world where adventures can find you.

Mercury in Taurus is methodical, practical and organized. You believe in the tried and true and try to make sense of everything before you make any choice at all. You don't commit yourself frivolously because you want to make sure your grasp of the facts is genuine, but once you make up your mind, you tend to maintain your point of view no matter what changes. You understand things like the stock market and can read complicated financial documents with no confusion at all. You're also careful about keeping your work area neat and organized. You can't quite comprehend those eccentric geniuses who work amid chaos and clutter. You're good at the details of life and can spot little mistakes that other people gloss over, making you an excellent proofreader. Your goal is to understand and organize your world so that you can be in touch with the information you need and not be overwhelmed by all the unnecessary hype that's out there. You speak slowly and thoughtfully and you like to take your time.

Mercury in Gemini is in its own sign and functions perfectly there. With Mercury in Gemini you are speedy, smart and have a raging thirst for knowledge all your life. You're an avid reader and always will be. Your tastes in reading material may vary, but you will always want to swallow many words and ideas. You're so flexible that you're an ace multi-tasker. You work out on a treadmill while reading a book and watching television simultaneously and find it perfectly comfortable and acceptable to do so. Depth and focus are not your specialty; you seek breadth of knowledge and as much information as you can filter through your eyes and your mind. You are up on current events, even in faraway places, you know what's on television and you've been to the latest movies. In other words, you're a media darling! You speak quickly, pepper your language with jokes and puns and crave being out and around interesting people and events.

Mercury in Cancer is as much about feelings as it is about ideas. You have a need to make sense not just of the ideas involved with any situation as with the emotions that lie under the surface. Your own ideas come out of your mouth in a jumble sometimes because you're overwhelmed with the feelings involved and find them complicated to express in words. You rarely organize your thoughts before you share them, you just let them gush forward. To you communication is something imprecise, something that must be absorbed as much as heard. Likewise, when you listen to someone else, you get the sense of what they mean more readily than the actual information, and if asked to repeat what you hear, you will put your own slant on the comments rather than repeating them by rote. You speak with bubbly enthusiasm and share your important thoughts only with people you trust.

Mercury in Leo is cautious, deep and wise. You recognize that your word is also your honor, so you're careful about what you say and you always want to keep your promises. You like to understand the true nature of things and you put a lot of effort into learning not just what's on the surface but what any situation really means. You like the fact that you're intelligent and you're proud of your good mind. You may even enjoy taking tests and showing that your grades are better than those of your pals. You're usually more interested in reading fiction than material designed to teach and inform, but that's not always the case. You're quite demanding where written material is concerned; you're not the sort of person to read trash or pulp fiction. You believe in quality. You speak carefully, but you always try to be interesting to your listener. You like the give and take of communication as long as what you're hearing is honestly expressed.

Mercury in Virgo is precise, analytical and organized. You know how to take a bunch of seemingly unrelated details and to assemble them into something coherent. You're always interested in the meaning below the surface and nobody is better than you are at making sense of information. People whose minds are chaotic or unfocused irritate you to no end because you hate having your time stolen by nonsense. Although you're very smart, you're not usually a game person nor do you indulge in intellectual frivolities like jokes, puns or limericks. Instead you enjoy making sense of the world around you and using the information you have for practical gain. You're an excellent teacher because you can break anything down into its basic components and you think through any idea before expressing it. You're good at keeping orderly files or organizing information for other people. You speak precisely and thoughtfully and you make sure you're understood before continuing. You enjoy new ideas but only if they have a use.

Mercury in Libra is artistic, companionable and changeable. In your world, communication is really the servant of art and you enjoy so much experiencing a variety of artistic expression. You read novels, attend concerts, find poetry in the most mundane of song lyrics. Speech is a blessing, but it would be meaningless without someone to talk to; sharing your thoughts and ideas with the people around you is your way of enjoying life and celebrating yourself. You're always interested in your companions' ideas and you learn about them and yourself as a result of this intellectual interaction. Gaining new perspectives is a valuable pursuit because you like being intellectually flexible. Sometimes the act of simply exchanging thoughts is more important than the ideas themselves and perhaps that's why you often change your mind when you hear an opinion that is in conflict with your own. You speak softly and gently and try to put sparkle into all your conversations and you need to be out among people and excitement.

Mercury in Scorpio is deep, reflective and pensive. It's your nature to examine reality constantly but not always to share your thoughts. You recognize the subtext below the surface and realize that what people say isn't always what they truly mean. Because you're so astute, you know the difference between those who have trouble articulating exactly what they mean and those who are deliberately veiling the truth. You're a master of the spoken word, perhaps because you're so cautious about what you say. You never want your own comments to come back and haunt you. You take your time in formulating your own beliefs and you remain committed to what you know is true despite many obstacles or naysayers. You're interested in knowing the truth and you never give up until you've actually gotten to the bottom of any situation. You're an excellent detective as a result. You speak passionately but with caution and precision and you enjoy hearing about the mini dramas of life.

Mercury in Sagittarius is lively, expansive and needs movement and change. You love learning of all types and will read pretty much anything except books asserting prejudice or useless dogma. You believe in justice with your whole heart and will go out of your way to see that right is done. You never follow rules blindly because you'd rather think about what should be done, case by case. You're a champion of the underdog most of the time. You like the idea of adventure and long to be on the go. Reading exciting stories is a fun pastime but you also feel a need to have some of the thrills yourself. Foreign places and different people appeal to you and even with a language barrier, you're pretty good at making sense of what someone is telling you. You have a deep intellectual curiosity and a flair for knowledge. You speak with verve and are filled with a sense of fun and excitement. The world is your playground.

Mercury in Capricorn is organized and practical. The world must make sense to you, not mainly in an ideological way but in a down to earth, common sense fashion. You like information that is useful and which helps you achieve your goals. You're not the sort of person to stand around cracking jokes when something must be accomplished. You have a dry wit and a controlled manner and you appreciate when people don't inflict their nonsense on you. You're not a dumping ground and you can't quite comprehend why someone would share private details when it's inappropriate to do so. You like organizing and using information and you're an excellent accountant. You really understand the bottom line! They way people do things is endlessly fascinating to you, whether they excel at their technique or are hopeless wrecks. You always see a way to salvage a situation and make it pay off. You speak with authority when you know something and remain silent when you don't.

Mercury in Aquarius is visionary and intelligent. Your mind likes far ranging ideas, whether they have any use at all and you are quite content to sit and think your deep thoughts. You like high tech gadgets and people whose minds challenge your own. Nothing is more irritating to you than someone who repeats over and over ideas which were learned but never truly contemplated. You'd rather be taught nothing at all than to be expected to memorize a bunch of useless pap. The very act of thought and discovery is so enthralling and so very thrilling that it makes your whole life worthwhile. If you were confined to a small, empty space, you wouldn't like it but you'd survive by amusing yourself with your thoughts. You're a natural inventor and you can see new ideas that the world needs. It can be hard sharing these advanced concepts because often nobody else is on your level. You speak distinctively and you want other people to respect your ideas whether they understand them or not.

Mercury in Pisces is intuitive, sensory and sometimes confusing. You get a sense of the meaning of things and that guides you more steadily than the actual concepts involved. Your inclination is to follow your gut more often than your head and sometimes you turn your thoughts off altogether and just go with the flow. Music is very important to you and motion is soothing. A person can tell you one thing yet you might come away with the opposite impression of the meaning involved, because you are reacting to energy below the surface. If you get too involved with concepts and lose sight of the intuitive side of your nature, you tend to follow other people rather than to challenge them. It's better to trust your instincts instead. You speak softly and although you like to share your impressions, you don't want to overwhelm anyone with your own ideas. You like the traffic outside your window and it's fun to experience the panorama of life.

Mercury Through the Houses

Mercury is about movement and communication of ideas. Wherever we find Mercury in a horoscope, we see the areas on which you focus your thoughts and the ways in which you share them. Mercury also has to do with short term travel, so there may be more physical activity and general running around connected to whatever house in which Mercury appears.

Mercury in the first house is immediate, outgoing, and energetic. Whenever there are planets in the first house, they represent energies that you are working to learn and become more accustomed to in this lifetime. The first house is how you project yourself into the world — the illusion of you that everyone else sees, although the real you may be rather different. With Mercury here, you reach out and try to connect with the people around you — intellectually, through the sharing of ideas. You are an enthusiastic conversationalist, writer and you enjoy local travel as well. You crave a steady stream of intellectual stimulation and find dull moments when nothing is happening to be rather burdensome. You like to read and you enjoy all aspects of the media — in fact you may opt for a profession in one of those fields. You are probably a bit impatient and equally fidgety because you just like to keep on the move. People regard you as intelligent and interesting.

Mercury in the second house is practical and financially oriented. The second is the house of money. With this placement, you think about your financial situation, read financial books and may be interested in the stock market. You understand the ebb and flow of money as a commodity and regard it as an intellectual exercise to balance your own budget. You might enjoy one of those financial computer programs that allow you to create fancy spread sheets detailing your bank accounts. You also enjoy taking classes designed to help you manage money. Other people turn to the comics or the headlines when they first open the newspaper; you flip to the financial section.

Mercury in the third house is outgoing and communicative. The third is the natural house of communications and it also relates to education, your neighborhood, and siblings. With Mercury here, you love to talk, read and write and you may choose a profession in one of these fields. The world is an exciting place to you and you always want to know what's going on — pretty much everywhere. You might be a news junkie. No matter where you go, it's natural for you to strike up conversations with everyone around you and you find something of interest in just about everyone. Studying new things is always appealing and you're never quite as stimulated as when you're learning something new. Travel is another pleasure and even if you just stroll down an unexplored street, you feel like an adventurer, out for a thrill. Understanding your world and communicating about it makes you feel alive.

Mercury in the fourth house is pensive and private. The fourth is the house of home, childhood and your mother, and the teachings of childhood will always play a large role in the way you view the world. You like to be surrounded by books and feel quite comfortable in a cozy chair at home, reading about whatever subjects most interest you. You might have quite a collection of cookbooks, crafts books or volumes on decorating. You also enjoy things like scrapbooks and diaries and if you don't create your own, you're still very interested in those your friends and family members share with you. Thinking about your childhood is always meaningful and someday you might want to pen a memoir of the events of those long ago days. Movies and books recapping other people's childhood memories are always appealing to you. Discussions with friends and family members help you to make sense of what you think and believe.

Mercury in the fifth house is romantic and creative. This is the house of romance, creative endeavors and children and you enjoy reading novels, seeing movies and watching television programs. Entertainment is stimulating to you, and even if you have to do some deep thinking, you don't mind the hum of the TV in the background. The things that children say particularly appeal to you and you're probably quite a fan of those programs and books that feature comical comments made by kids. You also enjoy romantic stories, even if they're not very believable. Whether or not you consider yourself a creative person, it's fun for you to try writing stories. Even if all you do is tell your children fanciful bedtime tales, it feels like you're using your mind in a positive way to create something that brings pleasure and stimulation to other people. Short trips to local amusement parks or other fun places keep you happy and excited.

Mercury in the sixth house is practical and work-oriented. The sixth is the house of day to day activities at work and of health. You like focusing on material that can help you accomplish something. Self-help and how-to books particularly appeal to you and you feel that you can learn just about any skill with the help of a book. Health and diet books are another source of interest and you might keep them on your bookshelf right next to the cookbooks. When you get a new gadget, you're apt to look at the manual first and that way you save yourself the trouble of getting annoyed with it and heaving it out the window. You keep professional manuals close at hand at work and you keep your work materials and files organized and available for ready access. You enjoy traveling to attend seminars or business conferences and find it a good way to get to know your coworkers.

Mercury in the seventh house demands interaction with other people. The seventh is the house of partnerships and so you feel a need to talk to other people. You enjoy collaboration in all sorts of projects and never feel there's enough conversation before beginning a task with someone. You really learn a lot as a result of the things people share with you and sometimes you're willing to change your point of view in order to be congenial and accommodating. If you do feel strongly about something, you can usually find a way to share your point of view without alienating anyone around you. Marriage is one of the aspects of the seventh house and you realize the importance of communication within a relationship. You want to understand your mate and you work hard to share your own points of view with him or her. Having good communication and someone interesting to talk with is essential for you to feel alive and connected.

Mercury in the eighth house is probing and analytical. The eighth is a complicated house dealing with sex, other people's money and the deep connections we make in life. With Mercury here, you're always interested in digging below the surface. You enjoy talking to people about the intimate details of their life and often you can see what they truly mean when they say one thing yet really mean something else. You're interested in understanding what motivates people and you enjoy reading psychological books, whether texts or thrillers. You're also interested in finance and can understand the way money works. You find books on financial approaches helpful to you in planning your own investments and you make sure that all the details are on the table before you agree to any financial partnerships. Someone with Mercury in the eighth house probably invented the pre-nuptial agreement! Sex is another area of interest, and whether you're discussing sex with an intimate or reading books like the Kama Sutra, you're not just titillated but enthralled.

Mercury in the ninth house is expansive, exploratory and intellectual. The ninth is the house of higher education, philosophical ideals and long distance travel. Your mind seeks not just information but ideas. You like to ponder things and to make sense of them on your own. All sorts of philosophies appeal to you and it's interesting to you to determine why people buy into the various dogmas that keep them going. You're more apt to be an independent thinker than to accept without question religion or other doctrines. You like learning and you like teaching and you're always willing to share information with other people. A rousing discussion about ideas is always a fun way to spend your time and you never take it personally when someone disagrees with you. Instead you respect an individual's right to have whatever opinion he chooses. You believe in justice and enjoy following legal cases, though you don't always agree with the outcome. Travel to foreign places really appeals to you because then you see life being lived differently.

Mercury in the tenth house is ambitious and career-oriented. The tenth is the house of not just your profession but also your father and your standing in the outside world. With Mercury here you focus on what you want to achieve and you use whatever tools are necessary and at your disposal to make progress. You believe that getting an education is important to further your career, and chances are so did your dad. You want to be considered a person who is intelligent and informed and you try to express yourself in a dignified and responsible manner. If you don't know something, you will do your best to get more information before piping up with any opinion. You strongly believe in that old adage: *it is better to remain silent and be thought a fool than to speak up and remove all doubt.* You're interested in reading books about your career and you particularly enjoy those books which instruct you in ways to win friends and influence people.

Mercury in the eleventh house is intellectual and loquacious. The eleventh is about long-term goals for the future and social interactions with friends. With Mercury here, you enjoy talking about all sorts of things with the people around you. Communication is an important skill and you're interested in learning to do your best to be a pleasant conversationalist. Chances are you've succeeded because people generally enjoy talking to you. You have deep ideas and you enjoy expressing them. It is worthwhile for you to take the time to make sense of where you're headed in life and you may opt to make lists, keep a journal or use other ways to keep track of your goals. Books that inspire you to do more with your life or to overcome obstacles particularly appeal to you. It's also fun for you to hear people's life stories and you are willing to listen to the problems of those you know in order to help them see solutions that will help improve their lives. Visiting new and different locations is also fun because you enjoy the panorama of life.

Mercury in the twelfth house is deep, mysterious and intuitive. The twelfth is the house of the unconscious, buried events from long ago and feelings you can't quite understand rationally.

With Mercury here, you sense things and get impressions as strongly as you acquire concrete knowledge. Your thoughts are entwined with your feelings and sometimes they're so deep it's hard to articulate them. But you also find that you can understand other people on a gut level and know the essence of what they mean even when they haven't expressed it all that well in words. Your dreams are, of course, very significant and particularly so to you. Perhaps you keep a dream book beside the bed in order to record your dreams and make sense of their symbols. Books on dreams are quite interesting and meaningful to you, as are books about psychology. You may even be interested in hypnosis. Music is very inspiring to you and helps you think more clearly. Sitting alone and doing intellectual work or coming to grips with your thoughts is a comforting and meaningful activity.

VENUS
Venus is the planet of love and describes the way you express affection.

Venus is the planet of love and affection. In a woman's chart it describes the way she shares her heart and what she wants from love; in a man's chart it describes the women who appeal to him. The things that you like and enjoy doing and the objects with which you surround yourself are determined by Venus, which is also about pleasure, art, culture and taste. Venus rules Libra, where it loves romance and seeks harmony and Taurus, where it is sensual and seeks pleasure.

Venus in Aries is assertive, passionate and self-involved. Whether you're a man or a woman, you understand the motivation of the caveman who clubbed and dragged a mate back to the cave. When it comes to love, subtlety eludes you. Instead you like to overwhelm the object of your affection with evidence of your interest as well as many tales about that wonderful and loveable person — yourself. Patience is not your strong suit; you don't want to take your time and see how romance works out. Instead you race forward, ablaze with passion and determined to capture the heart of a potential lover — not someday but this minute. In addition to instant gratification, you like the new and unusual and your tastes are rarely conservative. Perhaps because your ardor is so quickly ignited, it's not always long lasting. But when your attachment ends, you cut the cord and move on without too much misery or regret.

Venus in Taurus is sensual and pleasure-seeking. You know what it is to enjoy the earthy pleasures of life, whether you're making love for hours, stroking a pet's soft fur or savoring a delicious morsel. Your affections are strong and long-lasting and you seldom get bored with a partner. Because your pleasure receptors are so developed and your approach to love so sensual, you're always willing to invent new ways to satisfy and be satisfied by a lover. You are also willing to take your time when beginning a new romance. There's something quite thrilling about going slowly enough to enjoy each sweet new moment, and even if you've driven yourself (and your partner) to distraction by prolonging the momentum, that's all right with you because you feel every nuance so intensely that you're constantly stimulated. You love comfortable surroundings, lush and sensual objects and good food. If you're a bit overweight, who cares; life is too sweet not to enjoy every little bite.

Venus in Gemini is flexible, changeable and a bit distracted. You fall in love at the blink of an eye and just as quickly get over a broken heart. In your life, there's no tear-soaked lingering by the phone. There are many people out there who appeal to you and you like taking advantage of each attraction, even if they're meant to last only a brief time. Talking to the one you love is very important to you because you share what's in your heart and mind through words far more often than those tender, smoldering glances that the less verbally agile must rely upon. You love entertainment and the media and spend a great deal of your life with the television humming in the background. You might even be one of those people who make love with a talk show going in the background and find it amusing when you finish along with the monologue. You love books and would be lost without your telephone.

Venus in Cancer is tender, nurturing and family-oriented. You care about the deep and important values in life and you have a great deal of respect for people who feel similarly because they know what's genuinely important. You rarely seek just a date. You want to find your perfect mate so you can settle down and raise a family together. Nothing is as beautiful to you as a cooing baby and if you could you'd have a dozen children. You like taking care of the people you love and you're always there when someone is in need. It actually pains you physically to think of a loved one suffering and because of that you're likely to overindulge your children. Cooking is very rewarding to you; the world feels like it's in perfect harmony when you're in the kitchen preparing a meal or a treat for loved ones. You have a real sense of life and its specialness and want to imbue each day with magic.

Venus in Leo is opulent, generous and beauty-oriented. You love the majesty of life and anything gilded or fancy appeals to you. You are quite affectionate and you love buying presents for the special people in your life. In fact, sometimes if you're feeling insecure, you might be tempted to overbuy where others are concerned in an effort to win their affection and gratitude. You love long and completely but with dignity. You want to do what's right for a lover and you also want to be treated with respect. Although you know that it's what's inside that truly matters, you also like the outside to be attractive. You do your best always to be attractive and you enjoy being around people who are good looking and well dressed. You also love children because of their vivacity and the beauty that radiates from them. Cultural pursuits are important and meaningful to you and you enjoy the theater immensely.

Venus in Virgo is helpful, modest and cautious. Showy displays of affection are distasteful to you. You're a subtle person and you show your affection by doing a kindness for someone you love. Whatever a lover needs, you're willing to pitch in and lend a hand until the problem is solved. You often ignore your own needs and instead put those of loved ones first. Sometimes you're so self-sacrificing that you're content to remain in the background, playing the part of the loyal friend, while the person you love dates someone else. That is a tendency you might want to rethink because love needn't entail quite that much sacrifice. Good taste is as important to you as is discretion. You like classic lines, soothing colors and nothing too discordant. The decorating style *less is more* was probably developed for someone just like you! Despite your subtlety and modesty, you can be quite sensual and earthy and your desire to see a partner happy makes you very good in bed.

Venus in Libra is romantic, artistic and tasteful. You believe in true love with all your heart and you enjoy daydreaming about romance in all its glories. When you're not in love, it feels that something is missing from your life. You enjoy social interactions and it's fun for you to get to know a new partner, but he or she must be tasteful for you to maintain an interest. A coarse, sloppy or uncouth person is not someone on whom you'd choose to bestow your favors, and even if someone has seemed all right for a while, once he or she crosses the line, you'd prefer to part company than deal with the possibility of a reoccurrence. You love fine art and beauty is very important to you, not so much for shallow reasons but because it feeds your very soul. You don't mind being assertive in wooing a lover, but your technique is so subtle that soon enough he or she is wooing you.

Venus in Scorpio is intense, passionate and sexual. You are like a lightning rod for love and when it strikes you feel the vibration immediately and intensely. It sometimes feels as though you are in the grips of something stronger than yourself and that you have no control over your own actions. You are bewitched and absolutely must posses the object of your affections. This generally isn't a problem, because you have a passionate vibration that is pretty hard to ignore and potential partners rather easily succumb to your charms. When you fall in love, it feels like destiny and you have a sense of commitment to your mate forever. If it ends, you find it quite devastating and may even come to hate your former true love. You rarely go on to have nothing but bland disinterest between you. Your tastes are as extreme as your passions; you like bold colors, vibrant art, and anything that stirs your passions.

Venus in Sagittarius is freedom-loving, outgoing and puppy dog friendly. You are not only a people person, you also love animals and plant life. You're just naturally affectionate and you see good things in just about everyone. You're probably the most accepting and least judgmental person around. When you fall in love, it's with an open hand and you're rarely possessive or jealous. You want your lover to be happy and you make few rules to control his or her behavior. Often you're just as content to keep a relationship casual as to make a commitment because you're quite happy spending time with a variety of people. You're interested in many types of partners and may have the fantasy of traveling far away and falling in love with someone from a completely different culture. Your taste is far from subtle and you like life to be casual and easy going.

Venus in Capricorn is practical, conservative and decorous. Although you can fall as much in love as any other besotted fool, you'd prefer not to be thought of in that way, so you try to control the outward manifestations of affection. Public displays seem tacky and just plain wrong to you. After all, someday you will be a parent and you have responsibilities to your children, your parents and the community. A tastefully lived, solid life is always your goal. You choose your partners carefully and seldom are ready, willing or able to fall in love with some eccentric flake who's sporting blue hair or covered with tattoos. Instead you are careful to see just who the person is and what he or she stands for before you'll consider a first date. You plan to fall in love only once — with the person you marry, and you also intend to remain together forever. Your taste is traditional and that's how you want your life to be.

Venus in Aquarius is friendly, eccentric and idealistic. Romantic love doesn't always make sense to you because the concept of friendship is so much more important. You can't quite imagine how some people fall so madly in love that it's like they've gone insane — over someone they don't even particularly like. You'd rather have a friend for life than a passionate affair that sizzles and fizzles. You really care who the person is and what he or she stands for and a mutual sense of values is a good foundation for affection. You meet your lovers in unusual ways, perhaps because your interests are so diverse. You love gadgets and may spend time online flirting before you actually meet in person. Commitment isn't always terribly important to you, but once a person has your affection, he or she remains in your heart a long time.

Venus in Pisces is tender, sensitive, and romantic. You believe not just in true love but in destiny, magic and universal oneness. When you fall for someone it's as though the world stops and you forget to breathe. You life has come into focus at last! You see great things in the one you love and even if he or she has many flaws, nothing can dissuade you from your idealized vision. In fact, you may discover at some point later on that you erred in judgment and you feel quite sad in discovering that this person you thought so special is nothing more than just human. You are a people person and you need social interaction. People often make demands on you and you want to give what you can; you're a bit of a soft touch for the needy. You like music and the ocean and love to snuggle with your lover, even hugging him or her while you're sleeping.

Venus Through the Houses

Where Venus appears in your chart determines the ways in which you seek romantic involvement and what you expect from love when it arrives. Venus in a house generally makes that house a little nicer and the affairs of that house a bit more pleasant.

Venus in the first house is soft, sensual and attractive. The first house describes the way you seem to other people and your physical body, so if you have Venus here, people regard you as attractive, no matter whether you consider yourself good-looking or not. You just have a nice vibration that attracts people to you and often you receive compliments without expecting them. First house planets are important because they represent energy you need to learn to assimilate. With Venus here, on a Karmic level, you are learning to be more sensual and to allow more love and beauty into your life. Pleasure is an important component of your life and with this placement you're rarely a workaholic or a driven person. Instead, you stop and smell the roses because you want to enjoy life. You also want to be loved and appreciated and chances are you receive a lot of positive, self-affirming feedback from the people in your life.

Venus in the second house is rather material. The second house is about money, and with Venus here, you're generally rather a spendthrift. You like buying things and will often buy a present for a loved one as a way of smoothing over troubles between you. In fact, you may feel that buying presents is the right approach when trying to woo a new lover, but eventually you will learn that no matter how much you spend, you can't buy love. Your taste is usually rather opulent and you're not usually the sort of person to deny yourself. Things are important to you and shopping is a favorite pastime. It's also possible that you make a living in some creative or artistic field, and if so, having Venus here is a blessing because it will help you attract the right sort of patrons into your life. Venus can also bring promising financial opportunities into your life and people who want to see you succeed.

Venus in the third house is gregarious, friendly and culture-oriented. You are very outgoing and you may even meet your lovers while passing on the street or racing for a bus. You naturally reach out to the people around you and it's easy for you to make new friends. You're popular and just about everyone enjoys your company. Socializing is important to you and you put effort into being charming and friendly. You like greeting cards and email and all sorts of ways in which you can communicate your affection to the people you love. The phone is permanently attached to your hand! You enjoy attending cultural events of all types, particularly while dating. You just enjoy experiencing the various ways in which people express artistic inspiration. Seeing beauty all around you helps you feel happy and more alive. You want your world to be a beautiful place.

Venus in the fourth house is personal, emotional and family-oriented. The sanctity of your home and family mean so much to you because they provide the safe oasis of love that is your emotional foundation. You're very attached to your mother and likewise to your children. You realize that life changes, people come and go, but family is the most important thing. Just looking around at your family fills you with tenderness and hope for the future. Having a cozy and pretty home is very important to you because that's where you go to retreat from life's woes and to restore yourself for tomorrow. Decorating may be a hobby or even a profession because you just know what it takes to make pretty surroundings. You love knickknacks and treasures of all sorts and enjoy saving little mementoes that remind you of the special events in your life. Entertaining at home is also fun for you. You're more of a homebody than a gadabout but you love having the world come to your door.

Venus in the fifth house is romantic, pleasure-loving and creative. You know what it is to live the good life with Venus here. Being involved romantically gives real meaning and pleasure to your life and if you're unattached, it usually isn't for long because you have social skills and a real knack for attracting interested romantic partners into your life. Basically, you're a party animal and you wouldn't have it any other way. You also love children and make the sort of fun parent who knows how to enjoy playing with children as well as raising them well. You may be quite creative or even a professional artist, but even if you're not, you appreciate the creativity of other people. To you creative activity is not only pleasurable, it's genuinely meaningful in that it feeds your soul. The nuts and bolts of life are important, and they may be important to you, but more than that you need the things that give life flavor—love, passion, and art.

Venus in the sixth house affects your life at work and your health. With Venus here, chances are you love to work and you put a lot of your heart and soul into your everyday chores. People at work tend to like you very much and they may be your pals as well as your colleagues. You have an easygoing, charming manner and that makes you pleasant to be around; you're rarely driven or frenzied even if you do have deadlines. You may actually fall in love with someone at work, or meet your mate through a colleague's introduction. The sixth house is also about health and with Venus here you may be a bit lax about your diet and lazy about getting exercise. Just be careful you don't overdo the sweets because that's never a good thing. Small pets are another aspect of this house and you may find yourself falling madly in love with your cat or dog—but pets are very lovable, so who can blame you.

Venus in the seventh house helps you with partnerships. With Venus here, you really want to be married. You feel that being part of a couple is the only way to live and if you're single, you feel quite lonely and needy. You know how to reach out to others to meet your emotional needs and you're genuinely quite popular and well liked, but having a million friends is still not enough for you. You want love and you want marriage. Your goal may be to find your true love early and remain all your life with that same person. Nowadays that's a difficult ambition to fulfill but not an impossible one. You do very well with one-to-one encounters and business partnerships can be quite happy for you. You also do well in counseling situations, whether you're the one giving or the one seeking help. Because you realize how important other people are to you, you make the effort to make them feel more valuable and that enriches their lives as well.

Venus in the eighth house is passionate and financially lucky. The eight house describes ways in which you merge with significant others, and with Venus here, you have good sex. Your desire is to please and be pleased by a lover and more than that, you regard sex as a tool for transcendence of your earthly being and a way to transport your spirit into holier realms. So for you sex is not just about reproduction or even pleasure, but about a spiritual quest to merge with the infinite. Because you're so attuned to this higher vibration of sex, you send out a kind of buzz which attracts all sorts of potential lovers to you. Be careful how you use this energy because some of the people you attract will just want lust, not transcendence! The eighth is also the house of other people's money and with Venus here you may inherit money, marry someone wealthy or at the very least, find a mate who wants to pamper you.

Venus in the ninth house is scholarly, culture-loving and travel oriented. The way the world lives is interesting to you and you may have a desire all your life to go off to a foreign place where you can immerse yourself in another culture. Certainly you like people from distant places and you may end up married to such a person. You have a great affection for different lifestyles and you can find something to like in just about everyone. You're also very good at getting along with diverse people and you may an excellent mediator because you can help people see each other's points of view. You also like art and may teach or study art as part of your profession. Cultural events of all sorts really speak to you and you attend them to enrich your being as much as for entertainment. Even if you don't move far away, you will bring the world into your home via objects d'art and foreign movies.

Venus in the tenth house is artistic. This is the house of your career and your standing in the outside world, and with Venus here you tend to make an excellent impression on employers, colleagues and business contacts. No matter who you really are inside, you tend to inspire a great deal of affection in those around you at work. Even when they don't quite know you, people feel you're a special person and they want to help and support your efforts. The tenth is also about your father, and with Venus here you have a nice relationship with Dad. He is supportive, loving and nurturing and you will always remember him fondly. This is a good placement for people who want to make their living in a creative field. You may have artistic ability and if so, other people will appreciate and support your talents. You might also be in sales, as in someone who works in a gallery or sells other creative output.

Venus in the eleventh house is friendly and charming. You're a real people person. The people in your life are very important to you and you want to make the most of every social opportunity. You like seeing good things happen to your friends and they will usually go far out of their way to see that you are happy and taken care of. People really like you and want to spend time with you and you're content to return the favor. You care about being friends as much as being mates and you will rarely choose to marry someone whom you can't consider a best friend as well. The eleventh is also about long-term goals for the future and you never fail to make pleasure and happiness a priority in your life. You understand that no matter what else you achieve, being a happy person and radiating inner harmony is a very important life choice.

Venus in the twelfth house is veiled and private. Although you do have strong and loving feelings, you're not always willing to verbalize them. Sometimes you're content to remain behind the scenes as a friend rather than making your romantic interest known. Often you have dreams of beauty and love and it's fun to wake up and recall the intense feelings of love and romance that have flooded your dreams. You have a second sense about people and sometimes you find yourself liking a person whom others dislike. That's because you feel you really know who he or she is deep inside, and they do not. You're also rather creative and you respond strongly to music and art. They make you feel balanced and happy and if you're blue, singing a song will cheer you up.

MARS
Mars is the planet of action and describes the way you assert yourself.

Mars is the planet of energy. It describes the way you thrust yourself into life and how you go about getting what you want and need. It is also the planet of sexual desire. Venus is about love and affection and it combines with Mars to express that love physically. Mars rules Aries, and helps give Aries people that immediate, do-it-now, impatient, energetic quality. Mars is fiery, insistent, and self-centered. In a man's chart it describes his masculinity and in a woman's it describes the male energies that appeal to her.

Mars in Aries is single-minded and assertive. You know what you want and feel unapologetic about going after it. You feel entitled to have what you want and there's nothing stopping you from pursuing your heart's desire. You are very aggressive and often you take action first and think later, making life exciting or disastrous, depending. You like speed, instant gratification, fast machines, and people who don't demand that you waste your time. You're passionate and very in touch with your sexual drive. You get aroused easily and you want a mate who will say yes just as easily. You need an active lifestyle to keep you happy and emotionally balanced and if you spend too much time indoors at a desk you feel all twitchy and irritated. It's easy for you to fly into a temper tantrum at a moment's notice and just as easy for you to recover and be pleasant again. Being self-directed and assertive is essential to you.

Mars in Taurus is slow, sensual and controlled. You like to take your time with any project, and if that means lying on the couch eating candy for a very long time while mapping out a game plan, so be it. You like life to be orderly and for your choices to make sense before you act on them. You have a lot of stamina and stick with any project for as long as it takes to complete it. That's partially why you're so slow to make a choice — you know once you're committed you'll be stuck. Long and difficult projects are a challenge to you and you make it up that hill while the Jonny-come-lately's are dropping like flies. Although you control your temper, sometimes you just can't take it any more and then you erupt in a mighty explosion, sort of like a volcano. It's better to modulate your energies so this doesn't happen because it's not exactly good for your heart!

Mars in Gemini is speedy, impatient and changeable. You

realize that there are many ways to get to any goal and very often you change your approach mid-stream. You like trying new things and you feel no obligation to complete what you start. As long as you get the sense of something and then decide you've had enough, that's just fine. Long, tedious tasks bore you and boredom is not something you suffer gladly. Your reflexes are acute and you excel at things like arcade games and other sports that require lightning movements. You're usually late and often in a hurry and that's because you get interested in whatever flickers by in the moment and lose track of what you're supposed to be doing. You don't want to be mired in anything for too very long so your life must remain changeable or you opt to change it. You'd do well at an occupation that requires travel or flexible duties and hours.

Mars in Cancer is sensitive, nurturing and yet dynamic. You are a cautious person who cares how your actions impinge on other people, yet you still find ways to be assertive enough to get what you want. You're good at motivating other people to take action, and often you lead through showing people why it's best for them to do what you say. You understand that action isn't blindly motivated but that there are feelings below the surface that cause us all to do the things we do. Because you're in touch with your own feelings, it gives you greater power to accomplish your goals—without stepping on too many toes. Anger is a difficult emotion for you to express and sometimes you sublimate these feelings through overeating. It's important for you to learn to stand up for yourself and not to let anyone walk all over you. And of course, if you're annoyed, speak up!

Mars in Leo is demonstrative, generous and showy. You never mind being the center of attention, no matter what you're doing, and you enjoy your moments in the spotlight. You feel entitled to respect and when you go after something you want, it just seems appropriate that you should get it. You have stamina and will keep at something until you meet your goal, but you'd never want to behave stupidly or foolishly because being held up to ridicule for your behavior is too horrible a possibility to consider. You pride yourself in your lovemaking techniques and you enjoy being able to satisfy a lover, no matter how much effort is involved. Of course lovemaking, no matter how long it lasts, is not something you consider an arduous or odious task! There is a playful quality to your energy and you love having a good time with friends or with the children in your life. Your own spirit is lively and your inner child remains active all your life.

Mars in Virgo is organized, precise and efficient. You do things neatly and carefully and any with task you attempt, you think through all the details in your mind in order to do your best. You like developing your skills and will work quite hard to attain expertise in anything, whether something simple like painting an old chair or complicated like assembling an object with many parts. You are naturally helpful and will automatically reach out when you see someone in need. Sir Galahad probably had this placement and you know too well how easy it is to rescue a person in distress and set him or her on the right path again. You can be quite selfless when it comes to meeting your own desires because you get as much gratification from doing things for others as for yourself. You need exercise and enjoy using your body well and efficiently. You despise laziness and sloth and try to encourage everyone to follow your lead. They didn't write that Boy Scout creed for nothing!

Mars in Libra is indecisive, changeable yet an excellent leader. You are assertive, yet you never want to step on anyone's toes. Remarkably, more generals have this placement than any other and perhaps that's because they know how to inspire the loyalty of their troops through honor. You do go after what you want, but often you think you want one thing but later decide you want something else. It doesn't bother you if you don't finish everything you start, as long as you're courageous enough to keep starting new things. You enjoy pomp and circumstance and always feel that your behavior must reflect courtesy and good taste. You'd never allow yourself to be caught in a compromising situation. Sometimes you hesitate to make a commitment to a course of action because you can see so many possibilities that it feels your options diminish once you make that commitment.

Mars in Scorpio is formidable, determined and invincible. You have a great deal of inner power and you know when to use it. You're rarely showy and it's not in your nature to challenge someone else to a fight. But if it comes to that, your courage is legendary and you will fight to the death if necessary. The steely look in your eye is often enough to get an opponent to back off—way off! You have no compunction about going after what you want and if you need to manipulate someone else to do so and it's justified, you will use whatever means are necessary without looking back. You're stubborn and when you make your mind up, you get what you want because you never let go until you do. You are legendary in bed and no doubt have lovers lining up to sample your skills—and your stamina. Your energy inspires confidence and can be quite healing.

Mars in Sagittarius is playful, outdoorsy, and flexible. You understand what fun is all about and generally speaking, having a good time is tops on your list of priorities. You're rarely regimented or orderly and because you go with the flow, you avoid health crises that plague other, more constipated individuals. You love to be outside and if you are stuck indoors for too long, you get cranky. You know you need to be out in nature, running with your dogs and if you can, you choose an occupation that gives you that flexibility. You're not tied into any one course of action and will often change your mind in the middle of any task. Finishing what you start is less of a priority than giving energy to your newest flight of fancy. You're modest about what you need and rarely inflict ego-driven desires on anyone else.

Mars in Capricorn is organized, ambitious and practical. You are assertive to the max and will do whatever is necessary to get your own way. That doesn't mean that you use power frivolously or to subjugate others. You don't. You simply work hard to achieve your goals and take all the proper steps in order to make sure that you do get where you want to go. You are an excellent leader and are very good at making use of whatever resources are available to you. If you have a large task to complete and many helpers, you'll naturally take over and delegate the work until everything is humming smoothly. You have a strong sense of propriety and find offensive behavior that is blatantly showy or tacky. That doesn't mean you avoid self-serving actions however, because after all, you're no fool. You take great pride in your work and enjoy doing things with your hands.

Mars in Aquarius is determined, experimental and bossy. You like getting your own way and because your energy is so strong and unwavering, you usually do manage to prevail. You're like this locomotive that plows through objections until everyone else gives in. You have your own ideas about how things should be done and you're never unwilling to try something new — as long as it's your own notion to begin with. You like unusual approaches to living, but you're more inclined to expect other people to follow your innovation than to sample their approach. People who are stodgy or staid bore you and it's sort of a hobby for you to set them on their ear with a bit of outrageous behavior designed to stun their sensibilities. You have excellent stamina and can finish any task you start, although you seldom feel a compulsion to do so. You want your lovers also to be your friends and if you have nothing in common intellectually, what's the point of having sex?

Mars in Pisces is sensitive, apologetic and healing. You have a hard time being assertive because it's so easy for you to focus on other people's needs and points of view that often their desires substitute for your own. Ultimately, however, you will shortchange yourself with this sort of behavior if you're not careful. You do have a right to have your own way and it's important for you to believe this and to assert yourself when something truly is important to you, no matter how guilty you feel for putting yourself first. Sometimes you *should* come first! Your energy can be very healing and simply by touching a person who is ailing, you can make a difference. Be careful of the sponge effect, though, because you can absorb other people's negative vibrations when they're ill or depressed and you will then feel under the weather yourself. Music and dance helps you balance your own energy.

Mars Through the Houses

Mars is the planet of energy and sexual drive and where it appears in your chart, you are more active, more energized and sometimes more driven by the concerns of your ego. The house that contains Mars describes the ways in which you assert yourself naturally throughout your life and the issues that will always stir you up.

Mars in the first house signifies an active, passionate, sometimes hot-headed person. As first house planets represent energies you're trying to learn more easily to understand and incorporate into your nature, with Mars here, you're learning the value of action and assertiveness. The only problem is that in this lifetime you will probably over-compensate and be a bit too aggressive, a bit too confrontational, a bit too domineering. It's important to remember that most life lessons take a whole life, so right now you're exploring the sensation of Mars and eventually, on a spirit level you will master the proper use of force and energy. Right now, you're definitely an active, outgoing, masterful person who radiates energy and sex appeal. People find you exciting and usually you seem to be the one in charge in any situation. Whether you're sure about what you want or not, you act on impulse—quickly and with few concerns for the consequences.

Mars in the second house focuses quite a bit on money. You recognize that it's important to make a living and you want to do even more than make a living—you want to be wealthy and you generally expend quite a bit of energy in making money and in maintaining a lifestyle you consider appropriate. Money is a real frame of reference to you and you make behavior choices because of it. For example, you might choose one social event over another simply because of the cost or choose to live in a certain place only because of financial reasons. The problem is that your ego is closely tied into your back account and you feel that your personal worth is also measured in dollar signs. If you pause and think clearly for a moment, you'll realize that of course this is untrue, but it doesn't stop you from wanting to impress people with your wealth, your lifestyle and the shiny car you drive.

Mars in the third house seeks unlimited freedom to come and go and enjoys the pursuit and sharing of knowledge. The third is the house of communication and of siblings and neighbors. With Mars here, you enjoy participating in the media, whether you're an avid reader, a TV junkie or a fan of culture. You spend time and energy sharing activities with the people around you. You love adventure and find excitement in ways large and small—even a drive down an unexplored street can feel like an exciting event. You love cars and other machinery and like to be on the go. There's always a feeling in the back of your mind that there's more to see, more to experience, and you certainly want to be there, right at the front of the line. You may have some competitive feelings toward a sibling or a sense of disapproval of a neighbor. You like to be top dog in whatever arena is yours.

Mars in the fourth house is home and family oriented. You're an enthusiastic putterer and you love to fiddle around at home, making improvements. You probably are a good handyman, whether you're a man or a woman and wielding a hammer is fun for you. Organizing your tools in the garage, or for that matter, keeping your home in order appeals to you. That doesn't necessarily mean you live in a pristine showplace, but rather that it's a constant work in progress because it's the work you enjoy more than the perfection you create. Your family is very important to you and you love organizing family outings, holiday events and gatherings that bring together the people you love. You just can't help it—you're sort of a scoutmaster at heart and it's just your nature to want to see the whole family hiking, picnicking, barbecuing or building a tree house together. You may have some resentment toward your mother, and if so, work to understand the sources and then release the pain.

Mars in the fifth house is athletic, passionate and focused on fun. You are an outgoing and energetic person and you know how to enjoy life. You're playful and doing fun things is always meaningful and rewarding to you. You love sports and have good muscle development. Even as a small child, you walked earlier and could master physical tasks more easily. Your inner child remains vibrant today and you always enjoy sharing fun activities with the children in your life. Romance is another fun pastime and you're willing to go on a date at the drop of a hat. You put a lot of energy into your social activities and you're rarely too shy to make your interest known to the object of your affections. You might be a bit too much of a party animal and you like playing the field, but you figure life is short so why not enjoy it. You're also a bit showy and may enjoy performing in front of others.

Mars in the sixth house focuses on the day to day chores at work. You're a hard-working person and you love to dig in and get a task done. In fact, you tend to turn everything into work. A hobby or an important career task inspire in you the same sort of focus, devotion and determination. You like working on your own better than working for or with other people because you are most comfortable when moving at your own pace. You know that you will give any project your all as completely as possible and you don't want other people and their demands slowing you down. You may also have an interest in health or even be a devoted health nut. Either way, you recognize the importance of exercise and proper diet. You know that your body is a machine and that proper maintenance is essential if it's going to work as hard for you as you need it to do.

Mars in the seventh house is a mixed blessing. This is generally considered the position of one-to-one combat. Although partnerships are very important to you, and you want to work very hard to make a relationship function, sometimes it seems that you gravitate into relationships that are more like battlegrounds. If this is the case, it signifies an ego issue. With Mars in the seventh, you struggle because you know that you have your own needs and desires and that you want to have them met. You also have a tendency to merge your desires with those of a significant other. So you have what the psychologists call the approach-avoidance dilemma. What choice do you make? This confusion leads to frustration and ultimately to quarrels. The less sure you are about your own strength as an individual, the more likely you are to engage in battles in which you overexert your power. The key is to get in touch with these issues and feelings in order not to let them overtake your love life.

Mars in the eighth house is both passionate and financial. You're very in tune with sexual energy and impulses and you can feel whatever chemistry exists between you and someone else immediately upon meeting him or her. You have a lot of personal magnetism, and no matter what you look like, people consider you sexy. You understand about energy currents below the surface and can use your own charisma to get what you want from other people. You're rather demanding where sex is concerned—you know what you want and when you want it and usually that translates into a good bit of sex on demand! Other people's money is another issue. You have a certain degree of ego invested in your financial status and you like it when lovers spend money on impressing you or on fancy gifts for you. You may be involved with high finance as a career, but you're certainly determined to manage any joint funds with a good deal of control.

Mars in the ninth house is intellectual. You are passionate about the world of ideas and you like unraveling concepts until you get at the true nature of what's been said. You're an excellent teacher and it's very enjoyable for you to share knowledge with other people. Your nature is quite philosophical and it's fun for you to work at understanding deep and complex ideas. Like knights of olde, you live by your credo and make your point of view reflect your life choices— and vice versa. You may or may not enjoy political, philosophical or religious debates. Generally speaking, you're a good debater but depending on how secure you are in your own points of view, you might opt just to live and let live where other people's opinions are concerned. Traveling is very rewarding to you and it may be your goal to travel all over the world. Certainly you enjoy being in distant places and seeing how the other half lives.

Mars in the tenth house is hard working. Success is so very important to you and you are willing to give your all to get somewhere in this world. You like being self-directed and you feel more comfortable when working on your own projects than when working for someone who constantly oversees your progress. Your goal may be to be self-employed. Your ego is invested in your position in the world and if you haven't achieved as much as you think you should have, you feel rather bad about yourself and determine to double your efforts. It's important to you to be thought well of in your community and within your profession. You have a strong connection to your dad; you think about the things he taught you and his approach to tasks and to life and in a lot of ways you try to be a similar person.

Mars in the eleventh house focuses dynamically on long-term goals for the future and social obligations. You're the sort of person who always has a blueprint for life. You have a five year plan, a ten year plan and so on and it's very useful for you to look back over your previous plans to see how on-target you were at the time. The point is that you are a very self-directed person and your natural inclination is to be in charge of your life. People who just drift from moment to moment completely unaware seem like fools to you. Life is complicated and you want to stay on top of it. You're quite assertive in your social life. You like spending time with friends and you're also a great volunteer worker. Being on committees and boards seems worthwhile as long as you don't feel that you're being bossed around by someone else. You can definitely be a force for good in the neighborhood.

Mars in the twelfth house is rather shy and understated. You don't like charging forward and making demands on your own behalf. Instead you stay on the sidelines, quietly working for whatever it is you want. Sometimes your way of being assertive is to do things subtly so that other people bring what you want to you, rather than you having to go out and get it. You just don't feel right in being too demanding, but sometimes you wish you could be more aggressive, particularly when you're overlooked. If you do have some anger, it may manifest through your dreams. Intense situations where you're struggling, fighting or killing someone in a dream are signs that you need to work through more of your feelings and to take more direct action. It also helps to become completely in touch with your own feelings and desires. Working on behalf of others is rewarding too.

JUPITER
Jupiter is the planet of expansion and describes areas of ease, and perhaps luck, in your life.

Jupiter has traditionally been considered the planet of good luck, but it's really more about positive expectations being met with happy responses. In other words, when you expect good, good comes to you. Jupiter is the principle of happiness, of gifts, it is Santa Claus, the benevolent parent, the loving mentor, and the blessings of life. Jupiter rules Sagittarius and it gives that sign a love of justice, the outdoors, a calm sense that life will be good, and an affection for animals. Jupiter's energy is warm, expansive, and glowing, like a helium balloon floating off into the great beyond. It has an affiliation with law, medicine and teaching. Where you find Jupiter, life is easy and comes naturally; it's where you excel without having to strain.

Jupiter in Aries is courageous, speedy, and impetuous. You feel that anything is possible and that nothing can stand in your way. That can be a wonderful asset unless you go too far off the deep end by deciding you're invincible and letting life show you that indeed you are only too human. Jupiter in Aries can be wonderful for courage though, and this is a good lifetime to learn to become a fair and just leader. Your strength can mean a lot when deployed to help those weaker or less fortunate than yourself—often just about everyone else! You like fast cars and machinery of all types and you may even invent or build some sort of speed machine.

Jupiter in Taurus is indolent, pleasure-loving and wealthy. This is an excellent indication that you are prepared to live the good life and have the financial resources to do so. You love the pleasures of life—food, comfort, sex, money, and you enjoy every moment of pleasure that you receive. If you're a careless person, you may overdo and find yourself overweight and surrounded by empty Godiva boxes. But with a little heart and soul, you might opt to throw yourself into good causes—such as school lunch programs or feeding the hungry with food banks. You realize that living in the flesh on the earth plane is a wonderful thing and you want to share that good life with others.

Jupiter in Gemini is intelligent, hungry for knowledge and a good teacher. This is one of the best placements for teachers because you love learning and enjoy sharing what you know with other people. You can make any bit of information sound interesting because you know how to express yourself with verve and sparkle and are attuned to the responses of your listeners. You also enjoy travel and may spend many happy hours tooling around the neighborhood on your bicycle, pedaling for fun and stopping here and there to chat with all the people you spot along your route. You're a bit of an information junkie and have piles of books, newspapers and catalogs all over the house.

Jupiter in Cancer is warm and nurturing. You have the heart of Mother Nature and you love helping something live. Whether or not you have children of your own, you adore youngsters and are a wonderful role model for the kids in your life. There's just something magical about watching a child grow and you feel the spirit of life blooming all around you. You're also an enthusiastic cook and you love offering treats to everyone you meet. You just naturally know how to take care of other people. Your family is very important to you and you reach out regularly to the people you love so that they remain warm and cozy and a tight part of your life.

Jupiter in Leo is showy, outgoing, and dramatic. You love being the center of attention, and whether you're a professional actor or not, you're an excellent showman/woman and in your heart of hearts you know you belong on stage. The theater is a world of magic to you and you will retain that sense of glamour and happy expectation all your life. Children are also very special and you love going on fun outings with the kids in your life. Using your own creativity is very important, so be sure to pursue those areas of interest, whatever they are. Doing something creative reaffirms your sense that life is wonderful and that God is in the world.

Jupiter in Virgo is practical, helpful and healing. You like making the world a better place and you like to help other people get their lives in order. You're good at giving advice and helping a friend see in what direction he or she needs to go in order to make life better. You may actually work in medicine or even if not, you have an interest in health. Reading up on natural approaches like herbs and medicinal teas is meaningful to you because you feel that health begins inside, in the soul and radiates outwards to the body. You're right about that. You don't always worry about your own needs because you get so many good feelings from helping others.

Jupiter in Libra is artistic, romantic and loves the whole world. You are quite romantic and you love everything about romance, perhaps going so far as to dot your with little hearts. You like things to be pretty and life to be pretty as well and you're always planning a social event or attending one. Getting along with other people is very important to you and you have quite a knack for it—in fact you may be a bit of a matchmaker or even work professionally matching singles up. You learn about yourself through your contacts with other people and you grow as a person as a result of your social interactions.

Jupiter in Scorpio is transcendent, healing and magical. You adore the mysteries of life and thinking about religious or philosophical issues really makes you understand the deep truths that are so important to the way you live. You have a great deal of personal power and can provide a healing through touch or by sending energy. You like all sorts of transformations and even something as simple as watching the water boil in the kettle causes you to think about the way the universe works. You also see what's under the surface in the people around you and because you know what makes them tick, you know how to help them. You have similar insights into finance.

Jupiter in Sagittarius is expansive, philosophical and a happy wanderer. Jupiter here is in its own sign and it functions perfectly. The Jupiterian quest for justice is fulfilled here and you may be quite a crusader for the rights of the underdog. You just like to see justice done—and you generally can listen to other people's points of view and see who's in the right—or what compromise needs to be made. Perhaps you're a judge or a mediator or even a union activist. You feel a bond with many different sorts of people and you can see the beauty in life in so many different ways. Travel is broadening for you because you see how life can be lived in other cultures.

Jupiter in Capricorn is success and status oriented. Jupiter's natural expansiveness is somewhat limited by the caution of Capricorn. You tend to believe that a person makes his own luck rather than expecting any windfalls from the universe. You're focused on success much of the time and although you'd enjoy a lucky break now and then, you're much more used to plugging away and reaching for every opportunity you can create. You really want to achieve the highest level of success possible and can envision yourself at the very top of your game, whatever that is. You understand authority figures and aspire to be one yourself.

Jupiter in Aquarius is idealistic, inspirational and a little eccentric. You want to see justice done, but your idea of what's right for everyone isn't always in sync with their own idea of what they truly want. It's your challenge to learn how to help people without burdening them with your own unwanted truths. You believe in the future and can imagine huge leaps of growth in whatever area you're considering. Your imagination is boundless in that way and you can envision a future that most people don't even dare to dream. You love your friends and will do anything for them. In fact, you're surrounded by pals day and night and you love it that way.

Jupiter in Pisces is religious, artistic and traditional. You adore the pomp and circumstance of religion and may be quite involved in whatever religion is your own. Although you can see the merits in alternative schools of thinking, the traditional approaches have so much meaning and depth for you that you're content to remain immersed in the teachings of childhood all your life, or if you were raised by free spirits, you're likely to seek out a system of belief on your own. You love art and music and gain perspective and healing from them. A stained glass window or a hymn can move you to tears. You like to help those in trouble and to take care of those less fortunate.

Jupiter Through the Houses

Jupiter is the planet of good luck, and natural expansion. Where it appears in your horoscope, life is a little easier and you do well without having to try. It's your easy ace and the benefits given to you by Jupiter are like the natural resources that are yours to build upon. Jupiter in a house gives you a sense of confidence and positive expectations about the affairs of that house. These are the things you expect to go well and which you count on to sustain you when other elements of your life are going poorly. It's also where you can be generous and give to others.

Jupiter in the first house gives you optimism and a sparkling personality. In this lifetime you're learning to trust that things will be good and generally they are good for you. People like you and life gives you many rewards and pleasures. It may also give you a little extra in the way of avoirdupois—those love handles that you can't seem to shed and which nobody minds but you. You can relate to many people from all walks of life and you number among your friends a wide assortment of interesting folk. Traveling is a passion and may also be part of your work.

Jupiter in the second house brings good fortune with money. Does this mean that you're rich? Maybe or maybe not! What it means is that you have faith that money will flow in your life and generally that is true. How you manage the money that flows to you determines the level of your wealth. You may be rather lax about taking care of finances, and if so it's because you feel comfortable with your life and refuse to worry. That's positive. You may also decide to make your money work for you and if so, that could lead to more of the good life. You're usually willing to help those in need, whether by donation or with financial advice.

Jupiter in the third house brings loving siblings, pleasant neighbors and a great deal of intellectual curiosity. You like to explore your world, whether through local travel or by reading all sorts of books. You're smart and you do well in school without having to try too hard, although you're casual about your good grades and never smug about your success. You enjoyed playing with siblings or neighborhood kids as a child and you never lose that love of adventure. Being involved with local activities is fun for you all your life; those block parties are so much fun and you attend as many as you can find. You make an excellent teacher, even if it's not your profession because to you learning is an adventure you love to share.

Jupiter in the fourth house gives you a sense of security that nurtures you all your life. Your mother loved you and looked out for your welfare, or perhaps your dad took on a role that might be called maternal, but either way you felt safe and cozy and because of that early care, you now usually expect that things will work out for the best. You have a positive attitude about life and that gets you through all sorts of difficult situation. Your nature is sunny and people love having you around. You will never want for a home because even if you're out in the world traveling, someone will take you in and declare mi casa su casa.

Jupiter in the fifth house brings abundant creativity, warm and loving children and a general zest for life. You know how to enjoy everything from your own natural talents to the children running about under your feet. Life to you is rather magical and you see the pleasure and sparkle in every aspect of it. You are filled with joie de vivre and like to make every moment as special as possible. Entertaining and dating are great pleasures and you never lose your love of the theater and cultural events. You just like to enrich your life with every wonderful thing available to you. Because of that sparkle, you pass on a love of life to your children.

Jupiter in the sixth house brings a pleasant outlook at work. You are willing to give your all to your job and you're well regarded by coworkers and your superiors. Even if you're very busy at work, you never feel terribly pressured because you know you can handle everything in your stride and that it will all work out. You might work in law or medicine and if so, you feel good about the fact that you're helping people. Taking care of your own health is important, but it's often a low priority. You feel healthy and invincible, and while that's positive, you still need to eat properly and exercise, just like everyone else.

Jupiter in the seventh house brings partners who dote on you. You're not the sort of person who will put up with a lover who walks all over you or a business partner who usurps your authority or steals your cash. You expect to be treated fairly and well by other people and you have the good fortune to attract partners who make your happiness and success their priority. There is some risk that your approach to love is as a good time Charley who bounces from one mate to another, but that's probably not something that will be a lifelong problem. At least you know if one relationship ends, it won't be hard to begin another one, and that's comforting.

Jupiter in the eighth house is excellent financially. You attract mates and business partners whose resources are not only abundant but also completely available to you. It's easy to get credit of all types, insurance companies pay off when they're supposed to, and your investments do well. You might even inherit money or win the lottery. The eighth is also the house of merging and with Jupiter here you're an enthusiastic and generous sexual partner who has as much fun giving pleasure as receiving it. You're willing to try most anything a partner wants, all in the spirit of good fun. If you meditate it may be quite easy for you to connect with those little angelic voices of your spirit guides and their messages will always be life-affirming and loving.

Jupiter in the ninth house brings many adventures and a lifelong love of learning. Your mind is expansive and you love to explore ideas and the world itself. Travel is a great passion and chances are you will visit many foreign places in this lifetime. You feel as comfortable in a distant place as you do right at home in your own backyard. Despite the fact that people live different lives in other cultures, there is a sense of humanity and you easily tap into that brotherhood of mankind (or sisterhood of womankind as the case may be)! You're an excellent student and you may have many advanced degrees. Whether you use the knowledge to teach or in another profession, broadening your mind enriches your life.

Jupiter in the tenth house brings large success. Your career is a source of happiness and satisfaction for you and you are well regarded by the community. You have a great deal of affection and admiration for your dad and you feel that he prepared you well for the life you are now living. You are in touch with what you want to achieve and it seems not only possible but likely that you will be able to meet all your goals. Law or medicine are good choices for a profession, but acting is another possibility and despite the odds you could become a world-famous movie star, like Harrison Ford, who has this placement.

Jupiter in the eleventh house brings loving friends and a sense of positive expectation for the future. You like thinking about what you truly want not just today and tomorrow but also ten years from now and with Jupiter here, you can clearly envision how to manifest those goals and turn them into the happy reality you wish to live. Opportunities present themselves to you without you having to search for your lucky break. Friends love you and desire your company and they will always reach out to help you when you're in need. You can do your part by helping out with community do-good projects.

Jupiter in the twelfth house gives a quiet sense of security below the surface. Daydreaming is fun for you because you get a boost of energy from unknown sources when you do—perhaps you are connecting with your spirit guides or some sort of universal energy then. Actual dreams while sleeping are also pleasant as you tend to sleep easily and have pleasant dreams. You feel that you're okay most of the time and because you do, you're willing to reach out and help other people who are needier than you are. Religion and spirituality are meaningful to you because you want to make sense of the deeper truths that define you and your world.

SATURN
Saturn is the planet of Karma and limitations and describes lessons to be learned in this lifetime.

Saturn is the planet of Karma and earthly life lessons. It relates to timing of major life events and is always there to help you make revisions in your life. Saturn is the stern taskmaster who requires you to redo a project when it's incorrect, it's the ticking clock, the architect, and those situations in which you feel a sense of deja-vu. Saturn rules Capricorn and its somber nature helps those people to focus on achievement. Saturn is about doing it right and building something that lasts. Its energy is cool, steely and dry. The sign of Saturn shows the Karma you are trying to clear and also the fears that you are working to overcome. Oftentimes Saturn teaches by helping you overcome natural tendencies that lead you to make mistakes that ultimately must be corrected.

Saturn in Aries indicates a Karmic need to learn the positive qualities of courage, self-reliance and leadership. Perhaps in a past life you were too dependent on other people and let them lead you around by the nose. Now you must learn not to do that and through a series of challenges, you learn that standing on your own two feet makes you a stronger and a safer person. You may have some issues with authority figures, and if so, you will have to learn how to handle orders from other people. There's a difference between responding appropriately to authority and being walked over.

Saturn in Taurus indicates a Karmic need to trust in your own heart. In other lifetimes you've too easily sold out for the almighty buck and now you realize that money can't mean everything to you. Sometimes in this life you experience financial troubles, but that's only so that you will release the hold on you that money represents and look around at life in order to see what truly matters. You also have issues about pleasure. You're afraid to let go and just let yourself enjoy life because you fear giving in completely and becoming a libertine. Now you prefer austerity and control.

Saturn in Gemini indicates a Karmic need to learn to use your intellectual abilities. You're too easily distracted and have spent some lifetimes indulging in so many material pleasures that you forgot how to amuse yourself with your brain. Now you may not have a dime—

or may be unable to manage money effectively, but that's all right because you're determined to focus on intellectual pursuits. You may spend so much time reading that you neglect your career and find yourself trapped in menial jobs. Once again, it's all right because you're here to learn to communicate and to think effectively.

Saturn in Cancer indicates a Karmic need to get suckered into situations or relationships that are not in your own best interest. You've been overly needy in other lifetimes and now you have to learn that neediness is not the best way to get your needs met! You have to find ways to take care of yourself and to be responsible for your own security, because if you don't do it, nobody else will. Your tendency now is to find someone to cling to and to put your energy into making that person safe, secure and successful, but unfortunately, there is no guarantee that he or she will take care of you as a way of returning the favor. Love with your heart but not because you're terrified.

Saturn in Leo indicates a Karmic need to express yourself. You've been very shy in other lifetimes and have hidden your lights from other people. That has led to feelings of loneliness and despair. Now you must learn to be your best self and to share those qualities willingly with the people around you. There are many rainbows inside of you and it's up to you to discover and maximize on them. That's not to say that you should be a show off or an ego-maniac. Instead you should strive to be a warm and successful person who uses all your talents to their best effect. You also need to learn to curb a tendency for meaningless opulence.

Saturn in Virgo indicates a Karmic need to have a healthy mind in a healthy body. In other lifetimes, you have been either totally intellectual or utterly physical, and now you need to balance both. Your body is more than an instrument for frivolous pleasure and you need to take care of it. Likewise, a good mind is a tool for success, but more than that it can provide you with endless hours of recreation in a silent, empty room. It's your task to find a way to use your body and your brain to the best effect and to take care of both your physical and intellectual needs so that you're a balanced person who can make a difference in the world.

Saturn in Libra indicates Karmic issues where love is concerned. In other lifetimes you have abandoned mates and lovers and now you might find yourself on the receiving end of some pretty callous romantic behavior. It's really unfair, because in this lifetime you probably haven't hurt a soul, yet a mate disappears from your life without a word. Karmically this is part of the give and take of energy, so if a love leaves you, be philosophical, shrug your shoulders and move on with your life. As long as you give your heart honorably and do your best always to treat people with kindness and consideration, eventually you will be all right.

Saturn in Scorpio indicates a Karmic need to understand the power of the soul. In other lifetimes you may have been rather careless and rather promiscuous. Perhaps you regarded sex much too casually and thus you didn't realize the power it has as a tool for spirituality. Sex is, of course, lots of fun, but it can be a source of transcendence and the tool by which we all connect with God. Through merging with a mate, you can feel the infinite power of God. Likewise can you do this through meditation. All it takes is the ability to give up yourself and open to the universal. Learning how to do this is your task now.

Saturn in Sagittarius indicates a Karmic need to trust in your own instincts and desires and to follow them. In other lifetimes, you were a slave, or someone who simply went along with the suggestions of other people. You neglected to live your own life. Now it's up to you to learn the value of reaching deep inside yourself in order to ascertain who you truly are and what life you must lead. Your life should reflect important choices—your actions show who you are and what you stand for and the life you lead should be congruent with what's in your heart, mind and soul. You also need to learn the value of play and of keeping your inner child alive.

Saturn in Capricorn indicates a Karmic need to learn to respect success. It functions very well here because this is its own sign. In other lifetimes, you had great success and tossed it all away, for whatever reason—perhaps because of insecurity. Sometimes people who make it to the top too quickly don't trust their success and they sabotage themselves. Now you will have to take your time in achieving your goals, although your temptation will be to try new things rather than sticking with something that is going slowly. Avoid that approach because it will just prevent your success. Deal with your issues, whether fear of failure or of success and remember that something that takes a while to achieve usually lasts.

Saturn in Aquarius indicates a Karmic need to learn

selflessness. In other lives you have been too self-centered and it's been hard for you to focus on the needs of others. Now you must learn to do so. It may be quite hard for you to become a joiner because you feel ill at ease in groups, but it's important for you to realize the power and the benefits of association with others. Charity work can be very meaningful to you now and in fact, it could become a career. You feel an obligation to help those less fortunate and it's good for you to share your abilities in whatever way you can.

Saturn in Pisces indicates a Karmic need to get closer in touch with the Spirit inside you. In other lifetimes you have lived a rather soulless, material existence and you have been the poorer for it. Now you must learn that the earth plane is a wonderful, fulfilling place, but without ties to God and other universal energies it's not nearly as wonderful as it could be. Learn to reach inside yourself for inspiration so that you can follow your heart and express your true self, in ways both profound and beautiful. Art is very important and meaningful to you now and if you open up to universal inspiration, you can channel in something quite beautiful for all to share.

Saturn Through the Houses

Saturn is the planet of Karma and earthly life lessons. Where it appears in your chart, you must deal with various insecurities and fears. The fears arise because you have had problems with this energy in other lifetimes and are trying to master it now—except you're insecure about your ability to do so. In addition, Saturn describes obligations to other people you must meet—whether you truly have the resources or not. It's where you will be judged and where you must learn to try hard to do the best you possibly can.

Saturn in the first house requires you to work hard and to take care of your health. In other lifetimes you were a bit of a slacker, but in this lifetime you don't have a moment to yourself. No matter what you do for a living, you're always busy with things you must accomplish. It just feels comfortable for you to be busy and you're willing to volunteer your time in order to keep pumping along. Lying in a hammock simply doesn't feel like a comfortable way to spend your time. Because you're such a hard working machine, be sure to eat right and to exercise. It's also good to take vitamins and other supplements to prevent colds.

Saturn in the second house requires you to work particularly hard for a living. Money is hard to come by, and you must learn to respect its value. In other lifetimes you frittered away your money, so in this one you're a bit of a miser, always planning for the future and terrified you won't have enough to get you through. You have a deep desire for a solid financial foundation and you can certainly build one through hard work. If you suffer financial losses, be calm and know that you always have the ability to keep on plugging away to acquire more money and more security.

Saturn in the third house requires you to be there for your siblings and your neighbors. No matter what your position in the family or the neighborhood, you're the one to whom people come when they need a favor or a shoulder to lean on. You know that you do more than your share and that's all right. In addition you are a hard-working student and you enjoy gathering knowledge of the useful variety. How-to books may be your specialty and you can certainly teach. You're probably also good with science and math, and even if you're not, you knew you had to study them diligently because they are, indeed, important.

Saturn in the fourth house requires you to deal with your childhood issues. Perhaps your mom was too stern or a bit foreboding and if so, you felt a little out in the cold as a child. That sort of thing can affect your whole life if you let it. It's important to develop self-reliance in order to assure yourself that someone reliable is taking care of you. The only truly reliable person for that job is none other than yourself. You have a reverence for old things and you may find yourself living in an old home which requires many custodial duties. You're the caretaker of your home and of your family and you learn that these are the ties that bind.

Saturn in the fifth house requires you to learn to be a devoted parent, no matter what soul comes to you as your child. Chances are you weren't the best parent in other lifetimes, perhaps because you were too frivolous and involved more with your own pleasures than with parenting. In this lifetime you must learn to take your responsibilities seriously. Perhaps you have a child who is particularly needy, and if so it's your chance to develop those parenting skills for a long, long time. You have a real sense of obligation to this child, and that's as it should be. You will also need to learn to take your own special talents seriously and to develop them to the best of your abilities rather than taking them for granted and leaving them underused.

Saturn in the sixth house requires you to learn the obligations of working for a living as well as to care for your health. This is another situation in which you were a bit of a layabout in another life and now you must be responsible and get a job. In this lifetime you work quite hard, and sometimes it almost feels as if your work is a calling. You tend to turn things like hobbies into work as well, because being a worker bee is comforting to you. Although you tend to drive yourself (or feel driven by an employer), it's important to balance work with pleasure and to get exercise and proper food. It's also possible that you will have some obligation to a beloved pet who needs special care.

Saturn in the seventh house requires you to become responsible to a partner. In other lives you have abandoned spouses, and perhaps children and now it's essential but rather difficult for you to make a marriage work. It's hard for you to know if a date can become the right sort of mate because your tendency is to attract people who are needy and demanding. It may also be that you are the demanding one and you spend your time trying to decide who's the boss and whose needs must get met. Learning to balance selfish actions and selfless ones is the answer. Love can be totally selfless only when you've found a mate capable also of selflessness.

Saturn in the eighth house requires you to learn to let go in a manner that is both healthy and reasonable. In other lifetimes you abandoned yourself too easily to the needs or desires of other people and you suffered the consequences. Now you're a bit standoffish and afraid to connect intimately, whether sexually, emotionally or by merging your finances with another person. The goal is to learn whom to trust and who is worthy of your intimacy. You need also to work on your fear of leaving your body. In a state of grace, we flow into and out of our bodies through sex and death and there can be little pain or remorse, but instead a knowledge that although physical life ends, the spirit always endures. That is your lesson now—to trust in miraculous rebirth and not fear change.

Saturn in the ninth house requires you to develop a philosophy that is meaningful to you and to live by it. In other lifetimes you were too much the follower and too easily led astray by the ramblings of incoherent or dishonest gurus pretending to teach.

Now you are suspicious of such folk and with good reason. You may dislike religion, philosophy or even astrology, preferring instead to focus on the concrete ideas you can really see in action here on earth. That's going a bit overboard. Your challenge now is to find a system of belief that is your own and which truly resonates for you—intellectually, spiritually and emotionally. You may become a teacher.

Saturn in the tenth house requires you to build a solid career and a stable position within the community. Your dad taught you to create a foundation of ethics and to stand for something, and that is a lesson very meaningful to you. In other lifetimes you've taken the easy path and haven't achieved as much as you know you could have. Now you really want a high level of success but must constantly combat your fears of inferiority or the resistance of those in power. You must learn your profession well and work hard and long at practicing it. Stability is the answer.

Saturn in the eleventh house requires you to get in touch with your long-term goals and to be there for the friends who need you. In other lifetimes you were too casual a person and you lived in there here and now, never worrying about tomorrow. Even today, your tendency is to retreat into escapism when it seems too hard to accomplish your goals. But you need to fight that tendency and to remain focused on your blueprint for the future because only then will you feel safe and secure. Time has real meaning to you and you always want to live a life that is age-appropriate. Your friends seem a bit needy but you love taking care of them because you fear being all alone.

Saturn in the twelfth house requires you to face your demons. In other lifetimes you may have given in far too easily to the fears that plagued you. It's natural for children to be afraid of the bogeyman, but you can't allow those fears to define your life as an adult. Now you must reach inside yourself and learn why you have these issues so that you can give yourself a pep talk and move forward. Doing good deeds or working on behalf of the less fortunate not only makes you feel that you're doing something meaningful, but it also helps you see how really well off you are. Remember to keep a dream journal beside your bed because the mysteries of your mind are greatly revealed through your dreams.

URANUS
Uranus is the planet of sudden change and describes your tendency to rebel.

Uranus is the planet of sudden change and personal eccentricity. Its energy is crackling, sparkly and explosive and it has an affinity with electricity, computers, and other high tech gadgets. Uranus rules Aquarius and it gives those people their eccentric bent toward genius and their love of electrical equipment. Uranus moves very slowly — it takes 84 years for it to move once around the sun! At the current moment, Uranus is in Aquarius, its own sign, and that may be the hallmark of the Age of Aquarius, in which we have begun our brave new world. Uranus likes disruption, individuality, and change. It provokes new ideas which were never before considered, and change that often has no rhyme nor reason. Often the energy of Uranus will hoist you out of a rut and set you on a new course of action, whether you really want the change or not. Ultimately though, it is liberating.

Uranus in Aries is rebellious, self-centered and demanding. You want what you want when you want it and are willing to mow just about everyone down if they stand in your way. Speed is one of your great thrills and they haven't yet invented the amusement park ride too extreme for your tastes. You're always seeking new ways to go faster and have more fun.

Uranus in Taurus is conflicting. You have some disdain for the financial establishment, yet you also want to have security — just not in the conventional way. You might opt to make money in computers or high tech sales on the web. You're interested in outrageous cuisine and style and wonder why so many people cling to outworn lifestyles of commitment and monogamy.

Uranus in Gemini is impatient, brilliant and changeable. You like all forms of information and the moment a new gadget is invented, you own it. Those cell phones that also connect to the internet really appeal to you, whether or not you have an actual need. You speak in a sort of shorthand that only your most intelligent friends can decipher.

Uranus in Cancer is uncommitted, detached and seeks solitude. Although you may be quite a nurturer, on some level you also require your privacy. Being around people who need you constantly is draining because you have your own agenda and need time to pursue your own interests. Divorce is upsetting and quite traumatic but sometimes you just have to be on your own.

Uranus in Leo is outrageous, eccentric and showy. You love doing things that knock people on their ear. Unusual forms of art appeal to you and you might even be some sort of performer. You have wild ideas about fashion and might have dyed a blue streak in your hair. You think people cling too strongly to what they're used to and you want to try new things.

Uranus in Virgo is scattering, innovative and inspirational. Your need is to stop and think about the way your world is ordered and then to find new and better ways of keeping track of things. You're very good at dreaming up new systems of organization, even though it feels that you're plunging into chaos before you erupt with the scheme that changes everything.

Uranus in Libra is liberating, self-involved and reticent. You have a need for a new type of relationship, perhaps an open marriage, because you don't like the way things have been done so far. People can annoy you and sometimes you confine your best affection to the people you meet on the internet because you know you can always turn off the computer and walk away.

Uranus in Scorpio is kinky, manipulative and self-serving. Your mind accepts a lot and you rarely want to limit your behavior to the tried and true standards that everyone else demands. You have your secrets and you like it that way. Your sex life may be completely outrageous and something about you that nobody knows. You like persuading other people to try things they never before considered.

Uranus in Sagittarius is unfettered, free-roaming and eccentric. Your taste is rather outrageous and you may opt to live a completely odd life—perhaps as an outdoor worker at a nudist camp. You just need a lot of freedom and you find new and different ways to seek it. Your philosophies come and go and you may be something of a religion junkie, embracing new causes as you live your life.

Uranus in Capricorn is uncomfortable. You want to upend the establishment but you may not have the wherewithal to do so—as in the case of one of those people who plays a huge computer prank, makes a million bucks online and then gets arrested. Avoid that sort of behavior! Instead decide to find your success in a way that is completely comfortable to you. You don't have to break the mold inhabit it!

Uranus in Aquarius is in the sign of its rule and it functions perfectly there. It's eccentric, self-centered, inventive and genius. You can see the future as it should be rather than the way it's heading and you want to make brave and sweeping changes in the world. You love high tech gadgets and will own as many as you can. Youth is your emphasis and no matter how old you get, you don't see a reason to become stodgy or an old fogey. Instead you embrace new things and new ideas all your life.

Uranus in Pisces is disruptive, divisive and forward-thinking. Your tendency is to become attached to any number of odd ducks, many of whom need your help on a temporary basis. You like being part of a peer group known for something unusual and you may attach yourself to people who are vastly different from yourself. You like unusual music and art—that techno music created on computers really speaks to you, even if everyone else is wearing ear muffs to keep it out!

Uranus Through the Houses

Uranus is the planet of sudden change and eccentricity. It brings great intelligence but also a need to shock, rebel and change. Where it appears in your chart, your life is a little less solid, a little less reliable. It's where you do things differently or deal with other people inflicting difference and unreliability on you. Where Uranus is you must learn to expect the unexpected and to relax and go with the flow rather than demanding that things stay the same.

Uranus in the first house makes you taller than the rest of your family and usually gives long legs. In this lifetime you're learning to be more flexible and to accept new and different ideas instead of clinging to the tried and true. You may go a bit overboard, becoming a very different person than your family expected you to be. You may choose a profession that is outrageous, eccentric companions, or just live a lifestyle that is considered out of the ordinary in your circle.

Uranus in the second house brings some financial upsets. Money comes and goes in your life and you never quite feel that you have a handle on your finances. You don't have to be confined to a life of poverty because you might opt to make a living doing something different—computer work, electronics or even as an astrologer. You spend your money on whim and have huge ups and downs in your bank balance.

Uranus in the third house brings scholarly brilliance, although you may have been one of those twitchily eccentric kids who is so smart but bored in school. Studying what interests you is much better for you than being forced to memorize useless information. Your siblings may be rather eccentric people or you could opt to live in a neighborhood far different than the one in which you were raised.

Uranus in the fourth house keeps you on your toes. Your childhood and your mother were unusual in some way and you reminisce about events that are far different from those your friends recall. You have some issues about closeness and may prefer living alone to living the traditional family life. You have rather austere tastes and fill your home with high tech gadgets and modernist furniture.

Uranus in the fifth house brings different and unusual lovers and keeps you a bit distant from your children. You like mates who are not the people you're expected to marry and may hook up with someone from a different background or ethnic group. You like exploring diversity in all things, are creative in many different ways and are fun loving. You prefer your kids to be independent and not too needy because you feel rather like a kid yourself and don't want to be smothered or tied down.

Uranus in the sixth house puts you in unusual lines of work, surrounded by coworkers who seem eccentric enough to be characters on a sit-com. Even if you're not a computer geek, high tech gadgetry is part of your field. You might be one of those med techs who regulates the machines that keep people alive in hospitals. You like unusual health regimens and are often interested in fad diets, but hey take care with that because most of them are unhealthy in the extreme.

Uranus in the seventh house brings many relationships with a variety of eccentric partners. It's hard for you to have a stable marriage and you need to learn caution about the people whom you attract. It could be that you have your own agenda and need to be on your own rather than tied down with a mate—if so, that's okay, so don't feel badly about yourself. At least you know that you can see good things in people that others reject. Often you elope or marry suddenly.

Uranus in the eighth house makes it hard for you to have a mate who is there financially for you. Financial matters are difficult for you and you may be rather irresponsible in the way you use credit. The eighth is also the house of sex and you find yourself attracted to people for reasons that are different from those most people choose—often you like the buzz of chemistry more than any prospect of a future. Kinky sex appeals to you and you're rather liberal in your standards.

Uranus in the ninth house brings much sudden travel and an affinity for eccentric systems of belief. You love being out in the world and may opt to live in a distant land, feeling as much at home there (or more so) than in the place of your birth. Foreign people fascinate you and you like learning languages. You're also interested in unusual philosophies and may want to overthrow the current order, like one of those people who starts a commune. Perhaps you're into metaphysics or astrology because you feel that's the source of real truth. You're right!

Uranus in the tenth house requires you to be flexible in your profession. Although it's possible that you will work happily for someone else, you'd be better off working for yourself, setting your own hours and being independent. Your dad may have been a bit of a slacker or one of those eccentric geniuses who can rarely provide a traditional home. You may work in computers or astrology or another field in which brilliant thought and technical skills pay off.

Uranus in the eleventh house brings sudden insight into the future and eccentric friends. Your tendency is to go with the flow and not worry about tomorrow and sometimes you get a flash of information that shows you where you are headed. Your goals may be different from the usual and the life you want to live far from traditional. You have a collection of wacky friends who like to be outrageous.

Uranus in the twelfth house brings unusual dreams and inspirations. You might doze off and wake up suddenly aware of how to program that pesky VCR. Or you could hear the voices of your spirit guides in odd moments. You feel as if you're channeling in information from the great beyond and that is what you're doing.

People around you behave in sudden ways that are not always to your liking.

NEPTUNE
Neptune is the planet of illusion and describes areas in which you seek an ideal.

Neptune is the planet of illusion and delusion. Neptune is also the planet of music, film, psychics, high ideals, deliberate lies, drugs, drink, universal love, self-sacrifice and the ultimate that anything can be. Neptune is the fog, the mist, the soul-lifting lilt of an aria, the soul-denying rush of heroin, the thrill of putting aside your own needs for a lover's, and the crusade that never works out. Neptune's energy is hard to comprehend because its truths are greater than we really understand here on the earth plane. Here we live in bodies that decay and die; here everything has limits and finality. Neptune is the limitless universal energy that we feel only in spirit and although its truths are higher and more real, they often don't play out as we expect here on earth. Neptune rules Pisces and makes those people creative, sensitive and attuned to universal forces. Neptune's energy is wet, soft, filmy and changeable. Because Neptune takes almost 165 years to travel around the Sun, it reflects societal changes more than personal ones.

Neptune in Aries casts doubt on individuality and personal leadership. It encourages the abdication of power and the release of the importance of the self. With Neptune here, there is a need to tap into universal energies and to merge in a spiritual way with all that is. Neptune moves into Aries in 2024 and there should be some effect on the military and more commune-type living.

Neptune in Taurus brings new and possibly negative focus to earthly pleasures, as in the days when people frequented opium dens. It also brings detachment to financial dealings, and that can sometimes be a good thing because great sums of money can be made with detachment. It's only grasping insecurity that blocks wealth, and with Neptune here, there is potential for riches. Neptune moves here in 2038.

Neptune in Gemini challenges old forms of communication. This energy encourages telepathy, astral travel, and gathering information in ways that are subliminal rather than organized. Perhaps by the second half of the current century, with Neptune here, there will be computer chips in our brains, helping us to make phone calls without phones!

Neptune in Cancer creates illusions about family life and childbirth and describes the generation of women who first fought for birth control. It was here in 1901, through the World War I years, in which psychotic prejudice brought death in gas chambers to a race of people. There are issues about security and home as well and a sense that a family is greater than the nuclear groups we had always sanctified before, thus the extreme nationalism of Nazi Germany.

Neptune in Leo brings new energy to the arts and from 1914 saw the development of motion pictures and a change in the sort of stars we the public celebrated. It also casts doubt over the ego and saw the era of the flapper — wild, fun-loving, party animals who lived for thrills. Neptune helped challenge the laws of propriety by casting doubts on standards of the times.

Neptune in Virgo requires new approaches to medicine and health care and from 1928 saw the early developments of many miracle drugs — and ushered in prohibition to regulate alcohol consumption. Neptune here also challenged out expectations of daily work and described the great depression, when there was no work for people who wanted it.

Neptune moved into Libra in 1942 and describes the baby boomer generation in which divorce became the norm. With Neptune here, the nature of relationships became cloudy and this generation was the first to cohabitate openly without marrying. There is also a sense of challenge of the social graces and as a result people became more informal and less demanding about propriety.

Neptune moved into Scorpio in 1955 and inspired confusion about sex and merging with others. During this period, there were many acts of suburban rebellion, casual sex, and eventually people with this placement natally grew up to fear the AIDS epidemic. Merging with another person became dangerous — because of the risk of disease. Neptune also inspired many New Age disciplines which were positive.

Neptune was in Sagittarius as of 1970 and inspired new approaches to philosophy, religion, and spirituality. We saw the world getting smaller, and as national boundaries changed, there was a sense that we were less isolated, more connected. Psychic phenomena, talk of soulmates and other previously specialized schools of thought became commonplace.

Neptune moved into Capricorn as of 1984, affecting large business in ways both positive and negative. The 80s are considered an era of greed because of all the huge deals that made equally huge fortunes, some of which were done deceptively, essentially robbing the poor and giving to the rich. Money was fluid and how to make it not so clear. But there were also huge fortunes lost in market crashes and a Neptunian sense of chaos.

Neptune was recently in Aquarius, and there is a greater call for brotherhood, charity and responsibility to less fortunate people. We all look to world events and the atrocities that take place far away are immediate to us, and we feel a need to intervene. There is a greater sense of spirituality now, with many people involved in ideas that used to be merely available to occult enthusiasts. The development of the DVD has allied high technology with music and motion pictures. With Neptune here, we endeavor to create that Age of Aquarius with all its high ideals.

Neptune moved into Pisces in 2011, and that will bring new and interesting techniques in moviemaking, film, and music. The arts will be filled with experimental approaches that will thrill some people and baffle others. There will also be greater development in psychic phenomena and with the broadening interest in New Age theories, maybe your average Joe will be taking classes in channeling his spirit guides and Reiki healing. It's also likely that there will be more dependence on drugs, whether medicinal or recreational and more insanity but there could also be inspirational new ways to deal with these issues.

Neptune Through the Houses

Neptune is the planet of illusions and delusions, and where Neptune appears in your chart, you seek the highest possible ideals, but often find it difficult to manifest them. Perfection isn't that easy to attain! Often Neptune brings confusion to your efforts and a sense that you're not quite in touch with the reality of the situation and that's because you're focused on such high ideals that they're not at all congruent with reality. Compromise isn't really in the nature of Neptune, but rather an insistence on maintaining the dream at all costs. Even though the Neptunian ideals seldom work out as we initially envision, it's hanging onto them that brings the perfection of God into our daily lives. Where Neptune lies, be prepared to detach your ego and wish for the greatest good and highest possible manifestation and you will get better results.

Neptune in the first house requires you to get more in touch with universal energies. You may be psychic or musical and in using these talents, you channel inspirations from God. You need to release concerns of your ego and realize that you are not detached from all that is but a part of the whole, connected on all levels and able to merge with the infinite. Because of this spiritual vibration, other people sometimes find you confusing.

Neptune in the second house demands detachment from money. Often investment bankers have this placement because their financial detachment allows huge sums of money to flow through their lives without causing them to be nervous. The more detached you are from an ego involvement with money, the more cash you can make, but if you are desperate and insecure, you'll probably lose some money until you release its hold on you.

Neptune in the third house gives you unusual conversation skills—perhaps you're quite a story teller or a movie-maker. Fiction and reality get mixed in your mind and it's hard for you to repeat details of an event without changing them each time. Your siblings may be creative or even a bit nuts, and if you can use water transportation, such as a ferry, you will enjoy doing so.

Neptune in the fourth house requires you to find your own inner strength. You often feel a bit needy and that your mom is neglecting you, but being a bottomless pit of need isn't healthy, so work to fulfill your own needs by achieving security on your own. You have many interesting memories, although some may have been fictionalized in your mind as time passed.

Neptune in the fifth house brings a love of the arts and entertainment and also, unfortunately, a tendency to regard drinking alcohol as recreation. It would be better to immerse yourself in the theater or other forms of culture than to be a booze hound, so keep a grip on your drinking. Your children can be quite creative, psychic or intuitive in other ways.

Neptune in the sixth house is good for people working in health professions as long as you're not tempted to use recreationally any of the drugs surrounding you. You can be quite healing but also have to remember to release energy of the sick people for whom you care, because, like a sponge, you can absorb their ill vibrations.

Neptune in the seventh house brings confusion about your partnerships and often makes you feel that your own needs are not as important as those of your mate. Avoid a tendency to attract needy partners who are drunks, druggies or a little out of whack because no amount of love can ever cure such a person. Instead share love openly and remember that ruining your own life never heals another's.

Neptune in the eighth house brings great spirituality to your sex life and allows you a real sense of the infinite during love making and orgasm. It can be a bit cloudy, however, so be careful about whom you allow into your bed—be safe, not sorry. There is also a sense of confusion with a mate's finances, so don't count strongly on the resources of others.

Neptune in the ninth house brings a gut-level understanding of various philosophical tenets and may involve you in foreign religious disciplines. Avoid those preposterous gurus who spout clichés and have large followings. Trust instead in what resonates for you and maintain a clean and heartfelt love of God. Long distance travel is also indicated.

Neptune in the tenth house can bring some confusion about your career, but it may also indicate a career in the movies, once you actually get started. You have high ideals about what you can achieve, but also a sense that it may be impossible, and this is something you need to overcome by working to develop greater faith. Meditate and see what vision of your career comes to you, then manifest it.

Neptune in the eleventh house brings some confusion to your friendships. Often you feel you're friends with a person who isn't really that great of a pal, or somehow the relationship dissolves when you discover that your friend really feels one way about you rather than what you'd been led to believe. Spiritual people come into your life and that can be rewarding as long as they're not lost souls looking to be rescued. You have a real sense of your life purpose and know that you want to do good and help others as a part of your destiny.

Neptune in the twelfth house is very comfortable. It promotes psychic ability and prophetic, or at the very least, unusual and interesting dreams. Your life seems to lose the sense of a time line, and like a Vonnegut character, you float through time in your mind, revisiting the past and gaining flashes of the future. The less fortunate really speak to your soul and you want to do as much as possible to help those you can. Do remember however that not everyone can be helped and that we all make our own destiny rather than have it thrust upon us.

PLUTO
Pluto is the planet of extreme change and describes where and how transformations will occur in your psyche and your life.

Pluto is the planet of birth, death and all transformations. The smallest and most dense planet in the solar system, it requires over 240 years to orbit the Sun. The ruler of Scorpio, Pluto is about matter turning into energy and vice versa. Its energy is dark, seductive, sometimes manipulative, sometimes liberating. Pluto is magnets, psychotherapy, orgasm, sexual perversion, nuclear energy and all obsession, for good or evil. Because Pluto moves so slowly, it affects whole generations. It is always about the breakdown of energy patterns and the rebirth of that energy into something new and hopefully better. Pluto is a pure force for power. It represents the big bang, the atom bomb, the power of creation, even in something so small as a one-celled animal dividing into two. In your chart, the sign Pluto is in isn't personal because everyone in your generation has the same placement. It's about society's energy as a whole, about what you and the people born within a twenty-year period are feeling, doing and striving for.

Pluto was not in Aries at all in the last century and it won't be there for more than fifty additional years. But Pluto in Aries will be about the transformation of the self and about changes in leadership and the way leaders are perceived. There could be a break down in systems that rely on presidents and a change to a committee. There could be the end to power-seeking megalomaniacs, though maniacs will always make attempts to rule.

Likewise, **Pluto won't move into Taurus** until close to the end of the current century. Pluto in Taurus will be about the breakdown in current systems of agriculture. It will be about wealth and its power and changes in the balance of haves versus have nots. It will also herald changes in art, plastic surgery, and cooking.

Pluto was in Gemini as the 20th century began. If you have Pluto in Gemini you're 85 or older. Pluto in Gemini is about transformation in systems of travel and communication. It's about the breakdown in the transmission of information and energy. It inspired electric light, the automobile, the telephone and countless other aspects of the industrial revolution, if not the entire revolution itself.

Pluto moved into Cancer in 1914. It represented the breakdown of the family, change of family values and a decaying sense of security. An important aspect of this placement is women's suffrage in which birth control became important so women could control their destinies. It also described World War I, in which many families were wrenched apart or destroyed.

Pluto moved into Leo in 1939. It represented the breakdown of the ego and it took World War II to trounce the egomaniacal tyrant, Hitler. It also described the baby boomer ME generation of people who were determined to be all they could be. During this period there were new art forms developed, like performance art, a new mod style and a new emphasis on youth.

Pluto moved into Virgo in 1957. It represented the breakdown in ways to organize and manage information. It also described a new interest in self-analysis and the popularity of therapy. New forms of healthcare and health management became prominent during this period, with people eating better, exercising more and trying to live a more healthy life. The Virgo modesty was challenged by a call for free love and multiple sex partners.

Pluto moved into Libra in 1971. It represented the breakdown of marriage as an institution and its replacement with new and different ways of managing relationships. People began living together without marrying and the palimony suit appeared in the courts. Along with marriage falling out of favor was the need for each person to be a strong individual rather than an incomplete part of a team.

Pluto moved into Scorpio in 1983. It represented the breakdown in the way we view sex. The Aids crisis came to prominence now, ending for most people the acceptance of promiscuity begun decades earlier. During this period, new forms of healing and a broader interest in psychic phenomena attained prominence. There is a stronger need for God and angels to be a presence in daily life.

Pluto moved into Sagittarius in 1995. It represents the breakdown in systems of religion and philosophy and a search for something better to believe in. It's also about finding new and better systems of travel and there have been some major plane crashes and the retiring of the Concorde. Hopefully there will also be a successful end to the oppression of peoples and hate crimes.

Pluto moved into Capricorn in 2008. It's about the breakdown of big business as we now know it and a search for better ways to manage the resources of the globe. There are serious issues about allocation of resources, including intensive changes in the way high finance is structured. There could be a call for a change in the way buildings are built and how people are housed. Chances are some major earthquakes will challenge structures that can't withstand them.

Pluto moves into Aquarius in 2023. That will signal a breakdown in ideals. By then we will have come to grips with what the Age of Aquarius meant and we will be searching for new and better ways to create the brave new world of the future. High technology will go through a major revolution and computers will be vastly different than they are now.

Pluto moves into Pisces in 2043. That will bring about changes in art and psychic energies below the surface. Perhaps by then we will have mastered astral travel, telepathic communication or perhaps those things will bring about destruction and will need to be restructured. There will be a change in religion and spirituality and we will see God differently.

Pluto Through the Houses

Pluto is the planet of birth, death and transformation and the house where it appears in your chart describes areas of your life that require work. These are the issues you must confront and must learn to change within yourself. This is where you will be tempted to exert power over other people or where you will allow others to have power over you. Ultimately you should learn you have power only over yourself. In this lifetime, these temptations will always exist but recognizing them helps your Karmic growth.

Pluto in the first house makes you aware that other people have power over you. Sometimes you're attracted to dark forces because you like the feeling of being out of control. This can lead to muggings or being a puppet for someone else. The Karmic lesson to learn is to stand up for yourself and not enjoy being out of control. Also it's important not to engage or participate in manipulative behavior.

Pluto in the second house indicates large ups and downs in your finances. You're always being forced to decide just what you're willing to do for money and the Karmic lesson is to learn what you truly value and what you stand for as a person. It's also important to learn to trust in the universe and to know that your needs will indeed be met. You won't starve in this life unless you choose to!

Pluto in the third house indicates some resentment and power struggles with siblings and neighbors. There is also a need to manage the way in which you communicate so that people understand you clearly. You are a magnetic speaker and the Karmic lesson is to learn that if you give into the temptation to manipulate people, they will turn on you eventually, leaving you alone and lonely.

Pluto in the fourth house is a need to restructure your feelings about your mother, the background from which you came and your very need for personal security. With this placement you have many fears and it's your Karmic challenge to learn that you and only you can take care of yourself and meet your needs. You also need to learn how much power you give to people whom you need emotionally. There may also be structure issues with the home in which you live.

Pluto in the fifth house is quite magnetic and you have no trouble attracting lovers, but the Karmic lesson is to learn caution about the people to whom you entrust your heart. A power-mad Svengali may be hard to resist, but resist you should because he or she will only destroy your self-esteem. The value of children is important to learn and you might want to give to a children's charity or volunteer your time, particularly if you have trouble conceiving.

Pluto in the sixth house affects both your work and your health and they're related. Your temptation is to surround yourself at work with people who are manipulative gossips, although it won't feel to you as if you've made that choice but rather that it was thrust upon you. The Karmic need is to choose positive people and situations that are on the up and up in order to avoid emotional stress leading to poor health and digestive upsets.

Pluto in the seventh house is a tendency to play master-slave scenarios within relationships. There are always issues about who is really in charge and who has the power within any partnership. The Karmic lesson is to learn to let go of your need to control and to eschew the thrill of being controlled. Love with an open hand is the only answer and manipulation, jealousy or power plays always backfire.

Pluto in the eighth house is about intense sex and financial disentanglement. It's easy for you to become enraptured with someone sexually and to lose money because of it, but the Karmic lesson is to be more careful about what energy you allow to merge with your own. Sex can be a very powerful tool for spiritual and psychic healing with this placement—and a partner you can truly trust.

Pluto in the ninth house is about the breakdown and recreation of important ideas. It requires you to learn what you truly believe and stand for and to make your life a reflection of the principles on which you stand. The Karmic lesson is to avoid the temptation to follow religion by rote or to give yourself over to the teachings of a guru. Find your own truths and make them holy. Share what you believe but avoid the temptation to hold yourself up as invincible to others.

Pluto in the tenth house is about the power of dealing with the public. You have the ability to touch a nerve in the society in which you live and it's your Karmic lesson to learn to use this energy for good. Being responsible about how you build your career is the answer. For example, having Pluto in the tenth and becoming a drug dealer is bad, but a motivational speaker could be a positive choice.

Pluto in the eleventh house is about belonging to a group without sacrificing your individuality. You're tempted to give in so that you are a well-entrenched part of your peer group, but your Karmic lesson is to learn that if you lose yourself in the group, you lose something more valuable than you gain. It's also about helping your friends become all they can be and about being true to yourself when choosing your long-term goals.

Pluto in the twelfth house is about the transformation of the unconscious mind. It works under the surface mostly, but you have a sense of what's going on as a result of the dreams that filter through. Perhaps you have dreams of being overwhelmed by forces stronger than yourself—if so you need to get in touch with your own personal power base. The Karmic lesson here is to trust in the process of birth and death as it exists within you. You change on a constant basis and by trusting in God and the powerful forces of the universe, you allow yourself to release the negative and to embrace the positive.

Chapter Three:
Astrological Symbols

Now that you have a good grounding in astrology, take some time to delve a little more deeply, to ponder the symbols involved and the essential meanings involved.

Part One: Astrology in Action

Years ago I watched a documentary on Henry Ford, and as I was watching it I kept thinking, gee here's Aquarius, there's Virgo, etc and so I rushed to my database, pulled up his chart, and all the vibrations I felt were represented. This is astrology in action. As I was getting to know my future son-in-law, his quirks were the source of many jokes. My daughter dieted and he appropriated control of her eating, keeping track of every mouthful she swallowed and ultimately causing her to threaten to leave him. "He must have a Moon-Pluto aspect," I said, laughing, and sure enough he did.

A while back I found myself trapped at a social event next to a ho-hum guy who, when he learned I was an astrologer asked me if I could guess his sign. It was an easy task. With his large head, full beard, and leonine features I might as well have trucked him to sit in front of New York's 42nd Street Library. "Leo," I replied without a moment's hesitation and his jaw hung open in shock. Of course maybe I was just lucky that night because he clearly was not only a Leo but also Leo rising and rising signs are more physically representative of the sign.

This is astrology in action. Nowadays no matter what I do or where I go, it seems like the astrological symbolism represented by any individual or bit of action is abundantly obvious. You can do it too and it can be lots of fun. Watch television and try to imagine the astrological configurations behind the behavior you're seeing dramatized. As you chat with casual acquaintances, consider who they are astrologically and what it all means. It'll keep you from falling asleep when your companion is a clunker.

Even the smallest action, gesture or event can be regarded as astrology in action. For example, a paper boy glides down the street on his bike, delivering the news. What would we call that? Gee, how simple! It's Mercury in Gemini, perhaps conjunct Mars. Mercury is movement and communication, the ruler of Gemini, the sign of communication, and incidentally a dual sign—representing the two wheels of the bike. And of course Mars is action. And we might even say that since the paperboy is working, not just pedaling along for fun, that there's a conjunction to Saturn as well.

If we were screenwriters, we'd be seeking some drama to add to the equation. So suppose a monster truck comes careening along the road, and because the driver is drunk at the wheel, and it's early morning and quite foggy, the truck barrels right at the innocent paper boy. We hear a sound! Screech! What does all this action represent? The truck might be considered Pluto, making an opposition to the triple conjunction above. Pluto, the planet of birth, death and extreme change is a vibration of tremendous, very frightening force. And because it's foggy and the driver is drunk, we also suspect that Neptune, planet of illusion, drugs, drink, and yes pea soup, is involved.

We've set up a scary situation and now it's up to us to determine what really may have happened. There are rules when playing the astrology in action game. You must stick to the rules of astrology. So that means you can't say OK this sounds like a person who has Sun trine Venus. Why can't you do that? Because it's astronomically impossible for the Sun to be 120 degrees apart from Venus. They are always closer together! Another rule involves where the planets can possibly be. Since I already postulated that we had a triple conjunction in Gemini, the Pluto transit had to be an opposition, because that is where the planets currently lie. If I'd said OK maybe it's a square, then you'd say gee what decade are we talking about. You can take some license, though, because after all it's a game, an intellectual exercise. When postulating the planets of a fictional character, it's okay if you can't find an example to match in the ephemeris. Maybe that's why the character is fictional, not real. As long as you're practicing good astrology, you're following the rules of the game!

So now, back to our hapless paperboy, trying to earn a few bucks and the victim of a drunk monster truck driver. If Pluto is precise enough, perhaps he's squished like a bug. Or maybe we could say, OK it's a freak accident, so Uranus, planet of chaos, is involved. And if we say that, we could say OK, the boy's lightning reflexes (Mars plus Uranus) cause him to veer up onto a customer's lawn, setting off the sprinkler system, (Neptune). Or better yet, the boy crashes into a storefront with only minor scrapes (Mars plus Uranus plus Jupiter), an alarm (Mars plus Saturn) goes off, causing the driver to snap momentarily out of his stupor and bringing the police (also Mars plus Saturn).

I have this obsession for "Gone With the Wind." I've read the book many times, seen the movie many more times. Years ago, when I was new at astrology and pretty obsessed, I wanted to do Scarlett O'Hara's chart. I spent a long time thinking about what her horoscope would look like and what Rhett's would be and also Ashley and Melanie's. I was certain Scarlett was a Leo, with Moon (emotions) in Capricorn. It would explain her belle of the ball personality and money-loving heart. But when it came to filling in the positions of the outer planets, I was at a loss. Those were the days way before everyone had access to a computer, before astrological software existed. So I had to find an obscure bookstore and get some ephemerides (the book that details the planets' positions through a specific time period) from the 1800s. It was a hard job. The civil war began in 1861, the beginning of the book, and at that time Scarlett was 16 years old, so she was born in 1845.

Nowadays we have it easy. I was able to pop up my astro software right now and input a date, randomly chosen on the spot, August 15, 1845. Amazingly, the luck of the draw did give me the Moon in Capricorn on that day, but it also showed Venus in Virgo conjunct Mercury, and while that would explain her ability to sweet talk the people in her life, there was no aspect to Neptune, and her years' long obsession with Ashley Wilkes could be described by no other planetary configuration. Plus people with Venus in Virgo are giving, helpful and somewhat self-sacrificial and Scarlett was none of these things. I liked the fact that the Capricorn Moon was squared by Pluto, indicating Scarlett's raw determination and reverence for her mother, a powerful woman who did healing. But still it didn't feel right. So I told the computer to flip back a few days to July 26, 1845.

On that date, Scarlett is still a Leo, but her Sun is square Jupiter and trine Uranus, making her a bit of a rebel, like her danger-loving dad. I randomly chose a noon birth time, indicating someone who is independent and self-employed and that fits Scarlett's persona as a woman who worked all those centuries ago when women barely dared to venture outside the home. With that position we find the Moon, now in earthy Taurus, conjunct Jupiter in the 7th house. Are you nodding your head? Moon in Taurus can be quite material and the Jupiter conjunction plus the 7th house placement pretty well describes the way she benefited from her marriages — to men far more congenial and devoted than she!

On this date we find the Venus-Mercury conjunction in Leo, describing her love of parties and fashion, but opposed both by

Neptune and Saturn. This would describe her hardship during the war, the necessity to work, deprivation and yes, the obsession for a man she could never have. And, in a stroke of luck, Mars had just moved back into Pisces, via a retrograde, so that would describe her fascination for a man who seems sensitive and otherworldly—in short—Ashley! In addition, the conjunction to Neptune described her love of dancing and with Mars opposing Venus-Mercury, it made her attractive to men and quite an adamant and persuasive conversationalist.

I've had a theory for a long time. I don't think Scarlett is a fictional character at all. I believe she was a real woman, who lived that misguided love story that Margaret Mitchell somehow tapped into—perhaps Mitchell channeled it! In any case, I think we'd certainly say this chart that we've created matches the personality of the character quite well and since it is a real chart, it could surely have belonged to a real life Scarlett O'Hara.

Let's take the example of two brothers, close yet locked into a perpetually antagonistic competitiveness. The older felt neglected since the moment of his brother's birth and frequently complains this his position in the family is a lesser one. While his younger brother has a happy marriage, a home and children, he is a childless divorcé, living in an apartment and unable to reconnect successfully enough to make a commitment. He feels he's behind the eight-ball, from start to finish. What sort of planetary pictures might this sad sack have?

The Moon is the planet of emotions and always the answer when considering someone's emotional outlook. Perhaps he has a Moon-Saturn opposition, describing his difficulty with women all the way back to mom. And to describe his inability to commit, could be that opposition is really a T-square with divisive Uranus at the focal point. With such a configuration he would seek an abundance of contact, but feel hesitant to make a commitment to any one person. And a Saturn-Moon opposition would make him feel lonely and a bit insecure.

Because this man is extraordinarily tall, we might assume that Uranus is in his 1st house, so perhaps he has Moon in the 10th house (outside world, father) and Saturn in the 4th house of emotions, childhood and mother. In that case, we could say his perceived childhood emotional traumas were indeed debilitating, but in fact they provided the necessary impetus for him to maintain independence and alienation—Uranus in the first. That would indicate a Karmic need to learn to depend on himself and not to rely too strongly on other people.

What sort of Sun would we imagine this man to have? It seems natural to assume his Sun is in the 12th house, giving him emotional awareness and making it a bit easy to overlook him. With this sort of picture, it's easy to see why he's more focused on his emotional life—or the lack thereof—than on personal achievements.

The case of the younger brother is interesting as well. Whereas his brother is dour, he is generally cheerful. He loves having a family but would rather play golf or watch sports on television than visit the zoo with his kids. His mother is still the primary authority figure in his life and he married a woman who is clearly the boss of his household. Basically he's a big kid always trying to extend his playtime into perpetuity. It's easy to imagine someone like this with a 5th house Sun, indicating love of fun and pleasure, and maybe a 5th house Mars (action, sports) as well. As a sportswriter, it would make sense for him to have a Sun-Mercury-Mars conjunction in the 5th. That would also give him a love of children, but might explain in part his personal selfishness. Chances are, though, there's more to his Solar configuration than this, perhaps an opposition from Neptune. He tends to weasel out of responsibilities, perpetrate small trickeries on his wife and beg a lot for sex!

Planetary contacts often run in families like hair color and body types, so we would pretty well assume he too has some yin issues. First of all, because he has a good sense of humor and a congenial nature, we might expect a pleasant aspect from expansive Jupiter to his Moon. Although he is a jokester, he's still insecure; he just covers his flaws better than his brother does. I would expect a Venus (love) conflict with Saturn, perhaps an opposition. He feels undeserving of love and lucky that his wife cares for him at all, but because of the Moon-Jupiter aspect he rebounds quickly and doesn't obsess too much. It's likely too that he has some sort of lesser Moon-Saturn aspect, perhaps a trine or sextile, giving him the feeling that women are authority figures but not a depressive nature.

What about the long-suffering wife in this equation? She rules her roost, competes with her domineering mother-in-law, whose domestic skills far outpace her own and constantly demands that her husband be her equal, her partner, rather than her dependent. He loves her no matter what, and she frequently calls him an idiot. As someone engaged in power struggles at just about every turn, we can assume she has a Mars-Pluto aspect. She and her husband are always jockeying to get their own way.

What's really going on in her life can better be described by her Moon. With a challenging Moon-Saturn aspect, she didn't get enough attention from her own mother, learned few of the domestic joys and finds cooking and cleaning meaningless chores. She does work hard at mothering, and that too can be described by Moon-Saturn. Her compulsion to be an authority figure can be indicated by a Sun-Saturn contact. Perhaps she has Sun opposite Moon, making a T-square with Saturn. That would indicate difficulty in balancing her outside life—a career—and her home life—without her doing a lot of work. On occasions when she's tried to work outside the home, it's always been a failure and her guilt at leaving her young children probably undermined her efforts, causing her to manipulate the situation into failure so she can go back home and work at being a better mother than her own parent was.

In addition, these configurations (Mars-Pluto and Sun-Moon-Saturn) would explain her competitiveness and the problems she has in relating to the women authority figures in her life—both Mom and Mom-in-law. It would also explain why her environment is filled with so much criticism. Her mother in law constantly chides her about poor housekeeping and cooking skills. She constantly chides her husband about his absentee parenting style. We might also wonder if maybe she has Neptune in the 4th, another indication of maternal neglect or absence.

The interesting dynamic in this sort of situation is the factor of choice. With planetary pictures like this, the person would very likely choose a partner who is substandard because it gives her a sense of power and of superiority. If she's with someone less good than herself, she doesn't have to worry that maybe there's something wrong with her. And, of course, if she had chosen a perfect hub and father as her partner, her mediocre cooking and housekeeping skills would make her the lesser mate. This way she has leverage, identity, and control.

Of course we couldn't leave this situation without considering the horoscope of the mother-in-law, the pivotal figure in the family. We could say that a woman of her generation gained her primary identity as a wife and mother, so that explains her need to continue mothering her grown sons so assertively. But how do we explain it astrologically? First of all, we'd expect a Moon-Pluto aspect, giving her a desire to control everything within her domestic sphere. There might also be a Moon-Jupiter contact, explaining her love of cooking and domesticity. And, interestingly, we'd find a Sun-Neptune conflict. Without her home and family, she has less of an identity; she is who she is because of other people. That would also explain her marriage to a man who was an absentee father. What would describe her critical nature? The Moon-Pluto would be one aspect of it because that tends to generate a bit of paranoia, the expectation that things will not work out perfectly—or at all—and that's why people with this aspect need so much control. In addition the Sun-Neptune aspect might make her want to lash out so that nobody notices she feels insecure about herself. Perhaps, though, she also has a Mercury-Saturn aspect, and that could provide an instinct to teach as well as the tendency to point out flaws.

We see these dynamics in the popular television comedy, "Everyone Loves Raymond." It's amazing, isn't it, that such deep and complicated emotional portraits have been created through a 30-minute sitcom.

In another example from real life, a college friend of my daughter's is always calling her to bemoan a difficult and complicated love life. It seems that by the second date, she's already calling the guy her boyfriend and by the fourth date she's wailing about the nasty qualities she's discovered in him that require her to break up. A week after the breakup, she's distraught because the guy took the breakup seriously and staged no mini-drama to regain her heart. "He said he loves me," she cries, "He can't take that back can he?"

I've known this sweet girl for quite a few years, but as she's not a client, I don't have her chart in my files. I just had to speculate about what her astrological indicators were with a love life like that. It wasn't hard at all! First of all, we think about the intensely romantic side of her nature, the side that allows her to believe she's found true love—all on the first date. That to me indicates Venus aspected by Neptune, the planet of illusion. Love seems to cost her something, and she seldom finds a man on whom she can rely. With a Saturn opposition to that Venus-Neptune conjunction, there is always a seesaw about how much to give, how much to get, what's good for the heart, what's good in real life. Plus Saturn and Neptune rarely combine happily. They are the two most incompatible planets in the zodiac. Saturn demands practical reality and Neptune promises dreams, fantasies which most often are unrealizable. Thus Saturn and Neptune together add up to emotional war. It's a call to live spiritually in the real world, to make dreams come true, and that's pretty hard because by their very nature Neptunian dreams are better left unworldly.

This girl is very athletic—Mars in the first house— and, very sexy, so that would indicate a Venus-Mars aspect. With Mars in the first at the focal point of a T-square involving that Venus-Neptune opposite Saturn picture, she tends to be attracted to men who seem dreamy (Neptune) but can't live up to her expectations (Saturn).

There have been decent guys in her life, but something has always gone wrong. They're bad in bed. They're too clingy. They're too emotionally needy. They let her walk all over them. So she dumps them. What sort of pattern would cause her to look for excuses to push away guys who really are nice and who dote on her? That would be a Moon-Uranus problem, always a source of alienation and distance. And with Moon in fire-hot, impetuous Aries, it's quite natural for her to race forward into relationships and then come to a screeching halt because of Uranus.

In another relationship example, a superior-feeling graduate student enters a bar with her fiancé, an older professor who is also her supervisor at work. When the prof runs out on her, she decides to take a job in the bar, a milieu far beneath where she could conceivably belong. The bar owner, a studly ex-jock, falls for her and they begin a romance that is constantly up and down.

The bartender, tall and handsome, has specialized in women long on legs and short on brains, and is perplexed to find himself enamored of this geeky, perpetual student who regards him with scorn. Although he is the hero among the crowd of drunks and losers in his bar, he comes from a childhood where he could never please his father and was constantly outshone by his successful older brother.

As an athlete, we might expect to find his Mars in the 1st house of identity, although his Sun is probably in the 5th house of pleasure, perhaps making a trine. A man who is a sexual legend would probably have a Mars-Pluto aspect, so let's say he has another trine. Assuming Pluto to be in Leo, he'd have a grand fire trine, with Mars in Aries and Sun in Sagittarius, and that suits his mostly easy-going nature as well as his love of the single life. And I suspect he has Saturn squaring his Sun, accounting for that sense of childhood inferiority and paternal disapproval.

Right now you might be running to your ephemeris to see if it's possible that a Sag with Pluto in Leo could have Mars in Aries and Saturn squaring his Sun. Although it's astronomically possible, it didn't occur in this century.

When we consider his yin elements, it seems plausible that he might have Venus in Aquarius, astronomically possible with a Sag Sun. That would give him affection for many types of women, including brainy intellectuals and total flakes!

If we place that Venus opposite Pluto, we've created a kite configuration, and all that macho, masculine energy is filtered out through Venus, explaining his thousands of conquests over the years as well as his obsession for women. Let's assume that Neptune is in the 6th, explaining his bartending career, and trining his 11th house Venus, describing his love of friends and association with people who drink. He would be a man who loves women of all sorts, dreams of true love but settles for hot sex.

Where would you place his Moon? I think it's in the 6th house, in Libra, conjunct Neptune. That would give him a dreamy, romantic quality as well as some issues with Mom, who may have seemed absentee. With this Moon and a Venus-Pluto, it is as though he was waiting for a woman to come along who could stimulate his imagination and spark something more than just a physical connection. And an emotional connection via work also makes sense.

That brings us back to the supercilious barmaid. She chose to rebound from rejection by immersing herself in a world far beneath her. What sort of chart might she have? As an intellectual, she might have Sun conjunct Mercury, and that combo is probably squared by Jupiter, explaining her love of education and inability to communicate without a massive amount of verbiage. I can envision an opposition of Saturn to her Sun, explaining the need to engage in actual work as a form of validation. But there must be something else to explain her unstable life, rebellious nature and inability to choose a major and stick with it. Perhaps she has Uranus making a T-square to that Sun-Mercury opposite Saturn. She would always be involved in a struggle to build something substantial versus her desire to run away and begin again with something new. But wait! We said she has Sun-Mercury square Jupiter, so perhaps we're looking at a grand cross, four planetary points at 90 degree angles. This is a sign of ongoing chaos in life, many choices, and a need for perpetual excitement. Such a person would have a difficult time in the staid world of academia.

In addition, we have her love of powerful men, in positions of authority in her life. That would indicate a Mars-Pluto aspect, or a Mars-Saturn aspect, or both.

What sort of yin pictures might her horoscope reveal? As someone who loves culture and art, perhaps she has a 3rd house Venus, possibly aspected by Neptune. Being an obsessively neat perfectionist, we might expect a Virgo Moon, and perhaps we could postulate that it lies unconnected in her horoscope, explaining her feelings of emotional alienation but not describing someone who has difficulty sustaining emotional connections. Her issues aren't emotional, are they?

In this romance, although there is strong sexual chemistry and love on the part of the bartender, the real story is about ego and power. In falling for the intellectual barmaid, the bartender put himself right back in the same position of his childhood—always seeking approval from someone who considers herself his better. And as she is a person who always seeks chaos and change, he's the perfect partner for her. No matter how attracted to each other they may be, the fact that they have no common frame of reference pretty well guarantees an eventual split. People who need freedom or chaos do tend to drift into relationships like these. They feel below the surface that there is a fail-safe, an out, something that will ultimately set them free, on toward a new course, new challenges and unexplored excitement.

We saw these dynamics in the classic comedy, "Cheers," and now we know why it was inevitable that Sam and Diane shouldn't end up together!

Let's do a few more quick takes in the astrology in action game. A girl bakes bread with her mother. Could we describe that as Moon plus Mars (nurturing, mothering, women in action, plus of course the Moon is also food) trine Jupiter (inflated energy), describing the rising of the dough plus the nourishing effect it will ultimately have.

A salesman comes to your door pedaling vacuum cleaners. That could be Mercury, (communication) plus Neptune (lies, salesmanship). How would we describe suction? What about Saturn plus Mercury—work applied to movement. Maybe we could say it's Jupiter—a bunch of hot air! Then if he empties a pile of dirt on your carpet, it's Pluto, both pressure to buy and transformation of your clean carpet. Assuming he vacuums it up successfully, it's Virgo, (cleaning efforts) plus Mars and Saturn (energy for work). And if you buy his product, it's Neptune again.

The thing that's so wonderful about astrology is that it is a system of encodement for all the energy in the universe. Think of any situation and there will be a set of astrological symbols that describe that energy. Astrology is God's code book!

Part Two: Combining Astrological Symbols

Astrology is difficult and complicated and that is what I've always loved best about it-it's the hardest thing I've ever studied. Students of astrology begin by memorizing the meanings of the building blocks of any horoscope-the planets, signs and houses. That is a relatively straightforward process, and while there are many nuances to every definition, most beginners can grasp the essential truths with time and effort. It's only when it's time to combine the planets that it gets complicated and yes, much more difficult.

How do you really know what it means when one planet in a horoscope aspects another? You can understand that Mars means action and that the Sun is "the ego," but what does the ego really mean and does a Sun-Mars contact mean an active ego, or just how should you look at it? It gets even more complicated when more planets are involved. If there are two planets 180 degrees apart, that's called an opposition, and if a third planet lies at their mid-point, that's called a T-square. But how do you know what all those planets mean to each other and to the person whose horoscope you're examining?

These are the questions that intermediate students must ask. Astrology isn't just about memorization, or all those people who describe themselves as "really into astrology" would actually know something and might someday call themselves astrologers!

The first step after you've memorized all the definitions of signs, planets and houses is to familiarize yourself with the actual energies involved. It's one thing to know what a planet means, and quite another to relate to it as a buzz, which is a truer way to understand astrology. Mars is probably the easiest planet to understand because it's about action. Mars is like your car-it gets you from one place to another. Mars in Aries is the archetype, and with Mars there you easily reach out for what you want without a qualm and often without thought of anyone else. You want what you want and you go get it. So what would that vibration be like? It's not too hard to imagine the hum of Mars, a fireball heading in a direction that best suits itself. And of course, it's pretty obvious that when we think of action that benefits the self, we also think of sex because everyone wants and desires sex, not just in an emotional way but in a way that is purely physical, a product of physical need and of the need to propagate the race. Whether or not there is an emotional connection, the population needs to reproduce itself, so there is Mars, planet of lust, generating sexual desire.

Another planet that is relatively easy to understand is Venus, planet of love. Venus is how we express affection for other people.

Venus is that pit-a-pat in our hearts when we think of that special someone. We all know what this is and we understand the buzz of Venus. So it's not terribly difficult to contemplate Venus and Mars in combination. Love plus Sex. We understand only too clearly what it means and how it feels because we've all been feeling those energies since grammar school or even before.

So if you're studying astrology, and you see a horoscope where Venus and Mars are connected by aspect, you conclude that the person is sexy-and creative. It just makes sense. And if you look at a couple's chart and see a connection between one person's Venus and the other's Mars, then you say who-ha they have the hots for each other. And if you look at transits to your own chart and see your Venus and Mars receiving a lot of energy, you say wowie, people will find me sexy and I might get the hots for someone over the next few days. It's about the easiest astrological concept and one of the most popular reasons why people look at horoscopes in the first place. Venus and Mars are easy to understand, individually and in combination.

When we look at other planets it gets more complicated. What about combining Mars with another planet, Saturn. Saturn is about Karma, earthly life lessons, rules and regulations. It's not too terribly hard to picture these planets in combination. If Mars is action, a whizzing fireball, what is Saturn? Saturn is the crossing guard with the whistle, the big stop sign and to power to arrest. So what happens when these two energies combine? The buzz that is Mars is fast, uncontrolled, desiring freedom, and self-involved. On the other hand, Saturn's buzz is about control, order, precision, rules, appropriateness, society and so on. Could we really say that we feel these energies are similar? No, they're not similar and thus are not terribly compatible. If you're whizzing down the street on your roller blades, showing off for pedestrians and in a world of your own, you find it annoying when that crossing guard blows the whistle and brings you to a screeching halt. Of course if you're on a bike and you see a new bikes-only lane, you might just appreciate the city council who voted to create that passageway just for you.

So we would have to say that Saturn in combination with Mars creates controlled energy, sometimes blocked energy. To express it in graphic terms that match the nature of Mars, Saturn is the condom in sex-it doesn't prevent sex but it certainly changes its nature and its outcome. If you picture a raging stream and a funnel, you have another image that goes with these two planets. Saturn directs the raw impulse, and Mars doesn't always like being directed.

Does that mean that Mars and Saturn are always at odds and if someone has this aspect, he or she will be miserable? It's important to realize that we are all our horoscopes and what we have feels normal to us. Thus someone with a Mars-Saturn connection would prefer orderly action, enjoy doing chores, appreciate the military, may join the police and in general would try to fit in with society. This person will feel comfortable in this role. It's only other people who have dissimilar aspects who would regard that behavior as annoying. For example, I have a Mars-Jupiter aspect, and that makes me impatient, assertive, cheerful and so on, and I find Mars-Saturn energy anal. So see, it's all in your point of view!

To take another example, think of Neptune, the planet of illusion, delusion, spirituality, and a million other qualities. When we define Mars, we can easily use one word and in that definition are quite clear about what we mean. Neptune is more difficult because its energy is filmier and more ethereal. Neptune is the ocean, drugs (both medication and addition), film, art, and so on. It takes dozens of adjectives to encapsulate the complexity of Neptune. But when we try to understand the vibration involved, it's a little easier.

Think of a melody, of dancing and swaying to the music. Of Ray Charles at his piano, swaying sightlessly to the vibration as he plays and sings. Think of a hymn and people involved in a religious ceremony, floating out of themselves on the music, to reach for higher connection and spiritual truths. Think of the ocean, vast and mysterious, life giving yet dangerous. Think of a drug addict, being lulled into the pleasurable coma-like state of a high. With all that it's not too difficult to understand the buzz that is Neptune, and from that to extrapolate on its energy. Neptune is illusive, wet, foggy, confusing yet also enlightening. Neptune is a conduit to other realms.

But what happens when we try to combine the fireball that is Mars with the fog that is Neptune? If Neptune is the ocean and Mars is a fireball, does Neptune extinguish Mars like a stray asteroid blazing to earth only to plunge to the Atlantic's watery depths? It is in looking at astrology that way, by focusing on the vibration of each element, that we can understand in very clear terms just what happens to the symbols in combination. If Mars is action and Neptune is illusion, would a combination of the two planets create indirect or dishonest action? If Mars is selfish and Neptune is spiritual, wouldn't a combination create behavior that isn't quite so self-serving? And, since Neptune is film and dance, and Mars action, wouldn't a combination indicate acting ability, cinematic charisma and rhythm?

Of course the answer to all those questions is a rousing yes, all true. So now you're nodding your head and saying, yes make sense, I see it all clearly now. I understand Mars plus Neptune. But then, just like my students, you'd raise your hand, say "Ahem, excuse me, but how do I know which of these manifestations will occur in this life? How do I know whether the person will be a con artist or a socially-conscious ballerina?"

And of course the answer is in looking at the entire horoscope, at all the planets in combination and seeing what that lifetime is truly all about. Any one planetary combination is a single clue about the person and what he or she is capable of. So with that in mind, you can assume that at some point, there is behavior from the best to the worst of anything indicated by any individual planetary picture. Thus a person with a Mars-Neptune aspect can be a bit tricky, sometimes underhanded, often spiritual, a good dancer and a photogenic movie star. How extreme the behavior is, depends on the aspect in question and other issues in the chart.

To examine one more Mars combination, let's look at Pluto, the planet of birth, death, and extreme change. Pluto is like a nuclear explosion, that destroys everything in its wake and paves the wave for something completely different. Pluto defines the moment at which we enter our bodies in birth and leave them in death. Pluto is about power, manipulation, and it is intense and sometimes scary. Pluto is said to be a higher octave of Mars, so their energies are similar. If Mars is a fireball and Pluto is a nuclear explosion, it's pretty easy to envision that energy in combination.

Pluto confers power, dominance, creativity and intensity, and when it hits Mars, the action is amplified to quite a greater degree. Thus a Mars-Pluto aspect would be more powerful, sexier, more domineering and creative. It's Mars amped up!

So if we wanted to look at just the combos we've defined so far, we'd have Venus-Mars as romantic attraction, Mars-Saturn as controlled action, Mars-Neptune as indeterminate action and Mars-Pluto as explosive action. But what happens when we have more than two planets working together? This is the point at which most people grow confused.

We mentioned that a T-square is a configuration of three planets in which two are at 180 degrees, or opposite each other and the third is at the midpoint, making a mutual right angle. So let's say we have a horoscope with Venus opposite Mars. As the opposition is an aspect of relationship, we'd say the person is sexy (Venus plus Mars), but may have a bit of conflict (opposition) in interpersonal relationships. That's easy enough to understand. Now we have to examine the third planet. In a T-square the energy of the opposition is filtered out through the third planet. If it were just a simple opposition, the energy would be like a seesaw. It would go back and forth with no outlet, but with the T-square there is a way for the energy to be focused and expressed definitively.

Suppose we have Saturn at the focal point of this T-square. Can you envision what would happen? The Saturn in combination with Venus would make you feel insecure about getting the love you need. And with Mars would block action. So maybe you'd attract partners who seemed okay but turned out to give too little or to have too many flaws. Love would require you to give more than you took and it wouldn't be easy to have your needs for sex to be met simply or without complications. This would be true in a horoscope with this natal combination, but if it were simply Saturn transiting the Venus-Mars opposition, it would be a trying period but not a permanent annoyance. In the case of a transit, what might happen? Envision a happy couple in bed, beginning to make love. Suddenly the lights flip on, a toddler walks into the room and cries, "There's a monster under the bed." The demands of responsibility have halted their ardor. Or perhaps the couple is in a college dorm and in walks the proctor, saying "Hey Miss Venus, no guys allowed in the room." Or could be the parents call and say "We're not supporting you as long as you're shacking up. Get married already."

What if we placed Pluto at that focal point instead of Saturn? That person would have the same set of romantic conflicts caused by the opposition, but would be having transcendent sex-at every possible opportunity. Sex would be a source of healing-or disease-and self control would not be an issue or the behavior of choice. In addition we might worry that this person would be attracted to shady, unsavory or deviant characters and use kinky sex as a way of heightening emotional intensity.

It's a huge difference, isn't it, by simply substituting the planet at the focal point we see vastly different behavior patterns. And of course, if we'd started with different planets than Mars and Venus, we would have drawn still other conclusions. That is the magic of astrology-it can explain just about everything.

A T-square is a relatively easy configuration to understand because the thrust of the energy goes out through the planet at the mid point. But what happens when there is a cluster of energy? For example, I have a client with Mars conjoined by explosive Uranus and domineering Pluto. With this configuration she should be a real dynamo. She should be determined to get her own way at all costs and that really is her desire. But the simplicity of that triple conjunction is affected by an opposition-Saturn opposing all three planets.

That's an interesting life predicament isn't it, and as astrologers, how do we determine which energy will hold the most weight on the seesaw of that opposition? The problem in her life is that other people let her down. They make promises they don't keep, or they do underhanded things to bring about her downfall-things she is sure are undeserved. Her life has been filled with drama and much of it has been unfair and unprovoked attacks against her.

Because the planet involved is Mars, this is a power issue. Can she really express her own power? A person with a Mars-Uranus-Pluto conjunction should seem quite powerful to other people, but in this case the problem is that those Mars-Uranus-Pluto energies are being expressed against her rather than by her, something that is always a possibility with any planetary picture. People start rumors about her and she ends up fleeing, choosing to abandon the struggle instead of facing it. Her sense of her own power is not great and when push comes to shove, she runs. She can't seem to hold her own in the battles of life, despite that intensely aspected Mars. She feels she has to fight for what she wants and unfortunately, life is proving that fight to be a losing battle.

Once again we come to the issue of Saturn at the opposition. Something about her energy is inspiring other people to put up a wall against her. It would seem that the constraints of society are preventing her from the very self-expression and individual freedom promised by her Mars. She feels like an outsider at every turn and unable to get what she wants. So the real question she has to answer in this lifetime is how to express personal power and still manage to live within the rules of the society she wants to accept her.

Even with complicated planetary alignments like this, we would still have to look to other pictures within her horoscope to discover why this is happening and why her life is such a constant struggle against frustrating odds. There are other difficult aspects in her horoscope so that would provide the explanation why she doesn't own the power promised by her Mars.

Let's review another configuration, one considered lucky. Suppose you had a grand trine, three planets at 120 degree angles from each other, forming a large triangle in the sky. Say you have the Sun, planet of identity, trine assertive Mars and trine Jupiter, planet of luck and expansion. That's a really snazzy planetary picture. You'd be optimistic, genial, outgoing, properly assertive and confident of your own success. The planets involved are congenial and harmonious and they're configured in a way that is favorable. The only fly in the ointment comes when we decide to transform the grand trine into a kite configuration.

A kite occurs when there is an opposition between one of the planets in the triangle, forming a large kite shape in the sky. This too is considered a lucky and dynamic configuration. With the grand trine, the energy radiates among the planets happily but has no real outlet. With the kite, the outlet is at the point of opposition and it creates a very dynamic point in the horoscope.

Suppose the opposition occurs between the Sun and say, Neptune. A Neptune opposition to the Sun tends to cloud the ego a little. Who are you and to what are you entitled? These are the unspoken questions you tend to ask. There is less confidence. But with that grand trine, the energy would be shored up-a lot. You would be more hesitant, more modest, but you could also succeed quite well.

What if the opposition occurred between Mars and Pluto in that same grand trine? With a Mars-Pluto opposition, you're used to functioning within the atmosphere of power struggles-people constantly challenge you and you have to see who comes out on top. So in this case we would look to the sign Mars is in. If Mars is in a less well suited sign like Pisces, you would always be seeking a compromise in order to effect positive (Jupiter) self-expression (Sun). Of course that doesn't mean that you would always act in an above-board manner. Some of your behavior could be a bit underhanded, but ultimately with the grand trine boosting you, you would learn that you catch more flies with honey than with vinegar-an apt translation of that particular kite configuration.

If Mars is in a stronger sign like Capricorn, you might be a great deal more powerful and even ruthless. You might seek success at all costs and chances are you would ultimately learn that it doesn't matter how much you succeed if you don't have your own self-esteem. For every configuration, every tiny corner of every horoscope, there is a life lesson to be learned and there are as many life lessons as horoscopes.

Another issue to consider when studying planetary combinations is transiting energy. When we talked about planetary combos above, it was mostly about natal combinations. But what happens when the energy is planets transiting, hitting points in your chart and then moving on? Do you turn into a whole other person? No you don't, but don't try to tell that to your annoyed spouse who feels that you've gone from Dr. Jekyll to Mr. Hyde after a long Pluto transit. Sometimes it's hard to distinguish between who we are as basic human beings and who we seem to be as a result of action we take during transitory upheavals. Or as the poet Yeats says, how do you tell the dancer from the dance.

Another issue to consider is the quality of energy hitting. If you are a Moon-Jupiter person (like me) you find a transit of Saturn to your Moon quite uncomfortable, but if you have a Moon-Saturn aspect natally, that feels much more acceptable to you. A lot of what hits and how it affects you depends on what you have already. That's why it's a bad policy simply to look at a chart to see what will "happen." Nothing just happens. We interface with energy and the only way to know the outcome is in seeing what's there in the first place.

So if we were to return to a previous example, we already discussed Saturn transiting a Venus-Mars opposition, forming a T-square and how it affected romantic expressions. But suppose that T-square were the natal aspect and then transiting Saturn came along to aspect that whole configuration. Because of Saturn's 28-year orbit through the horoscope, we can assume that it would hit the various planets in that configuration at 7 year intervals, and in a way it would provide the timing for various romantic attachments and disentanglements in that person's life.

What if the person had Pluto at the focal point in the T-square? Then if Saturn transited, it would be just as serious. For example, Saturn could cross Pluto and end a relationship, amid cries of infidelity, or even VD. That's complicated, difficult and unpleasant energy. Even if there wasn't a sex-related health crisis, Saturn's energy would be quite an intrusion on this Venus-Mars-Pluto person. This sort of person wouldn't want to be accountable where sex is concerned and Saturn would demand accountability. So in a way, this person would have a much harder time with the Saturn transit than the person above, who is used to that vibration.

Suppose we returned again to the same Venus-Mars-Saturn example yet this time it was Uranus, the planet of upheaval, transiting the combo. As Uranus crossed Saturn, there would be a huge desire for change, for freedom, and this energy would produce a sort of grass-is-always-greener phenomenon and behavior designed to break free of that life's limitations. You might leave a solid relationship because it was unfulfilling and after Uranus moved on, feel lonely and unhappy at the loss. After the transit ended, you would want what you used to have-stability even if it were imperfect. Of course that's not to say it would be a bad thing to let go and move on because it's possible that after such a transit you would be ready to find a better partner and greater happiness, and that of course is always the goal of change. It would just be a question of courage and whether other factors in the horoscope indicated an ability to be independent for a while.

The question of transiting energy is an interesting one. Many astrologers feel that any two planets in transit will create the same effects. So that would mean the difference between Saturn hitting your Mars and Mars hitting your Saturn would be one only of degree and longevity. Is this really the case, though? I don't think so.

We have to agree first that any transiting energy will stimulate the vibration already present in the chart. Anything hitting that Mars-Venus opposition will have effects related to the issues described by that configuration-love and sex-in the specific way they're expressed in that particular life. So first you would have to look at the horoscope and see what it contains, what the reality of that person really truly is. Then you will understand what the issues are that a transit will stimulate.

Suppose in your natal horoscope, you have Mars, in the 10th house of career, making a positive and healthy trine to Jupiter. That would give you high energy, athletic ability and optimism, and the desire to work independently. It's a nice planetary picture, you are generally happy and feel your efforts will be rewarded. Then suppose Saturn comes along to cross your Mars. Well, we said it before-you're a Mars-Jupiter person and this isn't terribly comfortable. You are under pressures, feel you have to follow too many rules and that you're working way too hard. Plus Saturn transiting the 10th house is always difficult as you have to reassess your whole life and your career. The good news is, Saturn is also trining that Jupiter and that's a sign of new opportunities. So maybe you are working harder, but you see the value in it and in years to come, you look back on this period as difficult but worthwhile.

Suppose instead you have a 10th house Saturn, an indicator of slow but steady career progress with diligent effort. Assume the Saturn is well aspected and not in and of itself a source of conflict. What happens when Mars crosses Saturn? The fact that Mars is transiting the 10th house does indicate more deadlines and hard work, but it also brings speed and opportunity. With Saturn there natally you may be stumbling along, feeling you have to give extra effort to gain the slightest momentum. But when Mars comes breezing through, you speed up a little. Your limitations are lifted. Does it mean that the effects of Saturn in the 10th are lifted and suddenly people are beating a path to your door offering success and opportunity that you barely have to work to achieve? C'mon!

We said that any transit will stimulate the energy already present. So we know that with that 10th house Saturn, you have to work long, hard and diligently. That never changes throughout your life-it's who you are and what you are all about. But when Mars comes along you get a little nudge forward, a chance to move a bit faster and to achieve more. You get more work, more opportunities, but they will still be hard, demanding and time consuming. Even though the transiting energy we're discussing is between the same two planets and same house, the effect is not identical.

Another interesting example is with Venus, planet of love. Transits of planets to Venus bring various types of romantic interest, in keeping with the planet itself. Pluto transits and there is creativity-pregnancy-lust, obsession, and love that rocks your soul. Uranus transits and you fall for someone not your usual type or who will challenge your family. Neptune hits and you find a love that is ideal or a delusion of perfection. Saturn transits Venus and you want a love that equals commitment and permanence; your desires are for substance. But what happens when Venus transits these planets?

It's often written that pretty much the same thing happens when Venus hits as when she is hit, but again I disagree. I think when Venus transits Pluto you find ways to get along better with people and to neutralize challenges-Venus softens any situation. Venus transits Uranus and you consider buying a new gadget, you get along with people you'd normally avoid and you're more tolerant. Venus hits Neptune and you reach for culture or good deeds. Venus hits Saturn and you're more willing to give of yourself-to do favors for other people and you take your responsibilities more willingly.

Thus it seems to me that transits to Venus inspire different aspects of love while transits from Venus do involve love but more in the way of applying social skills in a beneficial manner. They're not about lust, desire or coupling.

The final thing to consider when focusing on planetary energies in combination is the purest of all-transiting planets in the sky that are simply connecting to each other. For example, right now as I write this, there is a kite in the sky. The grand trine involves the Moon, Neptune and Saturn and the kite is focused through Pluto, opposing Saturn. What better time to contemplate deep spiritual truths and how they work in life and in astrology, and to debunk old notions of what planetary energies can do?

Chapter Four:
Delineating A Horoscope

Nothing is more helpful when learning to unravel the meaning in any horoscope than to see how it's done, bit by bit. Here are some eye-opening examples.

Part One: Delineating a Horoscope

Reading a horoscope is a lot like building a house from scratch. There's a lot to learn in advance, you have to assemble everything in front of you, and then you must begin carefully in a slow and methodical way. I've said many times that astrology is the most interesting thing I've ever learned because it's so intricate and complicated, and I still enjoy making discoveries about it as much as I did over twenty years ago.

In this book, we've been discussing the ABC's of astrology. So far we've learned meanings of the signs, planets, houses, and major aspects. Even if you didn't know any astrology when you began reading, you're now ready for the glamour; you're ready to read a horoscope!

This is an exciting moment. Perhaps you have astrology software that will let you enter the data and print out a chart in an instant. Or maybe you went to the web to get a chart calculated for free, but either way, you have in front of you a circle filled with symbols, ready for you to decipher it. I've chosen a few horoscopes from my own data base for us to consider today. It's a lot easier when you're not looking at your own chart!

The first step when looking at a horoscope is, well, to *look* at it. What do you notice first?

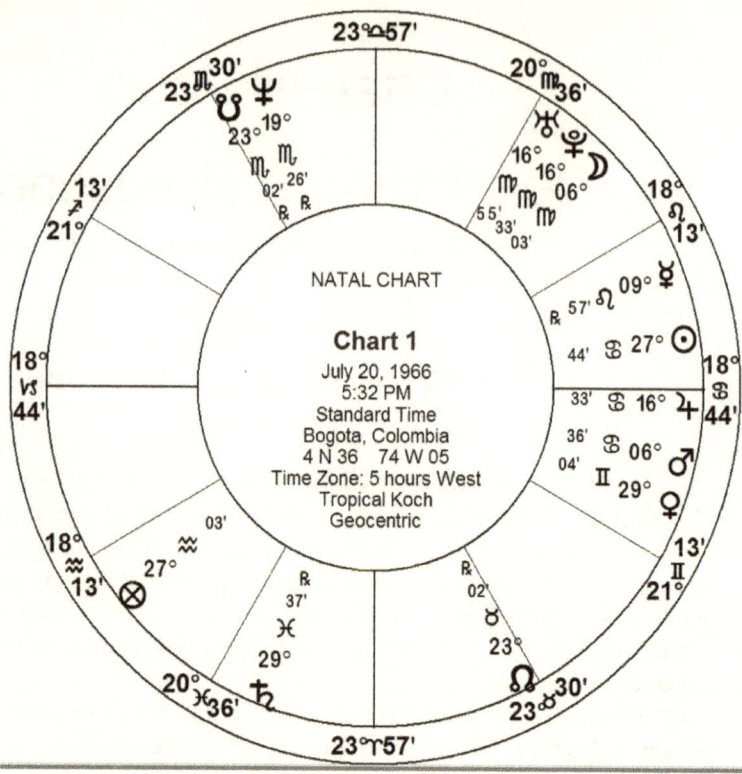

In Chart one, we see a Cancer horoscope of a man, and notice immediately that most of the planets are clustered at the right side of the chart, indicating a person whose life will very strongly involve other people. Also on first glance, we observe a lack of oppositions (planets 180 degrees apart, plus or minus 10 degrees), which would indicate a difficulty in understanding the need for compromise. Right there, almost immediately, we have a strong idea about this person, and we haven't even begun our analysis. We see a people person who automatically expects to get along with everyone.

Now let's get on to the methodical process, and look at the chart, bit by bit. The first step is to notice the Sun — in Cancer, in the seventh house, so that would indicate a sentimental need for security (Cancer) through a connection to partners (seventh house). The Sun makes a major aspect, a trine (an angle of 120 degrees, plus or minus 10 degrees) to Saturn (Karma), indicating a sort of personal stability and the willingness to assume responsibilities, perhaps often to siblings and neighbors (third house). There is also a trine to Neptune (spirituality), indicating creativity, sensitivity, and increased emotionality, and a tendency to seek ideals and self-expression in his career (tenth house). Also we could say that his dad was a source of inspiration as often the tenth represents the father. All together these planets form a grand trine in the chart, (three planets in a triangle configuration), indicating ease and cooperation among the energies in question. In this case, we'd say he is emotional and sensitive, but need not ignore the practical side of life.

Sometimes the next logical step would be to examine the Moon, but sometimes I like to look at all the Yang or masculine, outgoing energies, then at the Moon and all the Yin or receptive energies together. I think in this case, as we've already explored the Sun's grand trine, we should look at the Moon. That's the thing with astrology—the best way to unravel a particular chart will be communicated to you by the horoscope itself.

The Moon (emotions) is in the practical, earthy sign Virgo and lies in the passionate eighth house of sex and partner's resources. This would indicate a person for whom sensuality is a means to an emotional connection. Although the Moon appears closely linked to Pluto and Uranus, they are not in fact conjunct because there are greater than ten degrees separating them. The moon is sextile (an angle of 60 degrees, plus or minus six degrees) Mars (action), making the emotions even more intense. It's also widely sextile Venus (affection), giving him a nice connection with women, a tender side, and an affinity for sweet treats.

Now let's move on to the rest of the planets. Venus is in Gemini, indicating an ease with finding interesting companions and conjunct Mars, making him sexy and creative. With the planets of love and energy in the sixth house, we might assume that this man could work in a creative field, or at least will have pleasant interactions—and perhaps affairs—with colleagues. This conjunction is widely conjunct Jupiter (expansion), giving optimism, energy, and charm. Jupiter hovers right at the Descendant, and that brings energy to relationships. We also have Mercury (communication) in the outgoing sign Leo, also in the seventh house. Mercury makes a very wide square to Neptune (illusion), indicating some creative writing ability, and an occasional tendency to spin a tall tale. With Neptune in the tenth house of career, we might wonder would he want to work in film, photography, or chemicals. Actually he works in Human Resources, which makes a lot of sense considering the rest of the chart.

Now let's look at the few remaining planets. Saturn, the planet of Karma, is in Pisces, indicating a need to trust his heart and follow his talents, and perhaps that coordinates with the tenth house Neptune. Perhaps he has creative talents he isn't expressing, which the Venus-Mars would confirm. Uranus (sudden change), is in the practical sign Virgo, indicating a need to be more flexible about his desires to organize and control everything, and in the eighth house, suggesting many financial ups and downs. Pluto (transformation), lies conjunct to Uranus. That's a great deal of intense energy for personal change, and sexual encounters. Clearly we can look at this horoscope and say this is a man who will develop and grow via his encounters with other people.

In coming to that conclusion, it's interesting to note that Sun sign astrology has a lot in its favor. Simply by knowing that a person is a seventh house Cancer, you could pretty much come up with a similar conclusion. That will always be the case. A person's destiny is never at odds with his or her Sun sign. That's why we choose to be born during that particular time. The rest of the horoscope will give many other details and will develop the ideas of that life. This particular chart is not terribly complicated though, is it? There are few inter-aspects between planets, although no planet is completely unconnected. There is no major configuration. I always feel the more complicated and more connected a horoscope, the more evolved the person is. Our next chart has some recognizable configurations.

Chart two, also a man, shows Sun in Aries. As we first glance at the chart, we notice a T-square involving Moon, Jupiter, and Neptune. We also notice several clusters of conjunctions. Many elements of his life will be intertwined because of all the connections among the planets. Now let's begin with the Sun.

The Sun is in Aries, indicating a need to develop the self. Saturn conjoins the Sun and reinforces this message, suggesting a new Karmic cycle. We also have Mars, the planet of energy, and ruler of Aries, in its own sign. It's a good thing when an Aries person's Mars is in a strong sign, and significant when it's in Aries. It means that he will not only *be* an Aries, but will take action in that same Aries manner. As Popeye might say, "I yam what I yam." Also aspecting the Sun is Uranus, forming a wide, out of sign opposition. This would indicate the need to be independent, to forge his own way in life, and would also promise a bit of a temper. Thus far we see many indications of individuality, which is what Aries is all about.

An interesting question to ask is this—if Uranus opposes the Sun and is within the orb for that aspect, what about its close conjunction to Pluto? Because all of the Uranus energy will be tinged by its connection with Pluto, we have to assume that some of that shading will also apply to the Sun-Uranus opposition. A Sun-Pluto opposition indicates a tendency to get into power struggles and to deal with people who want to boss you around. So we can assume there will be some of this in his life.

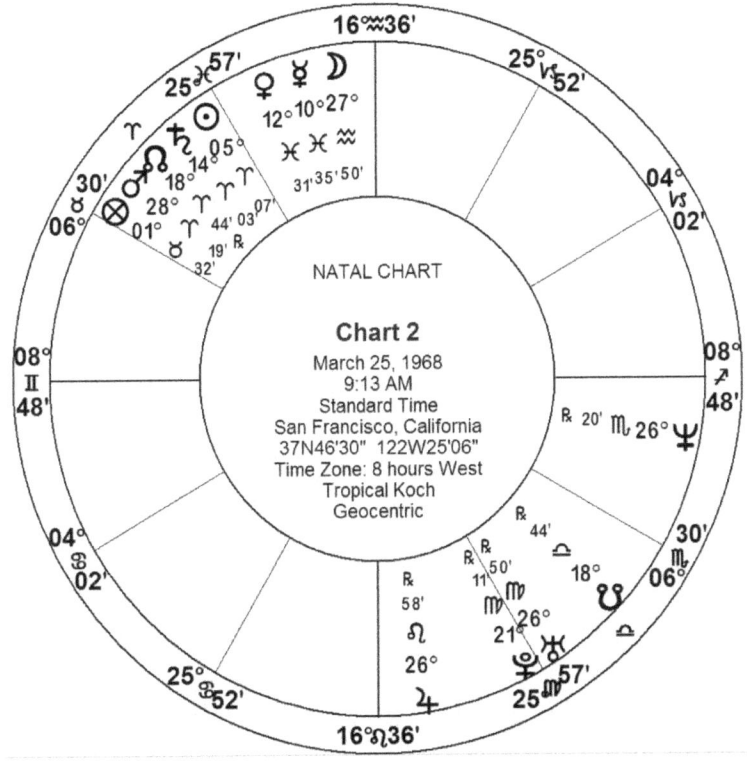

We also notice Uranus and Pluto in and hovering near the cusp of the fifth house, and that provides an interesting dichotomy. With Sun in the eleventh, he is friendly and people-oriented. He cares about his personal ties and wants to fit in. That opposition in the fifth indicates romantic partners who are either unusual (Uranus) or domineering (Pluto), so he would have to make choices based not on peer pressure, but on what feels right to him. He must follow his own instincts, reinforcing the Aries goal of the chart.

Also among the Yang elements of the chart, we have Mars trine Jupiter, nice for energy and athletic ability. We also have Mars quincunx (an angle of 150 degrees, plus or minus 3 degrees) Uranus, and Neptune, and also by association once again with Uranus, Pluto. That's a lot of energy! Male movie stars often have this sort of multiple Mars hits because it makes them sexy and charismatic. The

Mars-Uranus tie gives individuality, some quirkiness, a little sexual kinkiness. The Neptune hit brings musical abilities and sensitivity. The Pluto tie can bring power struggles and more sexual kinkiness.

Among these outer planets and Mars we have a configuration, called a Yod, involving two planets in sextile (Neptune and Uranus), both of which are quincunx a third (Mars). Some people consider this a Karmic aspect, one giving power and a shadowing of destiny.

This chart has a great deal of Yang energy, and it would imply a person strong enough to face life on his own terms. But what about his Yin side? With all this Yang energy, if he doesn't have decently soft Yin planets, we'd end up with a bombastic blowhard.

The Moon is in socially conscious Aquarius, indicating a need to have women friends and a desire to make the world a better place. In the tenth house, it suggests that a man might meet his mate through work, or that he'll have a personal sense of identity with his career. We might also assume strong female role models. The Moon is opposed by Jupiter, giving a cheerful personality and a great deal of optimism. This is one of those cases where an opposition isn't a bad thing. I feel Jupiter can rarely do harm no matter what aspect it makes, but it could give an excess of optimism, I suppose and thus an inability to deal with crisis because too much time is spent looking for the silver lining. This man is unfailingly positive and seldom says a bad word about anything or anyone. He believes in focusing on the good.

Neptune is in the sixth house of work and health, and could indicate a career in the health field, or at least a strong interest in healthy living, and perhaps some allergies. Neptune makes a square to both Moon and Jupiter, forming a T-square (two planets at 180 degrees, and a third lying at the midpoint of the opposition, squaring both). In other words, all the passion and energy in that Moon-Jupiter opposition filters out through Neptune. This can be a mixed blessing. It can indicate a sense of idealism and a personal desire to make the world a better place. But it can also describe relationships with women who have emotional problems, drinking or drug problems, or are deceptive. He has experienced quite a few of these issues, but always remains positive and holds good feelings in his heart even after a relationship ends. The worst thing about this aspect in a man's chart is an inability to see women clearly and to assume that each new woman is the embodiment of the goddess energy he imagines he wants. So balance—and honesty—are definitely essential.

The other Yin planet, Venus, is beautifully placed in Pisces, indicating a deep ability to love at the most profound level. It's conjunct Mercury, making for what I like to call "sweet talk," or a tendency to say sweet things. Often Mercury functions poorly in Pisces, because it gets bogged down in emotion and otherworldly fuzziness, and this man often says he doesn't have the words to express his thoughts. But he does express himself in an interesting way and says very sweet things.

We should note that both Moon and Venus are in the tenth, and that weakens the Yin energy just a bit. It brings it out into the outside world, making those sensitive planets less emotional. It might also indicate a sort of professional creativity, or the likelihood of working with women, which he hasn't really done. But because they're anchored by Jupiter and Neptune, that brings Yin elements into many parts of his life. Plus, a fourth house Jupiter is like a treasure trove of good things. It brings a happy childhood, love of mother and other females, and most importantly, a sense of emotional security that provides a strong foundation to deal with whatever life crises may emerge.

This is an intense and very interesting horoscope. Both Yin and Yang energies are well represented and are strong and well-developed. You might say that the task of this lifetime is for him to express himself without losing sight of the value of other people in his life.

The next chart we're going to consider has some of the elements of the last, but to quite different effect. Chart three is a woman, born under the sign of Pisces. On first glance we notice another T-square involving the Moon, plus a grand trine. This chart also features Gemini rising, and as the two people are of approximately the same age, we notice once again Uranus and Pluto at the fifth, making an opposition to eleventh house planets.

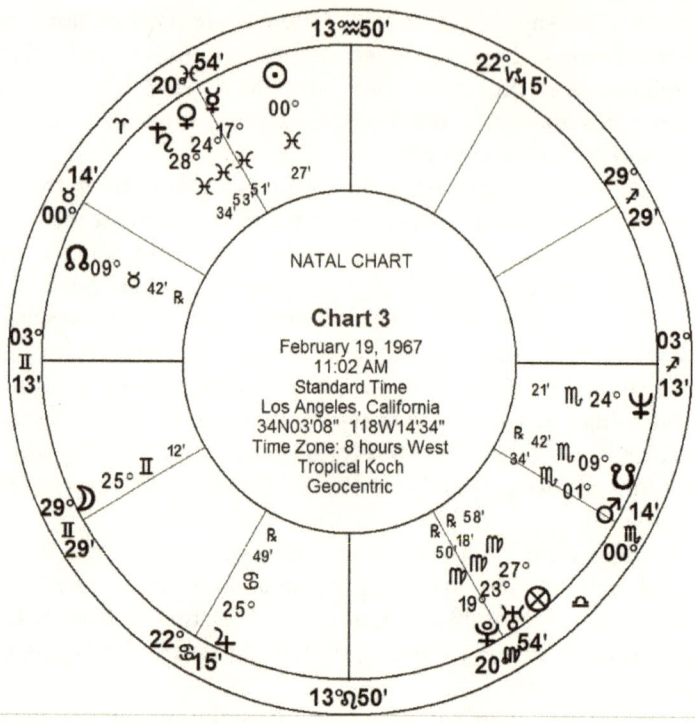

The Sun in Pisces is in the tenth house, describing someone whose emotional nature is right out there in the world, perhaps as an artist of some sort. The Sun makes an out of sign trine to the Moon, granting an expectation of harmonious relationships, and perhaps a childhood with parents who got along well. As the Moon is in the first house, emotions once again are emphasized, but it's in the decidedly unemotional sign of Gemini, so there may be a bit of a case of mood du jour in this woman's life. The Sun also makes a trine to Mars in Scorpio, another emotional placement, signifying actions dictated by feelings more than thought. Who she is and how she feels—and behaves—are very closely related. This is the first grand trine (a triangle of three planets, all of which are 120 degrees apart, plus or minus 10 degrees) in the chart, and in this configuration the energy flows in a sort of circular manner, connecting all the vibrations together. Mars also makes a square to Jupiter, giving energy and courage, perhaps too much so. A Mars-Jupiter square can also bestow a bit of klutziness.

In addition to these aspects, the Sun is squared by Neptune, creating an identity crisis. It's very hard to know who she is and what she wants with this aspect, but it does confer some creativity—and spirituality. We could say that her self-image is blurry so that she can more readily get in touch with her inner impulses, instincts, and can allow herself to be guided by the universe. Then she expresses that energy through the grand trine just mentioned. This is a very emotional, subliminal chart.

The Moon is in an Air sign, and it lies at the focal point of a T-square, similar to what we saw in the previous chart, but in this case the energy is a bit more strident. Once again we have Venus and Mercury conjunct in Pisces, but they're restricted by Saturn, also closely conjunct. This might indicate some writing ability, but perhaps in a scientific field. The Venus-Saturn conjunction in Pisces implies some lifetimes in which love was mishandled or caused emotional trauma, leaving a residue of romantic fear. In addition to this, we see an opposition by the Uranus-Pluto conjunction from the fifth. That would bring sudden (Uranus), ill-fated (Saturn) romantic encounters with a fated and very intense (Pluto) nature. In other words, she's suddenly in the grips of a passion that she can't quite control, and which feels threatening. This opposition indicates a very complicated—and difficult—love life. And we have all this energy bursting out through the Gemini Moon. It's as though she has intense, Karmic romantic encounters, all of which affect her emotionally (Moon), but which flow through her and don't remain (Gemini). If the Moon were in a more emotional sign, it would be extremely difficult to deal with the residue of all her romances.

We also notice with interest, a tight trine to both Jupiter and Neptune from the Venus cluster. That indicates an affectionate nature (Jupiter) and the desire for true love (Neptune). There is a huge amount of emotional, romantic energy in this chart, isn't there. But unlike the previous grand trine, this one has an anchor—the opposing planets Uranus and Pluto, out of which all this energy flows. Sadly it's quite disruptive. It indicates sudden break ups.

The Moon in this horoscope is very complicated. The happy go lucky Gemini nature is a tool for the heavier elements in the chart. First of all, lying there in the first house, it attracts emotional entanglements. The Venus square gives a desire for pleasant social interactions. The Saturn square brings loneliness, and although much is written about the alienation produced by Saturn-Moon aspects, in fact those people seek out companionship quite compulsively, because they're so lonely they need the distraction. The Uranus square is far more alienating, because it prevents intimacy and closeness, the very thing the Saturn craves. And then the Pluto comes along and becomes quite grasping, possessive, and demanding.

The scenarios aren't hard to envision. She desires closeness and companionship (Venus and Saturn) but can't relate intimately (Uranus) so either does things unconsciously to push lovers away, or attracts lovers who have the same Uranus issues and who push her away. Then she becomes insecure and starts grasping (Pluto) and the relationship blows up. Because the Moon is in Gemini, she feels the pain, but lets go quickly and moves on to her next conquest. Otherwise this lifetime would be much too painful to endure, and she wouldn't have as many opportunities to confront her Karma. You might say she's over consuming at a romantic schmorgasbord—and the Gemini Moon provides the Alka Seltzer!

So what would you say this lifetime is all about? It's about learning of the consequences of unconscious, ill-thought out choices and random emotional entanglements. All her energies lead her into relationships she really isn't prepared to handle, then they blow up in her face, and she is left with a fleeting sense of the consequences. This is one of those horoscopes in which the person is immersed in lesson after lesson, never mastering them in this lifetime, and then when the life ends and the afterlife review process begins, there's the chance to come to a reckoning and to make sense of all these disruptive impulses. We might even say that a chart like this symbolizes a lifetime that could be a precursor to the lifetime described by the chart we analyzed previously. We all work our way up to greater levels of evolution. It's instructive but not always fun.

An interesting and very dynamic configuration in any horoscope is the grand cross (4 planets lying in two sets of perpendicular oppositions). Chart 4 illustrates this configuration.

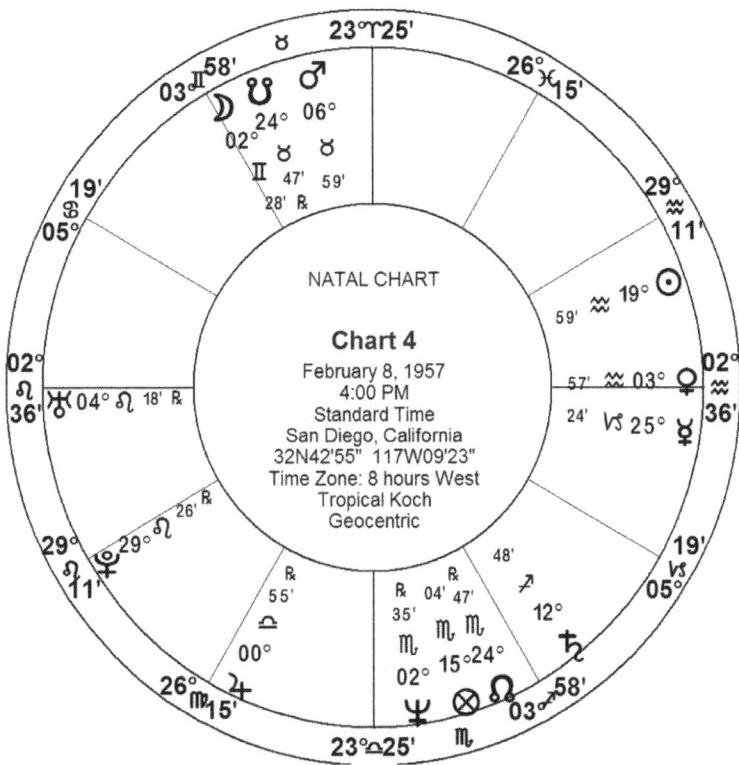

On first glance, we observe planets in many houses of the horoscope, indicating much activity and interaction in this lifetime.

There are many balls to keep in the air with this sort of horoscope. We also notice Uranus right on the Ascendant, and expect this man to be a live wire, a bit quirky, and perhaps tall.

He is an Aquarius, so we already know he's a little eccentric, and that coordinates with the Aquarian ruler, Uranus, on the Ascendant. As a seventh house Sun, we assume this man to be partnership oriented, whether through marriage or business alliances. We observe a single aspect to the Sun — a very wide opposition from Pluto, indicating some challenges from other people. Immediately we notice a see-saw effect in this chart. He desires independence and longs to be a bit eccentric so he can express his individuality, but Plutonian conflicts keep him tethered — or they provide something to rebel against!

The Moon is in Gemini, and we already know that means he's an emotional butterfly, enjoying multiple emotional interactions. The

Moon is trine Venus, giving him an appreciation of women—and sweet treats—and also trine Mercury, which conjoins Venus. This is truly the gift of gab in a man's chart. He enjoys talking to women and interacting with them, something confirmed by the third leg in this configuration, a trine to Jupiter, bringing friendliness and optimism. This is a very social grand trine, isn't it, and based only on what we have so far, we'd assume this man to be a pleasant charmer.

The Moon has some more complicated aspects, however. It receives a tight, out-of-sign square from Pluto, which is very intense, and tends to imply the people with whom he connects emotionally demand more than he's willing to give. Pluto aspects both of the lights, and in both cases it's there to remind him that other people have needs, feelings, and demands. Despite that Uranus rising, he can't always do just as he likes in his personal interactions.

It's important to understand the difference in this Moon-Pluto aspect and one involving another sign. For example, a Moon in water with a Pluto square would be much more tenderhearted, and would desire closeness, and might even cling. So the sign of the Moon determines just how unfriendly the challenge from Pluto will become. If the depth it seeks is basically against the nature of the Moon sign, it will feel as though other people are infringing on your life. If the Moon seeks depth, Pluto will simply increase that, although with a square aspect, there are bound to be some challenges either way. It's just a question of how discordantly it will behave and how much it will feel as though other people are making unreasonable demands. And, if the Moon is in emotional water, the person in question might do the clinging rather that receive it from others. Either way though, there would be lessons to be learned about the perils of clinging and possessiveness in human interactions.

The Moon is quincunx Neptune, giving more emotional depth and some psychic ability. And it's sextile Uranus, creating a desire for emotional independence, and basically reducing the Neptunian sensitivity. The Moon is a very important planet in this horoscope. It aspects six planets out of a possible nine, so it's very connected. But is it a particularly emotional Moon? Not at all. It's a social Moon, and a playful one. That's the thing with the Moon in Gemini—it likes connecting with a wide range of people but doesn't want to wallow in feeling.

We already noted the Mercury-Venus conjunction, and that is another friendly aspect. It's the sweet talk aspect, but with Venus in Aquarius, it's more likely to be friendly chatter. The conjunction is opposed by Uranus, giving sudden attractions (Venus) and intellectual impatience (Mercury). It also gives him the urge to meet women on the internet.

Mars, in the stable sign Taurus, is square all three planets above. With both Venus and Mars in fixed signs, we'd assume he'd want to linger in relationships, and he has remained married for many years, despite being separated for most of them. The square from Uranus gives a quirkiness and reduces the normal stability associated with Mars in Taurus. It also gives a temper and a tendency to seek sudden, outrageous, or shocking sexual encounters. Plus Venus square Mars usually is out there expressing itself via a desire to connect romantically — and sexually — as often as possible.

Mars is opposed by Neptune, and that is an extremely challenging aspect. It makes it hard for him to act assertively without worrying he's on the wrong track. People with this aspect often get into kinky sexual scenarios because they enjoy power play. Interestingly, the Neptune person often plays the dominant role, but it's really only a role, and usually this configuration indicates some passive-aggressive behavior. Remember Ben Affleck and the questionable tabloid reports about his sexual exploits with a stripper at his bachelor party? He has Mars opposite Neptune, and my feeling was he was trying to get JLo to break up with him, which he ultimately succeeded in doing through a number of ill-advised exploits. That's the Mars opposite Neptune personality. He doesn't want to just speak up and say honey it's over. He does things the partner will hate until she flees.

In this chart, Mars is also trine Pluto, and that gives a bit more confidence in his ability to be assertive, and even more sexual kinkiness. We notice that the planets of love and sex are very important in this chart, as they're involved in a grand cross. There is a huge amount of energy devoted to social, romantic, and sexual activity. Is he a babe magnet? I don't know, but he certainly spends a great portion of his life chasing women!

We notice Saturn in the fifth house of romance and children and that can indicate Karmic problems with children, a lifetime with a challenged child, or no children, as is the case with this man. With Saturn in Sagittarius, we suspect he has had lifetimes in which he didn't let his philosophy guide him, in which he knew the truth and ignored it. So we'd assume that he has some relationship Karma in this lifetime, and a tendency not to commit, not to give his heart, not to love.

Neptune in the fourth house is very telling. I call that the bottomless pit of need aspect. The tendency is to have an unhappy childhood, to feel that Mom was off attending to her own concerns and thus was neglectful. There is a sense of inferiority, too. So what does he do? He reaches out to women as a substitute for Mom, hoping to fill that void. But he lacks the emotional depth to fulfill a woman's needs, and in fact, mostly focuses on having her fulfill his. But we women can get pretty annoyed in such relationships, so then the woman speaks up, complains and starts making demands (Pluto square Moon), which he finds oppressive. He knows he's doing a bad job (Neptune opposite Mars) but he doesn't want to care (Uranus on the Ascendant) and so he rebels and either lashes out, or does passive-aggressive things to make the woman ditch him. Sometimes he has to do a combination of the two because with that Moon-Pluto, his tendency is to attract women who cling, so it's all about how far must he go to attain his liberation and try a new relationship.

I've often said that a fixed Mars in a grand cross will indicate a person who tends to live as a victim. The grand cross attracts lots of chaos in the life and no matter what comes, the person stands pat and sticks it out. This is just such a horoscope. He feels like the victim in his relationships and wants to burst free, but has to use passive-aggressive behavior to accomplish that goal.

What sort of life lessons might be indicated by such a horoscope? Perhaps he's learning that you can't truly be an individual unless you can also fit in with the people around you and also that his own behavior is what determines how others behave to him. It seems quite fitting that the golden rule would be a life lesson in an Aquarian horoscope, doesn't it. He can't get what he wants from other people if he doesn't give them something in return!

As I mentioned when we were considering the aspects, it's nice to have a number of connections among the planets, because it gives the lifetime richness and appealing complication. But I didn't want to imply that you must have one of the major configurations to have a "good" horoscope. In fact the whole concept of what's good in astrology is probably a bad idea because all it does it make people feel insecure. Some things are more challenging, but there is always a Karmic purpose for any horoscope, so it's wise just to see what's there without labeling it good or bad.

I find the concept "whatever is there" is my best guiding light. I look to see whatever is there, and I just notice stuff. I don't make too many rules, and many of the astrology rules I learned as a beginner, I've tossed out since. All that stuff about certain aspects being intrinsically bad, I ignore. The stuff about planets being in "detriment," or "exaltation," well I ignore it. But then I don't like following rules blindly. It seems wiser to me to observe what's there and to make sense of it individually. Perhaps life is more complicated when there are fewer rules, but for me it works better. I'm a Virgo, and to me details should make sense, one by one. And of course experience teaches so much. Once you see the same effect time and again in many horoscopes, you know what behavior will result from what planetary pictures. The best thing about growing old is that we've seen it all before and know what to make of it.

The final chart I want to examine now is a very important one. It's yours! So pull out your own chart and let's have a look at it. What do you notice first? Is there a bunch of complicated configurations, something simple and elegant, or just a few conjunctions here and there? Every possibility has meaning, and value in any lifetime.

Where is your Sun? How does the house placement shade the Sun sign's meaning? What aspects does it make to the other planets in your chart and how do they shade it? What could it all mean in terms of Karma?

Now what about the Moon? Is it in an extremely emotional sign or a barely emotional sign? There's no bad or good in this, and a reason exists for every placement in every horoscope, so just be honest, open your mind and be willing to see whatever is there in your own chart. How do the house placement and aspects shade the meaning of your Moon?

Then keep going. What's happening with your Mercury? And your Venus? How does your Venus work with your Moon? They are on the same, Yin team, and together they tell the story about what's inside your heart and soul.

What's the story with your Mars? Does it uphold the lessons indicated by your Sun's placement? It is an ally to you in your efforts to be assertive, or does it restrain you as in the chart above. What do your Venus and Mars do in combination? How do they paint a portrait of the lusty side of your nature. Are you a horn dog or a sentimental lover?

What about the outer planets? What does Saturn indicate about your past lifetimes and the lessons you are trying to learn in this one? How does it touch your personal planets? What about Uranus? Are you an eccentric maniac or in control of your urges to rebel? And Neptune—has it made you a little crazy or just good on the guitar? And Pluto, don't forget to see how this very powerful little planet is altering the power dynamics in this lifetime. Once you can answer all these questions, you are able to make perfect sense of your own horoscope and you might just discover some things you never before realized. That's the purpose of astrology! I know of no other tool that surpasses it for psychological awareness.

Take some time now to look at charts of friends, but don't make pronouncements or give edicts. Don't say "You can't be assertive."

Nobody wants to hear this. Ask questions. Ask "Do you feel you can be as aggressive as you like?" That way the person can say no, and if you've hit on a nerve, they're not obligated to accept information they're not ready to hear. Be gentle when sharing ideas, particularly at the beginning when you're just learning, because chances are you don't have all the answers and the way you're expressing the ideas may not jive with the outlook of the friend whose chart you're dissecting. It's always best to give people some breathing room. You may have the absolutely correct information but perhaps are choosing words that mean something else to your friend. Communication is complicated and it helps to be subtle when dealing with something as important as a person's life. The more experience you gain, and the more you observe your friend as you're sharing information, the better you will become at expressing ideas in ways people can accept. And of course, the better you will become at seeing the truth of any horoscope.

Part Two: Harrison Ford and Clark Gable: The Male Icon

I'm never sure if movies are my passion because I love the artistry of a flickering image on a screen in a dark room or because I'm a romantic who loves to fall in love with heroes. Either way, I love the movies and like most of the women on the planet, at pretty much any point in my life, I've been in love with one movie star or other. Often the qualities I perceive in my screen idols are qualities I seek in men to whom I relate in person. My screen loves seem to be divided into two categories—the ones I'd like to sleep with and those I'd like to marry! Over the many years of my movie going adult life, there have been dozens I could easily imagine in my bed but only a couple who seemed like marriage material.

Like most of the rest of the female population, my two all-time favorites are Clark Gable and Harrison Ford. It's interesting to think about these two megastars and to ask ourselves why, of all the men on earth, do they strike such a vibrant chord with so many bedazzled women. The qualities they define speak volumes not just about our fanciful female hearts, but about civilization in general and what we want our men to be.

In February, 2001, it was Clark Gable's centenary, and it was interesting to read some of the articles reviewing his career and his legend. In one article in the Los Angeles Times, the writer was debating if Gable would still be King if he were a movie star today. Her theory was that he would have to "get a body" among other things! There's no question that Gable's fine physique for the 30's wouldn't have been up to par in the muscled and underfed twenty-first century. In the popular hit movie Titanic, a plucky, diminutive-seeming (although DiCaprio is actually very tall) boy romanced a solid woman and millions of girls swooned and wept. The Times' writer correctly pointed out the difference between a star like Gable and the young Leo DiCaprio. My sense was that Titanic appealed mainly to young girls, and if Gable had been in the lead, it would have been a different movie, one that would have appealed to grownups, such as myself! But I felt that the Times' writer totally missed the boat when talking about the King. What made Gable so special would have stood up today and any other day.

I remember so clearly the first time I saw Gone With the Wind. I was twelve years old and the movie instantly became my all time favorite, so much so, that years later I took my infant daughter to a screening so in later years she could say it was her first movie.

Everyone loves Scarlett O'Hara's epic struggle, but the reason most women see that movie again and again is Clark Gable, the perfect embodiment of Rhett Butler. He captured so faultlessly Butler's rogue strength, his veiled sensitivity, his charisma and his powerful sexuality that the role and the actor have completely merged.

What the Times' writer failed to mention (perhaps she is too young to remember!) is that what made Gable so compelling for his female audience is the way he held a woman in his arms. Even though he was large for his generation, he didn't hold a woman casually, his hand somewhere in the middle of her back. When Gable held a woman, he held her! His arm wrapped tightly around the woman's shoulders, reaching all the way around to her other side. That would not have been a director's instruction but simply part of

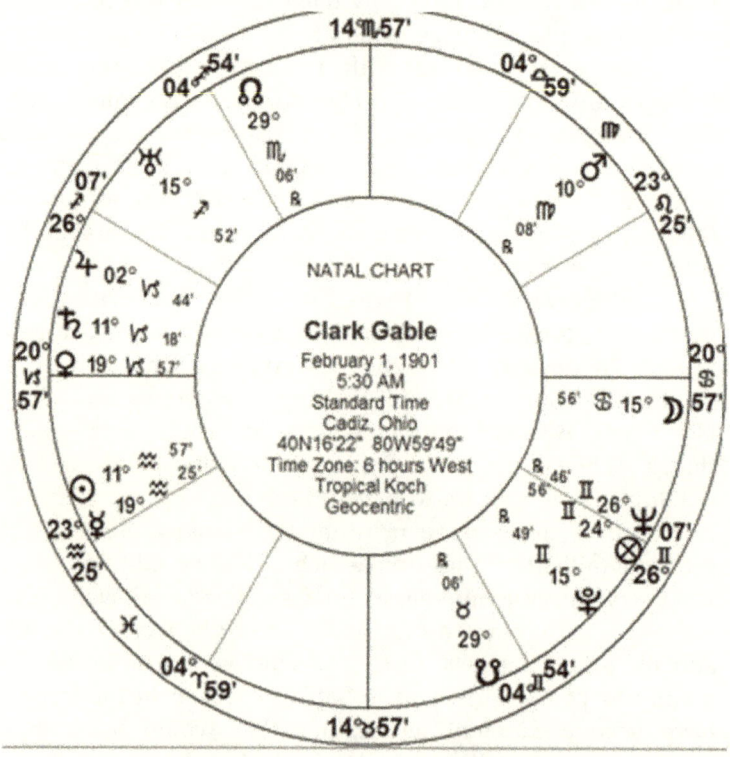

the man himself, because he did it in every embrace. In that simple gesture of tightly holding a woman to his chest, Gable conveyed the qualities we most prefer in our men: strength, solidness, reliability. Tough but tender, honest even when he was a rogue, intelligent but not bookish, skilled, principled and physically strong, Gable was a man's man in many ways. The one thing he wasn't was a boy.

Gable was an Aquarius, and to me that's the most masculine sign for a man. Aries are macho and studly, Scorpios are magnetic and sexy, but Aquarian men are guys—very different from us women! With Sun conjunct Mercury, he projected intelligence, and Gable played a journalist more than once. His performance as the wisecracking reporter in It Happened One Night earned him an Oscar and defined an aspect of his screen persona that lasted throughout his career. With a trine to Pluto, he seemed magnetic and powerful. His Sun was also sextile Uranus, making him an individual, but not necessarily a rebel. Mars also aspected his Sun—by quincunx—another aspect of power, strength and sexuality.

His Virgo Mars isn't necessarily a placement we would consider either powerful or sexy, although with Mars there, generally a man will work at being a good lover, and that was certainly Gable's reputation, plus of course it is in the eighth house of sex so that does amp it up. Gable had a t-square going out through his Mars—involving a Pluto-Uranus opposition, and that would certainly give intense power and sexuality to his energy. That scene in which he carried Vivian Leigh up the stairs is the embodiment of this energy. He swept her into his arms, and took the stairs two at a time as though her weight was nothing at all to him.

Mars is also aspected by trine by three other planets. A wide trine to Jupiter gives energy, good muscle tone, and a sense of boyish can-do optimism. A close trine to Saturn gives a sense of being in control, a reliable boy scout appreciation for responsibility and a military precision. Gable was well respected during his wartime stint in the Air Corps, even participating in several air raids over Nazi Germany and winning the Distinguished Flying Cross. Venus forms a very wide trine to Mars as well, giving even more sex appeal and some creativity.

Finally, the Moon is sextiled by Mars, giving passion and depth of emotion. Seven out of nine planets aspect Gable's Mars, so it's little wonder why he seemed such a masculine, manly man. In any chart, a planet heavily aspected will be quite strong and Gable's yang planets are all heavily intertwined. What that comes down to is quite a buzz—a sense of energy radiating from the person—in other words, charisma. No wonder women loved Gable because he seemed dangerous and manly!

Gable's yin aspects are also worth exploring. He has a Cancer Moon in the seventh house, and that makes him deeply emotional and sensitive and someone who needs a mate to feel safe and happy. The Moon is opposed by a Saturn-Venus conjunction, so we would assume Gable had some conflicts about women, starting with his mother, who died when he was only seven months old. The Saturn opposition gives a sense of loneliness and emotional neediness—often people who have this aspect fear being alone and they reach out again and again to people who can't quite give them what they need, so this is an aspect of unrequited love. The Venus opposition is generally nice—it would indicate a man who likes women—and food and the good life, as Gable openly admitted he did. But with the Venus-Saturn conjunction, once again he would be searching for love and commitment, something it might be difficult for him to achieve.

In addition, Uranus makes a quincunx to the Moon, and that creates emotional distance. With both Uranus and Saturn aspecting his Moon, Gable ran hot and cold where women were concerned, and probably felt that the women in his life didn't quite give him what he needed. Generally speaking, when there are hard aspects to the Moon from both Uranus and Saturn, there is a need to learn balance. Conflicting desires for closeness and freedom are usually played out through attractions to the wrong partner. The person is always yearning for love but is attracted to people who are distant; there is also the tendency to run away from those who truly want him or her. This pattern would indicate a Karmic tendency to become too much a slave to love and so in this lifetime, the person would have to confront those desires to love too much and be rescued by the Uranian need to pull apart. Gable's tortured portrayal of Rhett, hopelessly in love with Scarlett for decades until the time she finally returns his ardor, and he decides "frankly my dear, I don't give a damn," is the perfect illustration of this Karmic configuration.

Gable married a total of five times, first to a much older woman who helped him start his acting career, and that's not surprising considering the lunar contacts already mentioned. Most memorable was his happy marriage to Libra movie star Carole Lombard, and whose tragic death plunged him into heartbreak that endured all the rest of his life. It's romantic to assume that marriage would have been long-lasting, but considering these aspects, it's more likely that something would have intruded on the fairy tale if tragedy hadn't intervened. Gable's longest marriage lasted only eight years. But for us viewers, it was easy to fall in love with a man who was capable of love so deep that despite his incredible personal, masculine strengths that he could be so visibly wounded by unreturned affection.

With a horoscope like this, a man would have to develop independence and to learn to meet his own emotional needs. I feel a little tug at my heartstrings as I unravel this horoscope. Here was Clark Gable, a man who exuded all sorts of masculinity and genuinely appealing traits, someone whose very presence could define the word manly and yet I see a man with a tender heart, someone who suffered a great deal of pain over love, someone always in need of comforting that once bestowed would usually be wrenched away. It is no wonder at all that Gable was the King—even his horoscope has a larger than life quality of intense emotion, thrilling sexuality and personal charisma.

The life lessons of Gable's horoscope are important not just to him but to us all. He was here to learn to stand on his own two feet, to go on despite the pain, to live an upstanding life and to do what's right, to make something of himself. And one of his lessons was to realize that he could be adored by the whole world, but if he didn't have just one woman to care, none of the rest meant anything. We can learn from him that no matter how glamorous a person seems or how thrilling his life appears to be, that on a fundamental level, that person is just as human as you or I, and as such has just as many problems as we face. We might say that is the true measure of a man—someone who exudes Hemingway's definition of courage—grace under pressure.

I remember noticing Harrison Ford in college when I saw American Graffiti, and his bit part as the cute but menacing cowboy behind the wheel stopped more than a few hearts. I remembered him as the devastatingly gorgeous but slimy office assistant in The Conversation. But I didn't fall in love with him until Star Wars. His portrayal of the selfish and cocky Han Solo, who became a hero despite his self-serving intentions, made every woman in the audience swoon. In the more than two decades that have followed, Ford has never lost his place at the top of the box office. One wag even quipped that he's the most famous carpenter since Jesus!

Ford has had greatest success playing action heroes, and we feel comfortable with him in the role of father, cop, or president. Romance is somewhere a tangential part of most of his movies, but not the main story, whether he's fighting evil as Indiana Jones, fighting evil as the good cop on the lam fighting evil as the unjustly accused Dr. Richard Kimble in *The Fugitive* or fighting evil as the President in Air Force One. Yes, he's pretty much always fighting evil! The movies in which he has a different agenda have rarely done as well, including a turn with Michelle Pfeiffer in which he was the villain (*What Lies Beneath*).

My favorites of his movies are the vastly less popular feminist pic, *Working Girl*, the thriller *Frantic*, and of course *Presumed Innocent*, which did well. More recently he turned heads as the cranky news anchor in *Morning Glory*. Ford always plays a traditional, stand up guy. He's generally sexy, sometimes cocky, usually modest, never a showboat, and basically he's the sort of guy we women want to marry. Interestingly, he was a nerd in school, the object of bullies' aggression and someone who flunked out of college because he spent all his time sleeping.

Ford is a Cancer, born during a New Moon, Sun conjunct Moon. It's that Cancer energy that makes him seem like the perfect husband, father, neighbor and breadwinner. It makes him a bit stodgy but the sort of solid man women love and admire. With Sun, Moon, Jupiter and Mercury either in his tenth house of career or conjunct the Midheaven, Ford is a self-starter. People with tenth house Suns generally feel most comfortable working for themselves and they project responsibility and seem like authority figures. Interestingly, with no oppositions, it's hard for him to compromise because it's easier to assume his will shall be done.

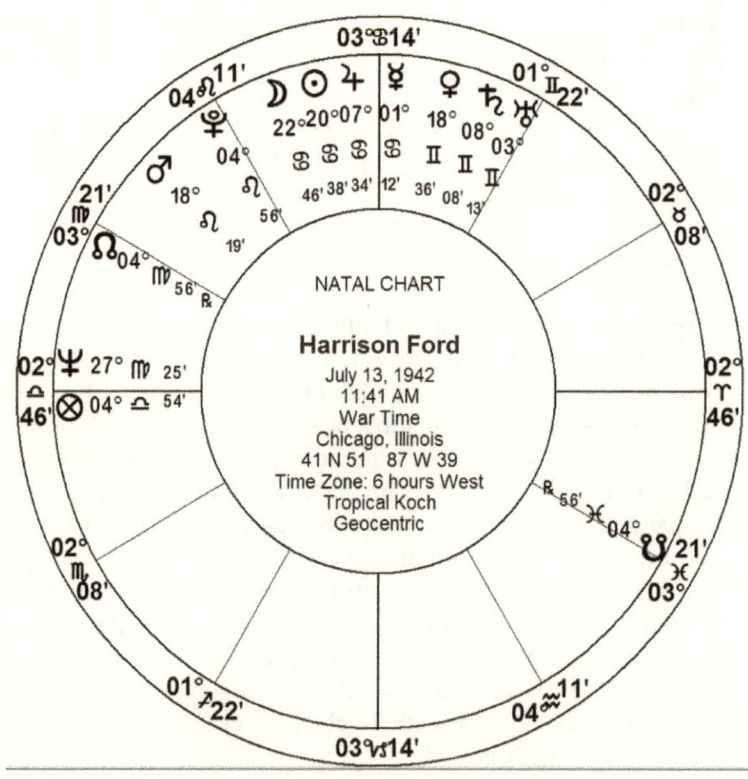

He is a man who wants to be prepared, respected and to do a good job; he's well known to be a perfectionist. Even when he was just getting started, he'd walk away from a project if something struck him as wrong. I saw him profiled at the Actor's Studio and found one comment most telling. He mentioned that prior to the interview, he'd purchased a biography of himself and read it in order to be prepared should he be asked questions on things in his own life he'd forgotten. That's commitment, diligence and thoroughness in the extreme! We would assume with this nice tenth house that Ford had an easy time getting his career started, but it did take him until after he was thirty to become a movie star. He was successful as a carpenter before that, however.

Ford's other yang aspects are Mars in studly Leo sextile Venus. Once again that confers sex appeal and makes him creative. If we think back to Clark Gable's many Solar aspects, Ford has far fewer. He does have quite a few hits to his ascendant, starting with a Neptune conjunction, which is excellent for acting. Early in his career he was told he showed no star quality in his portrayal as a grocery store clerk and he answered he was not trying to look like a star but a grocery clerk! He's also commented that he avoids publicity because it's his goal as an actor to convince us he's someone else, and having the audience know who he is personally is counter to that goal. That's Neptune on the ascendant—never quite knowing who the person is—and easily being able to draw a veil over the personality in order to project just about anything.

In addition, there is a trine from Saturn, giving a sense of stability and reliability, a trine from Uranus, giving a nice sexy and exciting buzz, and a sextile from Pluto, making him magnetic and sexy. Both Mercury and Jupiter square the ascendant, and with that aspect from Jupiter he might have a weight problem, something we've seen no evidence of in the many years he's been a star. The Jupiter-ascendant aspect coupled with Mars in Leo would explain his enthusiasm for piloting his own aircraft and doing many daredevil stunts over the years. The Mercury-Jupiter conjunction would generally make him a good conversationalist and able communicator. In fact, he learned carpentry by checking a book out of the library. That's typical of Mercury-Jupiter contacts—an ease at learning new things and a ready aptitude in applying what's learned.

Ford's yin aspects are also few. His Moon is conjunct the Sun and sextile Neptune. People with Sun and Moon in the same sign seem less complicated to others because they have no hidden agenda—what you see is what you get—and they are who they are—through and through. A Moon-Neptune aspect is rather psychic and often spiritual, though nothing has been written about Ford to indicate he's either. It would also give him deeper emotions and the ability to empathize with other people. He refuses to use his name to get special perks because he thinks it's inconsiderate and unfair. His ex-wife once mentioned that he forced the family to stand in line at Disneyland, like everyone else, rather than just getting in first on his celebrity clout. It's also likely that with this sensitive Moon, he'd rather not call attention to himself in a public situation when he's living his private life, so standing anonymously in line seems less threatening.

Venus is sextile Mars but is otherwise unaspected. The Venus-Mars aspect is one of creativity, and he was not only skilled as a craftsman but is also a good designer. He built his Wyoming cabin himself and continues to do carpentry as a hobby.

It's worthwhile to note the differences in Gable and Ford's yin pictures. Although both are sensitive, emotional men with Moon in Cancer, that's where the similarities end. Where love was concerned, Gable's ability to project misery and unrequited love echoed his personal life, and it inspired in his female audience the desire to make it all better. We could look at him and think, well gee, here is a man capable of love who just hasn't met the right woman—us—and that is a powerful response which kept him on top. Ford, on the other hand seems solid, safe, and even a bit stodgy.

On screen, he seems capable of having a solid marriage and a deep emotional partnership, and in real life despite two divorces he has had long marriages. My favorite scene in a thriller in which he searches desperately for clues in the kidnapping of his beloved wife, is when he discusses the kidnapping with a man who suggests perhaps Ford's wife has gone willingly with the suspect. Ford looks incredulously at the man and says, "You're talking about my wife! You must be thinking of yours." In that scene he projects the ability to know the woman he loves and to have absolute faith that only one conclusion could be drawn about her absence. It's that sort of devotion, ability to trust and sense of deep connection with another human being that we most love about Ford. He, like another Cancer, favorite dad Bill Cosby, seems like the happily devoted married man we all want at home.

It's interesting to stop and consider his past as fodder for high school bullies versus his phenomenal adult success. It's clear by his horoscope that he has a lot of positive energy, and he's far from a coward. But as a double Cancer, he's sensitive. Perhaps it was as an actor playing a role that he found himself. In being the rogue Han Solo or the determined and magnetic Indiana Jones, Ford could see in himself qualities he couldn't quite connect with as a youth. And in embodying those macho guys, perhaps Ford found the courage to connect with the hero inside himself. Who now could envision someone nervy enough to shove Harrison Ford down a hill? Carrie Fisher says of him that even when he's not carrying a gun, Harrison seems as though he is!

Ford's planets are much less compelling than Gable's. For one thing, there is promise of greater happiness. He is a man who is deeply emotional, someone who is private, but who can deal with his public life without making it his only reality. What he is doing is projecting positive energy as a male role model for the rest of the world, but he's also living his private life. In other words, he's less likely to buy into his own mystique than we are!

Ford is sexy and strong, but unlike Gable, he doesn't seem dangerous. The thing that they both have in common is personal strength, emotional depth, the ability to communicate their ideas, and the sort of charisma that inspires confidence. They are the sort of men we'd want on our side in a crisis, someone for whom we can envision cooking a special dinner, and someone who would make a good father. Even when they do things we might regard as boyish, those things are always boyishly charming, only because these guys are men, and we admire their grown up strengths as much as we enjoy swooning over their sexuality and charisma.

Part Three: Martha Stewart

The first time I saw Martha Stewart on television I had a good laugh. As an avid cookbook collector and home chef, I already owned many of her cookbooks and could spend endless hours turning pages and admiring the beautiful photos of perfectly prepared food. Martha's *Pies and Tarts* was the first one I bought, and sitting and reverently turning each pristine page, I ultimately found myself sated on pie—without ever lifting a fork. Those were the days before the cable Food Network—now a personal favorite—and also before celebrity chefs. We had all seen Julia Child and Graham Kerr, and of course I'd heard of some of the star California chefs like Wolfgang Puck and had eaten at some of his restaurants. But unlike today, there were not hundreds of chefs with personal cachet, cookbooks and mini-empires.

I knew that Martha was doing cooking and gardening and somehow I expected her to be a real-life replicate of Sue Ann Nivens, Betty White's hyper-feminine yet shrill character known as the Happy Homemaker on the Mary Tyler Moore Show. At that time Martha was on one of the daytime TV shows, but I'm a Virgo and watching TV is reserved for the evening. But one evening, lo and behold, there was Martha on, of all things, a television commercial. I recognized her pretty face from the covers of her cookbooks and expected to hear a high soprano voice and see a Suzy Homemaker demeanor. Then she spoke. Her voice was low and cultured and my eyes opened wide. She was no cupcake!

Martha was on television for Amex and she informed us that she had cut up all her other credit cards and used the shards to tile her swimming pool floor. Cut to the swimming pool and what do we see? A credit card mosaic replica of the celebrated Renaissance masterpiece, Botticelli's The Birth of Venus! Then came the laugh! I gained a lot of respect for Martha at that moment. She was game, she enjoyed poking a little fun at herself and when we laughed at her, she laughed right along with us.

Even to this day, after all Martha's legal troubles, I get joke emails from women who poke fun at Martha. But it's my suspicion that these are the gals who just keep a stack of emptied delivery pizza boxes near the couch in order to avoid the trauma of coffee table shopping. Gracious living is not what they're all about, and Martha knows this and she doesn't mind.

Born into a large family in a working class New Jersey neighborhood, Martha worked from her teens, first as a model, then after earning a degree in European and architectural history, she married a lawyer, had a daughter, became a stockbroker, retired to a Connecticut farmhouse, and then her real life began. She started a catering company in her basement and within ten years turned it into a million-dollar a year business. That's a lot of canapés!

It was because of her style and flair for presentation, and her vision of the future that Martha kept going onward and upward and became the premier lifestyle guru in America. Nobody has influenced Americans in terms of what we eat, how we live, and how we entertain as much as Martha has. Because of her determination, her vision and an ability to work hard with little sleep, Martha created a company worth billions and made herself a multi-millionaire in the process.

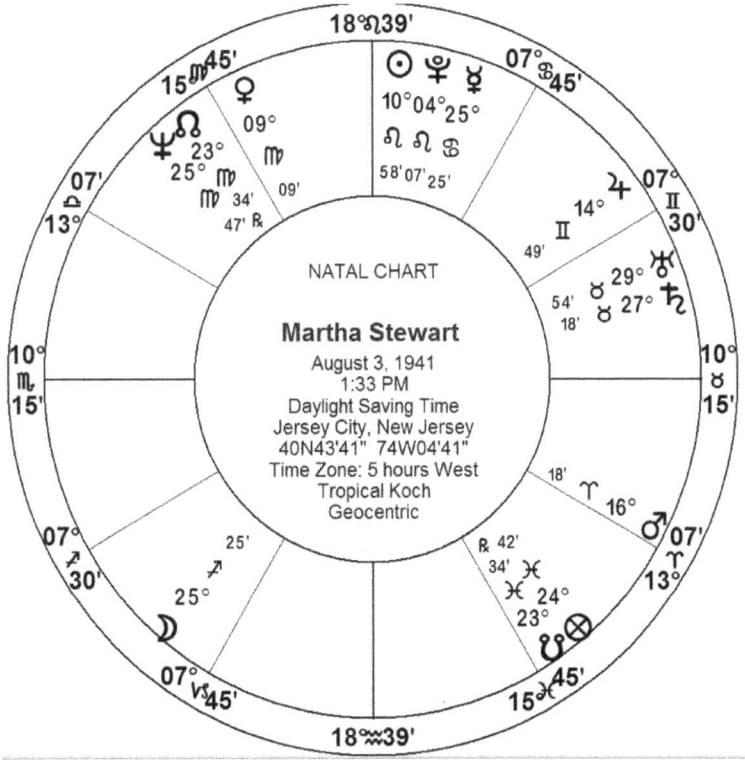

Born August 3, 1941, Martha is a Leo, with Moon in Sagittarius and Scorpio rising. Her Sun, planet of identity, is in the ninth house of higher education and long distance travel. Martha has said she wanted to be a teacher like her mother. An avid reader, she is interested in many subjects, considers the people who share information with her as mentors, and regards the educational process as a worthwhile, lifelong occupation. As anyone who watches her shows knows, Martha is an excellent teacher. She explains each step of the process clearly and makes whatever she's doing look easy. A conjunction to her Sun from Pluto, planet of birth, death, and extreme transformation, gives Martha her need for power and achievement. Pluto is one of the planets connected to big business, so desires for achievement that can be traced back to Pluto are usually quite large in scope. A little success is never enough, particularly when one can envision a much grander level of achievement. She has always wanted to be a person of substance and comes across as one. It's likely as well that her reserve comes from this Sun-Pluto conjunction. Nobody ever hugs Martha on the show as they might do to some of the other TV chefs. They shake hands, smile decorously, behave civilly.

The humor, good cheer and ability to make fun of herself and her work comes from Jupiter, planet of expansion, making a sextile to her Sun. That is another aspect both of teaching and of achievement. A trine from Mars, planet of action, gives Martha all that energy, the get up and go for which she is famous as well as those amazingly steady hands. She has said that if she hadn't chosen her current career, she might have become a surgeon. I marvel at Martha, cooking in a silk shirt and never getting messy. I cook in an apron so besmirched it looks like a Jackson Pollack painting!

With Mars in Aries, its own sign, Martha is a self-starter. In addition, all these yang elements form positive ties to the Leo Midheaven, the point of career and one in which we all exert ourselves in the outside world. With these planetary pictures, it would seem that Martha has the get up and go to fuel her natural drive and although Mars in Aries does sometimes lose interest before a task is done, with a Sun-Pluto conjunction in steady Leo, one of the fixed or stable signs, it's likely that Martha will simply apply discipline to her life and force herself to follow through on whatever she begins. Wherever there is Pluto, there can be discipline, healing and transformation, but also power struggles, sexual deviance, and underhanded behavior. Often it's a matter both of personal choice and Karmic development which way the Pluto goes. With a conjunction, we can usually assume that those very powerful Plutonian energies can be used for good and will result in greater achievement.

Mercury, the planet of communication, is in the sentimental sign Cancer, and the same ninth house of education. Cancer is one of the signs that very strongly reveres the past. Think of the Cancer people you know—they all seem to hang onto every possession acquired from the moment of birth and to love old stuff because of its history, cachet, and attached memories. It makes sense then why Martha would concentrate on history and architecture. The past has interest and sentiment for her and it enriches her present.

The aspects to Mercury are very important for a teacher and Martha has quite a few interesting connections. There is a very wide conjunction to Pluto, and that indicates someone who looks for depth of meaning rather than shallow ideas. This is also a salesman's aspect—with Pluto on your Mercury you can sell anything to anyone, be persuasive and get your point across. I can just imagine meetings with ordinary caterers for those high-profile business clients—they must surely have assumed they would be dealing with Sue Ann Nivens. But then—enter Martha—cultured, intelligent, and radiating an aura of control and power. She was born to consort with these people and deal with them on their own level. In fact, Martha has said that when she began as a caterer, she detested how she was treated— as a servant. In short order, her clients began to realize that they were dealing with an equal and she elevated the levels of respect due to someone in her profession. That would make her quite a trailblazer, which is well in keeping with a Mars in Aries. And of course the ultimate revenge was watching her own success exceed that of those for whom she began as a mere caterer.

Mercury also receives a sextile from Neptune. This is an aspect both of creativity and imagination. Often people with these contacts are fabulous story tellers and they delight in fictional tales and flights of fancy. You can't always count on the promises they make to be absolute gospel, though. With both Neptune and Pluto aspecting Mercury, there is a lot of intellectual pizzazz and depth.

Mercury also receives a sextile from Uranus, giving impatience, intelligence and techno-savvy. Martha does email first thing in the morning and last thing at night (just like I do!) and she travels with not one but two laptops—in case one breaks—and of course she adores social media and the tiny phones on which a person can remain up to date at any moment or in any place. A Mercury-Uranus contact demands instantaneous information and is impatient with slow-witted types. Life is just too short. Martha is perpetually stepping in to help her guest chefs and her willingness to do the little jobs to move things along is admirable. She has been teased for her haste, but when you live your life in 10-minute segments, life has to perk along. On one episode a guest chef struggled briefly with a jar, and before he could pop it, Martha said, "Let me do it," took it out of his hands, gave it a twist, and voila, the moment was saved! It didn't occur to her that dainty little gals don't wrest jars from the hands of men. She's just too capable and no-nonsense for that.

Saturn, planet of Karma, and earthly life lessons also provides a sextile. Mercury-Saturn aspects bestow a sense of form and order, give scientific and mathematical skills as well as a love of precision and details. This is a nice counterbalancing effect. The Mercury-Uranus likes speed but the Saturn ties slow it down, demanding that things be done properly. These would be the energies that allowed Martha to work as a stockbroker despite a background in history and architecture. This is also another aspect of appreciation for ancient times, techniques and artifacts. Saturn is the planet of time and it provides an awareness of history as it passes as well as the desire to maintain a record of what has happened.

In one episode, a viewer called in for advice about how to save her grandmother's recipe cards and Martha offered her a variety of options, including lamination. "I just love my laminating machine," said Martha, "Do you have one?" Of course the viewer did not, and the whole process struck me as funny. It seemed as odd as asking someone who cooks prepared frozen food if they possess a duck press, but although I do collect family recipes, I don't much care if I save the cards they're scribbled on. But that's the magic of Martha — she is involved in every aspect of living and loves incorporating the treasures of the past into the fabric of daily modern life.

Another, very important aspect to Mercury comes from the Moon in Sagittarius, forming a quincunx. That connection provides an awareness of feelings but a difficulty in expressing them. Emotions sometimes seem rather jumbled and can't be conveyed easily. That is another interesting aspect of Martha's chart. The connection between mind and emotions is muted, whereas the more yang contacts are strong and direct. I suspect she is much more comfortable discussing ideas and good things than she is talking about her own heart. The reserve she projects is not just about power and achievement but is also a form of self-preservation.

The yin, or feminine elements of a horoscope are very important because they show who the individual is, deep inside. These elements provide the solid emotional foundation that allows each of us to go out into the world feeling safe and secure enough to reach for our goals.

The most significant yin element in any horoscope is the Moon, planet of emotions. Martha has Moon in the freedom-loving sign Sagittarius. With this placement it's quite natural to feel an affinity for distant places, exotic people and other cultures. This is another knowledge-seeking indicator, and with it Martha likes to explore life as it's lived in different places and by other people. Moon in Sag is not terribly emotional nor sensitive. It's a sort of outgoing, puppy-dog emotional quality that gets plenty of satisfaction from casual social contacts. Being with other people is very important, but as long as there are enough contacts, the more intimate ones are less of an imperative.

Her Moon lies in the second house of money, and generally speaking, people with this placement need financial security and they make emotional decisions based on practical or financial reasons. For example, a homemaker with this placement wouldn't divorce a man who was providing her with the good life, even if the relationship were in deep trouble, because her security would be too important. Of course Martha was married nearly thirty years and she worked throughout the marriage, so chances are this was not her situation. In fact, we could regard her as a product of the liberated 60's in which all women realized it was as essential to earn a living as it was to be involved in marriage and family. We could also say that with this Moon in the house of money, it would be quite essential for Martha to make her way in the financial world. She would need the sense of security that earning her own money would provide.

There's no question, though, that the divorce was hard on her. Her entire professional world is built on the idea of living well, entertaining at home and within the family and certainly being married is at the center of that image. So with that second house Moon, she must certainly have feared for her security at the time of the divorce and perhaps that explains the difficult three-year separation she endured.

Another aspect of this placement is the desire to waste nothing, to conserve, and to make the most of one's assets. Moon in Sag is often quite a spendthrift and there is little worry about security inherent in that sign. The second house makes quite a difference in the way that energy manifests. Martha talks often about her childhood, about her mother, probably her strongest role model. Big Martha, as her mom was called in the family, worked hard inside and outside the home, she cooked everything from scratch, grew food in little gardens on their land and in general exemplified the waste-not-want-not values of her forebears' Poland. Big Martha didn't believe in waste and Martha learned that first hand. Using supplies well, conserving and of course making the most of what's at hand is a big part of Martha's ethic. She knows how to make the most of everything—whether a huge tin of Beluga or some scraggly veggies rescued from frost in the late-fall garden.

It's easy to see how this sort of outlook could have led to the stock sale problems that landed her in jail. Despite the verdict against her, Martha insists she did nothing wrong, so perhaps it all happened as she said it did. We do know that she would certainly keep a close eye on all investments, and with Jupiter posited in her eighth house of investments (other people's money) we would expect her to do well in the stock market. Saturn, planet of Karma, was transiting that house as the scandal broke, certainly not a good time for any sort of financial improprieties, because Saturn has a way of making us pay for financial miscalculations during its two-year eighth house visit. When Saturn moved in Martha's ninth house of legal matters, she went to trial and ultimately opted to serve her sentence rather than wait to see if her appeal would succeed.

In addition to the Moon-Mercury aspect already mentioned, Martha's Moon receives a square from Neptune, planet of illusion and delusion. This is the psychic's aspect and people with this placement very often have visions, hunches and a sense of knowing about various things in their own and other people's lives. Neptune on the Moon deepens it, gives stronger emotions and a love of art and music. It is also an excellent aspect for traveling because it is quite easy to fit into other cultures and feel them a part of yourself. Although there is a certain depth of emotion with a Moon-Neptune contact, we wouldn't say there is an excess. We would note, however, that with Neptune in the eleventh house of friends squaring this second house Moon, it's quite possible that Martha could get bad, deceptive, or confusing financial advice from friends, and at the very least we can assume that's true of the IM Clone stock mess.

Saturn makes a quincunx to the Moon from the seventh house of partnership. That's an interesting aspect. Saturn on the Moon is rarely a happy aspect. It creates a sense of loneliness, a need for companionship but not necessarily the ability to pick and choose good companions. It's an any port in the storm sort of aspect. It's also an aspect of responsibility and yes, achievement. With Saturn on the Moon, there is a need for security, and a sense of not being safe. This would provide additional impetus for Martha to work hard (Saturn) to achieve financial stability (Moon in two).

That this aspect comes from the seventh house is interesting. Partnerships of all sorts are defined by seven, so whether it's marriage, a business partnership or even a non-romantic relationship with a therapist or lawyer, the issues remain the same—can you meet each other's needs. Saturn in seven is always about meeting needs—getting yours met and whether or not you have what it takes to meet the needs of the particular significant other in question.

Saturn in the seventh house is believed to work acceptably well, but I have found that it demands a lot of the people who have it. It always seems that somebody is disgruntled and compromises are necessary. In Martha's case, with business deals, it makes a lot of sense — she has to hammer out agreements with the others who are involved. For example, one business writer wondered why Martha agreed to the "sweetheart deal" with K-Mart when she might have done much better financially with Wal-Mart or Target. Her answer was simple — she gained control in the deal with K-Mart.

It also makes sense that with this Moon-Saturn contact, Martha and her husband bought their Connecticut farm together and restored it over time, adding onto the land, planting orchards and so on. The partnership was emotional, as marriage always is, but also financial, and together they enhanced real estate (the Moon).

Also in the seventh house is Uranus, planet of eccentricity. With Saturn in the house of marriage, the goal is a long, stable union. With Uranus there, the tendency is to have many short-lived attachments. Generally speaking, when Uranus is involved with romance, it's likely that you become involved with people who aren't "the right type," but who are different, outrageous or somehow ill-suited. We can certainly conclude that a Yale-educated lawyer would hardly have been considered an eccentric match. But the interesting thing about this seventh house is that it's not all about one thing.

Andy Stewart must have felt confident when he married Martha. She was pretty, well-educated, had been cooking all her life at her mother's knee, liked owning and conserving old properties and was good at entertaining. When you describe her like that, she does sound like Suzy Homemaker, and chances are that's what he wanted. It was only after she ascended to the limelight that the marriage crumbled — and then we could say that it was Uranus describing what happened. Andy thought he was getting one sort of mate — as described by Saturn — but his wife turned into something quite different — Uranus — someone with her own identity, own agenda, and a level of success that surpassed his own.

Venus, the planet of love and beauty, lies in Virgo, in Martha's tenth house of career. Venus is about the unfettered giving and receiving of affection and about the enjoyment of pleasure. Virgo is about organization, restraint and service, so Venus there is not considered the perfect placement. People with Venus in Virgo are good at helping other people — they show affection by pitching in and being of service. Whenever Martha has a guest, she's right there in the background, doing the smaller job, facilitating the movement of the project and providing support. This is the perfect embodiment of this

Venus.

Venus in Virgo loves what's useful, practical and neat. Martha scours tag sales, rescuing treasures from ignominy and adding them to her collection. She finds and develops ideas to share with viewers and dubs them "good things." On her cooking show she often takes the time to teach ways to maintain and preserve the elements of the kitchen, whether how to sharpen a knife, how to oil a soapstone counter or how to clean a pastry bag. This too is emblematic of Venus in Virgo and of that waste-not-want-not Moon.

Venus in the tenth is very nice for a career. It generally means that your coworkers will like you, the workplace will have friendly, social elements and that there is a congenial atmosphere. It's also nice for a career focused around art. You could simply describe it as making a living from what's beautiful, and that's certainly true of Martha. I'm always amazed at the stuff for sale on her website. It's mostly beautiful, but there's so much of it. One day, I spotted pink light bulbs on the site! Pink light bulbs! That seems to me to be a pretty idea, but more than that, it shows a remarkable level of thoroughness. We'd say everything but the kitchen sink is Martha's domain, but she's got that covered too, and how very Venus in Virgo in the tenth is that!

Venus receives a single aspect, a square from Jupiter in the eighth house. That is certainly a sign of generosity, and Martha loves to show how to wrap gifts, how to make special little hostess presents and how to make even the simplest offering special. With Venus in Virgo, it's not likely she would imitate Elvis and gift wrap a Cadillac. Instead she finds beautiful tangerines at the market in a retro wooden crate, inserts some unshelled nuts, tucks in a nutcracker and wraps the whole thing in plastic film. Her generosity is filled with warmth, homeyness and effort.

Another manifestation of a Venus-Jupiter square is the love of shopping. Stuff is a big deal and lots of fun, and that explains how Martha is always unearthing those "good things." And with a square from the eighth house to the tenth, we can assume that raising capital for business ventures is easy to accomplish.

It's very important to note that the yin elements in Martha's chart are downplayed on a personal level. The planet of emotions is in an unemotional sign, in the house of money. The planet of love is in a conservative sign in the house of career. Martha's emotional life is there to support her efforts to achievement.

And to understand that, examine the nature of Leo. Much is written about the showy, ego-centric nature of Leo, but it's really only the most shallow and unevolved expression of that energy. Leo is really about becoming and expressing one's best self, about being a positive role model and about sharing those wonderful inner lights with everyone else. Yes, Leo is about living the good life, but it doesn't have to be a frivolous good life. When we read about those foreign princes whose bathrooms are adorned with solid-gold fixtures, yes that is the Leo energy, but it's Leo energy gone amuck. To find what's good in life, to live it to the best possible degree, to make things pretty and to share them with loved ones, that is Leo energy at its best, and certainly that is what Martha has tried to embody throughout her career.

Leo with Scorpio rising is a powerful combination, one Martha shares with another well-known icon of style and flair, first lady Jacqueline Kennedy Onassis. Jackie was avidly interested in decorating, was an expert on furniture and style, and redid the White House until husband Jack entered an elevator that was topsy-turvy with paper hangers and made her slow down. She was also known for her ability to connect successfully with foreign people and her love of exotic cultures. Eventually she worked in publishing, just as Martha does, but she never had her own empire. Nobody ever thought of Jackie as a homemaker, nor did we assume she could whip an egg white with one hand, but then she was a product of her times and her class. If she had been born a decade later, she might have decided to capitalize on her style and flair by "brandifying" herself as Martha has done.

It's interesting, isn't it? Our foremost expert on style at home isn't a Suzy Homemaker, but a divorcee. She is an expert on food and its presentation but she isn't a trained chef. Women's work has always been meaningful, but it's rarely been valuable in terms of dollars and cents. If a woman says she's a homemaker, she usually says, "Oh, just a housewife." Years back a wag calculated what it would cost to pay people to do all the jobs around the house a traditional mom performed and the total exceeded her husband's income. Yet, still that traditional mom was "just a housewife."

It has taken someone like Martha, a woman who is more of a dynamo than a cupcake to elevate women's work into a business. She saw the value in the day to day at home, and by putting her tasteful thumbprint on every facet of that life, was able to carve a huge empire. She is a modern woman and it was her yang skills of business, marketing and promotion that allowed her to use the raw materials of homemaking as the magic carpet that transported her to success.

Chapter Five:
Relationship Astrology

This is why most people study astrology—and you're probably no exception. Once you know what makes someone tick, you want to know what makes him or her a good partner, true love, or best pal..

Part One: Jane Fonda's Three Marriages

Astrology is probably the best tool available for unlocking the psyche of any human being. Our horoscopes show who we are, what we need, how we function, and how we feel. Astrology also provides a very astute road map about where we're going Karmically and what life lessons we're here to learn. With all that psychological insight and spiritual depth available from a horoscope, is that why most people come to astrology? Not hardly!! Most people want to know about their love lives.

I remember years ago when I divorced and was meeting lots of men. That was when the astrology bug bit me—I wanted to know what was coming up in my love life! And to this day, most clients consult me about love life issues, although some are also interested in finances. Astrology is just as good at helping you make sense of your love life as it is at giving you insight into your psyche.

Relationship astrology isn't simple, however. It's just as complex as we are as human beings. And it doesn't tell the whole story. If you have a hankering for hunks and you meet a dweeb whose planets connect remarkably well to your own, are you gonna fall for Mr. Dork? I wouldn't! But you might connect positively and like each other as friends. At least you'd be able to reject him kindly. In a world of the blind, astrology would be the perfect tool to match people up, because what matters would show up perfectly. Chemistry is important, and often we get dazzled by the physical and are blind to the message from our souls. Astrology does show sexual chemistry, and as I said, if image didn't matter, it would be flawless.

Of course when people come for readings, they already have a candidate in mind, someone who has passed the initial litmus test of image. Then it's up to me to share the relevant information. And a horoscope is a great tool in that case.

Novice astrologers are often tempted to look first at the

synastry in two charts — the inter aspects between the two charts — but that is the lazy approach to relationship astrology. It doesn't matter initially if her Venus is conjunct his Mars and so on. The first step in relationship astrology is the same first step when analyzing any horoscope: look at each person as an individual, because that's where you'll see that person's potential for romantic interaction. A relationship is defined by the characters and personalities of the two people creating it and by examining each horoscope first, we see the individuals and what they're capable of on an emotional level. Only then does it make sense to move forward and to look at what happens between the two people's horoscopes.

I debated for quite a while about whom to use as examples and then hit on a good idea — let's look at Jane Fonda and all three of her husbands. We'll not only see relationship astrology in action, but also a progression of relationship choices as one person grows older.

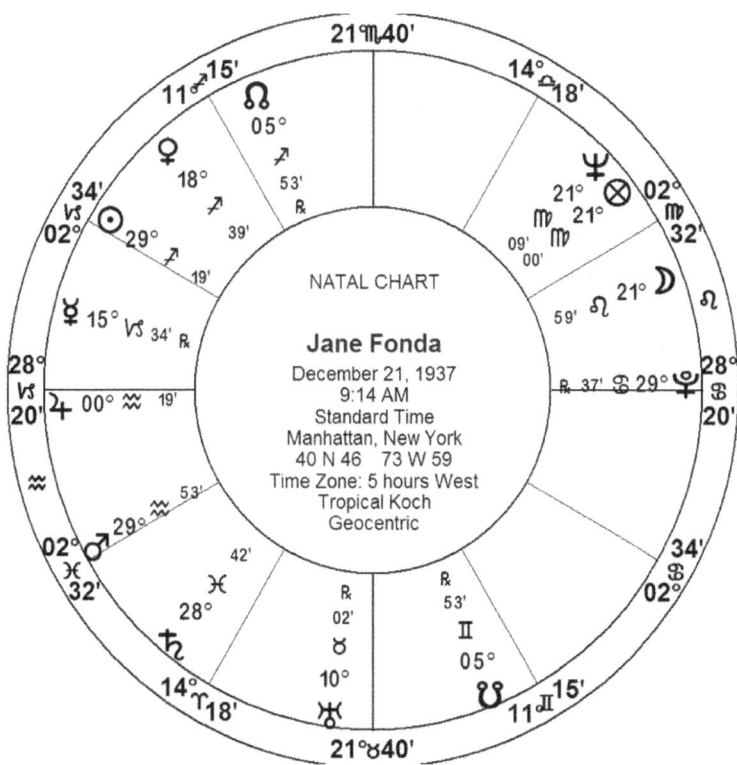

Jane is a Sagittarius, with Moon in Leo and Capricorn rising, although if she were born six minutes later, she'd have Aquarius rising. Most people's birth time is incorrect by a few minutes, even if they have a birth certificate record, as they're recorded by medical personnel, not astrologers. However, most births are a few moments earlier than recorded rather than later, but a small difference like six minutes could go either way.

Upon first glace at Jane's horoscope, we notice several oppositions (two planets lying 180 degrees apart, plus or minus 10 degrees), particularly the one teetering right at the Ascendant-Descendant axis, and a T-square (an opposition bisected by another planet lying 90 degrees from both the two opposing planets) with her Sun as the focal point. This is a dynamic horoscope with much energy involving and directed toward (and from) other people. As we take a first glance, we see Jupiter, planet of expansion—and ruler of Sagittarius, lying right on the Ascendant, giving optimism, height, and personal charm. Often people with first house Jupiters tend toward overweight, but perhaps Jane's lifestyle as an exercise maven has spared her that problem. Opposing Jupiter, is Pluto, planet of transformation, in the seventh house of relationships. Seeing only this aspect, we can already make a conjecture: Jane's life is a bit of a seesaw between her desire for independence and self-expression (Jupiter) and complicated partnerships that feature dominant men who try to transform her (Pluto). Now let's look at the rest of the chart, step by step, as we always do.

The Sun (identity) is at the end of Sagittarius, in the eleventh house of long-term goals and friendships. This is another indication of the importance of other people in Jane's life. The Sun is trine (120 degrees, plus or minus 10 degrees) the Moon (emotions), giving a sense of inner harmony and the expectation that relationships should be calm. Often this indicates a childhood where the parents got along well and were happily married, however Jane's father was much-married and her mother committed suicide, something that was kept secret from her until she discovered it accidentally by reading a magazine at school. Nevertheless, Sun trine Moon is a nice aspect and probably gives her a sense of happy expectation where relationships are concerned.

The Sun is tightly sextile (sixty degrees, plus or minus 6 degrees) Mars (energy), providing sex appeal, athletic ability and physical energy. Saturn (limitations) squares (ninety degrees, plus or minus ten degrees) the Sun, and this is a very difficult aspect. It creates a sense of challenge, and some personal insecurity. There's the feeling that she will have to work extra hard for whatever she wants. And as Saturn lies in the second house of money, it would seem that Jane would need to work extra hard to earn a living at her dream job. I don't know if she felt that way in her life, because growing up as Hollywood royalty, she probably had many opportunities in movies that other people had to work much harder to achieve. But her father, Henry, said he didn't particularly encourage or help his children and what they achieved was done despite him not because of his parenting, so perhaps she did feel a sense of difficulty and burden. And of course, it's always difficult to enter a field in which a parent has achieved great success because the child worries about being good enough to measure up. This is certainly described by the Sun-Saturn square.

Also challenging her Sun is Neptune, planet of illusion, providing another square. Sun-Neptune aspects are sometimes rather creative and cinematic, but often the challenging ones—square or opposition—create difficulty in building a sense of identity. With this aspect she would ask who am I and what do I stand for? What must I build in my life? This certainly describes Jane's many about faces in her choice of identity, first as sex kitten starlet, then Hanoi Jane, political activist, exercise guru, and ultimately respected actress.

Also, we have to mention that the Saturn and Neptune squares to the Sun are actually a T-square with the energy focused out through her Sun. With Neptune in the eighth, there is the desire for transcendent sex, and some strange investments. There is also the possibility of losing money through partnerships, although I have never heard that her husbands cheated her financially. I did hear her say that her workout money financed Hayden's bid for public office. And of course other financial issues are raised by the Saturn-Neptune opposition in the money houses. With this aspect we would assume some financial losses at some point in her life, or perhaps a tendency to over commit financially to a much too idealistic cause. Saturn in Pisces indicates a Karmic need to live her life according to the genuine truths which should define her world. With a T-square like this, there's always the need to balance the ideals of Neptune with the practical reality described by Saturn, as part of her identity, means of self-expression, and through the people (eleventh house) with whom she surrounds herself. She will spend her life questioning her identity and the meaning of the choices she makes in her life.

A final aspect is made to the Sun by Pluto, a quincunx (150 degrees, plus or minus 3 degrees). This is another indication of power struggles with significant others and also the tendency on her part to try to reform other people who are close to her. Jane has a very dynamic Sun with many aspects, giving her much presence when other people meet her, and also making her life interestingly complicated.

To look next at the Yin elements of the chart, we note that the Moon is in the warm and outgoing but not terribly emotional sign

Leo, also in the seventh house of partnerships. This is an interesting placement, because it ties the emotions to one-to-one relationships. On the plus side, it indicates an ability to connect emotionally with significant others, but on the negative side, it can create a too-involved emotional connection, causing confusion between her own emotions and those of a partner. This is the I feel what you feel placement.

The Moon receives a trine from Venus (affection) and that is a very nice aspect. It brings warm feelings, love of food and domesticity, congenial ties with other women, and affection for children. With this tie between the eleventh and seventh houses, Jane feels comfortable entertaining, whether for business or pleasure, and is an enthusiastic wife and helpmate. She's been married to three high profile men and always had an agenda of her own while helping with theirs.

The Moon is also opposed to Mars, creating intense emotions, some tendencies to quarrel with women, or be quarreled with by significant others. This is also a health aspect—the tendency to let emotional upsets cause physical manifestations—like stomach aches. We note that Jane has aspects from Mars to both Sun and Moon, indicating a tendency to thrust herself into the world with energy and assertiveness, whether reaching for personal self-expression or through emotions. Whatever she is, she's intense! We might also say that with Mars in the first house (well, teetering toward the second) opposing that seventh house Moon, there's always a seesaw effect. She is the active, dynamic one (Mars) but always has to make accommodations (opposition) in order to relate to significant others (seventh house) on an emotional level (Moon). We could also say that her desire for emotional closeness and compatibility is sometimes disrupted by her need to express her own wishes and desires. This showed up strongly in all of her marriages, as we will see in depth shortly.

Venus in her birth sign Sagittarius is friendly to a wide variety of people and sustains affection for all different types of individuals and cultures, and would make it easy for her to befriend people from other parts of the world. Venus in the eleventh is quite nice because it encourages affectionate friendships. Venus is square Neptune, indicating a perhaps unrealistic desire for true love. It also indicates a love of the movies. We might also say that Venus, by virtue of the close Neptune square, is also conjunct the Sun, widely square Saturn, and thus part of the T-square connecting those planets.

It's a very interesting picture, isn't it? A Sun-Venus person is sweet and lovable and seeks happy connections with others. And

Moon in the seventh is likewise a people person. But with the conflicts described by Saturn-Neptune, Mars opposite Moon, and Pluto in the seventh, we see a desire for uncomplicated, peaceful relationships that is generally challenged. There are many learning opportunities here. Jane has the chance to work at herself and her needs as a result of her interpersonal connections. Well, that's true of everyone, but in her case it's an imperative.

To look at the other elements in the chart, we notice Mercury (communications) in the practical sign Capricorn, but in the dreamy twelfth house of the unconscious mind. Her thoughts sort of well up as inspirations, and only then does she approach these ideas pragmatically. Mercury is trine Uranus (innovation), giving intelligence, impatience, and high tech abilities. It's also trine Neptune, inclining her toward idealistic ideas as well as musical abilities. Would we say we have a grand trine here? In this case, I wouldn't read at as such because of the wide orb between Neptune and Uranus. If there were a personal planet at either position, I might be more inclined to consider that as a possibility. With Uranus in the third, there is much sudden travel and non-traditional intellectual activity. Balance is a very significant issue in this horoscope, and that will always be the case when many oppositions are present. We might say that in this lifetime, Jane is learning to express herself with courage, to follow her own star and own beliefs, but not to ignore the needs and feelings of other people—that she cannot just express herself wantonly without suffering the consequences of the disapproval of other people. That's the seesaw! She needs to be able to express herself, but not so insanely that she incites other people to rise up against her and vilify her, because if she does, she won't be happy. She needs self-expression, but she also needs the approval and good will of other people.

Now that we know all this about Jane, what would we say her potential is for a relationship? With both Moon and Pluto in the seventh house, we pretty well assume there will be relationships. But because her need for self expression is so strong, her tendency will always be to gravitate toward relationships that jive with that need. In every case, her marriages were not just personal romances, but lifestyles with partners whose interests reflected where she was at that particular time in her life. So in a way, a marriage is a bit of an accessory to Jane, not her whole reason for living but another outlet of personal self-expression. Now let's look at her three partners one by one to see how this plays out.

Jane married French Director, Roger Vadim, in August, 1965, just as her Saturn return was approaching. This is a very typical time to wed, because there's so much energy to be an adult and that's one of the primary grown up things any person can do. Also at that time, Neptune hovered right at her MC, which could indicate confusion about her purpose in life, but could also bring work as a movie star. And Jupiter was transiting her fifth, about to oppose her Sun. All in all, it was probably a fairly energetic period of time.

It's interesting to consider if Vadim, nine years her senior, was an attempt by Jane to marry a mentor, and maybe some of that is true, but she was already a fairly big star at the time of their marriage and her status always superseded his. He's known for his films, but is more famous for his romantic liaisons.

Vadim is an Aquarius, and upon first glance at his chart, we notice most of the planets lying below the horizon (the Ascendant-Descendant axis) of the horoscope. Most of his planets are clustered in two houses, the third and sixth, indicating some emphasis in the affairs of those houses—communication and work. Now let's go step by step.

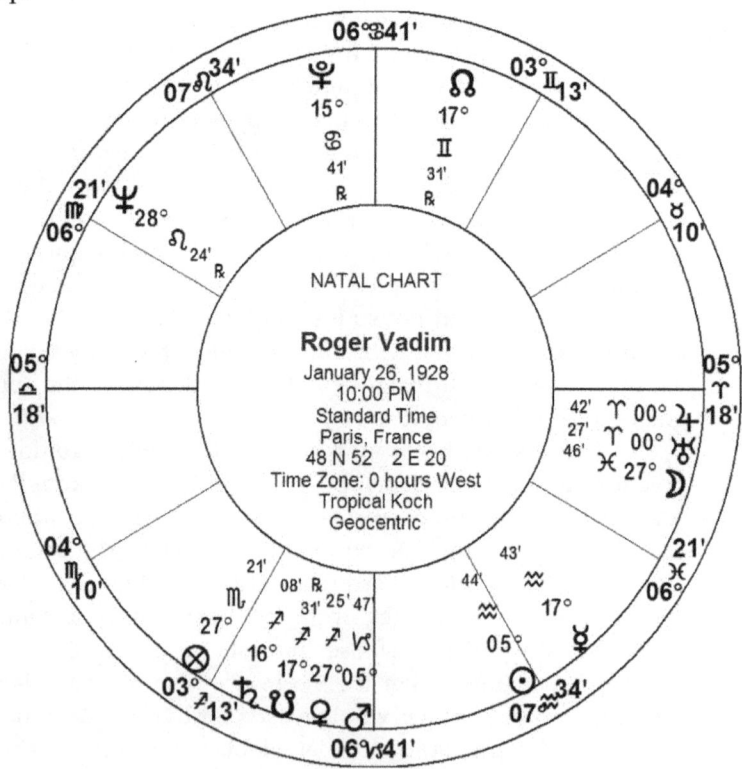

As an Aquarius, Vadim is forward-thinking and cerebral, but with Sun in the fourth house of emotions, home, and family, he's probably a bit more sensitive than the typical Aquarius. His sun is widely sextile Jupiter, giving optimism, and Uranus, providing an ease at expressing his individuality. He has far fewer solar aspects than Jane does, doesn't he?

His Moon is quite sensitive and emotional in Pisces, but in the sixth house that emotionality is diminished a bit—and might tend toward hypochondria. The Moon conjoins Uranus, creating a bit of a barrier for deep emotional contacts, and might incline him to fall for women who are overly independent or in some way rebellious— someone he wouldn't be expected to marry. It's also conjunct Jupiter, giving humor, optimism, and love of the good life. Venus is square the Moon, giving passion and an intense love of women. And because Venus is conjunct Mars, we have to say Mars too touches the Moon, amping up its intensity. Vadim's Moon is also quincunx Neptune, adding emotional depth, some psychic ability, and a tendency to romanticize the idea of women.

He was married first to celebrated sex kitten Brigitte Bardot, and takes credit for her unveiling in that persona. He said ruefully, "From the moment I liberated Brigitte, the moment I showed her how to be truly herself, our marriage was all downhill." So perhaps he was one of those men who liked the idea that he could take a girl and turn her into a woman. As a woman, I scoff at such a possibility as mere male ego, but we each have a right to our opinion! Certainly we can see in his horoscope that women would naturally play a big role in his life because so many of his planets connect to his Moon. There's a very rich and complicated emotional picture in this horoscope. A man with a Moon like this is good company and would be very attractive to women because whatever type of female she might be, there would be some aspect of him which could connect. So maybe his idea of being a Svengali for future sex kittens wasn't so far off, because he could encourage a woman to express the various sides of her nature, including the passion.

The Venus-Mars conjunction is a very sexy aspect, and a creative one too. Venus in Sag is outgoing and friendly, and Mars in Capricorn likes to be in charge, to be the boss. We also note the Venus square to both Jupiter and Uranus, bringing sudden, intense, and perhaps unreasonable romantic attachments. Venus is trine Neptune, giving a desire for true love and an affection for the cinema.

Mars is also square Jupiter, giving energy, enthusiasm, and some athletic ability, and is square Uranus too, making him freedom loving, kinky, and rather selfish. Pluto makes a very, very wide opposition, in fact, the only opposition in the chart, and I wonder if we really should count it at all. Most of the time there would probably be no effects felt at all because it's such a wide aspect. However, his Mars is definitely self-absorbed, determined, and bossy.

To look at what's left, we see Mercury in the scientific sign Aquarius, in the fifth house, giving creative abilities and perhaps accounting for the Sci-fi sexpic *Barbarella*. Mercury receives a sextile from Saturn, adding stability and technical expertise. It's also quincunx Pluto, indicating some verbal power struggles. There's a Yod configuration here—both Saturn and Mercury are quincunx Pluto and wouldn't that indicate determination (Pluto) to succeed at a career (10th house) through sustained effort (Saturn) via creative communications (Mercury).

To sum up our impression of Vadim, we'd have to describe him primarily as a ladies' man, wouldn't we. His Yin energies are the strongest in the chart. Jane's chart is about self-expression and is far more Yang, so perhaps that is a good basis for their interaction. Perhaps he provided her with some nurturing on an emotional level that she needed as a young starlet in a first marriage.

I always talk about resonance when looking at relationship astrology. It's not just about how your planets hit mine, but if we have similar things in our charts. Two Sun-Saturn people will feel a resonance. They're similar people. Venus-Neptune people will understand each other, whether one has the conjunction and the other the square, because that is a vibration they share. They seek love in a similar fashion. So it's really important to note those sorts of things when considering two charts.

Even though Vadim is strongly Yin and Jane is strongly Yang, they're both romantic Venus-Neptune people. They're both charismatic Jupiter-Ascendant people. They're both Venus-Moon people. Mars-Pluto people. These vibrations are very significant when considering a relationship. They each make sense to the other, have similar expectations, and thrust themselves into the world similarly. It's resonance or the "I see myself in you" factor. That is particularly relevant in young relationships because being young is all about looking for oneself. It can be a liability for partners to be too similar—out in the world where balance is needed, but internally within the relationship, it makes for more harmony. Nobody ever griped about a spouse, gee he's just like me and that screwed us up. Resonance is very meaningful in any sort of relationship and it makes us feel closer to a mate.

The next step would be to examine the charts together. Here's where we look at the synastry and see what interaspects occur between the charts. What I normally do is run a bi-wheel in my astrology software, which would show Jane's chart in the middle wheel and Vadim's planets surrounding hers. That is a very good visual for making sense of the synastry. There are also programs that will list the aspects between the two charts and then you don't need the visual, but I tend to like to look at things one by one. You can quite easily also look at the charts, planet by planet and see what hits what.

If we start with Jane's Sun, we see that Vadim's Venus is tightly conjunct, indicating deep affection for her. His Moon squares her Sun, and that is an aspect of some friction, but not a terrible thing in synastry. It's often a wonderful thing in a marriage chart when a man's Moon is conjunct his wife's Sun because it means she embodies his internal female nature. What is bad in this case is that his Moon lies right on her Saturn, which would mean that she would limit his emotional self-expression and in some ways play a parental role. That's an interesting idea since he is the older partner. We also note that his Jupiter and Uranus square her Sun, and that's not such a bad thing because it means he encourages her to express herself and perhaps that's the sex kitten thing at work. Whereas her own Neptune squares her Sun, his trines it, and that is another aspect of acceptance, for her own spiritual and creative nature.

It's important to note that another person's planets will affect you, but if you have your own planets in the same aspect, then you won't feel much. So if you have Sun conjunct Saturn natally, someone your own age will also have Saturn conjunct your Sun, but it won't affect you at all. In the case of the Neptune above, we could say that the easier aspect of his Neptune giving a trine could help Jane deal with her own more difficult one. She could see his acceptance of her nature and say OK, well gee I did lack confidence and identity, but now I see it's OK to be whatever I am, just do it.

Vadim's Venus trines Jane's Moon, another aspect of love and harmonious domesticity. And his Neptune conjoins her Moon, perhaps inspiring her to relocate to his country to live as man and wife. His Saturn trines her Moon, which although not technically a difficult aspect, does indicate some emotional restriction. They have double Moon-Saturn synastry here, and there must have been some emotional tension between them, or perhaps some sense of culture shock when trying to live as a couple in each other's countries.

Additionally Vadim's Saturn conjoins Jane's Venus, and in a partnership that isn't always light and flowers, but it also isn't a disaster because it indicates a serious and long-lasting partnership. Jane's Saturn squares his Venus, so once again we see a double Yin-

Saturn contact. It must have felt quite serious to them, and fated even, right from the moment they met.

Jane's Mars is in Aquarius, and although Vadim's Sun makes no major aspect to her Mars, it's in the same sign, indicating he embodies qualities that appeal to her in men. Women frequently gravitate toward men whose Sun sign matches their Mars sign for just that reason. His Neptune, which conjoins her Moon, also opposes her Mars, softening her energy. Actually we could say that the marriage might have restricted her a bit with this aspect.

Vadim's Sun is conjunct Jane's Jupiter, which is nice for affection and optimism, but he has a natal Sun-Jupiter aspect, so it will affect him less intensely. Her Pluto opposes his Sun, and that would mean she quashes him quite a bit and perhaps she railed at the permissive European lifestyle. Her Uranus is square his Sun, and that is quite significant because it means that a T-square is formed in both charts, with her Uranus as the focal point. In her case it affects the first house and her personal freedom, but in his it affects his eighth, and might cause him to feel overly pressured (Pluto opposite Sun) and to rebel sexually or financially (Uranus in eighth).

The Pluto symbolism continues with a trine of her Pluto to his Moon-Uranus-Jupiter, and that could increase the pressure placed upon him to conform in some way to her expectations. It could also bring more powerful people (Pluto) into his life via her connections. Jane's Neptune opposes Vadim's Moon, and that is another double synastry of Moon-Neptune. In this case, it creates a T-square in his chart with Venus as the focal point. That's a very dynamic aspect.

And then we get to the easy aspect — her Mars is sextile his Venus. Any Venus-Mars synastry in a relationship is good as it creates the hots and a good reason to make up after the inevitable quarrel. There are a great many energizing aspects in this relationship, aren't there? It wasn't nearly so simple as a young girl displacing Daddy by taking up with an older suitor, but two people who felt their relationship was fated and who stimulated each other on many levels.

The next step would be to look at the composite chart, which is one of my favorite relationship tools in astrology. To me it's almost a shortcut that will show the relationship and what it's all about, and it's much less complicated to understand than synastry.

A composite chart is a horoscope of averaged planetary positions. The two Suns are averaged to create a composite Sun. The two Moons, and so on. I run these on the computer and I'm sure all astrology software will do this. But if you want to do it by hand, the chart below will show you the way. Jane's Sun is 29 Sagittarius, so looking on the chart we see we must add 240 to it, making 269. Vadim's Sun is 5 Aquarius, so we add 300 to that and come up with 305. Then we add the two numbers together—269 plus 305 and we get 574. Next we divide by two (since we're averaging two planets) and we get 287. Capricorn begins at 270, so we subtract that and get 17 degrees Capricorn as the composite Sun. And so on with the two Moons, two, Mercuries, etc. And of course you'd have to average the two Ascendants and erect a chart with a table of houses, although you could average the corresponding house cusps I suppose. It's lots easier to let the computer do it for you and you'd save enough time to bake some brownies.

Composite charts make sense. If you look visually at the charts, you see his Sun in the fourth and hers in the eleventh, so it's natural they should meet in the second house, and that's where the composite Sun lies. Sometimes though, the math will play little tricks on you. I have an Aries friend with Sun in the eleventh, and my Virgo Sun is in the tenth, yet the computer puts our composite Sun in the fifth. When I see that, I tend to right the chart and flip the planets, also flipping the sign on the Ascendant. To me that makes more sense. This won't usually happen though, except when the planets are quincunx.

Sign	Start at
Aries	0
Taurus	30
Gemini	60
Cancer	90
Leo	120
Virgo	150
Libra	180
Scorpio	210
Sagittarius	240
Capricorn	270
Aquarius	300
Pisces	330

Now! Let's examine the composite of Jane and Vadim's horoscopes. We see a very dramatic chart. Sun in the second, opposite Pluto in the eighth, T-square Uranus in the fifth. Those are normal orbs, however, but it's a convention to use only three degrees in composite charts, so we wouldn't actually count the Pluto opposition. We would say as a couple (composite Sun) they were focused on making money (second house) through individual creativity (Uranus in the fifth). We also note a Mercury-Mars conjunction in the second, more energy (Mars) applied to money-making (second house) communication (Mercury).

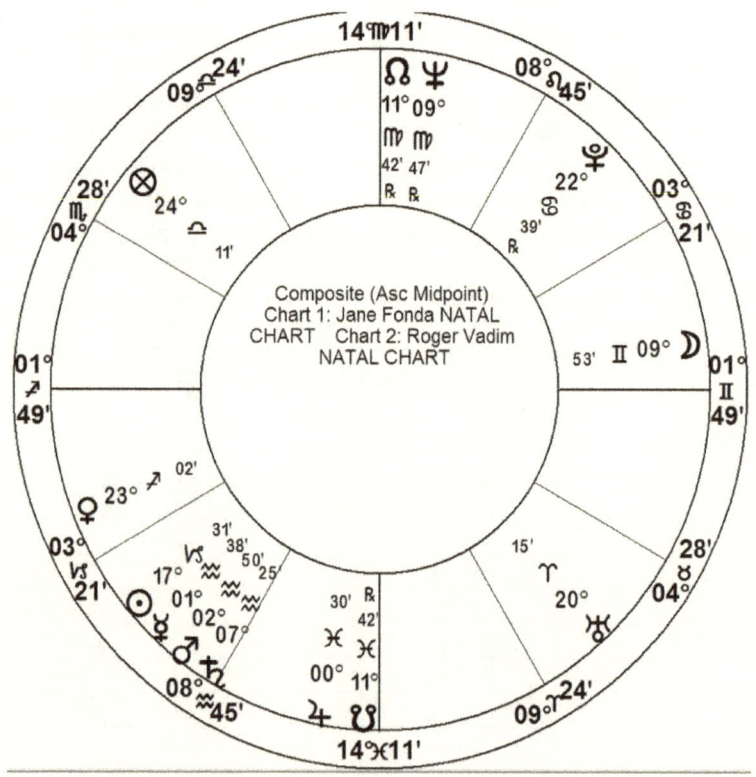

The Moon (their joint feelings) is emphasized in the seventh house, making them feel as though their partnership in some way completes each person emotionally. The Moon is square Neptune, making it more emotional, but also bringing some level of confusion. The Moon is also trine Saturn, which makes sense. Remember the double Moon-Saturn synastry? Any double synastry aspect will be reflected in the composite. Astrology is all about numbers and they never lie! This Moon-Saturn tie bestows a sense of gravity, making the relationship serious, but less fun.

Venus is nicely placed in the first house, indicating a love match, and it's (out of the 3 degree orb) trine Uranus in the fifth, giving them each the freedom to get their romantic needs met—and perhaps indicating a child who is different from what each expected. They have one daughter, but I don't know much about her. Pluto is quincunx Venus from the eighth, amping up their passion and sex drive.

So if we were to try to unravel this composite chart apart from the synastry, we might say it's a relationship that's loving and passionate, but also serious and responsible in which success and moneymaking are very important. With this sort of composite, we could assume they'd try to work together in some way or other. The one thing we can say for sure is it's far from frivolous.

This marriage lasted eight years, but by 1973, with Saturn transiting Jane's fifth house, it was over and she was re-wed, to political activist and future politico Tom Hayden.

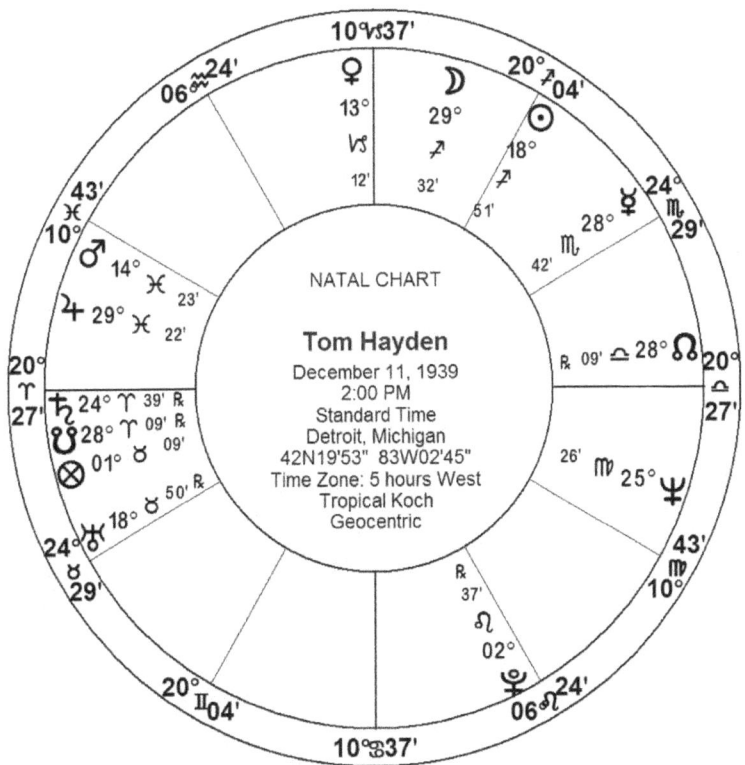

Hayden is a Sag like Jane, with his Moon also in Sagittarius. Whereas Vadim's planets lay mostly below the horizon, Hayden's are mostly above. On first glance we note Saturn right on the Ascendant and Venus right at the Midheaven. His Sun is in the sexy eighth house, and it lies at the focal point of a T-square of a very wide Mars-Neptune opposition. Even though the Mars opposition is wide, in this case I do count it, because of the power of the aspects hitting the Sun which pulls the configuration all together. Mars in Pisces is not particularly well favored, and it's weakened further by its twelfth house placement, and inclined toward passive-aggressiveness with the Neptune opposition. This is a difficult T-square because Hayden wants to express himself assertively (Mars square Sun) but feels a lack of confidence (Mars in Pisces) and personal insecurity (Neptune square Sun).

Saturn trines the Sun, demanding stability and consistent action, but the quincunx from Uranus makes him easily provoked and inclined toward rebellion. Basically with this sort of picture, he'd be likely to spend time plotting ways (12th house Mars) to get other people (Mars-Neptune-Sun) to carry out his plans (Saturn) for rebellion (Uranus). This certainly fits his profile as a college activist.His Sagittarian Moon is in the ninth house of law and philosophy, so clearly he felt his political beliefs quite personally. It's at the focal point of yet another T-square, involving optimistic Jupiter and idealistic Neptune. A trine from Saturn gives emotional responsibility and stability. Pluto is quincunx from the fourth house and perhaps his drive to reform the world came from things he learned in his childhood.

Venus is in the practical sign Capricorn at the top of the chart and can indicate a loving father or a career in the arts. It's sextile Mars, giving creativity and sex appeal, which is further enhanced by a freedom-loving trine from Uranus.

This chart is filled with personal, emotional, and even sexual insecurities, isn't it? He is far from a ladies' man and might be described as the anti-Vadim. His Mercury is nicely aspected by both Jupiter and Neptune, making him an inspired communicator.

The heavy planets are quite intense in this chart. Saturn right on the Ascendant indicates a Karmic need to learn responsibility and stability, and Pluto in the fourth certainly applies a great deal of pressure, both emotional and familial. It's very easy to see how he might be driven to political activism because by trying to change the world, Hayden could avoid having to concentrate on his own personal insecurities and could gain power and influence he might otherwise not have. It's interesting that ultimately he chose to work within the system.

Hayden and Jane have some personal insecurities in common with their Suns involved in challenging T-squares. They also have resonance with the following aspects—Sun-Mars, Mercury-Neptune and Mercury-Uranus. It all seems to be about action directed by idealistic thought, doesn't it?

As we examine some of the more significant elements in the synastry, we note Jane's Sun conjoins both Hayden's Sun and Moon, giving them much in common. Once again, her Saturn makes a challenging aspect to her husband's Moon, weighing him down a bit emotionally. And because Saturn sits right on his Jupiter, it affects quite intensely the T-square involving his Moon and Neptune. With this sort of aspect, and based on the limitations within Hayden's horoscope as a whole, we would really assume that he felt dwarfed by Jane and her celebrity, wealth, and achievement, although I've never read anything to that effect. Perhaps his successful political career in some way mitigated this because that sort of power is considered by many to be the ultimate aphrodisiac.

As they are close to the same age, her Neptune won't affect his Moon as his own aspects it anyway, and the same goes for his Neptune to her Moon. His Jupiter softens her Saturn and boosts her Sun, which is a very nice tie. Likewise, his Saturn trines her Sun, bringing stability and support. It also trines her Moon, just as Vadim's did. This is another case of dual Moon-Saturn contacts. Hayden's Uranus squares Jane's Moon and this is a rather disruptive aspect, in this case indicating that his need for free expression could challenge her emotional stability, and ultimately, the relationship.

Jane's Venus conjoins Hayden's Sun, a beautiful tie for affection. It's also square his Mars, great for dynamic sex, although some quarrels might be indicated. His Uranus is quincunx her Venus, and that could mean liberating pleasures, or disruption of the romance because of his self-expression. Actually the marriage ultimately ended due to his infidelity.

Jane's Mars sextiles Hayden's Moon, stimulating him emotionally, although it squares his Mercury, perhaps causing her to challenge some of his ideas or the way in which he expressed them. Likewise, his Saturn squares her Mercury, and even though his Venus conjoins it, it would seem that communication issues existed in the partnership.

As we look at the composite chart, we see Sun conjunct Mercury in the tenth house, indicating that their partnership (Sun) was very outwardly focused on their roles in the world rather than merely personal, and that communication was very important.

Neptune in the seventh is difficult, because it casts confusion on the foundation of the partnership itself, and it squares Sun and Mercury, increasing this factor. There is a nice sextile from the Moon, and this is pleasant for marital harmony. The Moon also receives a trine from Jupiter, creating a sense of joy and well being for them as a couple.

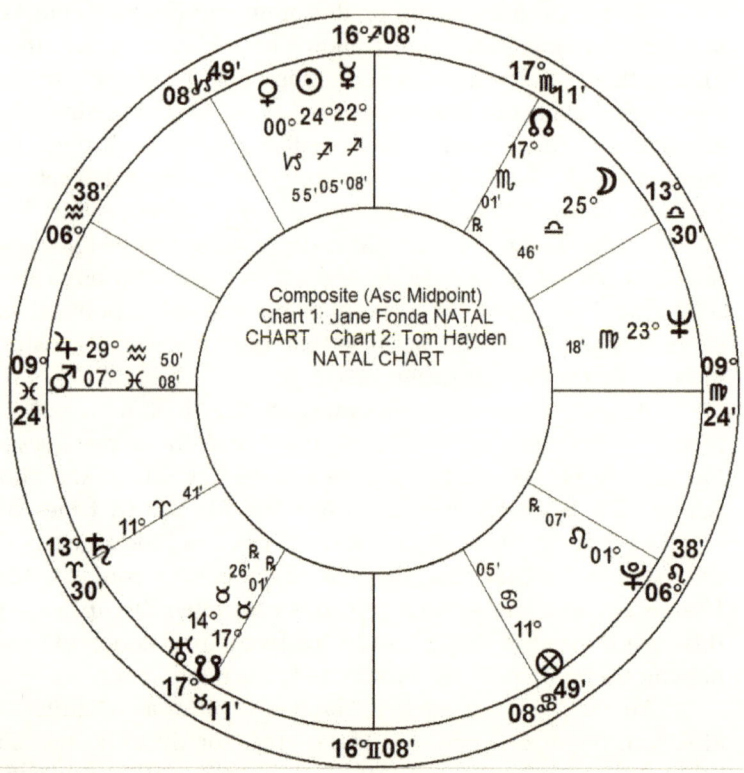

Mars is right on the composite Ascendant, indicating that they function best as a team when actually doing something together — tackling some project that demands action. Saturn is in the first, adding weight and seriousness to the relationship. Venus, planet of love, is placed in practical Capricorn, in the all-business tenth house, and it's sextiled by Jupiter, bringing joy and quincunx to Pluto, indicating some romantic power struggles but also deep passion. This was a long marriage, and by most reports a successful one, but it seems to me Jane was a much stronger person than both of her husbands so far. Her wealth and success exceeded theirs and she had more stamina and moxxy. The marriage to Vadim seemed far more passionate and personal than the alliance with Hayden, didn't it.

Perhaps they functioned so well as partners for sixteen years because they had what they felt were more important fish to fry—their mutual political goals. Nevertheless they share a child, so it was personal as well. But it seems to me that Jane was the leader at home, and her need for self expression was aided by marriages to two men who couldn't subdue her if they wanted to. Jane was naturally distraught when Hayden left her for a far less illustrious colleague in 1989, but

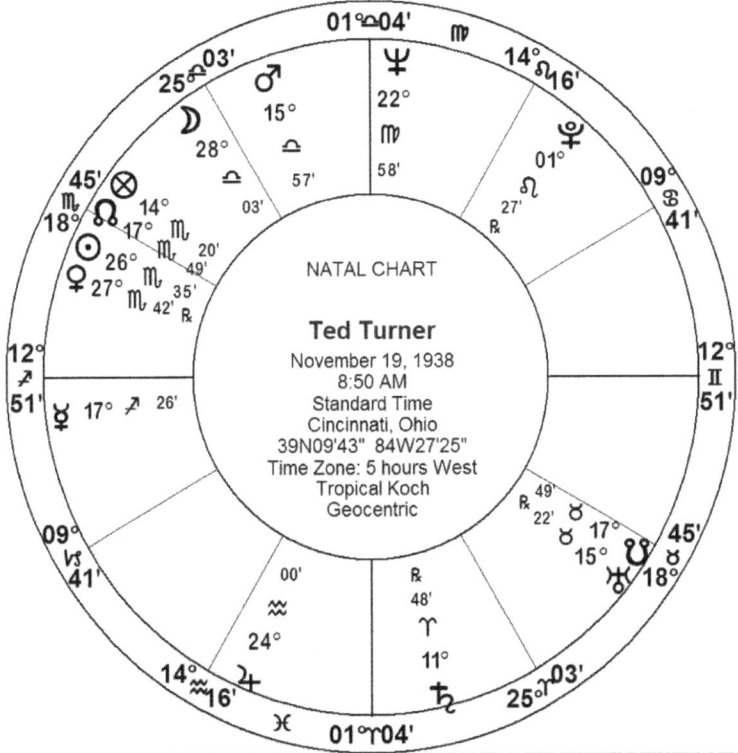

by 1991, as Pluto crossed her Midheaven, Saturn crossed her Ascendant, and Jupiter transited her fifth house, she announced plans to retire from the film business and married media mogul Ted Turner.

On first glance at Turner's horoscope, we notice a powerful opposition between Mars and Saturn at top and bottom of the chart. Immediately we get the impression of someone driven to achieve through tenacious devotion to work. Turner has Sun and Venus conjoined in sexy Scorpio, giving him charm and ladies' man type sex appeal, for which he is famous, although they're dimmed a bit by the shy twelfth house placement. In addition, Jupiter, interestingly placed in the third house of communications, squares the Sun, bestowing optimism and mitigating a bit of the twelfth house reticence. Neptune provides an uplifting sextile and Pluto a wide out of sign trine. With all this good stuff, we might say he trusts in the power of the imagination (twelfth house) to lead him to his destiny (Neptune at MC) via communications (Jupiter in three).

The Moon is in charming Libra, in the eleventh house of friendships, and often men with this Moon marry women who are friends as well as lovers, something we all agree is very nice. The Moon is trine Jupiter, bringing humor, optimism, and good cheer. It's also square Pluto, making him a bit clingy and possessive. Jane commented on her retirement after their marriage that you don't just go off to make a movie and leave a man like Ted Turner. Presumably with his Moon-Jupiter aspects he was capable of making a sandwich to sustain himself, so she was more worried about the temptations that might present themselves to him in her absence than her wifely duties as his caretaker.

His Mercury lies right on the Ascendant, and it receives quite a few aspects, as befitting someone interested in the media. It's sextile Mars, adding verve and passion to his communications. Saturn gives a trine, making him practical, business-like and perhaps interested in science. A quincunx from Uranus adds intellectual impatience and an interest in technology. And finally a square from Neptune gives a bit of the blarney and a vivid gift for story telling.

The only significantly difficult aspects in this chart are between Mars and Saturn and Mars and Uranus. Mars-Saturn describes a hard taskmaster and workaholic and the Uranus tie indicates someone who will go his own way despite disapproval. It's almost as though he would keep flogging himself until he achieved that empire, and that's exactly what he did, bit by bit.

In terms of resonance, Turner and Jane share less than she did with her previous husbands. But there is one chilling bit of shared identity-- the suicide of a parent. Jane lost her mom and Ted his dad. That's quite a difficult thing to endure and must provide a great deal of empathy between them. But she has Sun in the eleventh, and he has Moon there, and that's significant. They also share Sun-Pluto, Mercury-Neptune, Venus-Neptune contacts.

The first significant bit of synastry we notice is a sextile from Jane's Sun to Turner's Moon, a very nice tie. His Jupiter also boosts her Sun, and it opposes her Moon too, bringing a lot of joy into her life as well as an opulent lifestyle and access to unimagined resources. It must have been quite validating for her, at a time when she was worried that she'd aged out of Hollywood A-lists, to have a sexy billionaire seek an introduction to her as soon as he learned she was single again.

Turner's Moon is also sextile Jane's Moon, indicating domestic compatibility. His Sun-Venus is square her Moon, giving them a double Sun-Moon synastry. A difficult aspect is his Uranus, squaring her Moon, and she did disrupt her entire life for him, relocating to his Atlanta home to live.

Jane's Venus is sextile Turner's Mars, and her Mars squares his Sun-Venus, giving a double Venus-Mars contact, which is sexually incendiary and lots of fun. Her Venus conjoins his Mercury, nice for sweet talk, and is trined by his Saturn, giving romantic stability. His Uranus is quincunx her Venus, and that is problematic and can indicate disruptive infidelities, although I don't know if that was what ended the ten-year marriage.

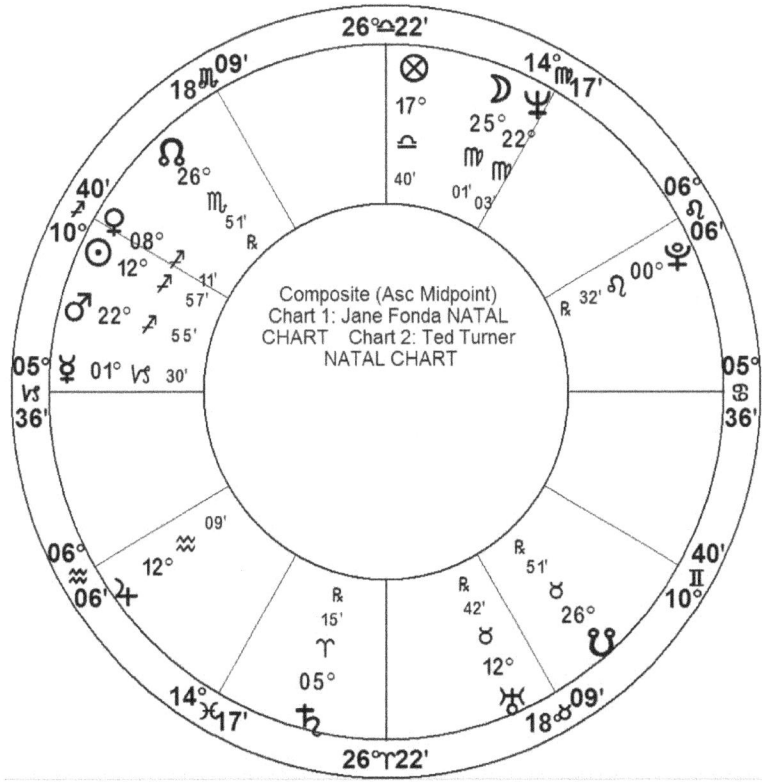

By all indications, this relationship was based on passion, fun, and good feelings, and must have seemed quite different to Jane after all her hard working years with Tom Hayden. She and Turner were hardly a frivolous couple, however, as he remained involved with his career, which suffered some ups and downs during the marriage, and she became seriously involved in charity work, as is befitting the grande dame wife of a billionaire.

The composite chart features a slightly out of orb Sun-Venus conjunction straddling the twelfth house cusp, and that's very pretty. It stands for love and friendship, warm feelings that never seem to subside. Even though they're now divorced, I bet if they're in the same room, they still feel a bit of a glow for each other. Recently she said she still loved him and had never stopped. Venus is trine Saturn, providing stable affections.

The Moon is in the ninth house of philosophy and travel, indicating the ability to share their deepest experiences, and it's enhanced by a Neptune conjunction. Mars squares the Moon, creating some quarrels, but also providing more passionate emotions between them. The Mars-Neptune square isn't the best for sex, but considering the synastry, I'd say in this case that it indicates physical passion that is also deeply spiritual and transcendent.

The worst thing in this composite chart is Uranus in the fourth house, providing a disruptive influence. Perhaps they were home together too seldom, she was uncomfortable living in Atlanta far from her children, or something about their childhood experiences separated them emotionally. I don't know what broke up this marriage, but perhaps Jane had retired too soon.

She is at this writing back in Hollywood, making movies, and has been single for longest period of time since she was a girl of twenty-eight. Some people speculate that her new interest in religion, as a born-again Christian, was a turn off for Turner, who finds religion pointless.

I think maybe this was her Hollywood romance, and because Turner was a much stronger person than her previous two mates, the liaison, although intensely passionate and loving, restricted her self expression. Just like the characters played by Streisand and Redford in *The Way We Were*, the marriage was doomed because they were two strong people who each needed to be allowed to take the lead. Ultimately a relationship, no matter how ardent and tender, can never supersede the person's Karmic journey as described in the individual horoscope.

Part Two: Matt Damon and Ben Affleck — An Enduring Friendship

Imagine this: what if you and your best friend went through school together with the same interests and the same dreams. And for years you dreamed together about making it big, becoming movie stars, Oscar winners, wealthy and hugely successful. It wouldn't be so unusual for two chums to spend their school days dreaming together of movie star fantasies, would it? It pretty much sounds like something every kid might do in idle moments with a best pal. But when it comes down to laying odds on the likelihood of these dreams coming to pass, most of us would just smile and say ok, kids will be kids.

In the case of Matt Damon and Ben Affleck, the dreams have all come true. They both struggled through their teen years, knowing they wanted to be actors and now they are bonafide successes. Their collaboration on the screenplay for *Good Will Hunting* won them a screenwriting Oscar. And through it all, they remain best pals. If they made a movie with this as a plotline, we'd all call it unbelievable! Of course everyone believes that these two golden boys became overnight successes, but that's not true at all. They've both appeared in dozens of movies, playing extras and bit parts long before they got their big breaks.

I saw Matt Damon in *Mystic Pizza* in '88, and he was right there in *Courage Under Fire* in '96, but I didn't fall in love with him until *The Rainmaker* in '97, followed by *Good Will Hunting* that same year. The thing I like about him is that he seems mature, wise beyond his years and seems to have a sense of humor about himself and his own foibles. And of course, there's the smile and the muscles!

Matt is a Libra, with Sun and a cluster of other planets in his eighth house. That often indicates someone who becomes a sex symbol — like John Travolta and Clint Eastwood, to name two. Matt's Sun is conjunct Uranus, making him a bit of a rebel and an individualist. It's also square his Capricorn Moon, and that describes some unease in relationships, beginning with his childhood; his parents divorced when he was two. Although, the Sun isn't technically conjunct the other eighth house planets, there is sort of a domino effect here. Uranus is conjunct Mercury, and Mercury is conjunct Pluto, which is conjunct Mars. So I would read this as a series of planets working together in a way that is similar to a conjunction. The Mercury-Uranus conjunction gives intelligence and impatience. Matt studied at Harvard, and left only a few credits short of receiving his degree. The Mercury-Pluto conjunction is persuasive

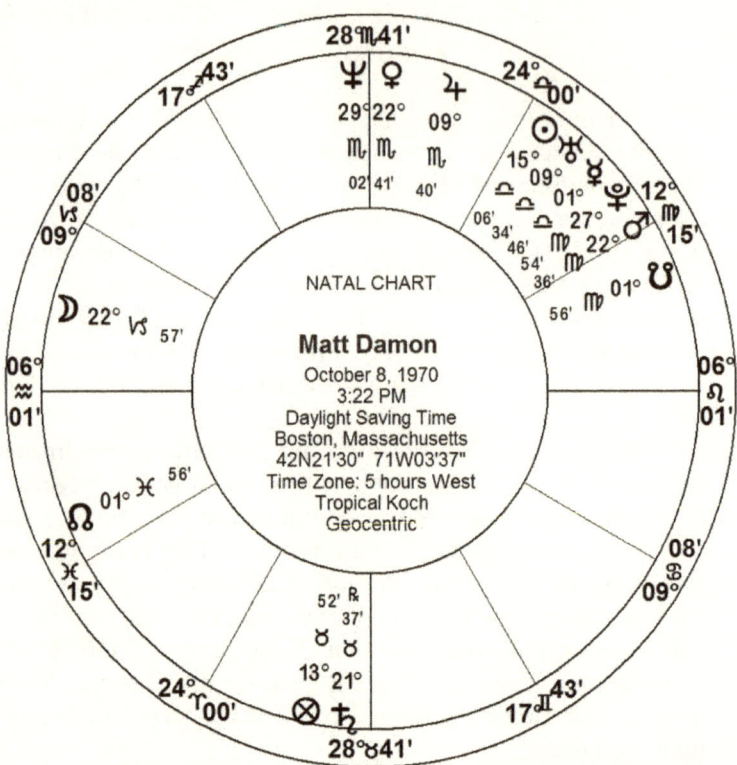

and deeply insightful, though it may seem a little verbally pushy on occasion. He definitely know what's on his mind and he has the courage of his convictions.

Also in the eighth house is Mars, conjunct Pluto in Virgo. This is an aspect of power and sexiness, of virility and fertility. I told one man I know with this aspect that he could easily impregnate a woman, and he confided how his wife became pregnant *after* her tubes had been tied! It definitely provides Matt with sex appeal. In addition, his Mars is sextile Venus, indicating more sex appeal as well as creativity. It's sextile Neptune as well, giving cinematic verve to his masculinity and some musical ability. Mars also makes a trine to both Saturn and the Moon, creating a kite configuration out through Neptune and Venus at the Midheaven. The trine to Saturn gives stability and a good boy scout quality and the one to the Moon makes him passionate. Matt will always be a staunch defender of the underdog with this aspect.

Mars is a very important and powerful planet in this horoscope, and that's great for a movie star playing masculine roles. He projects confidence, strength, and sex appeal, and Matt should play those sorts of roles. It's not surprising that in movies like *The*

Talented Mr. Ripley and *The Legend of Bagger Vance*, he was a bit miscast. We don't want to think of him as a psychopath or a failure. He is more believable as a hero and perhaps that's why he's done so well with the *Bourne* franchise.

Matt's yin picture is rather complicated. He has Venus in passionate Scorpio, conjunct Neptune, so we know he believes in true love and wants to live the dream, the fairy tale of happily ever after. Venus and Neptune at the Midheaven are nice for a career in art or film. But with Neptune at the MC, there is the possibility of making confused or poor choices, and I think Matt needs to work on which film projects he accepts. And of course the sextile from both Mars and Pluto make him even more passionate. When Matt falls in love, it's as though he's been felled by a wall of bricks falling directly on his heart! But he also has Saturn opposing the Venus-Neptune conjunction and that creates problems. Saturn seldom works well with Neptune; these two planetary energies are not compatible and usually there are problems as a result. With Saturn at the IC, there is a sense of insecurity, of modesty and the possibility that Matt's mother may have been too critical of him. So he might feel that he deserves less than he actually does deserve. What he won't be is an ego maniac, and by all accounts, he's a nice person and rather modest.

With Saturn opposing Venus in this way, there would be a need to become more level headed about love, and that's not such a bad idea. Because Matt falls in love so deeply, he could very easily get hurt, and I'm sure he has been disappointed in the past by romances in which his partner turned out to be much less wonderful than he initially believed her to be. Another dimension of this aspect is one of need. Matt's planets are very powerful, but he probably has some control issues. He feels vulnerable when he falls in love and then he loses his sense of control in the relationship. That is uncomfortable, so with this configuration he works through some of those issues by considering just how vulnerable he will allow himself to become with a specific partner. Also, the Saturn opposition functions as a set of breaks. He falls madly in love and is consumed by the hots for a lover, but with Saturn opposing Venus, he's too restrained to race off to the altar.

Another aspect of restraint is Matt's Capricorn Moon. That is generally a serious and solid lunar placement that indicates traditional values and a down to earth outlook. Because of the kite configuration, Matt's Moon has many tight aspects. The trine to Saturn gives maturity and stability. This is also an aspect of frugality and responsibility. Matt took his time buying a home and said he'd saved all his money, so that now he knows the people he loves are taken care of. The trine to Mars gives passion and emotional depth, and the trine to Pluto gives intensity and a need for control.

Matt is a very emotional person who can intuit other people's feelings. I remember being so impressed by *Good Will Hunting*. I don't normally shed tears at the movies, but I actually wept at one point. What impressed me most, however, wasn't the depth of feeling the movie inspired in me but that two boys, both under thirty, could write the part played by Robin Williams. His heartbroken widower rang so true, and the fact that those boys could write a monologue so deep about the loss of a beloved spouse spoke volumes about their depth and maturity.

Matt's Moon is also sextile Venus and Neptune. The Venus sextile would make him love and appreciate women, although with the Saturn opposition, he might find himself loving and mistakenly appreciating the wrong women some of the time. There is also a sense of appreciation for the good life, but with restraint, thanks to the Saturn opposition. This energy is most difficult in youth, because it makes it hard to resist the sort of women who find him appealing as a wealthy young movie star. But with the restraint and common sense built into this chart, Matt could gain perspective rather quickly and not be taken in by merely a pretty face for very long. After thirty, the women in his life would also be older and thus have the maturity lacking in girls he knew in his twenties. He did marry but not until his mid-thirties and now is happy and the father of several children. He also has Moon sextile Neptune, an aspect of sensitivity and psychic ability. This gives him a great deal of empathy for other people and the ability to read below the surface and know what someone else is thinking and feeling.

A kite configuration is always very interesting. It consists of a grand trine with an opposition, with the energy flowing out of one end of the opposition. With a grand trine there is a sense of luck and ease but often nothing dynamic enough to produce much action. With a kite, there is great luck combined with dynamism. In Matt's chart all the energy flows to his career. He has these dynamic, intense planets, but because the yin symbols all have built in controls, he's more likely to focus his energy on hard work than on a lifetime as a sex addict. That may be overstating it a bit, but without the Saturn to anchor him, he'd be more likely to give into random, fleeting, although intense passions.

In fact, he is someone for whom a committed relationship will always feel better. He would naturally be happier settled down with a partner he trusts so that he can know there's someone at home who loves him, and in knowing that, he has the emotional security to pursue that phenomenal career.

It's also interesting to note that Jupiter, in the ninth, is unconnected by major aspect. Often unaspected planets generate interesting life situations and I wouldn't be surprised at all if one day Matt decided to run for office.

When Matt stands next to best pal, Ben Affleck they look a bit like Mutt and Jeff, and everyone assumes that 5'11 Matt is really much shorter, because Ben is so very tall (6'3 or so).

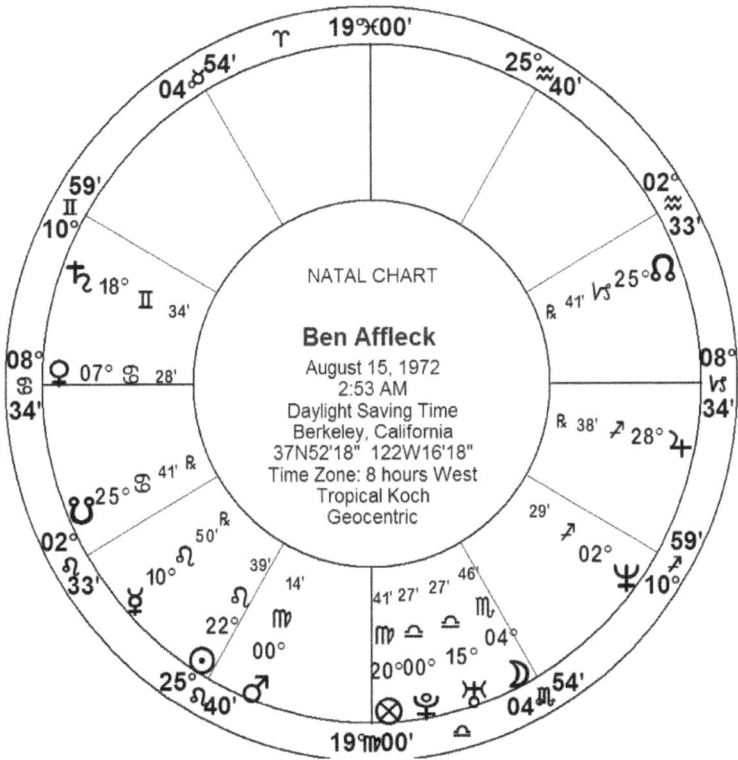

Ben Affleck has a Jimmy Stewart, decent guy quality and comes across as the sort of boy every mother would want to introduce to her daughter. I had seen him in several movies before *Good Will Hunting* but in that small role as the smart-alec, working class best friend of genius Matt, Ben really stood out. He's affable, outgoing, and when they appear in public, Ben is the one with the charm and ready bon mot, while Matt seems more shy and withdrawn.

Ben is a Leo with Sun in the second house and he's clearly money savvy. His Sun is conjunct Mars, an aspect of masculinity and great energy as well as sex appeal. It's trine Jupiter, giving him a nice optimistic, expansive quality that is also good for acting. And it's sextile Saturn, making him mature, responsible and steady. He is someone with a goal and with the stamina to achieve it.

Ben's Mars has some interesting aspects. A sextile to the Moon gives him passion and courage of his convictions. He also has a square to Neptune, which can sometimes cause problems. It's hard for him to be selfish, and after all Mars is the planet of unabashed selfish action. Ben tends to worry about other people's feelings before taking action and is a bit shy in that regard. He's said that he tips waiters so well because he remembers being in their position and wants to be generous now that he can. Mars-Neptune is a fairly common aspect among actors, making them able to project themselves into different roles and to express different motivations. With Neptune in the fifth, that is sometimes an aspect of people who drink for recreation, which has been a problem in his life. Mars is also trine Jupiter and that gives athletic ability, courage and youthful exuberance.

His yin pictures have some appealing aspects. Ben has Moon in deep and secretive Scorpio. Often people with this placement hold back emotionally unless they're with someone they trust and they prefer to keep private matters private. This could explain why there were so many rumors that Ben hadn't really broken up with actress Gwyneth Paltrow (and we saw this later with JLo.) Perhaps the couples opted to feign a breakup so they could keep their romance private! The Moon is square Mercury, and a Moon-Mercury aspect is useful when writing. It allows the writer to pen words that inspire deep feelings in the audience, something that touches the hearts of other people. Of course, with the square, there are more conflicts than the more harmonious aspects, so some of the time Ben feels it's difficult to express his feelings, probably because they're too deep and complicated to be accommodated by mere words.

A trine to Venus in Cancer is a very nice aspect. Men with Moon-Venus aspects really like women and they enjoy being in the company of women, usually offering respect and admiration. It's also a nice aspect for enjoying life, though sometimes it indicates a bit of gluttony—which after his JLo breakup was a well-publicized problem. We already mentioned the Moon-Mars aspect, giving depth and passion to his feelings. And finally, Ben has an out of sign sextile from his Moon to Jupiter. This is a nice aspect that gives congeniality, optimism, and a universal feel. Those with this aspect can get along with all sorts of different types of people, they love to travel and are well liked by foreigners. Despite the privacy-loving Scorpio Moon, Ben's an outgoing, friendly guy who likes and is liked by other people.

Venus in Cancer is a lovely placement, making him a nurturing person who is kind to other people. In addition, having Venus on the ascendant is an aspect of prettiness, and it certainly helps with those good looks that have made so many women develop crushes on him. Ben has a square to Venus from both Uranus and Pluto. The Uranus square tends to make him fall in love quickly—and perhaps a bit unwisely because he enjoys being excited by new involvements. The Pluto square makes Ben a bit possessive—he falls in love quickly and wants to be completely involved on an instantaneous basis.

These aspects form a bit of a conflict in Ben's life. On the one hand, he wants to be with a woman who is exciting and a bit quirky (Uranus) but he really loves sentimental, emotional women (Moon and Venus in water), and with the Pluto square, what can happen is Ben falls for a woman who seems sweet and tender but who turns out to be a bit of a flake—and then he has to leave her—something that the Pluto aspect makes very difficult. Ultimately it could mean that he will cling to the wrong woman because he's so nice and for the most part, rather tolerant, that he would allow a woman the space to express herself—even if it means she's behaving badly.

I wrote the paragraph above years before Ben's infamous tryst with Jennifer Lopez and we saw this exact thing happen between them as his passive-aggressive behavior with a stripper challenged the relationship he must surely have known was not meant to be. He seems now to be happily married to movie star Jennifer Garner, who's also a cooking enthusiast and mother, fulfilling the indications in Ben's Moon and Venus pictures.

It's important to examine Ben's 4th house as part of his yin picture. With the Moon there he would love his mother and of course have deep and private feelings. But with both Pluto and Uranus there, there is a sense of emotional turbulence and unrest—a sense that he feels his needs aren't quite being met. This is something that Ben has in common with Matt—they're both nice people who feel that they can't quite get what they need from the women in their lives, including their mothers.

This is emphasized in Ben's chart by the wide T-square formed with the Venus-Jupiter opposition, T-square both Pluto and Uranus. It's easy to see by this configuration why Ben is so outgoing and friendly. He's a bit of a puppy dog and this is his way of wagging his tale! But what happens when he does this too much is that other people get overwhelmed and back off. Then Ben has to cope with those feelings of loss and to learn to meet his own needs. This is an aspect designed to teach self-reliance and personal strength.

Just as in Matt's chart, Ben has to learn who to trust and to whom he should turn for emotional support. He has to learn that just because someone seems to like him, that person may or may not be a good choice as either a friend or a lover. It seems to me quite profound that these two pals have made it to the top in a very difficult business—together. They give each other balance and because their charts echo some of the same themes, there is a sense of recognition between them.

There are a number of ways to see just what to expect when two people come together. Of course, most of the techniques are aimed at determining what to expect where romance is concerned, but they are just as valid in friendship. The first one is synastry, in which we compare ways in which one person's planets impinge on another's. That shows the energy between the two people. As mentioned previously, a tool I really like is the composite chart, in which the midpoint is found between the sets of planets, and then a new chart is erected. We average the two Suns to get a composite Sun, the two Moons for a composite Moon, and so on. The resulting composite chart describes the relationship itself. I use these two methods but I also look at something else, what I like to call the buzz of the chart.

We all have certain vibrations and we send that energy out into the universe. People with a similar buzz feel that vibration and regard it as comfortable. So if you have a Moon-Jupiter aspect, no matter which aspect, someone who also has that aspect will have a harmonious buzz. If there are many similar aspects, there will be a great sense of compatibility, a sense that you and that other person are similar people and the energy is thus comfortable. Just for a second, let's examine the number of similar aspects between Matt and Ben. They have in common: Moon-Venus, Moon-Mars, Mercury-Uranus, Venus-Pluto, and Mars-Neptune. That would indicate similarities in their emotional patterns, the way they think, love and take action. Those are many similarities! In addition, having similar planetary contacts would indicate similar karmic goals, and in that way two people would be working on the same sort of life lessons and could provide each other with support. That is certainly the case in this friendship.

As we look at the synastry, there are many interesting contacts. Ben's Sun squares Matt's Venus and Matt's Sun squares Ben's Venus, an aspect that gives them deep affection for each other. They just like each other! Ben's Sun is squared by Matt's Saturn while Matt's Sun is trined by Ben's Saturn. This is an aspect of stability and Karma, although with the square we can assume that Matt tries to edit Ben's choices while Ben supports Matt's. In any case, it gives the friendship a professional tinge, so no wonder they collaborate and share similar career goals. Ben's Uranus conjoins Matt's Sun, encouraging Matt to try new things.

Ben's Moon conjoins Matt's unaspected Jupiter, revving up the Jupiter and increasing Ben's natal optimism. Matt's Moon is squared by Ben's Uranus, and normally this is a disruptive aspect. If Ben were to camp out at Matt's place, he might be a bit too rowdy, but since Ben traditionally was the host for Matt in their single days, that problem probably didn't arise. It could also indicate a dislike on Ben's part for some of the women in Matt's life. Ben may encourage the more sedate Matt to come a bit out of his shell and to experiment more.

Ben's Mercury is squared by Matt's Jupiter, and that is excellent for communications and writing collaboration. Matt's Mercury squares Ben's Venus, so they enjoy talking to each other and there is a real sense of energy in their communication—also good for collaborative writing.

Ben's Venus is trine Matt's Jupiter. Because Matt's Jupiter is unaspected, it's nice that several of Ben's planets contact it, because they activate this energy in Matt's chart. Matt's Venus is square Ben's Mars—an aspect of creativity and attraction, creating a nice chemistry between people and making them enjoy each other's company. Matt's Mars squares Ben's Jupiter, giving energy to Ben's chart.

As we look at the charts as a whole, we see that Matt's Sun falls in Ben's fourth house, making him feel like family. His Moon is in Ben's seventh, an aspect of partnership and emotional compatibility. Ben's Sun is in Matt's seventh, another partnership indicator. Ben's Moon is in Matt's ninth, as aspect of communication and shared ideals.

There's a great deal of symbiosis in this friendship. They each grow as individuals through the partnership and somehow they manage to nudge each other in positive directions, all the while maintaining the warm and friendly energy that exists between them.

In any relationship reading, I'm always interested in what the composite chart shows. There can be powerful and positive synastry, but if there isn't much of a connection in the composite chart it can indicate a relationship that begins and lasts, but isn't really significant, like some long marriages I know of in which the people have good synastry but the composite chart shows very little. In those cases, the couple might remain together, but in separate bedrooms and share very little of the important elements of their lives. In this case, it's a friendship, not a romance, so a strong composite would indicate reasons for the friendship to endure on a close daily basis as opposed to casual contact now and then. In the composite chart we use a tight orb of no more than three or at most four degrees.

Matt and Ben have a fifth house composite, which is nice for a

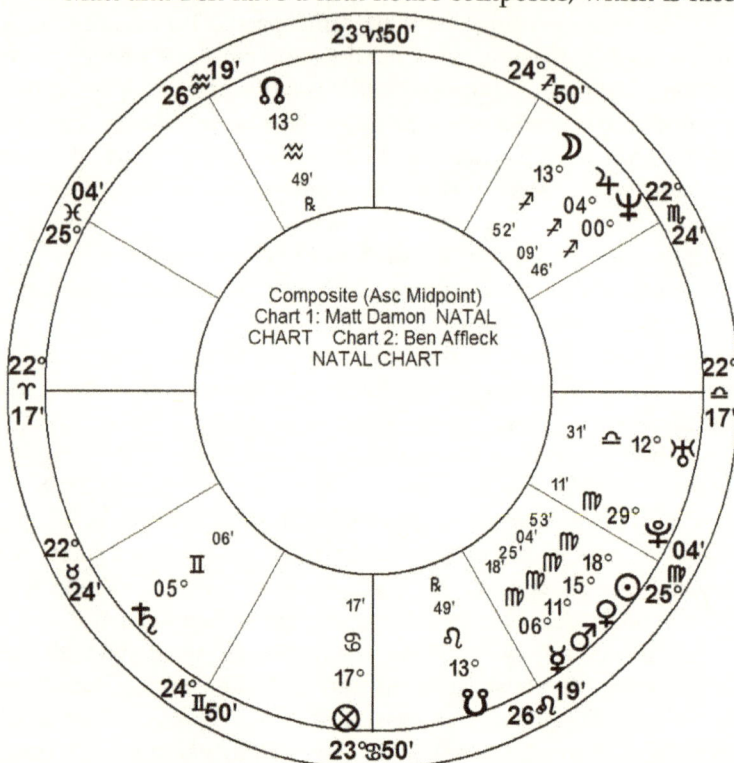

fun and pleasurable relationship. They have Sun conjunct Venus, one of the warmest and most affectionate connections. They also have Mars conjunct Venus, an aspect of attraction and affection which is excellent for a creative partnership. They can inspire and feed of each other's creative impulses and in general have fun together while trying to create something.

The Moon is in the eighth house, indicating a close emotional connection and the ability to share deep feelings. It is square Venus, an aspect of love and affection. It's also square Mars, so there may be some friendly rivalries and an occasional bout of roughhousing when there are unaddressed emotional issues or slights. Either way, they both have a strong stake in the relationship and in participating in it. And with Uranus sextile the Moon, they each give the other space and freedom. With two intense people like these guys, a little space is always a valuable thing.

It's interesting to note the T-Square involving Saturn, Jupiter and Mercury. Saturn in the house of money can often be restrictive, but Jupiter in the eighth is good for financial partnerships and since they form a T-Square out through Mercury, it makes sense that Matt and Ben would opt to work on a screenplay as a way to make money.

It's easy to see just how compelling this friendship is. These guys are as tightly linked as brothers, but perhaps their relationship is stronger because it is their choice to be friends and we can't choose our siblings. As they've entered a profession known for large egos (sometimes coupled with tiny brains), it makes sense that Matt and Ben would want to maintain their friendship because they know and trust each other. They are both solid human beings with good values. They can always be open, honest and they both know that they will receive the same treatment in return. They're two nice guys who can count on each other to stick to the same rules of helpful support and mutual integrity, something they've no doubt realized they can't always expect from everyone in Hollywood.

It must be all the richer for these two best friends to have made it side by side in show business and in my opinion, they deserve every accolade handed to them.

Part Three: Obsessive Love

Years ago, when I was in college, I wrote a paper for an advanced English class comparing Thackeray's *Vanity Fair* and *Gone With the Wind*. The teacher commented in her notes that I was so clever to compare a popular but insignificant novel with a Victorian masterwork. I remained silent since it seemed wiser to let the compliment alone, but it had never occurred to me that *Gone With the Wind* wasn't as significant a piece of literature. Now, okay I will concede that perhaps it isn't — well — *Vanity Fair*, but again and again I return to it because there's so much resonance there. Of course there are other stories that chronicle yearning and romantic obsession, but this Civil War novel seems to touch a nerve.

There was Scarlett O'Hara, desperately in love for decades with Ashley Wilkes, and too blind to see that he loved his wife, not her. And her husband Rhett was utterly devoted to Scarlett yet couldn't make her see or appreciate his affection. They were basically the same person — always yearning for someone they couldn't have! And what happened at the end — by the time Scarlett realized she actually loved Rhett and confessed it to him, he uttered his infamous line, "Frankly my dear I don't give a damn." He loved her less for loving him more!

I have Venus conjunct Neptune, and that accounts in part for my love of romance, love stories, and movies in general. But one day I was having a conversation with a wise old friend who's been an astrologer even longer than I have and in discussing my Venus-Neptune, she said, "That means you always want something you can't have." What an interesting insight, I thought. To me it had always meant that I wanted an ideal in love, true love, and that I knew what true love was. But to her, a Venus conjunct Saturn person, it meant something altogether different.

People obsess over love like nothing else. They can be broke, out of work, ill, whatever, and almost always will make love the primary subject of a reading. A client of mine is now going through a terrible separation and she's alone with several children, including an infant, worried about money because her dolt of a husband is off partying and enjoying his new single life rather than supporting his family to the degree that he should, yet the thing that disturbs her most is not the hardship, not even the wolf at the door, but rather that she now has nobody to make her feel special.

Love is the best thing around when we have it, but when there are doubts, boy oh boy does it cause misery, delusion, and yes obsession. Romantic obsession is an interesting phenomenon astrologically, and often what we see is a little surprising. Being a slave to love isn't always about getting love, and if that's so, what *is* it about? Let's look at the situation bit by bit.

Venus is, of course, the planet of love, so it begins there. Depending on the aspects to Venus, we have some idea of what approach to love a person will take. The simplest romantic aspect is Venus to Mars, and that's pretty straight forward. The planet of love connects to the planet of action, and we have a person who desires sex—or is very creative. Often they go hand in hand. But although the person in question may seek sex frequently, that's no particular indication of obsession. A Venus aspect to Jupiter, planet of expansion and personal growth, is very pretty and makes the person generous, and perhaps a spendthrift, but once again is not particularly obsessive. An aspect between Venus and Saturn seeks romantic security, and that can certainly lead to obsession when the person feels insecure, such as we might expect with a Venus-Saturn opposition. Uranus is the planet of sudden change, eccentricity, high technology, electricity—well you see where I'm heading! Uranus aspecting Venus can bring sudden romantic attachments, and it can also incline a person to break up too quickly. Neptune, the planet of illusion, delusion, spirituality, drugs, and drink, is a very mixed bag. At its highest, Neptune signals the truest of universal love but at its lowest, it's a drunk lolling on the beach. When Neptune hits Venus, we get some of everything, so someone with this combo might fall madly in love—with a sleazebag who seems like Prince or Princess Charming. Even though the choice of a partner is bad, the love is nevertheless real, so as I said, some of both! Pluto is, of course, the granddaddy of obsession. Pretty much anywhere in your chart Pluto lies is the chance for fixation. When it hits Venus, it can be quite intense. A Venus Pluto tie can indicate very deep love, but sometimes it also indicates depravity, such as someone who falls madly in love with a criminal or some other sort of Svengali who manipulates emotions.

Any single planetary tie to Venus will create effects, but behavior is defined not just by one aspect but by whole pictures of interlocking planets. Just like in cooking, the more ingredients you add, the more complex are the flavors produced. So, for example, what about my client whose husband's desertion has left her feeling "not special." She has Venus opposed by Saturn, and that is much more difficult than the conjunction. With the conjunction, a person will seek security and will usually find a relationship that provides it, barring any other challenges in the chart. With the opposition it's as though she's always begging for security that's often being yanked away. Or that she feels unlovable. Or that she loves someone who can't give her what she needs. Pretty much all these instances have been true in her life. But another challenge, brought about by Neptune, complicates her romantic situation even further. Neptune lies at the focal point of a T-Square in that Venus-Saturn opposition. I always feel that there are no two more incompatible planets than Saturn and Neptune. They simply don't relate to each other well. Saturn demands structure and security, while Neptune pushes to release these things. Neptune's truths are deeper and more universally profound, yes, but to earthbound Saturn, they're all smoke and illusion. To me, Neptune and Saturn at odds often means money loss, but when love is involved it's even worse. A square of Neptune to Venus would indicate a tendency to idealize the wrong people. I've had plenty of this with my own Venus-Neptune conjunction, but that is an easier aspect to handle. With the Square there's more confusion. In this case, she desires security, but doubts her own lovability (Saturn), and loves the wrong people (Neptune) who ultimately let her down—leading to bad marriages and money loss. That's also the thing about marriage—it's an institution defined more by Saturn than Neptune, since it's also a business partnership. To make matters more difficult, her Sun is involved in this picture—conjunct Venus, so not only does she feel insecure about her lovability, she is insecure as a person and often feels unequal to the demands of life (Sun opposite Saturn) and confused about her life direction, purpose, and value (Sun square Neptune).

Another interesting aspect comes from the Moon, which creates another T-Square with the Sun-Venus opposite Saturn picture. It's at a later degree, so Neptune doesn't touch it. The same issues of self worth defined by Sun opposite Saturn are much worse when described by a Moon square Saturn. That indicates loneliness and an extreme need for other people. Moon-Saturn people are often very popular, perhaps because they put so much effort into other people as a means of avoiding time alone. It's scary to be all alone with this aspect because the tendency is to inflict all sorts of self-criticism.

This is a person with a difficult chart, but we'd have to say her issues are more about loneliness and feeling unloved than about romantic obsession. Her husband is a complete loser, and she knows this, yet to her he's the whole world. She has many times described him to me as such, yet she says she loves him unconditionally. Why would this be? Okay, please remember that I have that Venus-Neptune aspect before you accuse me of being a cynic! She feels badly about herself, has a sense of being undeserving—unconsciously that is—so she's fixated on a man who's such a bad partner she feels safe. Nobody else would want him—as she's said many times. But that was no guarantee of success in the marriage, because he walked out.

It's a very interesting situation Karmically. Why would someone choose to incarnate with this set of challenges? To learn self-reliance is one answer. She must learn that she can't base her self-worth on sustaining anyone's affection. And of course the irony is that she always chooses partners who don't have the ability to sustain anything, guaranteeing that the relationship will ultimately fail. It's sad because then she feels that she's unworthy. She says things like "I'm a good person, so why does this always happen to me." She never sees that she's choosing bad people on whom to hitch her star, that their leaving her is not about her, but about them. So ultimately it's one of those lose-lose cycles that she would have to confront, but usually a person like this will live out her life and then only during the afterlife review come to the realization that she was instigating her own downfall. How could she fix the problem in this lifetime? She could give more attention to her children or could volunteer. By giving love without it being romantic, there's less of a need to be personally validated and ultimately that validation would come about through knowledge of good works and by receiving appreciation. She also needs to take a harder line when allowing herself to become involved romantically. If a prospective mate has walked out on several other women and children, she should wise up and move on — before she allows herself to fall for the guy. People do repeat the past all too frequently, so it makes good sense to pay heed to someone's romantic resume.

Planetary pictures describe romantic expectation very well, but it's also worthwhile to look at the houses because sometimes an obsession will be caused as much by house placements as a particular set of aspects. For example, think of what happens when Neptune is placed in the seventh house of marriage. This is a classic situation. Often the person will gravitate toward partners who need to be rescued, drunks, drug users, people who have mental problems, or in other words, partners who have some issue that prevents them from being one hundred percent involved in the relationship. Because of this situation, it's quite natural for the person in question to say, "If only," and to yearn after the partner, if only he or she would give up the addiction — or whatever — and invest in the marriage. Whether "If only" turns into an obsession or just a sad bleating depends on other factors in the horoscope.

With Pluto in the seventh house, we see power struggles. Somebody is the boss, somebody is the slave. There's a great potential for healing and self-knowledge here because Pluto tends to generate the sort of one to one conflict that involves us to the very soul. The needs and the quarrels are so incredibly intense that even someone who tries not to pay attention is bound to gain some awareness eventually. And just as with Neptune, it depends on what else is present. We could pretty much say that is always true about everything. It takes more than one little thing to create any complicated situation.

We seldom think of Uranus as involved in any way in romantic obsession because that planet tends to incline people to break up and move on toward the next passing fancy, so the worst we might hope for is an obsession with serial dating. But don't sell Uranus short, because sometimes it becomes a trigger. People who are inclined toward obsession, but who have a strong Uranus conflict will usually choose partners who ultimately desert the relationship. That way they fulfill both aspects of their charts — the desire to obsess and cling plus the need for freedom. We don't always directly act upon everything in our chart. Sometimes we rely on the bad behavior of other people to bring about situations! And if someone has this sort of obsessive-freedom dichotomy, there are many lessons to be learned about balance. Too much clinging is bad. Constantly letting go means always being alone. And so on!

I have a client who has Venus, Mars, and Pluto all widely conjunct in the eighth house of sex. Her tendency is to date men who are married, critical or abusive, mainly because they seem magnetic to her, but she says her reason for connecting with those specific guys is because the sex is so compelling. She never says it's love, or that her heart melts or any other Neptunian type explanation. She always talks about the sex and the chemistry, which makes perfect sense considering that particular configuration. Because of the personality types of the men she dates, during the course of any relationship she's always in a very tenuous position. Will he call? When will he call? Will they continue seeing each other? Her affairs are very exciting, not just because their foundation is always sexual, but because they're so transitory, so unreliable. She knows going in that there's no future — as there can seldom be when the partner is already married, but that never seems to bother her. The chemistry is just too strong, the sex is just too good. She has rarely admitted it, but there is a power dimension at work here, as we would expect with a strong Pluto involvement. She wants to see if she can "get" the guy, which really means, can she entrap him emotionally enough to keep him calling. Is she sexy enough to be the sort of human catnip that will drive him wild? Those are the feelings that are genuinely at the bottom of any of her relationships.

In addition to having the Venus, Mars, Pluto connection, her Moon is squared by Pluto. That's definitely an aspect of obsession. Holding on feels very natural with this aspect. One guy I know with this aspect was talking about his failed marriage and he said in the same paragraph that he was miserable with his wife and then went on to bemoan having lost her. I wondered why he was so sad to have lost someone who made him miserable, but that's the thing with Moon-Pluto — the misery is far less of a threat than the pain of letting go.

We would expect that this woman who has Pluto hitting her Venus, Mars, and Moon would seek a stable relationship, but she never has. She was married for a while to a man who drank and cheated and since has been dating the same sort of man. That's the thing with Pluto — the tendency is to put one's destiny in very scary hands. Her most recent relationship became more and more difficult, with the man doing worse and worse things, in an attempt to get her to break up with him, but with her Moon-Pluto aspects, she continued to cling. No matter what she'd take him back.

The pivotal thing in her chart is not Pluto, despite the Plutonian nature of all her entanglements. The most significant element in her chart is Uranus — in the seventh house. That brings her transitory relationships. She is an excitement seeker and Uranus makes it possible for her to keep exploring new territory. And that leads to an interesting conclusion. Very often romantic obsession is not about gaining closeness — it's about gaining — or maintaining — freedom.

What sort of Karma would a person have to come into this life with such a picture? One of her lessons is clearly about the perils of clinging, particularly when what she's holding onto is a very hot potato. But another is to learn discrimination. It's exciting to have lots of kinky sex, but as time passes, what do you end up with? Uranus in the seventh — nothing! There's a lot to be said for intense devotion, for loving wholeheartedly, with one's whole soul, but there's a big difference between love and those affairs of the heart that really are centered anatomically quite a bit lower! So ultimately this sort of chart might be for someone on a path of self-discovery because what she will learn in this lifetime is about herself, the depth of her own feeling, and the incredible experiences she might have here on the earth plane because of having placed too few limitations upon herself in terms of who and how to connect.

Romantic obsession is very often about freedom, which is hard for so many people to believe. By clinging and obsessing, usually the object of the obsession is driven far away, or is someone who by his or her own nature, will likely disappear anyway. Then there's all that delicious alone time spent day dreaming, wishing, praying, yearning, and in general wallowing in romantic fantasies that have no real grounding in reality. That's a Neptunian sort of obsession. Generally speaking, the Plutonian obsessions will require action, and because they amp up the sex drive, the person is motivated to move on toward the next thrill. With Neptune, there's a willingness to wait, to enjoy the delicious fantasy, and being alone isn't always a threat because those daydreams are sometimes more real than any reality. A person with a Moon-Saturn aspect will probably not give in to a Neptunian obsession because no matter how real the fantasies are, it's still too scary to be alone. Thus there are quite a few different ways to obsess romantically and different sets of behavior go with each.

Planets in the seventh house are important. With Saturn there, we would assume that the person will marry, although finding a mate won't be terribly easy — or fast. Wherever Saturn is, we pretty much always expect there to be some action because that is the planet of Karma and as such, events come about to generate the life lessons the person has incarnated to confront. A woman I know has Saturn in the seventh, and although she's far from young, she tends toward relationships that won't work out rather than anything that could or would lead to marriage. When an online romance went bust, she fixated for years on a coworker who was much younger, and although he was attracted to her, their relationship never even progressed to the point of actual romance. She felt there could be romance, but wouldn't even consider sleeping with him until some sort of guarantee of permanence was offered. As her guy was too young and inept to make any move at all, they were pretty much stalled in the "What if" stage.

She has a Libra stellium in the fifth house of romance and pleasure. Mercury, Mars, Jupiter and her Sun are all tightly conjunct, opposed by an Aries Moon. This is a high energy, very self-directed person, perhaps a party girl. Venus is in Scorpio, right at her Descendent, but it is squared by a fourth house Pluto. That Venus-Pluto could describe some of her obsessive qualities. And of course, Pluto in the fourth is rather uncomfortable — she feels insecure — life doesn't always feel safe and there's a great deal of pressure. Perhaps that accounts for the guarantee she seeks. Also at the bottom of her chart is Uranus, right at the IC. That's another aspect of instability.

She has an interesting configuration. The Moon is involved in a grand trine with Saturn and Uranus, and it makes a kite out through the Libra planets. There's so much energy here for freedom, that the other energy demanding love and commitment pretty much takes a back seat. Despite being a Libra, which is a very social sign, her chart has so much me-me-me energy that she's not exactly partner material.

Of course as Saturn is involved in the grand trine, we could say that she could build a stable relationship once she finds someone who accepts her and encourages her to be herself, providing lots of freedom as well as stability, but gee under those circumstances, who couldn't find happiness!

Saturn does send a strong message—it always demands that we put in effort and build something over time. Her task is to do so with a relationship, but her inclinations lead her in other directions. The Venus-Pluto is really a saving grace for her, should she choose to accept it. It's what's leading her toward love, away from her tendency to be a me-me-me party girl. The Venus-Pluto shows her what it's like to love someone, to be enveloped in those deep feelings, emotions that are far more thrilling than playing the field. But if she pursues and obsesses over the wrong person, what then? Saturn guarantees that she will be alone. In this case it's worse than Uranus in the seventh.

What is someone with this sort of chart trying to learn in this lifetime? Like all Libras, one lesson is to strike a balance. Her need to be social must be balanced with a desire to connect on a deeper, less casual level. The problem is that she tends to choose bad partners, and I feel it's a subconscious desire to avoid commitment—once again obsession being the tool of freedom rather than closeness. So ultimately the Uranus at the fourth will prevail, and she will be alone. And then she will learn that you can't build a lasting love by partying, but that's the sort of lesson that become clear very late in life—or in the afterlife review.

Transiting energy can come along to help the situation, and of course that's the whole purpose of life—experiences that bring home the life lessons we're trying to learn. But when transiting Pluto crossed her Descendent, she became more obsessed with this young guy rather than trying to connect with someone who actually might be interested in a relationship with her. When Pluto hit Saturn, she finally let go. This is very typical. Something comes along to point out that the delusion won't stand and the fantasy ends, but it doesn't always end for good. Once the transit ends, sometimes the tendency is to drift right back into the bad relationship, or to resume the fantasy, or whatever, depending on whatever behavior is involved. In the case of this woman, she's less motivated to let go and move on than some others might be because she has so much Jupiter, and the Moon in Aries isn't particularly fearful or lonely. You might wonder why, with the Venus-Pluto she didn't just seduce the guy, and perhaps it was the fear generated by that Pluto in the fourth that made her hesitate and wait for guarantees that were never likely to be forthcoming.

Sometimes romantic obsession is a function of just plain craziness, for lack of a kinder term. A woman I know has spent most of her life very sheltered and as a constant dependent, always living in her parents' home, with only a small hiatus in the form of a very brief marriage to a gay man who fathered her child. She's never had any sort of career to speak of, but one day she dreamt she would marry a very wealthy man twenty years younger. A fan of online chat rooms, she became involved in a cyber relationship with just such a guy, but every time he wanted to meet in person, she refused to let him come and visit, always choosing to put him off, using her father's health as a reason. Eventually her online boyfriend drifted away, but that never put a stop to the fantasy. She began getting readings from every psychic she could find, asking would they be together, never bothering to mention that they hadn't actually met in person. She did find one hapless psychic who told her sure, they had a future, and that bad reading fed the fantasy even more. She was absolutely certain he was her husband to be.

This woman has Mercury conjunct Venus, right on her Ascendant. Also in the first house is Sun conjunct Uranus. That's a lot of first house energy! And it's very youthful, in your face, rebellious energy too. She comes across as an impatient, somewhat deranged twenty-something despite the fact that she's much older. Mars is conjunct Jupiter in the second house, where Pluto also resides. The Moon and Neptune lie in the fourth, but are unconnected to each other. Neptune does square Venus and Mercury as well as the Sun and Uranus.

All those Neptune squares are very hard to handle. For example, a Neptune square to Mercury can make a person very musical, a talented writer, or a liar, and she frequently lies about absolutely everything, although she seems quite nice. Worse is the square to Venus, and worse yet to the Sun. And because these planets are in the first house being squared from the fourth, there is much more delusion indicated.

Her insistence that this young guy was coming to marry her was very strongly a Neptunian obsession. And it's a very interesting one too. Here's a woman who's basically always been nothing more than a girl, and she was yearning for her Prince Charming. Often women who are persistently immature, or who feel they've missed some part of their youth, will gravitate toward a much younger guy — someone who is at the stage of life where she feels she belongs, and that will allow her to relive the years that somehow felt squandered or not fully lived. The fact that he was also wealthy just fit into the Prince Charming mystique. He was supposed to ride up to her on his steed and spirit her away to his castle. It's a good fantasy isn't it, but one better suited to a girl of nine than a woman in her forties. If a life is defined by delusion, you can't really call something a romantic obsession, because basically it's one more make believe situation. Most romantic obsessions have some reality at their foundation, which is to say that the people involved have at least met each other in person. Of course women aren't the only ones who participate in such a fantasy. Look at all the older men who marry young girls to give themselves a new lease on life. They are not always as deranged as the woman above, but surely something is amiss when there are twenty, thirty or more years between partners.

The question is this—if you have all these obsessive patterns in your horoscope, does it absolutely mean that your love life is a minefield? Can you never find happiness? I would say that where these tendencies exist, some form of romantic problems occur, but they can sometimes be handled through conscious effort. Of course it is possible that some people out there who have these planetary pictures are off leading sane and happy lives and that's why I've never met them—happy people seldom contact astrologers.

I know in the instance of my own chart, that my Venus conjunct Neptune has always been an issue. Because it's also squared by Uranus, it inclines me to fall in love at first sight—often with someone who is ultimately not a good choice. I can actually feel myself falling, and it's a very strange sensation, that feeling of tumbling, the dizzying romantic energy taking over, intoxicating my brain. But I've learned to hold on, not to let go so easily, to wait and see. You don't have to fall if you're holding on! And by maintaining sanity for a longer period of time, I actually get to know the person and then it's not blind love, which essentially is romantic delusion.

That's the sort of technique anyone can employ. If you know your horoscope and see Neptunian obsessions, take charge. If a relationship ends, be willing to let it go. Don't obsess for years over someone who is no longer in your life. If you break up, believe it. Don't wonder or ask your psychic if he or she is going to call. Don't ask your astrologer to see when the next transit is coming that could pull you together. Take matters at face value. And when the urge to lie on the couch in your unwashed bathrobe and to daydream the hours away arises, get up, do the laundry, and don't let yourself wallow in sweet misery. It's so pleasant and tempting to enjoy the daydream, it's like being transported to another realm, one in which it all works out perfectly. Well why shouldn't it—you're the one writing the script. But that won't get you real love.

And if you're obsessing over someone who just can't be there for you, give yourself a reality check. Start at the beginning. If you're dating a married person, stop. A married person who is dating is a pig, and a cheater, and even if you're not the one with the wedding band, you're contributing to the cheating and pain on some level, so no matter how strong the chemistry is, say okay sorry no, and move on. If there's some unavoidable Karma between you and this person, wait until the divorce comes in. Because then you might actually have a chance for a relationship instead of a dalliance. If you find yourself repeatedly drawn to this sort of person, the question to ask is not why you have such bad luck, but why you need so much freedom. Ask why you are unavailable for commitment, because that's what's always at the bottom of any such situation. If you have a genuine need for freedom—because, for instance, your Karma is to build a career and romance is so distracting for you that it prevents you from focusing on your work, then at least you're aware of your situation and don't have to feel miserable when relationships come and go. You don't have to make it evidence of your lack of lovability but rather a situation that you yourself are at some level choosing, which is always the case in any life event anyway.

Consider the person to whom you're attracted. Do you love and admire him or her or is it basically a case of the hots? Do you actually despise the person and feel no respect at all? If so, you're obsessing up the wrong tree! A little good judgment at the beginning of a romance saves many tears at the end. And should a good relationship end, sure you're sorry, and perhaps heartbroken, but make getting over it a priority. Don't assume that this person is the one and only person on the globe for you. As your mother said, there are lots of fish in the sea. As long as you're clinging emotionally and psychically to one person, someone else won't come into your life. You need an open heart to attract a good mate. Of course you can easily attract a horny sleazebag, but that's what you're trying to avoid!

Do the work. Make the commitment to let go, but take a little time to mourn and a little more time to analyze the situation. Know what put you there and what you were supposed to learn. And then let yourself internalize that lesson. Once you do, it becomes much easier not to repeat the same patterns over and over. Nobody likes that out of control feeling of oh no—it's happening again. That's the nature of Karma—until we get it, it repeats. By knowing what you want, what you genuinely want that is, you're much more likely to get it. And by admitting that what you have in some way describes what you want, you make important strides because all of life represents choices that we ourselves make.

True love is a wonderful thing, but obsession is never any part of it. True love is simple—and kind. With true love each partner worries more about the other than him or herself. There is giving with no limitations—and receiving in equal measure. With true love, you meet, you love, you connect, and it just sort of works out. Your heart opens and there's no conflict, no reason it shouldn't. It's a safe, happy zone! True love lasts a lifetime and each day you're with that person you feel blessed to have him or her in your life. So make true love your yardstick. Fill your heart with love and positive expectation and know that love is out there, readily available for us all.

Chapter Six: Predicting and Planning Events

Astrology is as much art as science, as much intuition as supposition, but it's a great tool for planning events and predicting the future.

Part One: Using Astrology to Plan Events

Years ago I was chatting with a friend who worked in a metaphysical bookstore, and he dragged me over to the wall to view a horoscope posted on a bulletin board. It was the birth chart for the bookstore, and he smiled as he showed me the time of birth—midnight. The owners of the bookstore had opened their establishment at the witching hour, not because they belonged to a coven, but because, as astrologers, they wanted a good chart for their new business and the midnight birth time gave them Jupiter, planet of luck, right at the Midheaven, point of ultimate career success. Jupiter at the top of the chart is a good thing, and it augurs particularly well for a business chart.

People study astrology for one main reason. We want to know what's going to happen. By learning to decode astrological symbolism, we can make sense of the past, project that information into the future and feel a sense of power. We know what's coming next. Life isn't as scary when you have that sort of heads up.

But then, what follows from that? If you know what sort of events might occur as a result of certain planetary pictures, the temptation is obvious. Why not wrest the controls of life out of the hands of blind fate and back where they belong—into your own grasp. So those bookstore astrologers began casting charts into the future until they found a good day, then tweaked the time until the birth chart seemed destined for success.

Creating a new endeavor via astrological timing isn't a very complicated matter. You give birth to an entity that has its own energy. Of course we could also say that maybe they—however many partners there were—should also have looked at the transits to their individual charts in order to determine how propitious a time it was for embarking on a new business as well as at how their charts combined in order to see if they made a good team. Perhaps they did! In any case, that would make choosing a time much more complicated.

In the case of the bookstore, they had complete freedom. They could choose any day of the week they wanted as well as any time of day. Chances are they didn't have customers lining up around the block that fateful midnight, but never the less, it was the birthdate of the new business. In a situation like that, with complete freedom to choose date and time, it's very easy to maximize on astrological symbolism and to choose the best possible chart.

So, for example, suppose you wanted to begin writing a book. I've done that, but I've never used astrology to time the first moment I typed my opening sentence. I just sat down when I was ready and did it. But that's my nature—I tend to just let things happen and to do things when the spirit moves me. That's not a bad way to live because often you're acting upon the wave of those good transits of which you want to avail yourself anyway. But, if you really wanted to do that sort of thing, you could. You could cast some charts for the best time to begin a creative endeavor and make a pact with yourself to begin at that time, even if it were 3 A.M. on a Tuesday. Of course, you might also want to look at the transits to your horoscope to determine if writing were a favored pursuit at the time in which you planned to start. This, however, is a minor example because nobody really worries that much about starting a writing project or when to pick up the knitting needles for that new sweater.

An event that is worth considering is the purchase of a car. A client contacted me about her new car purchase because Mercury was retrograde and she was wondering if that would be a bad time to make the buy. Mercury retrograde is one of the most interesting astrological phenomena, not primarily because of the effects it causes but because of the superstition associated with it. It seems that everyone has heard of Mercury retrograde and is terrified it will inflict havoc on every area of their lives. Will it? No, not really.

Mercury is the planet of communication and although Mars is the planet of action, Mercury is about movement and travel, so cars have some connection to this energy. The God Mercury, the one with winged ankles—we can pretty well assume he traveled on foot, not in a Lamborghini. But what does the process of buying an automobile consist of? First of all there is thought and vision, a Mercury thing. We think ohh I need a new car, then there is the vision of us, tooling along in said vehicle, its shiny new paint glinting in the sun. So the initial desire lies in the province of Mercury and we would want a reasonable image. For example, I love those new SUVs. I like the way they're all square and boxy and how they have all that room. I could easily envision myself in one. But, to be frank, I'm not that great a driver. I need a car with a low center of gravity, and one that doesn't require a tank of gas to get to the supermarket. So in my case, I'd want Mercury to be working well for me to make a reasonable first vision of what I truly need.

The second step in buying a car is the test drive, and even with Mercury retrograde, you can pretty well assume you're going to navigate acceptably well along the 1-mile radius of the showroom. But then comes the negotiation and the contract, and those things are definitely Mercury, so it made sense to wait until this little stellar glitch ended. This is another situation in which the car buyer has total control. Even if you urgently needed a car today, you could opt to rent one for a few days until Mercury went direct.

A more serious situation arose when a pregnant client asked me to help choose the birthdate for her child who was to be delivered by Caesarian. This was a big and intimidating responsibility and I wasn't sure I wanted it. It can be quite scary to "mess with Mother Nature!" But I began looking at approaching dates within the timeframe and came up with the date and approximate time that looked the happiest. I gave the client a breakdown of each of the possible dates and what sort of person her new child might be as a result along with my suggestion about which was the nicest date.

In this situation there were constraints. We couldn't choose a weekend date because the doctor didn't work on the weekend. Ditto the evening. Sometimes I wonder if Caesarians are done nowadays to facilitate doctor's golfing commitments rather than mothers' health! So we hit upon a date that was reasonable for the doctor's schedule, or we thought we did. My advice to the client was just to tell the doctor that this was the day she wanted and not to give in. He didn't have to know why she was adamant or that astrology was involved. But the client didn't have the will to fight the doctor and the child was born on one of the dates I liked less well.

People have often asked me if a child born via Caesarian has that artificial date as a genuine birthdate, and the answer is yes, that's when the child was born. There are all sorts of agreements made under the surface at a psychological/Karmic level and one of those impels the doctor to deliver the child when the right time for that particular child has arrived. That spirit—the one who will inhabit that child's body is aware in advance of when the birth time will be and in agreement with it. In the case of this client, it made total sense why the baby was born on a less astrologically benign date. The client had a difficult chart, as did her husband and her older child. The new child was meant also to have a difficult horoscope — they had Karmic issues as a family and they fit together. So in this case, Mother Nature won out, and it was probably all for the best.

Part of the issue in using astrology to plan events is the level of power you genuinely have. In the case of the expectant mother above, she had little power indeed, which wasn't surprising as that was one of the issues in her horoscope. There is usually some degree of compromise necessary. Say we were planning a charity ball. We would clearly need a weekend evening, but chances are we could choose a Friday or a Saturday. As it would be a charity event rather than a personal one, we wouldn't have to concern ourselves with transits to any individual's chart, although we might want to look at the transits to the charity's chart. Even if the charity were going through a difficult time, there would be relatively little to worry about. The event could be under attended, I suppose, but it's not as though that single event would in any way define the course for the future of that entity — in this case the charity.

So, in planning this charity ball, what aspects might we look for? The bookstore's idea of having Jupiter at the Midheaven is a good one, because that blesses the event with both luck and generosity, with a sense of patronage and happiness. A combination of Jupiter plus the Sun, perhaps also plus Venus could be quite nice too. Now, obviously we can't assume there could be a conjunction at any given moment. Jupiter is in mid-Leo as I'm writing this, so as it is October, I'd have no possibility of finding a conjunction to either Sun or Venus until summer. But we could look for a trine or a sextile, and that too would be nice. Today Mars is in Libra, making a trine to Neptune, planet of music and that could be nice, plus with the planet of action in the sign of socializing and relationships, it leads to a cordial good time. But we realize something — if we're planning a charity ball, we can't plan today for a party in a day or two. We have to look a bit into the future. We could say okay, the holiday season is coming up and on one of those weekends on the way to Thanksgiving or Christmas, people might like to raise champagne glasses and pledge some money to a good cause. Or we might worry that family obligations would prevent solid attendance. Astrology could help with these issues, but it would really be just an advisor. As board members on the charity in question, we'd know our membership and their habits and could predict without astrology what general time of year would be good. Then astrology could refine it further and help select the best weekend for the event.

Generally speaking, for a happy event, I wouldn't necessarily want a Saturn-Moon aspect because that is not particularly light, carefree or joyous. In the case of a charity, a trine or sextile wouldn't be such a terrible thing. For example, years ago here in Los Angeles, a charity raised a bunch of money for world hunger. They did something quite dramatic. The A-list guests arrived and were given numbered tickets. Based on this lottery system, a small percentage dined elegantly on gourmet food, symbolizing the percentage of wealthy people in the world. A far greater number sat on the floor and were fed cups of plain rice, symbolizing the numbers of underfed across the globe. And some were fed nothing at all, to symbolize the truly hungry. In the case of a dramatic presentation such as this, a Moon-Saturn aspect would help point out the need in the world, but you wouldn't need such an aspect to have a successful event. You might even have a difficult Pluto event, which would give the event more of a sense of reality, but that could backfire as the planet of manipulation could make the deep-pocketed guests feel put-upon rather than generous.

One spring a special event happened in my own family. My daughter got engaged to her long-time, live-in boyfriend and she indicated a summer, 2003 marriage date was the plan, and it was up to me to choose a good date for the wedding. Well leaping lizards! Holy, buxom bridesmaids! This was the ultimate challenge in scheduling an event astrologically. I was terrified.

The question was this? Just how serious is the wedding date and what does it mean to the couple? Is that wedding chart going to define their entire marriage, whether it lasts or fizzles, produces little grandchildren I can baby-sit or screaming matches I won't want to witness? The only true answer is yes and no. Maybe if Xandy and Steven had never met until the day of some sort of archaic arranged marriage, and that was the true beginning of their connection, then the wedding chart would be the signa qua non of their life as a couple. But they had been a couple for a while, so there were more factors to consider. But when I resurrected the chart of my own long-ago marriage, I could see quite clearly that the chart described a relationship that really did match what I had experienced. So a marriage chart is a valid entity and does draw a picture of what that union will be like. Some astrologers say that the marriage chart goes into effect and then nullifies the chart that preceded it—in this case the one from when they first began living together and sharing a life as a couple.

I took some time first to look at their individual charts to see in a general way what transits would be hitting them summer 2003. Steven, who was born in 1971, had an easier time, as he had already passed his Saturn return. That summer showed Jupiter transiting his seventh house of partnerships, always a good thing. Saturn would still be transiting his fifth house of romance and children, but this is not a bad thing, as it often indicates a desire to get serious about love and make a commitment. I was a little concerned because Neptune, planet of confusion, was hovering at his Ascendant then, but this is a long transit, and will last years. In addition Uranus, planet of chaos, transits the first as well, so we can assume Steven is going through some ups and downs, but as they are part of a longer bit of energy, sometimes you just have to say okay roll with the punches. Pluto would soon be moving out of his tenth house and that could only be good for his career and as a future mother-in-law I say a quiet "Yay!"

Xandy's chart had me more worried. Summer 2003 would bring her Saturn return. All her life I'd told her, wait until after your Saturn return to marry. The Saturn return is the time at which the planet of Karma works its way back in the sky to the exact point it occupied at your birth, usually at approximately 29 year intervals. But September 11th had just happened and Xandy had adopted a carpe diem mentality. She would marry in 2003, just at the time of her Saturn return; she wouldn't wait. This isn't always a bad thing, because Saturn tends to nudge us toward what we should do. At the first Saturn return we realize it's time to be an adult and opt to embrace what's good for us in the future and to release that which is just a lingering remembrance of childhood. That's why so many teen brides divorce at this fateful moment. In addition to the Saturn return, Uranus would just have entered her seventh house. My feeling is that planets of upheaval create more chaos just as they enter a new house. Once they've been there for a while it's still ups and downs but not as extreme. It's hard to see how finally marrying someone with whom you've lived for several years will change your life so drastically, but there are usually events associated with Uranus, so we would have to wait to see what occurred. Neptune was still floating around in the middle of her sixth house of day to day responsibilities at work and Pluto in the middle of her fourth house of mother and home, and assuming that she didn't work me to death over this wedding, those planets will probably cause no grief. Pluto would be squaring her natal Jupiter, a natal seventh house planet, and that could cause dramatic results. One such imaginable result is that she at the last minute meets someone else and runs off with him instead. It's possible but she is a Cancer, and pretty loyal. It could also be growth to their mutual business involvements. There's never one and only one outcome to any transit. There are just waves of energy, as described by astrological phenomena, and it's wise to realize that many possibilities could emerge. In any case, we can all agree that the transits to her chart are more volatile than were those to the prospective groom's.

It made sense to look at the general transits first, but not to try to refine a marriage date based on transits to either of their natal charts or the composite chart. (A composite is a chart erected from the midpoint of each of the elements in the two individual charts. The midpoint of the two Suns becomes composite Sun; the midpoint of the two Moons becomes composite Moon and so on. It's a chart that describes what the relationship is all about and how the two people interact and its use is clearly covered in previous chapters.) The thing to do next was to look at the possible dates to see what sort of energy was available. I had visions of beautiful aspects, the Moon plus Venus, Mars plus Jupiter, the Sun in a nice place, happy trines, Saturn offering subtle support: basically the sort of perfection at which angels weep.

Here is where reality intrudes upon astrology. The kids were getting married and I didn't have the freedom of an astrological bookstore to choose any date or time at all. They could wed on a Tuesday at midnight, maybe, but they sure couldn't have a family wedding then. If we were going to avoid nuptials blessed by a Las Vegas Elvis impersonator, we would have to have the wedding on a Saturday night so out of town guests could arrive and attend. These are the limitations you have to face when planning special events. But, ok, that's life and the summer is long, so hey, we'd probably have tons of great Saturdays from which to choose. And there was also the issue of time. We could have an afternoon wedding if we wanted to, which we didn't, but we couldn't plan the ceremony for 10 P.M. because that's just too late. Once again, more constraints supplied by reality. Still, what were there, maybe 12-13 Saturdays in summer, 2003? There had to be a bunch of good ones. So, let's start at the beginning and see what we found.

June 7th. It would be cool and pleasant with ocean breezes and a little mist. That sounded positive but that information was climatological, not astrological. Venus in Taurus—it's nice when the planet of love is in a compatible sign and also nice that on that day it's conjunct Mercury. Mars (action, sex) is in the egalitarian sign Aquarius, widely conjunct Uranus (eccentricity) in Pisces. Would that mean the marriage would be plagued by temper tantrums? Those kids are volatile enough already! But the real deal breaker was the Sun—in Gemini, opposed by domineering Pluto, and making a T-Square out the Moon in Virgo. That sounded not only like strife and power struggles but surly waiters as well. Not only did we want to choose a time that would create a positive marriage chart, we needed one that at least indicated a nice party.

Fast forward seven days to June 14th and what do we find? The Sun is still widely opposed by Pluto—more power struggles, but the Moon is in Capricorn, opposed by Saturn. When the planet of limitations opposes the Moon, there are emotional issues, timing issues and sometimes even fertility issues. We didn't want that. Besides, Moon op Saturn isn't good for socializing either, so who wants dried out entrees and late officiants at a wedding?

Next we review June 21st, and by then the Sun is in Cancer, conjunct Saturn, which in and of itself isn't a bad thing for a marriage because it indicates responsibility, stability, and longevity. But where is the Moon? In Aries, squaring the Sun-Saturn combo. I didn't want a Moon-Saturn aspect for my daughter's wedding! Moon in Aries is considered not a bad thing, because it's a fertile sign, but somehow it seemed to me that it's not really a partnership Moon and that would be a better thing.

June was nearly over and the dates looked dismal. I began to worry and pointed out to Xandy that this is what happens when you don't listen to your mother. So although I felt it might be okay that she marry at Saturn return time, we had to face the fact that when you do opt to do that, there are limitations, delays and frustrations in the process itself. Details have to be nudged, labored over, whined about; they don't just fall into place.

Having said my peace, I moved forward in time. June 28th, the last Saturday in June. It contained a large stellium, or cluster of planets lined up like a row of dominoes, each one conjunct the next, starting with Venus at 23 Gemini, Moon at 29 Gemini, Mercury at 29 Gemini, Saturn at 3 Cancer, Sun at 7 Cancer. With Pluto at 18 Sagittarius, it made an opposition to Venus, and by association the whole shebang. And, with the approximate 6 P.M. marriage time, Pluto was pretty close to the Ascendant of the chart. My feeling was that it was nice to have that large cluster in the seventh house of marriage, and Venus with Moon and Mercury and the Sun, well that's all pretty nice, but with Pluto dominating the first, there would be a constant series of power struggles in every aspect of the relationship. It wasn't a terrible date, but it wasn't a good one either. So we moved forward into July.

The first Saturday was the 5th, and that wasn't a bad idea. It was a holiday weekend and people would have extra time off, more time for travel and vacation plus there would be fireworks on that weekend and who can say no to that. But it wasn't to be—Venus was in Cancer that day—excellent for love and for those grandchildren I want, but it was conjunct Saturn. Venus conjunct Saturn isn't a terrible thing, especially in a marriage chart. It indicates mutual Karma to be worked out, a sense of belonging, a reason to be together as well as a relationship that lasts a while. It's often a feature in composite charts of couples. The real deal breaker came from the Moon, very late in Virgo and about to enter Libra, making a square to the Venus-Saturn combo.

By July 12th, even though I was still looking at an approximate 6 P.M. timeframe, Pluto had moved out of the first house into the twelfth, which although considered the house of hidden enemies, still seemed like a better thing to me. Remember Venus moves relatively rapidly, being one of those small, inner planets, but it only moves about a degree a day, compared to Saturn, which moves much more slowly. The Venus-Saturn conjunction was still in effect, but it was at a lesser degree—the two planets now being five degrees apart. I still didn't like it but once again, the deal breaker came from the Moon, in Capricorn, opposing Venus-Saturn. Wow! What were the odds that every single Saturday would feature mostly bad Moon-Saturn contacts? I had no idea but that Las Vegas Elvis wedding was beginning to have some appeal. The kids were nagging me—where was the date—as I laboriously poured over all those charts.

On July 19th, Venus was now conjunct the Sun, which is excellent, and at 6 P.M. the two planets were in the seventh house, along with Saturn. I would generally rather not have Saturn in that house because it will just serve to emphasize whatever issues of compromise must be faced. Mars was now seven degrees away in its conjunction to Uranus, and in my opinion, the farther the better. But once again, the Moon, now in Aries, made a wide square to Saturn as well as a square to the Sun-Venus combo. Moon square Venus isn't such a bad thing—it can be an excess of love or too many sweet treats, but Sun square Moon in a relationship chart isn't something you want because there are basic strifes and a difficulty in maintaining a happy partnership at home, while working or just in general. Someone wants one thing while the partner wants another.

On July 26th, the Sun and Venus were still conjoined, and Jupiter was conjunct Mercury, which was wonderful for a pair of writers, but at 6 P.M., the Moon was Conjunct Saturn, hovering at the descendent of the chart. We couldn't have that. The summer was fast waning and I was getting more and more stressed. What if I couldn't find a good date? Could I let the kids marry on one of those dates I disliked and then worry for the rest of my short life about their welfare? I shuddered! And on a grander level, was every marriage made in 2003 going to fizzle because of all those nasty Saturday nights? We moved into August....

On August 2nd, a good thing happened. We were still looking at 6 P.M. but by then Saturn was moving its way down into the sixth house. The Sun and Venus were conjunct in Leo, which is nice for children and general happiness. The Mars-Uranus conjunction was getting tighter again, due to a Mars retrograde, and that combo opposed Mercury. That wouldn't be good—it would indicate some arguments, some delays when trying to work together, but it could also mean some lively conversation, which was something already in the kids' favor. But once again the Moon, now in Libra, squared Saturn. This was the first time I'd ever gone weekend by weekend to set a date, and if you had asked me if it were likely that week after week the Moon would be compromised, I would hardly have said yes. It was amazing!

We moved to August 9th, and the nice Sun-Venus conjunction held, along with the Mars-Uranus opposite Mercury. On that date, the Moon in Capricorn had just passed orb for the opposition to Saturn. It hovered at the Ascendant of the chart, which could make the marriage too emotional, but wouldn't necessarily be a terrible thing. It trined Mercury, which was nice, and made a quincunx to the Sun, something I didn't like but couldn't say I hated. It wasn't an impossible date, but it wasn't one I loved.

We move along to August 16th. Not only were the Sun and Venus in tight conjunction, they were conjoined also by Jupiter, which is lovely for just about everything—romance, love, money, happiness. Mars was conjunct Uranus, but they both trined Saturn, so even with some Uranian chaos, there would be Saturnine stability, in a congenial way. Mercury had moved away from the opposition, but was being squared by Pluto, and this could indicate some arguments and verbal power struggles. The Moon was in Aries, but at a late degree, and it trined the Sun-Venus-Jupiter stellium as well as Pluto, creating a grand trine in the sky, considered a lucky and harmonious planetary picture. What worried me most was Uranus. At 1 Pisces, it made an out of sign opposition to Jupiter and also the Sun-Venus, but the opposition was very wide.

I felt compelled to keep looking. August 23: Moon conjunct Saturn in Cancer in the sixth house. We have enough hypochondriacs in our family already, thank you very much. August 30: Tight opposition between Mars-Uranus and the Jupiter-Sun-Venus combo. The Moon was in Libra—good—but connected only by a sextile to Pluto, so that wasn't good enough.

By then the summer was over. I kept going through the end of the year, but knew the kids wanted to marry in the summer. So what would you do? We went back and revisited August 16th. I knew the date wasn't perfect, but it was better than the mostly dismal dates that were the alternative. As a mom, I had to do my best. My heart was pounding, my head ached. But then I decided to pull up the charts of their relationship so far.

Their first date, marked by the death of Princess Diana, was in August, 1997, and on that day Saturn opposed Venus and Pluto squared the Sun. They moved in together in February, 1998 and the Moon was conjunct Saturn and square Venus, the Sun conjunct Uranus, and Mars square Pluto. The day they got engaged in March, 2002, Mars opposed the Moon, T-squared by Neptune, Venus was squared by Pluto, and the Sun squared by Saturn. These are a bunch of very difficult aspects. They had muddled along on their own, falling in love, cohabitating and promising to marry during a lot of astrological chaos. So clearly the marriage date was so much better than any of these other dates, it seemed I could relax a little.

All that was left was to choose a time for the marriage. I decided to nudge the time just a bit to move Neptune down a little farther toward the middle of the first house, in order to lessen the square to the Midheaven. This also moved Jupiter into the seventh and Uranus out of the second up into the tail end of the first house. Altogether it seemed a good plan. They would say "I now pronounce you..." at 6:15 P.M.

The kids were content with the date I chose and we soon thereafter began visiting places to hold the wedding. The first spot we saw we loved. It was beyond perfect and our imaginations soared. At that time we had about eighteen months to plan. Except the spot was already taken—by someone else who planned farther ahead and who also chose the date because of an astrologer's advice! We agonized about changing the date to an available one in order to gain our location. Of course I once again gave my speech about the aggravations of marrying at Saturn return, but we survived and continued to plan the wedding—to be held at another location on August 16th. It made more sense to sacrifice a dream location than to compromise on energy that would affect the rest of their lives.

That same week, I heard from a favorite client who wanted to marry that summer and needed advice. They had already set a date but he wanted my input. My teeth clenched, remembering all those terrible Saturday nights. What was the date you were planning, I asked him. And casually he replied, August 16th, 2003! I breathed a sigh of relief. Mother Nature had come through and without even opening the ephemeris, I could tell him he'd selected the best date for the wedding of the entire summer!

As I amend this passage today in 2012, I can report that both marriages lasted quite a while — then fizzled. But what can you — these are modern times, more people divorce than stay married and relationships that endure past a decade can't really be judged failures. The marriage dates were the best available for the time, but time marches on and new transits come along to challenge even a well-aspected union. Such is life.

Part Two: Predicting the Future With Astrology

Astrology is the best psychological tool available. There is nothing out there that can give you deeper information about a person's psychological make up. With a horoscope, you can know essentially everything about someone, right down to the tiniest nuance of emotion. Nothing is better at helping a person confront emotional issues than a good horoscope reading. With all that going for astrology, you'd think it would be plenty. But there is something else astrology can do quite spectacularly — predict the future.

It's human to want to know what tomorrow will bring. We all have some germ of insecurity at our very core and thus we want and need assurances that everything will work out all right. We want to know what will happen, and basically if we'll be safe. Part of this desire to have advance knowledge of tomorrow is simply curiosity. Some of us are the type who read the last page of a book first in order to cut out the suspense and make the journey more relaxing and enjoyable. Astrology is very good at letting us know what to expect.

I do hundreds of readings a year and find it very gratifying when clients comment how much I help. It's also quite a kick to hear so often that the predictions I've made have come true. Do I have some sort of foolproof system that allows me to know exactly what's coming next? No, not really, but I do have some guidelines that when applied will lead to a higher rate of accuracy in predicting the future. Here they are:

Understand the natal chart. This is the first step in any reading. Never assume that you can ignore the natal chart and just breeze forward toward predictions, even if the subject of the reading insists he or she is interested only in what's coming in the future. Every horoscope is a blueprint of the life being lived and it provides the framework for the events that can and will occur in that life. The natal chart will show you the issues and goals the person is working on in this lifetime. Why is it so important to uncover these deep issues? Because nothing will happen that is not within the framework of the Karma of that lifetime. The whole purpose of life is evolution and thus each event is a nudge toward personal/Karmic growth. Everything that happens to you in this lifetime will relate to this purpose and there will be in your horoscope the framework that allows each particular event to occur. Thus the same energy pattern can produce a different event for different people.

I know of an astrologer who was desperate for love and who kept asking other astrologers for advice. He could have a spectacular love transit, one in which someone else would find true love and walk off into the sunset arm in arm with the perfect soulmate. Did that happen to him? Nope! The most he got from the most enormous love transit was a single date. That was because his horoscope was not about true love or coupling. He had other fish to fry. That's why you need to know what the horoscope promises before you attempt to predict the future, because if there is no promise, there will be no event, at least no event of magnitude.

Scale down your expectations. There are two huge events in any life: birth and death. There are a few large events in most lives: falling in love, marrying, having children, getting a job, getting some sort of award or promotion, leaving a job, losing a loved one, relocating. All of these events can happen more than once, but all in all, they are few in number. Then there is the rest of life — the day to day, humdrum events that keep life moving but really don't mean much in the great scheme of things. In fact, for all of us, most days are pretty similar — nothing happens. So please remember when you're going to predict something that life is filled with what the I-Ching calls the preponderance of the small. Small things happen.

I always remember back to a workshop I attended years ago in which we were discussing asteroids and their function in astrology. A woman in the group was having a transit by the asteroid that ruled the military and we knew she was job hunting. Everyone in the group was conjecturing about what might occur and their guesses were rather grand — she might join the army or the police and on and on. I, half in jest, piped up and suggested she get a job as a school crossing guard. The group started to smile until the woman spoke up and confessed that she had gone for an interview for precisely that job. The workshop leader declared I must be psychic, but in fact all I was doing was decoding the symbol into a small, reasonable potential event.

So don't look at a transit and predict death, dismemberment or the end of civilization as the client knows it, even though of course these things are possible. Look first for the smaller, more likely type of event because there are so many more of them in life. A person could be having a Saturn opposition to his Mars, and you could predict broken bones, but it makes more sense to predict car trouble since cars break more often than bones in anyone's life.

Yes, there will be big events in any one life, but most transits will not produce big events. You will need a cluster of transits or some sort of planetary configuration to produce a big event. Most big events occur within a long lasting planetary configuration. If one of the slow moving planets transits a house or a configuration in your chart, that sets up the situation. It's just like a play wherein the scene is set and an event is about to propel the characters into action. Look first at what scene is being set and then look for a hit from one of the faster moving planets to trigger some action. For example, Jupiter could move into your fifth house of children and romance, but not until Venus comes along to trigger your Mars do you begin the new romance. And once again, there would have to be the promise within the natal for a romance of magnitude for you to predict such an event. Otherwise that same transit could produce creativity, activity with children or some other manifestation of the same energy.

It can be very frustrating for a client to be told that something spectacular is going to happen and then when nothing much occurs, he or she feels a big letdown, as though there is some personal flaw at work preventing the good from coming forth. Likewise it can be equally stressful to worry a client with potential disaster when nothing more than car trouble is coming. Life is a process of tiny movement, and most of the time we're just floating forward, not scaling daily triumphs or gasping for survival from huge disaster.

Energy doesn't always produce events. I know some astrologers who make a slew of predictions, and they assume that every energy pattern will result in something happening. Well how exhausting! The simple truth is that sometimes nothing at all happens, sometimes there is personal growth but no event, and sometimes there is an event. Once again we have to return to the natal chart. If the chart indicates a person who needs a lot of activity, then there will be more events. For example, say the chart has a grand cross (four planets spaced in a cross, with each one 90 degrees apart from the next). That is a high energy configuration. People with that sort of configuration tend to attract people and situations that are challenging, complicated and energy which basically tosses them about rather chaotically. Thus if you read for such a person, you can assume there will be more events than in a horoscope with fewer or milder planetary contacts. Likewise if a person has a lot of Mars in a horoscope — many aspects from Mars to the other planets or angles of the chart — that person will have more events because that is an action-oriented person, probably someone who acts first and thinks later.

The level of evolution of the person is another indicator of events. A more evolved spirit will participate in the energy as it passes, and will get an insight or a great realization that spurs personal growth. Thus no event is needed. It's important to know what sort of person you are if the predictions are for yourself or who the client is, because then you can determine just how much of an energy surge is necessary to produce an event.

Understand Astronomy. An astrologer once read for me and she predicted a period in which I would be happy, happy, happy. On what was this based? The fact that there were many Venus transits then and few hits from the other planets. What really happened during that period? Nothing out of the ordinary. There are slow moving planets and fast moving planets, and the closer to the Sun a planet sits, the faster it will move. The Moon is the fastest of all, thus in any single day, you will have some lunar aspects. In any month you will have Mercury and Venus aspects. The rest is up for grabs, depending on what's actually happening in the sky and your own horoscope. So if there's a period in which you have few aspects from the planets Mars through Pluto, you will still have Venus aspects. Does that mean you will be wallowing in love and bonbons? Only if you're so inclined anyway. It just means it's normal life flowing by and that you're not being challenged too much by the other planets.

Remember always that the magnitude of the transit will match the speed of the planet. There is no lunar transit that will produce a huge event. The Moon's transits are like your breath, a steady rhythm of life flowing in and out but nothing worth writing home about. A Mercury transit won't do much either. Yes, you might read more, take a bus, ride a bike, etc, but in the grander scheme of things, who really cares? This too is just life flowing along. Venus transits are nice and sometimes a Venus transit can trigger a bigger event, assuming there is a planetary configuration already in place, or that you have a lot of romance stuff already in your horoscope. In the latter case, it means you're a person for whom any excuse for romance and pleasure is worth taking, and in that case I take my hat off to you!

Predict the future, don't create it. There is a huge responsibility that comes with being a reader. The client may too easily be inclined to give his or her power to you or to assume you have great powers that he or she lacks, so be sure to live up to that burden of trust. Never say that something definitely will happen unless it's a relatively small event and there are many indications that it will. It is better to sound a little hesitant, even when you're sure than to sound all-knowing. Even if you're absolutely certain a romance will ultimately flounder, say that no you don't *think* this is the person the client is meant to be with. That way the person still can pursue the relationship until it's ready to end of its own natural causes. The more definite you sound when making a prediction, the more energy goes toward that particular course of action, and if the client believes in you enough, he or she might opt just to make happen what you see happening. That is not in anyone's best interest.

A reading can change the course of the future, even when

you're giving your pronouncements humbly and meekly, as they should be given. By having a new point of view and a new piece of information, the client can opt to move forward toward a different course of action. This change can either create the future you've predicted or prevent it. Obviously this can be either good or bad. If, for example, a person is involved in a negative situation, like a relationship with a married partner, then being encouraged to let go can give him or her the courage to stop doing something that ultimately will lead to unhappiness. But in most life situations, it's not all that black and white, so it's best to offer guidance gently in order to inform without forcing the client to adhere to your own point of view and values rather than his or her own.

Allow for different possibilities. Life is wonderfully complex and there is a great variety of situations that can occur for all of us, so it's important always to remember that nothing is written in stone. There is no single energy pattern that will always produce a specific event. Likewise, the same transit can produce different events for different people. So when making a prediction, take into account all the possibilities and offer the client some variety as to what can be coming.

Remember first to note the natal because that will show you what's possible. Then keep in mind the larger energy patterns contacting that chart in the current time frame. That will show you the general situation surrounding the person in question. Then when you've honed in on the specific hit that will produce an event, you know what date to expect something to happen. Only then do you have the chance to offer your opinion as to what may occur. That is the point at which you can suggest some of the various possibilities. For example, you could look in the pantry and see butter, eggs, milk, flour and sugar and could predict the client will make a cake. When instead he or she makes popovers, your prediction is wrong. If you had predicted baking of some sort and had said maybe a cake, maybe pancakes or something else made with a batter, you'd be correct and a predictive marvel.

Decoding symbols is very rewarding because it can be as creative as writing a movie. You're seeing what the character (the client) might do and what might happen to him or her and there are many possibilities. If the person has a career type chart and you see a Uranus opposition to a ninth-house Mars, you might predict an earthquake, being electrocuted, a stroke, a violent attack. Obviously nobody wants to hear any of these possibilities and hopefully and most likely, they won't occur. Instead there could be a sudden business trip, computer problems or the need to contact distant/unreliable associates. Those are easier choices to confront and events more likely to occur.

In another example, if the same Mars-Uranus opposition occurred in a chart focused on relationship interactions, you'd be more likely to predict a quarrel with someone over ideals, travel plans gone awry, or the need to assert oneself in the face of personal opposition.

Always you'd be noting what is possible in that particular life before making a suggestion as to what might be happening now.

Avoid superstition and labels. It's rarely helpful to label an energy pattern and the resulting situation as good or bad. People live in terror of the Saturn return because of all the bad press that transit has received. There are people out there who know no astrology at all, yet they have heard of Mercury retrograde and blame on it everything from PMS to male pattern baldness. A person can go through a difficult period, and certainly that is something we all must endure at one time or another, but it's much easier to face difficulty with grace when your astrologer puts a positive spin on it. For example, if Pluto is about to square someone's Moon, that can be difficult, but there's no need for you to cluck worriedly and say you have sympathy for all the client is about to endure. No point in creating misery! Instead you can let the client know that there will be challenges and then explain the true purpose of such a transit, namely letting go of outworn patterns from the past in order to move on to a happier emotional period. Yes, someone may die during this period, but no you shouldn't mention it because it's more likely that nobody will die.

It's very helpful to take a broad view of life and of the future. Improvements come after challenges, and by focusing on the positive period that is the outgrowth of the difficult, the client has the light at the end of the tunnel and a sense of hope for tomorrow. In very difficult situations, that can be enough to pull someone through a disaster with courage and hope.

I'm not suggesting that you be nothing more than a Pollyanna. You can do as much damage by saying that you see only good things when in fact difficulties are about to occur as you can by focusing on disaster without mitigating it with hope. Honesty is the most important thing you can give in any reading, because after all, being accurate is important. Nobody appreciates hearing a love affair will work out splendidly when he or she ends up being dumped a week later. It discredits your reading and causes the client more rather than less pain. In the case of the Moon-Pluto transit, if the client confides that a family member is at the end of a terminal illness, then the more extreme manifestation of this energy is possible and you will need to acknowledge the possibility in order to help the client cope with the inevitable.

So the point is to find a way to express the truth in a way that is acceptable and leads to good choices, hope for the future and greater insight into the life at hand. It's important always to remember that every event, whether pleasant or unpleasant, has its purpose and each thing we do makes a difference in our lives. Focus on that aspect of what's coming and you will never have to label anything as good or bad.

Review the past. It's tempting to want to be the all-knowing seer when doing a reading, and of course you expect to be the one giving information, but remember that a good reader will ask some questions too. The best way to know what will happen in the future is to examine the events of the past. Often a client will come for a reading in the middle of a big transit. There could be an outer planet stationing on a natal planet or angle and some intermittent transits. A station is when a planet is moving forward, stops, goes retrograde (the illusion of moving backwards) and then moves forward again. Thus the same planet can hit the same point three times. This happens with all the planets and it happens every year, though not at every degree. Thus you can see what the station is and you know what the energy is all about and you can easily describe the potential situation. For example, if Neptune has stationed on Mars, you might expect some loss of vitality, some anemia, issues with medications or more music and dancing. And of course the energy pattern will be further complicated by other planets aspecting natal Mars and the houses involved.

After describing this general energy to the client, you will want to stop and ask him or her what happened the first time the station hit, noting the date and other aspects at the time. Then you can hear what the specific event was, and you can be much more precise in determining what will happen during the other two hits, plus you can give the exact date.

There will always be challenges in any life and certain energy hits will produce important events. As you get to know the client, you see precisely how the energy affects him or her. Likewise, this will allow you to make accurate predictions for yourself because nobody knows better than you do what happened when. All that's left is for you to note what energy was at play in the sky and then you can see when next that energy will occur. If you know that every time Mars crosses your Moon, you fight with your mother, overeat and end up in bed with a stomachache, you can take steps to avoid this pattern the next time Mars hits your Moon.

Allow for birth time inaccuracies. It's very difficult to get a precise birth time unless there is an astrology enthusiast in the family and the parents-to-be note the exact time the newborn draws the first breath. People often ask their mothers what time they were born, but mothers are rarely watching the clock while giving birth and years have passed between the happy event and the adult child seeking a horoscope reading. The planets will be accurate within a day, although the Moon can be off when the birth time is unclear. But the framework of any horoscope will change dramatically when the birth time changes. A difference of only two hours will put a different sign on the Ascendant, and sometimes it can be just a few minutes.

One good thing to do is to cultivate your own sensitivities to the buzz, the vibration, so if you meet someone whose birth time indicates Capricorn rising and you feel a Sagittarian vibration, you can say that no, perhaps this person was born a bit earlier. If only a few degrees are involved, that's quite possible anyway because most birth times are listed as later than the actual first breath.

What does this likely inaccuracy mean? It means that planets will move into houses a bit earlier than expected. For example, a client told me she was considering leaving her husband and felt quite driven to do so. I noted that Uranus was about to move into her seventh house of marriage, but based on what she described I had to conclude that her birth time was actually a bit earlier and that Uranus was already there or at least hovering on the descendent rather than merely preparing to move in a few months.

It's necessary to realize when giving dates based on transits through houses as opposed to transits to planets that the time frame will be off a bit, so say from June or July through next September or October or whatever applies, leaving a margin for error. Doing so doesn't mean you're being imprecise or fudging to cover your butt but rather that you're being more careful and allowing for a reasonable margin of error.

There is only one essence to anything. This is the most important thing to realize when making predictions. I know an astrologer who likes to use every astrological tool she can, not because she's seeking greater accuracy, but because she thinks different information will come from each. Her view is that the transits will give one picture, the progressions another set of events and the solar return other information. Does this make any sense at all? Of course not.

You are living one and only one life and are working toward certain specific Karmic goals. Any period of time has at its core certain challenges and certain growth patterns and the events in your life are geared to help you grow. Just as when you were in school, there was a course of study, tests along the way, and a sense of completion and moving forward to the next step when you completed the class. Your life is just like that.

In making predictions for the future, it helps to keep digging until you unearth what the current period of time is all about. There will be a life lesson to learn and the events you predict will be there to produce that specific life lesson. Every predictive tool will point to the same life lesson and the events will match.

The great thing about astrology is that it is a system of encodement for all the energy that is, and like in one of those oriental rugs featuring repeat patterns called arabesques, the same information is repeated again and again. A good reader would be able to look at nothing more than the transits and see just what sort of period you are in and what it's all about. And if that reader looks at your progressions, the same information will be revealed. Likewise will your solar return reveal the year's emphasis, and that emphasis will be echoed in the transits.

It's all just a matter of knowing what you're decoding and making sense of the horoscope and the life that is in front of you. It's a challenge but it's very exciting to be able to see a life unfolding through predictive astrology. It's rather like watching one of those time-lapse films of a flower opening.

Part Three: The Predictive Tools of Astrology

We've discussed all the essentials to consider before contemplating the process of astrological predictions. Now that we understand the philosophy of making predictions that work accurately, let's examine an actual chart and use some of the predictive tools of astrology.

There are many predictive tools that different astrologers use, but I have found that what works for me is to concentrate first on the natal chart in order to unravel its promise. Then I use a solar return (a chart erected for the moment when the Sun returns in the sky to the exact location it was in at the moment of your birth). A solar return describes the year from your current birthday to your next birthday. There is some debate about whether to use a classic solar return or one that is precession corrected.

Because the earth tilts on its axis, and because that tilt changes slightly over the millennia, the planets are actually in different locations; a precession corrected chart will compensate for this astronomical change. I spent some time studying my own chart and the two different solar returns and have concluded that the classic is most accurate from an emotional, personal growth point of view. However I did see merits in the precession corrected solar return, and because there were merits in both, it led me to conclude that the most important thing about a solar return is the aspects among the planets for the year. That is the same in both charts and will give a sense of the year's energy.

For example, many people mentioned to me that the year 2000 had been one of the worst years of their life. I thought this was a fascinating observation and it was worth considering why so many people reported 2000 as not just a terrible year, but one of the worst ever. There was a grand cross in the sky during part of 1999 and part of 2000, and that grand cross affected the solar return of many people, creating a complicated and annoying year filled with aggravation. That aspect formed the common denominator that made so many people report 2000 as a terrible year.

So when you look at a solar return, look to see how the planets interact, what sort of configuration if any is in the chart and how the general tone of the chart feels. Consider it sort of a natal chart for the coming twelve months. That will be more important than the house in which the Sun and other planets fall. I always run at least three solar returns for any reading. I want to see the previous year, so I can ask the client how it went, the current year for making predictions and at least one future year so I can see the overall direction in which that life is heading. I'm always interested in large swaths of time because that's the way really to see the life unfolding.

An interesting sidebar regarding solar returns is that there are patterns within them. The Sun will appear in the cardinal houses (ten, seven , four and one, going in that direction) for a number of years, approximately eight or so, and then will move into the cadent house (eight, five, two and eleven, also going in that clockwise direction) and then will move down to the remaining (nine, six, three and twelve). Basically that means that you have a period of seven or eight years to work on cardinal matters, and then you move to the next group. This is true from the moment of your birth and each following year. If you have a second house Sun, you will begin with the cadent houses, move to the succeedent and then the cardinal, and so on.

Of course if you move to a different time zone, this can change and it will flip you into a different cycle. The cardinal cycles are about beginnings and launching opportunities; the cadent ones are about persevering and moving forward in a controlled manner and the succeedent cycles are about mastery of what you've already begun and looking toward the future and the new beginnings when the next cardinal cycle begins.

The next thing I want to examine is the big transits and usually I do those first in sort of a cursory way. It's always good to see where the heavy planets (Jupiter through Pluto) are transiting and if anything big is changing houses soon as well as if any heavy planet will be forming a major aspect to a natal planet. That information will also give you the key as to the tone of the coming year and the themes being worked on.

Many astrologers love progressed charts. The classic progressed chart is called a day for a year, and basically that means that you can look in the ephemeris for your birthdate and then move down one day to see how your second year will unfold, and move down two days and see your third year and so on. Likewise do the degrees on Ascendant, Midheaven and house cusps advance.

A progressed chart is interesting to examine but its information is most useful when viewed over an entire lifetime. When I was first studying astrology and was more obsessive than I am now, I ran a bunch of progressed charts, one for every five years or so. Then in a concentric wheel, I surrounded the progressed chart with my natal chart. What I observed was quite interesting.

If you can imagine the chart as sort of a moving wheel, you can envision it clicking forward. The house cusps will move forward in a counter clockwise motion, and as they do, they will hit the natal planets, and then the natal planets will seem to be rotating clockwise.

This will show the process of the life unfolding.

For example, say you have a chart with Neptune in the eighth house. Eventually the angles of your progressed chart will move in such a way that the Neptune energies will spill down into your seventh house. That will last a long, long time and it means that your marriage years will be affected by Neptune, even though it didn't appear natally in your seventh house. For a person with a chart with relationship issues (for example a baby boomer with Pluto in the seventh and Neptune in the eighth, this will mean that the power struggle issues defined by Pluto in the seventh will be confronted through Neptune interactions with a weak, drunk, or unavailable partner.) Eventually the Neptune can progress down to the sixth house and by then that person should have worked through the life lessons described by the natal Pluto in the seventh. Of course, he or she by then would be perhaps fifty years old.

That's the point with progressions—they show the unfolding of the life in a very slow way, because after all life does unfold slowly. Most readings don't take into account the entire lifetime of the client because it's simply impractical to seek information over a timeframe so huge. Both the astrologer and the client would be exhausted. It's worthwhile to look at a progression, but if you're really paying attention, you will get the information you need from the solar return and the transits and will have enough insight to cover the relevant period the client is dealing with, whether one year or several. To cover decades is just too much.

You can look at the aspects of the progressed planet to the natal because that will provide some information about energy hitting and opportunities that will be presented to the client. That information should also be echoed in the transits, however.

Finally it's nice to look at the transits month by month. You will first want to see what major configurations hook into transits by large planets. Clusters of energy will always be where the events occur, so those are the most important things to note. And then there are the small transits, the single hits of individual planets that could lead to some predictions on the level of day to day. With something simple, like Mars conjoining Venus, you can have some fun predicting sex on a certain date and then enjoy having the client come back to you and say, well hey guess what, I *did* have sex that day. That's always lots of fun for me!

Now let's look at an actual chart and see how these techniques work. I have many clients who've been with me for years, and that's a great thing, not just for the validation of knowing I'm doing a good job, but because I get to find out how the energies have actually

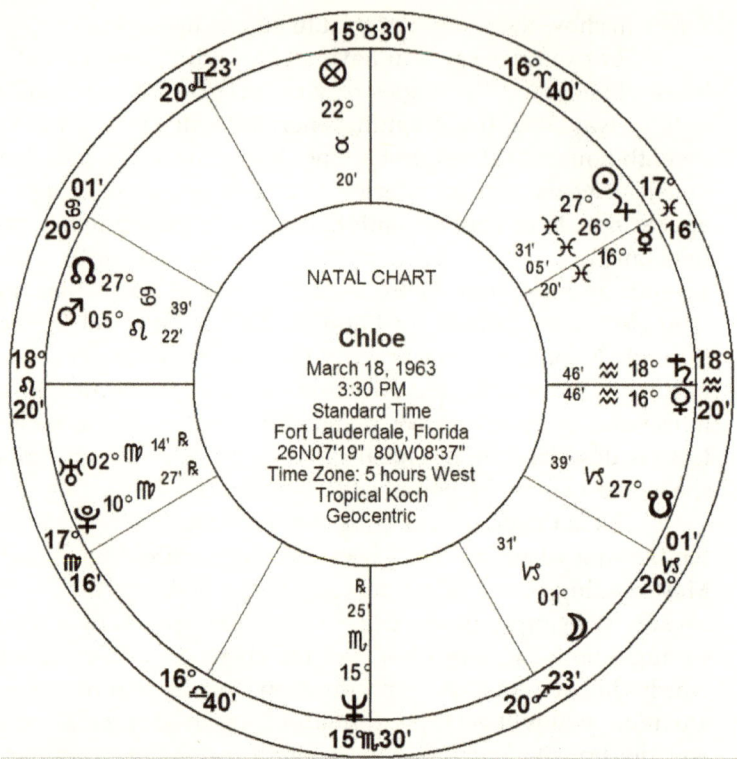

played out and whether what I saw came to pass.

"Chloe" is a medical professional who has been divorced once but has currently been married for 17 years. She is a Pisces with Moon in Capricorn and Leo rising. Pisces are always sensitive and that is enhanced by an eighth house Sun, twelfth house Mars and Neptune at the IC. With Sun conjunct Jupiter, trined out of sign by Mars, and with Uranus in the first house, she is also assertive, independent and positive. It's always important to note planets in the first house because that always represents energy that must be learned in this lifetime. It's energy with which the person had trouble or couldn't quite assimilate, so in this lifetime, they're going to have to deal with that energy in a very immediate way. Thus first house planets provide one clue to the Karma at work. With Pluto and Uranus in the first house, Chloe feels that other people can exert power over her (Pluto) but that she needs to rebel and go on her own path (Uranus). It's a matter of defining what she wants versus what other people demand of her.

Moon in Capricorn is generally practical, conservative, down to earth and there is always some emphasis on money. It is lightened a bit by the fifth house placement, and Chloe does love her children but she often complains about the money they cost her. This, of course, is somewhat of a universal complaint, but still in her life it's relevant. And the Moon is trine Uranus, another aspect of space in relationships and limits on intimacy. She has Venus in Aquarius, an independent, not very romantic placement, and it's conjunct Saturn, indicating a need to balance what she gives with what she gets. Generally speaking, Venus-Saturn people need safety, control and financial security in love. With this conjunction straddling her ascendant-descendent axis, Chloe values stability in marriage and takes commitment seriously, but she always wants to make sure what she puts into the marriage is returned equally by her mate.

Another yin indicator that is significant is the Neptune at the IC. Generally speaking this placement is difficult, because the person always feels that her needs are going unmet, no matter how much is given to her. And because that Neptune also squares her Venus-Saturn, there is the sense that her ideals will have a hard time being confirmed by reality. She wants a level of devotion that may be impossible to achieve. Saturn-Neptune squares are among the most difficult, in my opinion, as these are two energies that don't naturally work well together. There's always a need for balance when they occur and the Karmic task is to find a way to understand the nature of reality and what is genuinely possible on the earth plane. The person with this aspect will have come from a place of having gone overboard on dreams which couldn't materialize and now must learn to understand what dreams make sense here in this world.

Thus the real essence of this chart emerges rather quickly. Chloe is someone who must learn independence from other people and learn to take care of herself. She needs to balance what she gives with what she gets in return so that she doesn't feel that she's emotionally in the red. The way she will work through these issues is to attract people into her life who can never give her what she imagines she needs.

The Neptune will constantly make her feel she needs more and because of the Moon-Uranus, Venus-Saturn aspects, it's likely that she will prefer people who give her space. This is sort of a seesaw situation and everything of significance in her life will relate to this energy pattern. The ultimate resolution will be in her development of greater independence and her learning to take care of her own needs. She will need to become her own best friend before she can allow anyone else to take care of her.

This is a not uncommon Karmic pattern. Someone who was too in love with love or too giving in other lifetimes, for example a nurse who loved her patients so much that she eventually caught their illness as in the case of a healthy person who goes to a leper colony to heal others might come into future lives with this sort of chart. We are all meant to love, of course, but not to our ultimate destruction.

It is her current inclination always to put on the brakes when a relationship becomes too demanding or too unbalanced. And with the Moon in Capricorn Chloe is relentlessly upwardly mobile. She's always striving to improve her life situation.

Let's look for a moment at the recent past so we can be aware of how the important transits affected Chloe's life. At the tail end of her Saturn return, Chloe dealt with two separate issues. First she felt the marriage was floundering, and this is a common problem for people who marry young, and it's compounded by the natal seventh house position of Saturn. Generally at Saturn return, a person must look toward the future with adult eyes and plan for a tomorrow that will satisfy her adult nature, and if she's chosen badly, some of those choices will have to be released.

At this point in her life, Chloe opted to return to school for an advanced degree and that meant living apart from her husband for four years, seeing him only on weekends. That may be one reason why the marriage endured despite her perceived dissatisfaction. They were mostly apart during the difficult transit of Saturn through the seventh and eighth houses. The other reason is that she'd married a stable man who loved her and would probably love her forever, so even though she felt that she was not totally fulfilled in her marriage, she had something many people envy—a devoted mate who supported her choices, even at his own disadvantage.

By 1999, Chloe had completed school with flying colors and was then worried about obtaining a job in her field, something she did with great ease. At that time Saturn was at 4 Taurus, and it created a grand trine in her chart among her Uranus and her Moon, combining the first, fifth and ninth houses. Although that would not specifically be considered a career transit, the symbolism involved is that by concerted effort and study (Saturn in 9) she was able to follow her own path (Uranus) and build an improved and stable life (Moon). At the same time, Mars retrograded at 6-4 Scorpio, creating the last spoke of a kite configuration out through her third house. Any configuration is important but a kite is fairly dynamic and lucky and it's a good configuration to have when you've already worked toward a goal because it produces the resolution quickly and happily, particularly when it's Mars that is the focal point of the configuration. Everything just falls into place.

Chloe returned home, resumed the daily married life and worked hard to advance at her career, which she did, also with ease.

It was only her marriage and personal life that caused her problems, just as we would suspect because of the emotional dynamics in her natal. She kept working to improve her life while her husband was content to remain in the status quo. He did not see the need for any enhancements because he was happy as they were.

By 2000 Chloe was seriously considering a separation, but because she was worried about the possibility of having to pay alimony, she consulted a lawyer, who confirmed that yes that could be a possibility as she was now out earning her husband. It seemed to me that with Sun conjunct Jupiter in the eighth house, it would be unlikely that she would lose money because of a mate. It seemed quite telling to me that this was the thing about which she worried the most and it is very typical with her natal Moon and Venus-Saturn and the Neptune at the IC for her to fear a loss, particularly a financial one.

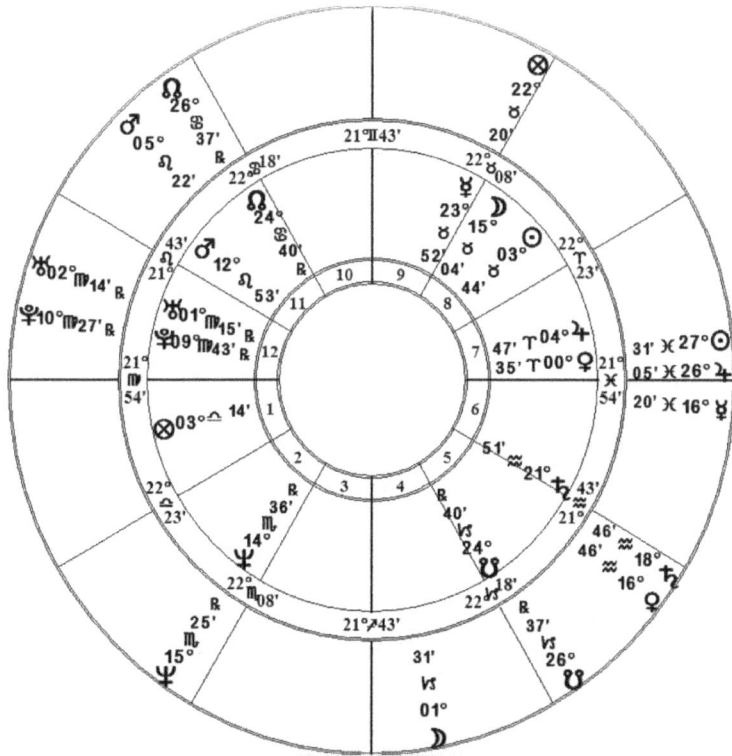

Inner chart: Progressed, outer Chloe Natal:

By the end of 2000 we discussed this situation seriously. Uranus had moved into her seventh house and she felt a sense of urgency to do something about the marriage. In addition, Saturn and Jupiter were now transiting her tenth house, and although most people would look at that and worry about what it might do to her career, I knew her career would be just fine. The significance of the tenth house is career and place out in the world, yes, but it's also about where you're going with your life as a whole, so in a way you can look at the tenth house and see that it pertains to your destiny in this lifetime and how well you're meeting the Karmic goals you set for yourself upon incarnating. Likewise the Saturn in ten also squared her natal seventh house Saturn, and that is always a period of review of the structures built into your life.

Now let's look briefly at her progressed chart and some solar returns before we look in more depth at the transits that will be hitting Chloe in upcoming months. As I mentioned above, I surround the progressed chart with the natal and observe when the angles of the progressed chart move, causing the natal planets to rotate clockwise into another house, that being the indicator of when the timeframe for resolution of whatever natal Karmic issues are involved. (What I'm saying here is that the house cusps are in the progressed chart and the planet movements I'm initially describing are of the natal planets.)

In Chloe's progressed chart for 2000, we see the following: Her natal Sun-Jupiter conjunction line up against the progressed seventh house, but as the progressed angles move forward, that Sun-Jupiter conjunction moves down into the sixth, probably by 2004. Also the Saturn-Venus conjunction, which had been lined up against the sixth house for many years had recently moved down into the fifth, probably around the time Chloe went off to school. This would also indicate some issues with her children, and she had plenty of those. It also indicates a desire on her part to be more fulfilled by love and to have a romance in her life that is solid, yet pleasurable. In essence, it reflects her desire to have the romantic marriage she believes is possible. This is also echoed by the square made by progressed Venus to her natal Moon. In other words, Chloe has prepared well and now wants to work hard, take her place in society and to live the good life, all admirable goals.

If the marriage doesn't work out, what is quite likely is that Chloe will search for that love for quite a while, until the Progressed angles move beyond natal Venus-Saturn again and the Venus-Saturn lies in the progressed fourth house. This process could last for another thirty years. Because at that time the Sun will have moved down toward the sixth, she could become a career woman who enjoys dating and her freedom. That's only one possible outcome, however.

Chloe's solar return for 2000 shows Jupiter and Saturn at the top of the chart, squared by Neptune and Uranus, indicating a need for her to work at making her life live up to the ideals she wants to create. There is a strong sense here of her being the architect of her life and having to confront her own choices. The Sun in the eighth house is an echo of the natal and it is inconjunct the Moon in the first house. 2000 is an emotional year. Venus and Mercury in the seventh house are pleasant and Uranus there echoes the transit of her natal. The 2000 chart has the same sign on the ascendant as the natal, and so that's significant. It's a touchstone year in which she can examine her life

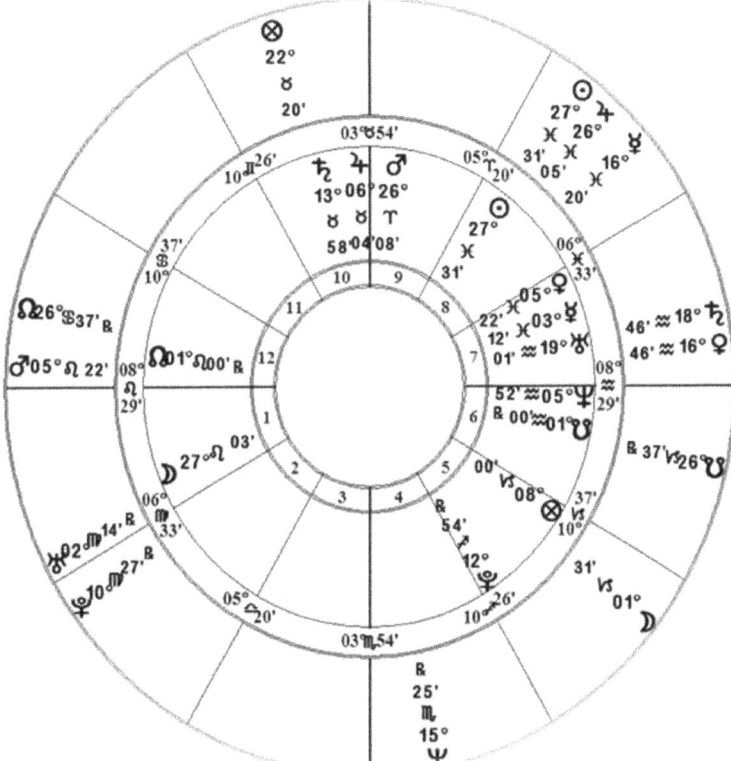

and her choices to see how she's doing.

Even if we don't consider so strongly the house positions of the planets in the solar, we do have to note the Saturn-Uranus square, which is the most important aspect in the chart, in my opinion, because it relates so strongly to current issues and natal issues. It calls for Chloe to build a stable life of which society approves (Saturn) without sacrificing her independent desires (Uranus). The question asked by this configuration is simple — will Chloe's marriage hold her back from achieving the life she knows she wants?

Her solar return for 2001 shows the Sun in the fifth house, sextile Saturn in the Seventh. I know an astrologer who says she's never seen an example of a solar with Saturn in the seventh in which the marriage didn't end. I have seen such examples, so I would never write off the marriage based on that alone. The Moon is in Capricorn, echoing her natal, and it squares Venus in the sixth, indicating pleasant work interactions and probably more socializing as well as some potential weight gain. Mars conjunct Pluto in the second could be some financial power struggles, but it's just as likely to be a desire for greater financial independence. Neptune and Uranus in the fourth could indicate a change of residence but can also be some emotional upheavals and the need to deal with childhood issues.

What we can conclude is that 2001 is a year of building toward

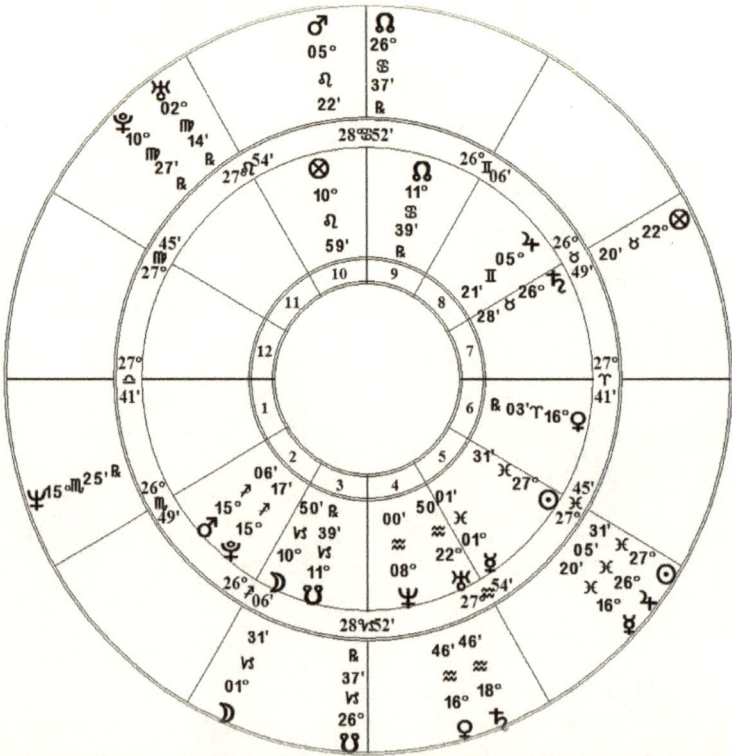

the future, in her own desired fashion and Chloe would work hard to create the life she wants to lead. Now let's look at the long-term transits and see what they show.

Uranus will be traveling through Chloe's seventh house until 2007-2008, so that indicates potential to seek excitement in relationships. This is not the time to look for a solid marriage, and I told her that should she decide to leave the marriage, it would be unlikely that, particularly at the beginning of this period, for her to find a solid new mate. If she wants to date and be free, there would certainly be that option.

Saturn moved into a square of first her Uranus then her natal Pluto by May through July, 2001. This indicates a period in which the challenges grow more severe. As Saturn contacts Uranus, there's a need for compromise. There certainly could be career changes, but the marriage remained an issue as well. During that same period, Jupiter squared her natal Sun-Jupiter and that could be a good thing in terms of her finances, despite the fact that squares bring challenges. She could threaten to quit her job and force her employer to give better compensation and benefits. In the case of a separation, she would press for what she wants financially, and she would have to give something to get more of what she wants, but all in all, I felt she would be all right.

We must factor into this equation the position of Mars, which was in Sagittarius, but going retrograde during this period from 29-15 degrees. Although it squared her Sun-Jupiter in May, it didn't complete the Jupiter configuration, and thus there was no T-square. If there had been, I would have felt the transit to be more strenuous and would expect more strident discussion over money and sex. Likewise if Mars had been part of the Saturn-Uranus square, it would have made a T-square out of Uranus and then I might have predicted more rebellious behavior and a more likely split, at least temporarily. That was not the case, however. Pluto, at 12-14 degrees during this period was enough out of orb to be a non-issue. Once again, if Pluto had been at 10, combining with transiting Saturn to make a T-square out through natal Uranus, that energy would have been the most explosive of all, probably forcing a huge change in Chloe's life.

While there are other transits we might have considered, the most compelling was the Uranus-Uranus opposition, hitting in 2003. This is the classic mid-life crisis transit. In May, 2003, it combined with the following energy. Mars transited Chloe's seventh house, and that can bring quarrels or your basic one-to-one combat. By June, 2003, Saturn opposed Chloe's Moon, often a time of separations, and certainly a time of health issues and dental problems, something that should always be mentioned in advance so the person can take care of her teeth before the transit hits. In June, both Mars and Uranus opposed natal Uranus. And Pluto sextiled natal Saturn, indicating a time of creative change and stamina.

Also during this period, Uranus stationed opposite natal Uranus and formed a configuration with the Moon, creating a transiting sextile with natal Moon. (A station is when a planet which had been moving forward, stops and then goes retrograde—seemingly in reverse. Of course this is an illusion based on our vantage point from the earth, as in fact planets always orbit in only a forward direction.) The configuration mentioned provided another surge for emotional freedom. By July, Jupiter moved into Chloe's first house, ultimately conjoining natal Uranus at the same time Mars opposed it, also creating an aspect that flowed out the natal Moon.

This is the sort of transit that is important because there is so much energy hitting and all of it is saying the same thing. There are confirmations all over the place. And if the marriage were to end, this is when it would happen. It would be smart to have a look at Chloe's husband's chart as well because it's nice to see a confirmation in the chart of both partners and very often that is the case.

In the previous section, I suggested making small predictions as well as large ones, and certainly the potential dissolution of a marriage is a large prediction. There are other prediction we could be making now, and in a reading, I would be making them at the same time. There is potential for job change or promotion, move to a new home, a business partnership, and of course issues with the children and I would certainly touch on all of these situations.

What we have left unresolved is whether the marriage will survive or not. I would not choose to tell Chloe that her marriage could end in 2003. First of all, in 1999 that possibility was still far away and that comes under the heading of creating the future rather than just predicting it. I did tell her there would be a period of challenges and after that period was over she would know where the marriage was going. I advised her to work on stabilizing the marriage so she could feel that she has done all she possibly can to make it last. And of course I reminded her that she was married to a man who loves her and always will.

As I look back on this situation today, I'm glad I made the choice I did. By encouraging Chloe to work on her marriage, she was able to take that advice, not fall prey to the ravaging Uranian energy, and the union survived. The smaller predictions I made did come true including the new job, new house, and issues with her kids.

The problem with her natal is that she will always feel she's not getting as much as she needs, so encouraging her to launch into a divorce during a period of turmoil would probably not increase her level of happiness. It may be that she at some point might choose to go her own way, and if so, with Uranus' long presence in her house of marriage, it will be difficult for her to find a partner who will be as stable as the one she now has, which could lead to some regrets. Ultimately she will need to work on her own life and to build in satisfaction in as many areas as possible in order to create greater happiness, and that of course is what I counseled.

The thing I admire about astrology is that it shows potential, not what will definitely happen, although many determined astrologers may disagree. I've seen too many cases where the energy indicated one thing and the person chose not to do it. Often it depends on how stubborn or neurotic the person is, and how determined to cling to the status quo. Of course, that does show up in the natal.

Astrology can absolutely show when something is going to happen — *if* it's going to happen, but there is always an element of free will, for good or bad. And in predicting the future it's always better to emphasize the choices the client can make so that the power of that person's life remains where it belongs — in his or her own hands.

Part Four: Outer Planets Transiting the Houses

Long ago my musically inclined high school friend told me about a very thrilling concert she'd attended. They were seated in the audience and on stage was a chair, some instruments, along with a scruffy looking guy, who was moving stuff about and arranging it all. Nobody took much notice of him or his activities, assuming he was just a porter of some sort, going about his menial tasks. In short order, the various items were arranged and to the great surprise of the members of the audience, the scruffy guy sat down and began to play. It was Bob Dylan! Apparently he had grown a beard and nobody recognized him.

As Astro folk, we always look toward upcoming transits and (often) worry about what they will bring. What happens when Saturn hits our Moon, or Uranus hits our Mars? Oh no, what's that gonna bring! That's pretty much the typical attitude of anyone in the know and expecting some sort of transit. But rarely do I hear people say, oh-oh, Neptune is about to move into my fourth house. Or Uranus just entered my seventh house. What I don't get is why not.

Just as during a play (or a Dylan concert) the mis-en-scene is arranged to host all the action, so does a planet's presence in a house create the atmosphere for what is to come. Slow moving planets like Pluto will spend so much time in a single house that it begins to feel like normal life. For example, if Pluto moves into your seventh house of partnership in college, for so many years it will be there shading all your deep personal relationships that to you it will feel normal to have power struggles as part of romance because you will have been too young to have had significant ties prior to its entrance. By the time all those years pass, your life will be very different and you won't know what to make of the change because your idea of norm will have been shaded by Pluto's presence. It will then take you a while to look at your love life from a non-Plutonian perspective.

Transiting planets don't always produce events as a result of entering a new house, but rather they create a sort of vibration, an energy that surrounds you that feels very different than the energy you were used to before. Of course the transiting planets will ultimately hit something and then there will be some events, but most of what happens as a result of a planet moving through a house is energy. For example, when Uranus, the planet of sudden change and high technology, moved into my fourth house of home, the building next door came under renovation and there was so much noise and disturbances, an annoying workman, dubbed by me the "Whistling

Monkey" because of his perpetual whistling and simian countenance. Years of this aggravation made me quite miserable, but unless you count various obscenities hurled back and forth through windows, no event in my life really can be listed. And then as Uranus was firmly entrenched in my fourth, the construction ended, and the Whistling Monkey moved on. Uranus' presence there marked a period of time that was consistent with its energy.

It's not that hard to comprehend. If you paint all your walls red, the energy in your home will reflect that color. There'll be more passion and more chaos. You'll be in a room and will feel differently (even if just below the surface) as a result of this red vibration. If the walls are a soothing green, the energy changes again. The same is true of the effects of transiting planets.

Even swiftly moving planets like the Sun and Venus create an effect during a transit of a house, one which isn't all that hard to note because it takes only a month or so for the energy to complete. You might decide now to do a little experiment, assuming you know your chart. Take a few months and track the presence of the Sun and Venus going through your houses. Just notice if you feel more energy connected to the affairs of that house while the Sun is there or more sweetness and light to go with Venus' presence. Certainly Mars, which can sometimes stick in a sign for months, will pep up the energy of any particular house.

In general, though, when we think of planets changing houses, we're really concentrating on the outer planets, Jupiter through Pluto. In a way, even Jupiter doesn't really qualify, since it's usually in a house no more than a year. Each planet will make a difference as it moves from house to house and this is worth noting. Let's just review the meanings of the planets and houses so we have a clearer idea of what sort of energy we're talking about.

Pluto, being the slowest moving planet, can visit a house for many years, and there's no question that transformations will take place. Pluto is about death and rebirth, so it provides a necessary breakdown before it can begin the rebuilding process. Most people look at this as a bad thing, because nobody likes the idea of something being broken down. Even looking at it from the perspective of transformation, which most of us admit is a good thing, it still doesn't seem like a fun prospect. In what area of your life would you like transformation? Most people will say none! Of course once you're on the other side of this energy looking back, you might concede that it was a difficult period, but you're glad to be in your current position. If you were renovating a big house, you'd go through a tear down phase and then a long rebuilding phase. There would be many problems, delays, and setbacks. But eventually the construction would be done and you'd be in your new residence and say how happy you were to have done it because of all the improvements involved. That's probably the best attitude you can have about Pluto transits. Shrug, grin, get through it and look toward the future when the rebirth occurs.

Neptune brings both a sense of confusion and idealism to any house it occupies. If you don't have many natal aspects from Neptune to your personal planets, this may genuinely feel like alien energy descending upon you. With a strong Neptunian vibration, there's a sense of not knowing what's coming, being unsure of your own beliefs, and confused about the people around you. If you think of Neptune as the fog, and yourself tooling along in the chic little sports car which is your life, well here comes Neptune rolling in while you're on the freeway in the fast lane, and suddenly you feel nervous because you can't see the road, the other cars, or even your exit. You basically have to use "the force" as they did in Star Wars to navigate and survive. Maybe that's why Neptune's alliance with the psychic world is so strong. It's the energy that allows us to close our eyes, tap into psychic forces and see even more clearly. Sometimes, though, it appears that we're seeing more clearly when in fact, we're basically hurling ourselves off a cliff. Neptune makes life seem different. Everything we once were sure of now seems much less certain. In a way, it can be a good thing, because this visionary energy opens us up to new possibilities by breaking down the foundations—and dogmas—to which we've long been clinging. Neptune wants to foster an ideal world, the life of our dreams, and although sometimes that means a crazy world, it also can be a better world, if we use its energy well. The key is to be open to new ideas but not be so insane that we substitute nutty ideas for good ones.

I admit it readily. Never mind being an astrologer and all, the art-science ruled by **Uranus**. This quirky, pain in the neck, is my least favorite transiting energy. It just brings so much wackiness into my reality, and since I have all the personal wackiness I need, what it brings usually comes from without, such as the Whistling Monkey, making me want to hold up my hands in frustration and yell, back Uranus, back! Uranus is all about change, and although I usually do like change, it's the sudden, unexpected, and downright irritating nature of Uranus that most irks me, perhaps because its energies are often expressed in my life via other people. We'd all pretty well agree that our own quirkiness is way more tolerable (read charming, adorable, appealing) than the thorn-in-the-side bad behavior of other people. The thing about Uranus is it likes to break down rigid perspectives. Am I rigid? It's hard for me to see how, considering how few rules and schedules I employ. There's no doubt, though, that a live and let live mentality fares better with Uranus at the helm. Flexibility really comes in handy during any sort of Uranus transits. When life gives you whistling monkeys, what do you do? Sing along? Maybe that's the wisest approach.

Most people hate **Saturn** transits, mainly because of all the rules, structures, and annoyances inflicted upon us. People lose things under this vibration—like their jobs—or that annoying spouse, who when he or she ups and departs suddenly seems more desirable. Saturn is all about building structure, and about working hard to create something viable. Most of us, being earth creatures, can understand this energy. We all know we must work, make a living, create a safe home with food on the table. It's not mysterious like Neptune, manipulative like Pluto, or kick-in-your-head quirky like Uranus. Good old Saturn is like that tough old bird, your gramps, grumpy sometimes, possessing skills nobody has any more, demanding you stick to values you think are outworn, and basically requiring you to be better than you want to be. Fun? Saturn isn't about fun. It's not the weekend, is it? Because Saturn pretty much makes sense, it's a bit easier to deal with than the more outer planets. You know you have to work harder, try harder, give whatever it is more of your all. You have to be all you can be, and that too makes sense because a Saturn transit lasts about as long as a tour with the military.

Jupiter, being the planet of expansion and sometimes good luck, is the bubble gum in this bouquet of thorns. Where Jupiter goes, opportunities follow. It provides the break you've been hoping for, a chance to make new and better things happen without feeling that at any moment you'll be placed in front of a firing squad. Jupiter's energy feels happily paternal. It's as though you're being supported by a loving parent who can see the good in you and who wants to encourage you to make the most of every opportunity, even if you're a little nervous about your abilities to do so. So much optimism comes with any Jupiter transit, and that's a good thing, because it allows you to feel that the universe is on your side.

The first house starts with your Ascendant, the point at which the world notices you. It's your energy, the buzz you send out into the universe, and it's also your physical presence, and that's why planets transiting through your first house can sometimes bring illness. It can also release illness. **Pluto** will attempt to transform your psyche as it moves through your first house, and if you're clinging to emotions with which you're not dealing, you could very well experience physical symptoms, such as something that feels like allergies, even though you're not allergic. Chances are that during this transit, Pluto will bring some people into your life—or people from the past will cross your path again, and whatever long-buried feelings you've been quashing will suddenly emerge, hopefully to be released, along with the allergies. Pluto can provide scary energy as well, and a transit through your first house can bring unsavory types into your sphere. This is not the time to roam through dangerous neighborhoods late at night. If you want to make changes to your physical appearance, Pluto might encourage this as well. Just don't get all Plutonian and start hanging out with a pierced tattoo artist who wants to turn your body into his personal canvas—not without thinking it through, because at some other Pluto transit you might end up employing a plastic surgeon to laser off all that ink.

Neptune moving through your first can be very confusing, or good for psychic ability. It can bring an interest in other worlds, other lives, or the spirit world all around us. It can also bring friends who want you to join a cult, bow to a guru, or move into a commune. Neptune is a strange vibration, for sure, and it always feels a little bewildering. Maybe you'll become a big movie fan at this time—or a movie star. The point with Neptune in your first is to understand your connection to the universe, sometimes by releasing your attachment to your own individuality. It's the perfect time to meditate because through that you gain insight into your own psyche.

Uranus! In your first! It's a trip! Notice all the exclamation points! That's how it feels! This is the itchy-feet transit for sure, and you will want to assert your individuality, even if what you're asserting is nothing even remotely similar to the person you've always assumed yourself to be. You want to change! Life is dull and you'll have no more of that—you want the thrills, chills, and excitement. Or maybe you're a regular, demure, normal person, a true individual but not a rebel. In that case someone odd and different could come into your life to make things much more exciting—in ways you never considered you wanted. Consider Uranus like one of those big buffet restaurants. There are a million choices, lots of items you never tasted before, and if you eat too much of it, you'll probably get sick.

Saturn in the first can be tiring—literally. This is the sort of energy that saps your vitality and can produce more colds than you're used to having. Usually, though, if this is the case, it's because you have things to consider which you refuse to think about and the cold is Saturn's way of focusing your mind on necessary things. It can be a very good time to take charge of your health, particularly if all those colds inspire you to head to the health food store and stock up on vitamins. Chances are life will feel more rigorous now, and you will be exerting yourself more. That's probably why you're so tired. It's a good time to consider how to implement new goals, how to build more of the structures you need in your life so you feel you're on the way to greater success and substance. Be serious. This is a serious period of time. Jupiter in your first is all about expansion, and yes your waistline is included. This is the transit where most people gain some weight. But you also feel happy, and you enjoy trying new things. Other people come into your life because you send out that joyous, yet responsible, kind, and caring vibe. It feels as though you can have fun and all the good things life has to offer at this time.

The second house is mainly about money, and **Pluto** usually breaks down your financial security when it enters. This is another one of those transits everyone hates, and I speak from experience. Pluto has been in my second for what seems like — and is — more than a decade. This is the time to cut back on what you need, because you will likely find your resources cut back too. If you have a job you hate, chances are that job could end, and although you'll rejoice about your freedom, your wallet will sing another tune. Creativity comes in handy during this transit, because you will have to live within your means and learn how to do so without being miserable all the time.

Speaking of creativity, having **Neptune** transit the second house can result in you earning money through creativity. Or cleverly spotted investments. Many people feel Neptune in a money house can guarantee losses, and yes that often is true, because someone will come along promising you great returns for your cash, and being greedy and not all that wily will definitely promote foolhardy choices. A different perspective can produce better results. Many very wealthy people who work in the money fields such as investing have natal second house Neptunes, and that tends to let them detach from the sense that this is important, this could be scary, and they toss those dice with a shrug and cash in. If you can do that, you can certainly make the most of Neptune moving through two. You might also decide to throw caution to the winds, quit that pencil pushing job and go for your dream of becoming a singer/actor/ jeweler. It might work, it might not. But it could also lead to the time of your life because you realize that what you value most probably isn't money.

Uranus in your second house will probably cost you money — it's the time when many of your gadgets go kaput and need replacing. If you work in a Uranian field such as computers (or astrology) it could be the time in which you begin making money in your profession instead of remaining a hobbyist. Money can come and go suddenly now, but try to handle it responsibly. Saturn in your second can also put a damper on your finances—at least at first. Usually with this transit people get fed up and decide to toe the line, to work harder and to build something. This can pay off by the second year of the transit, so hang in there. Obviously everyone loves having Jupiter in the second because it brings more money.

The third house seems far less frustrating, no matter what planet is transiting there. **Pluto**, having left your second house will probably feel like a blessing in the third house of your neighborhood, siblings, short term travel, and education, maybe until the building next door is being torn down, your entire neighborhood comes under gentrification, or is filled with some unsavory elements. Siblings can go through changes at this time or you might quit school—or return to school. **Neptune** in the third can be nicely creative because it allows you to use untapped talents in communicating. You might also go exploring to the neighborhood psychic, or become a movie buff. Uranus in three will logically bring noisy or irritating neighbors, who might also be very interesting. This could be the time that big box electronics store invades your neighborhood, and its customers use up all your street parking. **Saturn** in three could inspire you to work to make your neighborhood better, to study harder, or to help a sibling in need. **Jupiter** will of course bring fun events, like block parties, more social activities, and fun communicating about pretty much everything.

The fourth is the house of home, mother, and deep emotional issues. Any planet entering it will have to cross the MC-IC axis, and that could bring changes not only to your living situation but to your career as well. Likewise could one or both parents—or your feelings about them—be affected. Obviously **Pluto** moving here can signal huge changes, whether residence or job, or even the loss of a parent. Termites could eat up your home, or plumbing problems could plague you. But you could take this opportunity to create the home you've always wanted, even if it takes a long time and much work. **Neptune** here feels odd—I'm having it right now—and my mother did die during this transit—and I often find her in my dreams, often living with me, which she never did. I'm always doing decorating projects, so that seems no different. I did replace my dishes and flatware, designing a new tablescape and if that's the worst that happens, ok with me. Neptune will bring you a need to deal with your feelings, maybe going all the way back to childhood, as will Pluto. And the thing about Neptune is you might not really put two and two together. You could feel lonely, abandoned, and unloved and think oh wow I'm having a terrible time lately, or worse that your feelings are real and you aren't loved, but look to Neptune as the answer to these feelings of needs not being met. At least being able to lay the blame on Neptune could cheer you up.

With **Uranus** in the fourth, expect unexpected upsets, although you might buy new electronics for your home if you're a gadget person. Maybe a video cam will bring long lost relatives into your home for a chat. And don't forget, the MC-IC axis—a job change could be indicated. **Saturn** in the fourth brings work—necessary repairs to your home, perhaps a caretaker position for a family member, and also possibly a new job. **Jupiter** in four is very nice because not only can it improve your home, it can bring a better job. If relations with family members aren't happy, this is the time to restore them.

The fifth house is playful and relates to creativity and romance. Here's where we express the happy, individual side of our nature, and where we produce our children. Thus a planet here can affect your love life, or change the way you have fun, but it can also change your life via the behavior of your kids. **Pluto** here can bring an attachment to dark, deep, mysterious, manipulative, or very sexy types. It can begin or end a romance. And it can certainly change the way you express yourself creatively. Kids in your life can reflect this energy as well. **Neptune** has a kind of affinity with the fifth house because it aims for the highest possible love, true love, in which the other person comes first, but so do you in his or her value system. The fifth is about pleasure, though, so Neptune here can bring too much boozing, drinking for the fun of it, or maybe movie going. Likewise it can bring substance problems with your kids.

Uranus in the fifth is no fun at all—I'm having it now. I thought hmm, maybe something exciting will happen in my love life, but instead my daughter had an early mid-life crisis and although I approve of her changing her life if that's what she needs to be happy, it makes me unhappy to feel I'm no longer part of it. Kids rebel during this transit. They may not need you any more. Or you might decide this is your time to live and go a little wild. And here I am at the computer? I should be going wild too! **Saturn** in five can end a romance which is going nowhere because it feels you should buckle down and get serious about love. Likewise it could require more discipline for your children. Creativity may feel dampened as you focus on technique more than inspiration. **Jupiter** can do no harm and in five makes life—and your children—more fun. Of course there can be too much of a good thing, so don't party your entire life away. Do a little work now too.

The sixth house relates to the everyday routines of work, and it's also about health, which makes sense if you overwork yourself and thus your health will suffer. It's also about pets. Obviously **Pluto** moving here can break down both your job and your health. You could leave a job because it creates too much stress or because your health warrants it. Or maybe you might retire at this time and become a geriatric jock, walking to stay fit. You could remain in a job but your company could come under new management and thus change your entire work routine. Hopefully no little pets will die during this time, but it's not impossible. **Neptune** here can bring some confusion to both career and health. Avoid taking too many meds now, particularly if the docs can't quite identify what's wrong with you. And those liquid diets are tempting now but maybe not such a good idea.

Uranus in the sixth can bring some upsets to your career, the sort of thing where a non-techno person is forced to use a computer. One would think it could affect blood pressure too. And if you need a change in your life, it could take away your job altogether. **Saturn** has, obviously, the reverse effect. You'll be working harder than ever, and though it's wearying to have nose to grindstone, it's also satisfying. It's also a good time to take better care of your health. **Jupiter** in six can be nice, better work atmosphere, more money, congenial colleagues, and maybe even a promotion, although that's more a tenth house matter.

The seventh house is all about partnerships, and although most people think of that as the marriage house, it also relates to people with whom you work in tandem, like business partners, even doctors and lawyers. It's the one-to-one house. Obviously during a **Pluto** transit, some partnerships can end. Or there can be power struggles within what was formerly a congenial relationship, and if so it means all that sweetness and light was covering up some frustrations below the surface. It's possibly a good time to consult a therapist, as long as the doc isn't some Svengali type. The point is to learn more about how you interact with other people. **Neptune** in the seventh brings a desire for true love, but it can also bring a need to heal and be the transforming angel of a mate who's a drunk or druggie, obviously a thankless task.

Uranus in the seventh can upset a partnership, mainly because life seems so dull you want to experiment and that could send you running into the arms of another person. Singletons could attract new and unusual partners, people who shake up your life and make it more exciting, or who are much older or younger than is age-appropriate. **Saturn** brings its usual desire for seriousness to the seventh and many marriages end on this transit—but only the ones which essentially were already over. You want to work at a viable partnership now, something that supports your life and makes you whole. **Jupiter** brings its usual blessings to the seventh and can bring a cuddly, nurturing mate who offers much good cheer and personal support, perhaps even also tons of money.

The eighth is the house of death, but it also relates to other people's assets, which is why difficult transits ending marriages during seventh house transits move into the eighth house and describe acrimonious distribution of marital assets. Sex is part of the eighth house too, and any planet here can rev up your sex life. Obviously **Pluto** in the eighth can bring incendiary sex as well as financial losses, assuming it brings no loss of life. We can't always take astrology literally, though. Death isn't always physical death, and rebirth isn't usually reincarnation. Sometimes we go through life events and emerged a changed person—this too is a Plutonian death and rebirth, but not a physical death. In other words, don't toss out your vitamins and cancel your subscriptions yet! Look to ways in which you can change parts of your psyche through this energy instead. **Neptune** in the eighth can bring financial upheavals too, perhaps a partner who contributes no assets, whose estate is confusing to distribute, or investment opportunities that turn out to be a very bad idea. Obviously not everyone who fell into that Madoff scheme had this transit, but something similar no doubt. I always think that people who die in their sleep are dealing with Neptune-eighth house connections. Assuming no horrific dream is occurring, it's not a bad way to go.

Uranus in the eighth can affect your finances too—perhaps you've been burdened by too much debt for too long and now you decide to declare bankruptcy and wipe it all away. Uranus makes you feel that the pressure is too much to take and you need a release. A quirky affair is another means of eighth house release. Death by Uranus can be sudden, also not too bad a way to go. Saturn in the eighth brings financial responsibilities, a need to take care of any financial mess you're in, perhaps by paying off longstanding debts. You may also have take care of a partner, whether physically or financially. **Saturn** and death seems difficult, perhaps because fear of letting go holds a person alive, even when there's a very difficult illness. Trust would be the answer, but that's the sort of lesson that takes time, a typical Saturn issue. Obviously **Jupiter** in the eighth is pretty nice because it can bring financial blessings, sometimes from a mate or any sort of inheritance. It's hard to picture a Jupiter death though we'd assume it to be a peaceful one.

The ninth is a pleasantly intellectual house that relates to philosophy, travel, and justice. You don't expect the storm und drang that goes with transits to the more emotional houses. Of course there could be some negative effects to a transit here—if you've done anything wrong. Martha Stewart went to jail with **Saturn** here—and as my chart has the same houses as hers, the long arm of the law reached out for me too—for jury duty. Most people won't have legal issues worse than mine, though, and ultimately it was only a day out of a two-plus year transit. **Pluto** in the ninth can bring debates about systems of belief, whether philosophical or religious, or I suppose even intellectual. You might decide to follow one of those gurus I always rail against. It's tempting to think someone else has all the answers. If you're an alien in another country, you might be expelled at this point. **Neptune** in the ninth can bring a nice spiritual focus in which you feel a sense of deeper truths without having to articulate them. You might travel to vastly distant place, on some sort of quest, and it could be the time of your life, assuming nobody stashes a packet of drugs in your luggage as they did in one of the Bridget Jones movies.

Uranus in the ninth brings new ideas and revolutionary thinkers to cross your path. You might connect online to ideas you'd never encounter in your normal home base. Or you could decide to up and relocate to a very distant place. Whatever happens, it will feel exciting and come as a surprise. **Saturn** in the ninth could send you back to school. Watch Community on TV? In that fun sitcom a lawyer is discovered to have gotten his law degree without a real college degree and is sent packing back to college. That probably doesn't happen in real life but if it does it's the perfect example of Saturn here. Forced relocation is another possibility. **Jupiter** really belongs in the ninth and can bring some mind-expanding times during its transit. You could study and be enthralled, travel and be fascinated, or connect with people who open your mind in new and wonderful ways.

The tenth is the house of career, your status in the outside world, and maybe that's why it relates to the father. In days of old, when people's status was a family thing that was inherited, it really did make sense. The son of an earl is an earl. Now the son of even an unemployed drunk can be anything, so it's less relevant but the tenth is still the house of career, status, and dad. Obviously **Pluto** here can bring big changes in career, status, and for your dad, as a friend experienced when his dad's business tanked, the family lost their home, and fell into poverty for years. He was struggling to build a career in a difficult field and it felt like rejection and closed doors were the norm. Not until age thirty-eight did Pluto move on, so now we'll see if he finds more success. He will have to realize that his career expectations, which have been in place basically since college, now need to be revamped to a more happy outlook. **Neptune** in ten can bring much confusion, including the desire to change to a more artistic career. Clearly that could present financial problems unless it all works out. Maybe the career would be to help other people and not care about income, and if so it could be rewarding even if not lucrative. Relocation is also possible, because remember that any planet entering the tenth crosses the MC/IC axis. What affects the tenth house can also affect the fourth and vice-versa. A child with this transit could see a parent depart, even if not through death.

Uranus in the tenth can bring a new emphasis on Uranian careers and can be a good transit for someone in computers, but for most people it brings job upsets. It can also bring new technical skills, new gadgets to learn, and an increased emphasis on online business activities. The thing about Uranus here is it can totally change your plans. You can be on track to do something and suddenly you think forget it, I'm dropping out of medical school to do something that defines me much better. **Saturn** in the tenth is similar to Saturn in the sixth—you buckle down and work harder. Sometimes you get a promotion, sometimes you lose the job, particularly if you're ill-suited for it. Either way, you learn that life is serious and you need to become more stable. **Jupiter** in the tenth brings opportunities which you will enjoy and people who offer loving support to your efforts.

The eleventh is a nice house that we think of as about friends, but it's also about goals and long-term hopes. It's a house where you feel comfortable and where your dreams are cultured—and coddled. Obviously a **Pluto** transit here can bring about changes you might not like. Some friendships will end, perhaps because below the surface you discover things about people that you don't really enjoy. Goals can change now too, not always because you lose interest. Perhaps you're on track toward something and your life changes—as in a child whose parent dies and funding is lost for a long college career. That doesn't really seem eleventh house though, but if the remaining parent was forced to move to less tony surroundings and the child was thrown in with a new group of friends, the goals could change through peer interaction. **Neptune** brings confusion both to goals and friendships. You might become close to people who are more spiritual or join a cult. You could fall in with an arty crowd and become more creative. You could discover your talents and decide to make expressing them your career goals for the future. New things come along and you embrace them without too much analysis.

Uranus in the eleventh doesn't seem as worrisome although it can certainly bring quirky people into your sphere. Maybe you will turn your life around and make completely different choices for the future, something your new buddies will approve of but your parents will decry. It will ultimately be a learning experience. **Saturn** in eleven can bring the sort of friends who need to lean on you, and you could find yourself in a caretaker position. You might also decide to buckle down and take life more seriously—always the goal of Saturn—and thus you will forge ahead toward a goal that reflects this new attitude. **Jupiter** in eleven brings happy goals, which even if they're beyond your reach ultimately end up being possible, and cheerful friends who enrich your life in many ways.

The twelfth house is deep psyche territory and to me it's the distant past too, feelings and people long buried. They say it's the house of hidden enemies, although most of us have few of those. Remember in Grey's Anatomy when Owen told Derek not to hire Teddy when everyone thought he was going to bat for her? That would be a case of hidden enemies, although he really wasn't her enemy, just confused about his feelings for her. **Pluto** in the twelfth can bring about many psychological insights. Stuff long buried can be affecting your feelings and your behavior and this is your chance to deal with it, although you might just let it simmer until Pluto crosses your Ascendant. Certainly if you do have hidden enemies, they could do some damage now. **Neptune** naturally belongs in the twelfth house and is excellent here for all sorts of psychic abilities. Want to channel your guides, see your past lives, and maybe hear and compose music? Neptune here can make it all possible.

Uranus in the twelfth can bring sudden insights, and even visions about gadgets, as it once did to me about how to hook up some electronic equipment. I got a very clear picture of all the wires. Of course that's the sort of thing I can always do anyway but it was pretty cool. People from the past can suddenly reappear in your life—maybe via Facebook or other online sites. **Saturn** in the twelfth makes you work on your past as you think about your life, your situation, and whatever choices you have made to produce the current reality. Then you have the chance to work at fixing it all when Saturn is in the first. **Jupiter** in twelfth can bring some happy dreams, and maybe a reconnect with someone you loved and lost as in the movie *Letters To Juliet*.

Transiting energy through houses is very interesting. Just as Bob Dylan moved his equipment around before beginning to play, the planet enters the house, causes some change in your life, then the concert begins. The concert is the years in which you have to opportunity to deal with the new circumstances and continue your life, even if it has been nudged in different directions.

The thing to remember about transiting planets is that in considering the future, although we often gravitate to the largest event that can possibly occur, life is rich and varied and there are so many events, and energies, all of which are much smaller than say birth and death, and that is the stuff that is what fills our life. Transiting planets will create many vibrations in your life, some of them lasting for decades, but most won't be as horrific as you suspect. Most will be small things like little sighs, tiny insights, and brief moments of understanding. It's those small things that ultimately form the foundation of your life, and the more you pay attention to this preponderance of the small, the fewer giant and life irritating events you will have to endure.

Part Five: Outer Planets Transiting Themselves

All astrology enthusiasts know to approach with trepidation—and respect—two of life's most serious transits. They are the Saturn return at approximately age 28 and the Uranus-Uranus opposition, which generally encourages the mid-life crisis by 43. After considering those bits of energy, we generally zone out a bit and drift into the future with fewer expectations of crisis. We all certainly know that the Saturn return appears again at about 56, but I've rarely heard people stress over that transit as much. Perhaps it's because transits that hit after 43 seem less daunting, less difficult to confront, and in general kinder. It may just be that my nature is generally cheerful and I'm always expecting something wonderful to happen, but hey I felt that way when I was young too, and despite the disasters that have befallen me, I keep looking for the silver lining.

A better way to look at the situation of aging is to say that perhaps because age also bestows wisdom, that even the most daunting planetary configuration unleashed upon us will cause less trauma in middle-age than in youth only because we have the life experience to sit back, relax and to handle it with aplomb. Maybe. Or perhaps we just don't expect all that much to happen to people beyond middle age. This may not be true, but it does seem to be the expectation. I'm a movie buff and I find more and more that movies are being made about kids—surely a sign of my approaching dotage. The people my age in the film are the parents, comfortably ensconced in whatever reality suits the plot and they play supporting roles to the twenty-something actors who carry the story. There just aren't that many stories about spunky sixty year olds, I guess.

But it seems to me that just as much happens in the middle of your life as happens at the start. It must, mustn't it—or what would be the point? Whereas in youth we have a multiplicity of events and so many beginnings, in the middle things are perking along, humming in the background, and perhaps instead of all those life-bending events, we have thoughts, feelings, impressions, and life wisdom generated through them. In other words, by the time you're 45, you shouldn't need to be whacked over the head with a baseball bat to make sense of your reality and to grow as a person. Age is no guarantee of wisdom, however, and I see many middle-aged people in disastrous life situations, and it seems to me it all comes down to whether you're paying attention or not. The more thought and introspection you apply to your own reality, the greater wisdom you will achieve, and thus there will be fewer life crises.

I took some time this week to make a list of the stressful transit that can befall a person after forty, and it was very interesting. No matter how long we live, or to what elevated age we sustain our life, there is always a boot coming from the universe to nudge us in different and hopefully better, happier directions. From birth to death, there will always be opportunities for growth, change and self-awareness and we can hear these clicks on our own time lines by noting the various planetary aspects. As each of the outer planets makes hard aspects to itself, that forms a checkpoint in your life. Pluto hitting your natal Pluto, Neptune hitting your natal Neptune, and so on will give you those larger than life nudges in the right direction.

First let's take a moment to consider the planetary energies and how they function in any chart. Then we can go decade by decade and look at what you can expect as you march into the future.

Saturn is the planet of Karma and earthly life lessons and here is where you get your report card. A Saturn transit helps you see how well you've been doing and what parts of your modus operandi need revision. Saturn provides the tune ups in your life and helps you make the most of your opportunities. Uranus is the planet of eccentricity, innovation and sudden change. When you've been clinging to a rut for far too long, Uranus will step in and generate the upheaval you need. Although you may feel its energy is disruptive, Uranus helps you move forward in your life and it gives you the courage to try new things. Neptune is the planet of spirituality, illusion and delusion, and it provides a kind of yearning for more as it transits your horoscope. Here is where your imagination gets free rein, where you dream of the best of all possible futures and where you envision what you might do if only.... With Neptune you are prodded to aim higher, try for something better and to create more magic in your life. Chasing after the magical rainbows that Neptune helps you envision doesn't always lead to capturing that pot of gold, but it does provide a rewarding feeling that life can be wonderful, if only you'd believe. Pluto, the planet of birth and death and extreme transformation, is always about change. It helps you release old energy, people and behavior patterns in your life. Hidden things emerge and must be dealt with thanks to Pluto's insistence. This is the energy that brings the many rebirths that occur in any lifetime.

Now, let's look at your life, decade by decade and see what to expect when.

Because my mother was a marvel at 87 (sadly she died at 93), I used her chart to look back and see just when those hits occurred in her long life. The exact year in question may be slightly different for you or for me, depending upon your own natal placements, retrogrades and so on. But these are the approximate ages at which these energy patterns will affect your life.

I always like to joke that the first Saturn return is like an astrological bar mitzvah. Not until you've passed this landmark are you truly an adult. The thirties are about building a suitable adult life. Just as the Saturn return provides a marking post between your life as a child, much of which was created by other people and the circumstances in which you lived, the thirties represent the life you're building for yourself, according to your own choices.

By the time you've reached the big Four-O, you have to face a terrible truth. You're not young any more. Not only are you an adult, but you're middle-aged. Your youth is over—or it should be over. One thing becomes increasingly clear—you can't go back to the womb—or the malt shop—or the football field—and ultimately you will die. At forty we all face our own mortality, and that is the cause of the mid-life crisis.

The first transit that hits in this decade is Neptune square Neptune. It hits somewhere around forty to forty-two. Just as the realizations you might have while dead drunk seem profound at the moment and ludicrous in afterthought, Neptune casts a hazy film over your mind to cloud your current reality just enough to nudge you to think in different ways. This is a time of yearning for magic and deeper truths, for starrier ideals and happier moments. You want the ideal now, and because the illusion of Neptune is prodding you to cast aside all logic, you may feel you have found it, just like one business mogul I know who ditched his marriage, his New York co-op and ran off to a commune in Denver at this time.

If we think back to the old days, forty was a ripe old age. Most people died in the old West at the fateful age of 28—the Saturn return. So if you made it to forty, it was time to cast your mind over your life and to seek some spiritual redemption, to find inner peace—and perhaps God, as you prepared for the end of your life. For those who dread the milestone that is forty, it puts life in perspective to remember back to those times, less than two centuries past, when forty was a time to prepare to meet your maker. If that doesn't make you feel young at forty, nothing will!

One thing this transit can do, is bring more spirituality and trust into your life and encourage you to apply that trust and hope to the future, and that would be a very good use of this energy. Say to yourself, whatever befalls me, I will be fine and there will always be a good and true place for me here in the universe. Try to find the good and the beauty in your daily life, and if there is too little of it, enrich your life by giving of yourself to other people.

The classic mid-life crisis transit is the Uranus-Uranus opposition, occurring at about 41. This is the one that breaks up marriages, ends careers, sends men to Corvette dealers and women to plastic surgeons. Clearly this is the transit in which we bemoan lost youth, confront death and try to run screaming back into the womb. Does it work? Ask all the newly single, balding studs with candy cane spines lined up at the chiropractor hoping to get a back crack after squeezing their paunches into all those teensy sports cars!

Although many people react to this energy by trying to experience the unlived fantasies of their youth, (think of the character played by the amazing Kevin Spacey in the riveting movie, *American Beauty*), the true purpose of this transit is to allow you time to reflect on yourself and your own choices. Have you built a life that allows your inner lights to shine? Have you chosen a lifestyle that brings happiness and radiance to your every day existence? Are you still interested in the future and flexible enough to allow it to happen? These are the questions you must ask now and if the answer is no, it will be time to break apart the structures in your life in order to find an existence that reflects who you truly are, deep inside.

The final big hit of the forties is the Saturn-Saturn opposition. This is either a time of reward or a call for rebuilding. If you've been working hard, profitably and happily at the lifestyle begun after the first Saturn return, then you will feel firmly entrenched in the good life. You will receive the respect of your peers and your superiors will reward you. But if things go badly now—you get fired or dumped from a relationship, it's a sign that you have made a choice that suits you badly and that it's in your best interest to look in other directions and to rebuild your life differently. Although most people regard such possibilities with gloom, and of course it's normal to feel badly if you've been dumped or fired, a good outlook would be one of joy because it means you've won a reprieve, been given another chance and this time you can find the happiness you deserve.

The forties provide us all with a chance to reflect on our life and with the assurance that it's not too late to begin again if we're not happy. It's a time for reflection, confrontation and enhanced confidence or change and renewal. Although at forty we know we're not young, most of us still feel and look young. By the time fifty hits, there are changes that are physical and mental and we begin to feel older. This isn't such a bad thing because it takes a lot of the pressure off. Somewhere during our forties, we get our crap together and stop worrying so much about peer approval; we confront our childhood and become true adults. But by fifty, people around us are younger. Your doctor may look like a kid, your children may inflict grandchildren on you, and those up and coming, determined underlings in your wake at work want something from you—your job. It means one and only one thing—you need different things than you did a short time ago. At this point you are truly in the middle and you realize there will very likely be fewer beginnings now—this is the time to continue, not to start afresh.

The first transit of the fifties is the Saturn square Saturn which hits at about 50. There is a sense of frailty—you know you're not as young as you used to be and you realize that if you haven't been health conscious before, you should certainly start now. This is when you start thinking about your future, about financial security, about eventual retirement and the things you want to do for yourself. The question you ask is whether or not the structures you've built into your life will sustain the life you will want to lead ten years from now. You look back over your life and decide if in your own eyes you're a success or a failure. You measure yourself against the image of what you hoped to become and wonder if there's still time enough left for you to get there if you haven't already done so. Time goes faster now and you realize that you'll be sixty in the blink of an eye. Despite these worries, you also realize how skilled you are and how much good experience is under your belt. No matter what the kids coming up now know that you never thought possible, their high tech knowledge is no substitute for your decades of experience. If you do need more skills or knowledge, this is the time to get it.

At 54 or so, Neptune trines Neptune, and although it's not a hard transit, it's worth considering since Neptune (and Pluto) move so slowly that a trine is significant. This is a good time for reflecting on your choices and the life you have lived. Maybe you haven't achieved all you thought you would in the material realm, but it's quite possible that with some honest reflection, you will see that you have grown so much in a spiritual, Karmic, emotional sense that you can look at your life and yourself and rejoice. You realize now that you're not King Tut and you can't take it with you materially, but what you've achieved in terms of life lessons will be on your spiritual resume eternally and your efforts to give love and make the world a better place make you a better person and a stronger spirit.

By 57 or so, your second Saturn return hits and it's time to reflect on the life you've lived so far. If you've worked for decades at a job that provided little more than financial sustenance, you will probably grab that gold watch and get the hell onto a golf course somewhere. But if you've been on a path that has rewarded you, it will feel wonderful to look back over all you've achieved and to think about where you want to go next. The reaction of other people to you and your life's work is meaningful. This can be your chance to accept awards or to mentor someone else. Or it can be a new beginning of a different phase of your life, one in which you head in different directions. You realize that life is short and you want to make the most of it in every way you can. You're not willing to linger in a meaningless status quo because you realize this is it and that you have to think about tomorrow.

Pluto squares Pluto at 58 and this, of course, is a call for new beginnings. The idea that life is short is very important in this transit as well as in the Saturn transit above. Conflicts always arise because of Pluto transits because we tend to bury the stuff we don't want to confront—who can blame us? Then Pluto comes along to unearth whatever prickly emotional issues we haven't wanted to face and that forces us to gain some emotional perspective and the much-dreaded life lessons that are unpleasant but so necessary are inflicted upon us. If you're ready to retire, you'll have to confront the death of your accustomed status quo and to find a way to build a new routine. Perhaps you have a mate who wants one sort of retirement while you prefer a different lifestyle. And maybe you will have to confront the fact that you've grown a bit detached from each other and some open combat will help you both learn who you are all over again.

The fifties are about reviewing your life, taking stock of where you stand and what you've accomplished, sort of like inspecting the balance in your checking account before going on a spending spree. This is where you look to see what sort of foundation you've built for yourself and how it will hold up for you in your old age. There's a distinct awareness of the need for security because there is a sense that you can't work forever and that someday you will be old. There's also a sense of hope for the future because as you approach the sixties, there's a feeling that soon there will be time for yourself, that you deserve some fun, some freedom and the ability to invest yourself in the joy of living and after many years of being a worker bee, that you should now have some peace and pleasure. The fifties are sort of a bridge between the difficult working world of your youth and the leisure retirement time of old age—sort of like a period in which you anticipate loosening your belt or removing a girdle.

At about 63, Uranus squares Uranus and this is a time of change and reorientation. Although one of the manifestations of this energy could be enforced retirement, another one is a joyous new beginning of the fun life you know you deserve. Certainly there will be changes now. Your life is moving forward, and it's up to you to choose in what direction. If you cling to the status quo of going to a job simply because you can envision no other activities in your daily routine, that enforced retirement is a possibility, simply because it's important for you to think about who you are and to allow your external life to become a reflection of your inner truths. Another feeling that goes along with this energy is the sense that you've worked all your life, dammit, and now is the time for you to do what you please, time to concentrate on yourself and your own interests, whatever they are. It's time to attempt that hobby you always wanted to try, to travel, to learn new things and meet new people. It's time for a second childhood, shared with your grandchildren.

A few years pass and Saturn squares Saturn and it's certainly a time in which you consider if you really want to be working. Perhaps you want to work at something different, more challenging or less stressful. Perhaps you discover that you've accomplished everything you set out to do when you first tried to conquer your world. Whatever you conclude, it's a time for revisions in your game plan, for endings and tidying up the strings of the life you lived before so you can live a less demanding life as a senior. Perhaps you want to scale down by selling a large residence and moving into a smaller one. This is another one of those gold watch transits, and it's up to you to create a future that is just as full as your past, only one that suits the person you are now rather than the person you were decades ago.

By about 69, Pluto trines Pluto and this is a time for creative change. If there are issues from your childhood, it's much easier to confront them now, because you have the wisdom of experience and the ability to look back over your life and recognize all your previous foibles and frailties—and yes, your successes and triumphs too. The things that used to bother you so much bother you less now because you're wiser and more mellow and more inclined to live and let live. If you're one of those crotchety old people, this could lead to some confrontations with youthful members of your family in which you try to get them to cut their hair, or whatever seems right to you. Chances are they won't want to follow your rules at all, and this is your chance to see that love is a better choice than being an enforcer of silly rules. Live and let live and see the good and truth in all things and you will be happy and well loved.

The sixties are a time of acceptance of yourself and of planning for a future of peace. Chances are you won't have fulfilled all the dreams you had as a child when you were planning your future. Unless you're a millionaire astronaut ballerina married to a movie star with your own line of sportswear and a profile by Barbara Walters, you've probably lived a smaller life than the one you imagined at eleven. But you've also lived a life filled with small moments of richness, of love and tenderness, of memories that make you weep and smile, details that as a child you could never have imagined. And more importantly than that, you've grown so much as a person that you can look back on that starry eyed child and smile in amusement. Small lives are the norm, but they can be very rich and very beautiful. By your sixties, you're in touch with the wealth of complexity and pleasure in your own.

Saturn opposes Saturn again at about 71. This is the sort of transit that leads to one of those five generations in the same family photos in the newspaper. You've lived a long time, watched people come and go and this is what you have to leave behind—a group of people who wear your face and share your expectations of life. It can also be a period in which you focus on health issues, on financial security for your family by examining your estate and on what you need in your old age. Perhaps you are widowed and don't want to live alone any more. Perhaps you're the life of the party at your retirement community. Whatever physical manifestation of this energy appears in your own life, it's a time of reflection and of looking back at all you experienced. It's fun to review those scrapbooks, to dust off the favorite knickknacks or trophies and to say, well hey, I was quite something, and to realize that whatever you were, you still are right now, deep inside.

By about 78 or so, Saturn trines Saturn and brings you the concerns of aging. Is your body strong enough and healthy enough for you to do all you want to do or do those aches and pains require a lot more rest than you expected. It can be hard to reach this age, because you watch friends and loved ones leave this world, but you realize that well, ok, life moves on, but I'm still here and that can be a rather triumphant feeling. Look to the young people around you now, because they need your advice, your wisdom and your willingness to give them time and attention and love. You are someone valuable and everyone will see this about you if you let them.

It's a real landmark to reach your eighties. It means that you've been around for most of a century and can look back over times far different than the current day. It also means you're made of good stock, are sturdy physically and have the sort of even temperament that lets things slide without ruffling your feathers too badly.

At 82, Neptune opposes Neptune again, and surely that is a time of religious and spiritual awareness. You spend time reviewing your life, thinking about the deep truths of your existence and what it all meant to you. It's also a time to grow closer to God and to spirit, if you're so inclined. It can also signify that you've grown a bit dotty as they used to say in the old days and that you can't remember things as well as you should. It seems to me that becoming a fanciful old person filled with memories that never happened and goofy ideas could be rather enjoyable or at least charmingly whimsical. It can also indicate an increased need for medical attention.

Also at about this time Uranus opposes Uranus and that is another period of rebellion, of breaking down structures and trying new things. If you've lived on your own all this time, you might opt to go live with a child, and at this age you could have a child who is by now widowed and in need of your company and emotional support. What you don't want to do is to be saddled with the cares of everyday life. You've grown old and now you want to do whatever you please, and that usually doesn't include doing chores. You like watching your television shows, finding amusement in the antics of the younger people around you and in thinking about life and how amazing it can be. If you're one of those rigid old people, you might learn that it's better to be a bit freer and less rule oriented and a much younger person could come into your life to point the way. High technology is a marvel now, and even if you can't fathom how anyone can work the new gadgets that have overrun life, it's fun to see them in action.

At about 85, your third Saturn return arrives and the people in your life throw a party for you. It's a great feat to have lived so long and everyone is proud of your stamina and derring do. Children frolic at your feet and can't imagine the million years that have passed since you were as small as they are. And you look over the people who are coming up behind you, struggling as you have struggled and you shake your head at the mystery that is life on this planet. Who would have thought you could make it so far or so long? To you it seems like a minute has passed since you went to your first dance, yet it also seems like forever since you first fell in love. Life is a whole panorama that lies before you and you have the right to be impressed with yourself and all you've experienced. You're a person with gusto and you deserve some praise.

There are always patterns all through life. There is time for visions and revisions, as the poet T.S. Eliot wrote in *The Lovesong of J. Alfred Prufrock*. While we're living it, life seems like an unbroken line, day after day, but really it's more like chapters in a book, with confrontations, upheavals and restructuring. That is the basic pattern of the transits of the outer planets. Life is our choice and as we live it there is always time to review, accept or change, abandon one course in favor of another and to begin again anew. That way we have the full opportunity to be the person we are, deep inside, to express the self that existed at the moment of our birth, the self continuously refined through life's adventures and to become the self we hoped to be when we chose to incarnate in the first place.

If you live beyond 85, you shouldn't have to worry about transits. Just take life one day at a time and enjoy it all, just like my great grandfather, a Maryland farmer whose goal was to make it to 100. He hit 99 somewhere in the 1960s and was a marvel for his day.

Planets' Orbits Around the Sun in Years				
	SATURN	URANUS	NEPTUNE	PLUTO
	29.44	83.8	163.83	248.18

Major Aspects in Order They Hit And Their Degrees		
Aspect	Abbreviation	Degrees
Conjunction	CONJ	0
Sextile	SXT	60
Square	SQ	90
Trine	TRI	120
Opposition	OP	180

Age and Planetary Event — When Planets Will Aspect Themselves

Approximate Age	SATURN	URANUS	NEPTUNE	PLUTO
5	SXT			
7-8	SQ			
10	TRI			
13-14		SXT		
16	OP			
20-21	TRI	SQ		
23	SQ			
25	SXT			
26-27		TRI		
27-28			SXT	
29-30	CONJ			SXT
34	SXT			
37	SQ			
40	TRI	OP		SQ
41-42			SQ	
45-46	OP			
50	TRI			
52-53	SQ			
53-54				TRI
54-55	SXT		TRI	
55-56		TRI		
58-59	CONJ			
62-63		SQ		
63-64	SXT			
66	SQ			
69	TRI			
70-71		SXT		
75	OP			
79-80	TRI			
81-83	SQ		OP	
84-86+	SXT	CONJ		OP
88	CONJ			

Chapter Seven:

Astrology and Spirituality

Astrology provides information that is strongly psychological, but it goes deeper than that and helps us see what life lessons we must learn in this incarnation. It can also point toward former lifetimes and the journeys we're completing.

Unlocking Karmic Patterns with Astrology

For many people, astrology is about predicting the future. Although I enjoy using it for that purpose, to me it's a much more interesting tool for psychological awareness. Each chart has within it an encodement about the purpose of that life, the lessons to be learned, and the objective for that lifetime. It's quite exciting to work through a horoscope and come to the clear realization of what that life is all about and what life lessons are indicated.

Some horoscopes are quite dramatic in that they show clearly what must be learned in the current lifetime. In fact, some horoscopes point toward a single purpose—one huge life lesson that will impinge, again and again on every little facet of that lifetime. Of course, this is not true of every horoscope. Some people will have charts that show objectives in that life and some life lessons, but no overwhelming Karmic indications. That would be a sign of greater evolution. The person has come in with certain objectives, but on a Karmic level has moved past the Achilles heel stage of having to learn to overcome certain intense flaws.

In those charts where life lessons are very strongly indicated, it's also possible to see the sort of past lives the person might have lived—to a greater or lesser degree. It's quite fascinating to extrapolate the life situations experienced based upon the life lessons to be learned.

We all love short cuts, and it would be wonderful if I could offer you a little recipe to use when looking at a chart with an eye toward unraveling the past lives involved. If we could say Saturn in certain houses or certain signs always means such and such, it would be quite useful. In fact, to some extent we can do that. We have a good idea what life lessons are involved with Saturn placements in each sign, and I've written about that several times in the past. But to know specifically what lifetimes are indicated by a singular placement, and the details involved, would be to simplify something that is intensely complicated. Unfortunately astrology—and life—doesn't work that way. Perhaps it's because I'm a Virgo, but I feel there's only one way to get at this information—to start at the beginning and to work through the chart in an orderly fashion. Only then do all its mysteries begin to be revealed.

The way to begin is the same as the way you begin looking at any chart. Stop first and give the chart a glance to see what you notice first, then move forward in an orderly way, looking at the Sun (identity) and its aspects and so on.

This first example is of a young woman in her late twenties. She works in a questionable profession, is constantly falling for guys and pursuing them in a much too hasty or unreasonable manner, yet she is quite intelligent, and has a sweet nature.

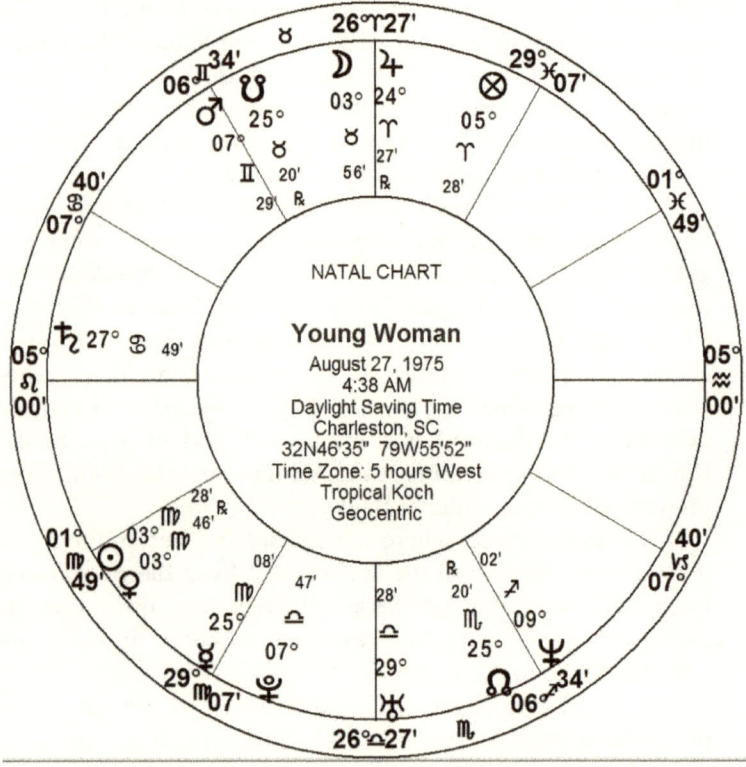

Upon first glance, it's interesting to note the number of angular planets. Saturn (Karma) very close to the Ascendant (image) is always very telling. Whenever you see this it's always an indication of someone who needs to learn responsibility, discipline, and steadiness in this lifetime. There is no more stabilizing influence in a chart than this one. Does it mean that the person is always solid as a rock? Not really, but rather that opportunities to work and to live up to responsibilities are always being presented. Someone with this aspect will seldom have to be unemployed.

Also on the angles are Jupiter (expansion) at the MC (life purpose), a very nice aspect for success. Generally this will indicate the opportunity to be given many breaks in life and the chance to begin new careers, to work at a level beyond which the person might be qualified. Also at the MC, and widely conjunct Jupiter is the Moon (emotions). Moon in the 10th is very interesting. Often it means that the person works in a domestic field—food service, supermarket, and so on. It can mean that the person is a wife, or if a man, that he marries someone who stays at home and takes care of him. It can also indicate that emotional contacts are made at work—the person marries someone met while on the job.

The house of the Moon is always very interesting because some are more emotional than others. For example, houses ten (career), two (money), and six (work) are much less emotional than other houses, and when any of the yin elements of the chart (Moon, Venus, and to a lesser degree Neptune) are in these houses, issues other than personal ones affect the emotional life. With Moon in the tenth, the person is apt to have a very personal connection to work and to displace emotions through a career. Those with Moon in the second house tend to make emotional decisions based on financial reasons. With Moon in the sixth, professional contacts tend to become part of an extended family.

In this case, with Moon in the tenth in the stable sign Taurus, she wants to achieve a secure financial base through working and derives emotional satisfaction from career success. So far her chart is set up to teach her that working hard provides personal satisfaction.

Also on the angles is Uranus (eccentricity) at the IC (emotional foundation). This is a very intense placement. It could indicate an unstable early environment, which was not the case in this young woman's life. It also indicates difficulty in gaining emotional support from her mother, which is an ongoing issue. Her mother tends to be too bossy and involved or not involved enough. More important is the fact that Uranus here is playing havoc with both her career and emotions. There is a pattern of constant upsets and changes both in career and her own feelings. The stability described by the Taurus Moon is challenged by the Uranus opposition. She desires stability and security, but it is always being yanked away.

We also notice that the seesaw of the Moon-Jupiter-Uranus opposition (two planets at 180 degrees) makes a T-square (two planets at 180 degrees bi-sected by another 90 degrees apart, concentrating energies) out through Saturn. This is very challenging energy and the most significant thing in this horoscope. With Saturn at the focal point of a T-Square, it's like putting a cork in a bottle of liquid and then heating the container. The energy heats up, things bubble, but are throttled until eventually something has to give and then there's an explosion. Saturn tends to block most of the expression of any energy in this sort of configuration, but not all. In every case, though, there will be major life lessons.

In this case, we could say a thwarted (Uranus) desire for security (Moon in Taurus) leads to hasty action (Jupiter) that doesn't always work out (Saturn). In other words — there are consequences for taking the easy way out.

Planets on the angles are always very significant because they seem to pack a greater wallop than those placed in the interior of a horoscope. In this case, we already see a great deal of information about this young woman. Now let's look at the planets in the usual manner.

Sun in Virgo in the second house indicates a need to earn money and an ability to be good with finance. We might assume she is good at accounting or some such field. Venus (romance) conjunct the Sun makes her pretty and popular, but with Venus in the second house, we see another downplaying of the yin elements. Although Venus in this house can be good for earning a living through creative means, it's not the best place on an emotional level for the planet of love. As we have already observed this with the Moon, we have to say that in this lifetime emotional connections are being downplayed significantly. She is someone who needs to earn a living.

The Sun-Venus conjunction is at the focal point of a T-Square. Mars, (energy, sex-appeal) is in the changeable sign Gemini, opposed by Neptune (illusion). A Mars-Neptune opposition is quite difficult. Although it gives musical ability, it tends to sap energy and to diffuse self-confidence. It's hard for someone with this aspect to be assertive enough, and with Mars in flexible Gemini, the tendency is to let things slide, and thus to take the path of least resistance.

The T-square complicates this further. Mars square Venus is a very sexy aspect, and Neptune square Venus tends to stimulate romantic fantasies. She is a whirlwind of sex appeal which she can't control very effectively. She can always find men interested in sleeping with her, but it's very difficult for her to get other needs met. Mars also receives a trine from Pluto (transformation), and that increases her sexiness even further. It also gives her a bit more strength and resolve about getting her own way and helps shore up the Mars-Neptune issues.

Another interesting configuration to the Sun involves the Uranus-Moon opposition. Uranus is sextile the Sun-Venus, making her independent and somewhat unconcerned about convention. The Moon is trine Sun-Venus, and that is a very nice aspect of friendliness, affection, congenial emotional interactions.

With this horoscope, she always uses her sex appeal to try to get what she wants from life. Although she's had several jobs in the years I've know her, she tends always to return to jobs in the sex industry — as a call girl or exotic dancer. She succeeds on a financial level then, but gets into trouble in her personal life. When she falls for a guy and he learns of her work, often the romance fizzles. Sometimes she hits it off with a "client," and then wants to turn her sex for cash approach to something personal, which never works out. It's very hard for her to see that men who pay for sex don't want a relationship or they'd get a date, not hire a call girl.

There are many life lessons in this horoscope. First of all, taking the easy way out doesn't pay off. Secondly people will value you as you value yourself, which is an interesting translation of the Sun-Venus in the second. But there is more here. Independence is valuable and a source of security. Another life lesson is that if you maintain independence and don't ally your destiny too strongly with someone else's you won't get hurt. But is this really a life lesson? No, because loving and taking risks are good things when done intelligently. It's fear talking. Who among us hasn't had a broken heart? That's the reaction we all tend to have to a broken heart — stay away from romance and we'll be safer. One message in this particular horoscope is that bad things happen when you take risks for the wrong person.

This horoscope tends to guarantee a large degree of unhappiness. Because of her Mars-Venus-Sun stuff, she will always tend to want to capitalize on her sex appeal and take the path of least resistance. But because of the Saturn T-Square, she will get slapped in the face, again and again. The only way for her to gain greater emotional security is to change her profession. She could go into sales and then not fraternize with the people with whom she works, although her chart does not indicate she would make that choice. Instead she might go into sales, but she would always try to turn clients into friends and then problems would ensue.

One of the Karmic tasks with Saturn in Cancer is to learn whom to trust — who is true "family," and who is not. With this horoscope we might conjecture that in other lifetimes, she was sold into prostitution by a family member, and it broke her heart. In this lifetime, she might opt to engage in that practice, but will always guard her heart to some degree. She does get hurt when she's been rejected, but bounces back amazingly fast. Another possible past life sounds like one of those scenarios in the books written by Pearl S. Buck. Perhaps she was a beauty who entered into a marriage with someone rich and powerful who wanted her because of her attractiveness and sex appeal, but as time passed and beauty faded, she was discarded and not cared for or supported. That life lesson would carry over to this one—beauty and sex appeal don't last forever, so don't assume you can earn a living based only on these traits.

With a horoscope like this, we can assume she will make only tiny strides in this lifetime, and it's part of a series of lifetimes designed to hammer home these ideas. It can take many lifetimes to learn these sorts of lessons, and the same behavior is repeated again and again. It's what you might call a vicious cycle. Eventually a glimmer of understanding dawns, and then the person will be born with a slightly different horoscope—there will be built in a solution to the problem. In this one, we see primarily the tendencies and the consequences.

In another example, let's look at the horoscope of a woman who's a success in a creative field, but who has a debilitating weight problem.

Upon first glance, we see two planets on the angles, Moon and Venus. Moon right on the Ascendant is very significant. It means that emotions color absolutely everything that happens to the person in this lifetime. Any planet on the Ascendant is very meaningful because it's an indication that this is energy that hasn't been fully actualized in other lifetimes by the person involved. They're not quite comfortable with the energy and need to become more acclimated to it. So they come in with that energy right on the Ascendant—basically a hit you in the face sort of approach. In this case, emotions are the issue, and she is learning to feel, confront, accept her emotions. Interestingly, Moon in Capricorn is not a terribly emotional placement. Generally that's a practical, security-seeking sort of approach to emotions. With Mercury (thought, communication) opposing the Moon, there's always a need to verbalize emotions. Although with an opposition, difficulty in expressing feelings is indicated, the desire to do so is very important because it means she will have to work to give words to her feelings, helping define them not just for the people to whom she speaks or writes, but also for herself.

Pluto sends a trine to the Moon, deepening her feelings and making them quite intense and important. Moon-Pluto aspects tend to demand control. They bring deep emotional involvements and the tendency to try to make loved ones do what is perceived as best. Of course a trine is an easier aspect than say a square, so in this case the emotional picture is just intensified. We could say though that some of the weight issues are described by the Pluto aspect because she may overeat when she's feeling out of control in the larger context of her life.

There is also a sextile from Neptune to the Moon, adding imagination, dreaminess, creativity and some psychic ability. This is a very beefed up Moon, and the planets connecting to it are quite intense, creating a very strong picture of an emotional world that impinges on every little aspect of her life. Food issues are always emotional, and it's likely that so much emotional energy sloshing around in her life is sometimes hard to take, so it's quite easy to lull

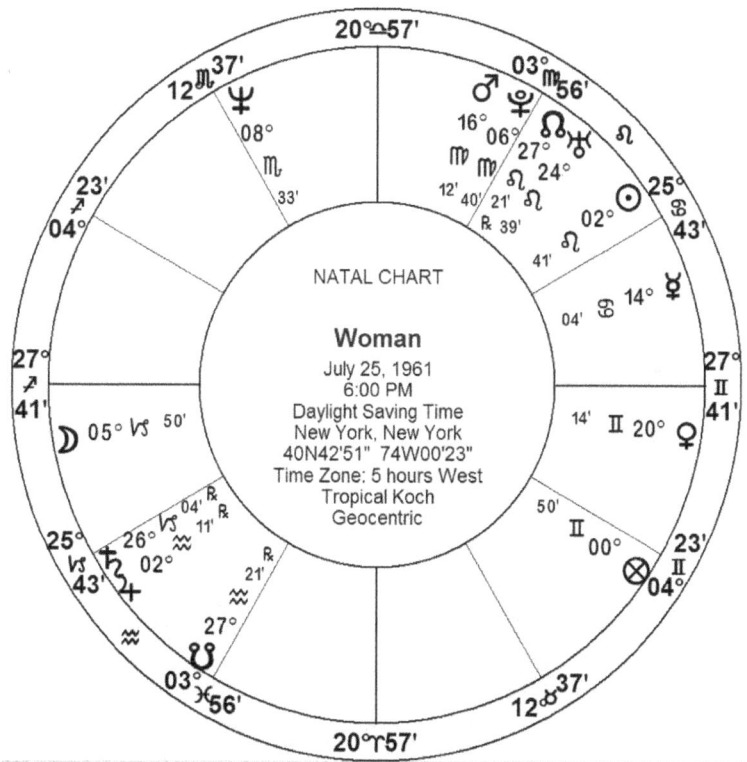

herself with food.

Venus, at the Descendant is similarly emphasized. This should bring her people who admire her, feel she's lovable and attractive, and also bring a mate who concurs. But once again, Venus in Gemini is less emotional than in some of the other signs, but it's quite artistic and good for creative self-expression. It does tend to fall in love too quickly but on the other hand, recovers from heartbreak equally fast.

I have this theory about the yin planets. I call it what you've earned the right to have. A person who comes in with Moon in Cancer understands emotions and feels comfortable with them and has been—for lack of a better phrase—emotionally proficient—deep— for many lifetimes. This person has "earned" this deep and sensitive Moon. Likewise, a person with Venus in Pisces is tenderhearted and very loving and has earned this placement through many lifetimes of giving and kindness. Not everyone can have these placements. Of course not every lifetime would need such intense yin elements, but still a person who has come in with a Pisces Venus would not follow that life with a Gemini Venus. It wouldn't be as deep and loving as they had become.

In this case, the yin elements are very emphasized, but they're not yet fully actualized. It's important for her in this lifetime to work on developing them. Then perhaps in other lifetimes she might move on—and up—to deeper placements.

Sun in Leo is creative and sexy and that is emphasized by being placed in the eighth house of sex. Both Saturn and Jupiter oppose the Sun, offering conflicting pictures. With Jupiter opposing, there tends to be an excess of optimism, which isn't always such a bad thing because it gives a creative person the confidence to put her ideas out there and risk the rejection that always comes in a creative field. With the Saturn opposition, the reverse is true. She has to work harder than other people might have to and she often feels she's behind the eight ball. To combine those elements, we might say that even when life is hard, she has the urge to be creative, so she picks herself up and tries again.

It's important to note the emphasis in the money houses, two and eight. Money will always be a significant issue with this many planets in these houses and we can always assume there is a strong need on her part to make money and build security. Plus, Saturn, as the ruler of the Moon, is present, and Saturn in Capricorn has its own Karmic indicators. With this placement, the person had success in other lifetimes but didn't sustain it and in this lifetime it takes much time and effort to build a solid financial base.

Completing this picture is a difficult T-Square formed by Neptune at the focal point of this opposition. Neptune square the Sun is extremely problematic. It makes it very hard for her to have self-confidence and to know exactly who she is. Neptune always brings the fog and there is always confusion. Neptune squaring Saturn usually brings money problems, and when the second house is involved, this increases. The real question with this planetary picture is can she actually stand up for herself?

We find Mars in the practical, methodical sign Virgo, which is not a terribly selfish placement. Mars here tends to want to help the world get organized. But because it's widely conjunct Pluto, it becomes stronger. People with Mars-Pluto tend to be sexy and self-determining and they don't apologize about wanting their own way. In fact, this is a very seductive combo because the tendency is to seduce other people into giving her what she wants. It's significant that the conjunction is very wide. She is reaching toward this energy, trying to learn to be more assertive, more selfish. If she had a closer conjunction, this would be a different chart.

We also notice that Venus is square this conjunction, increasing sex appeal and creativity. The thrilling thing about writing and any sort of creativity is that you get to let go and lose yourself in the work. You open up, release control, and let the work filter in through you. It's like being driven and it feels very exciting, just as being a sex object can be very exciting because you get all the thrills and someone else does much of the work! That is the essence of the creative process—to release yourself to the muses who inspire and drive you.

This is a very good chart for that because the Neptune square allows her to open up and let creative inspiration in, and the Moon on the Ascendant is very receptive as well. One message of this chart could be that good things come when you allow yourself to be a vehicle for the creative forces of the universe. But that is not the Karmic lessons involved. We would have to modify that and say instead that although good things can come when you allow yourself to be a vehicle for the creative forces of the universe, it's also important to develop your own identity or you will not have a life. Also that it's important to be able to distinguish your own emotions from the vibrations that circulate all around you—and us all. That you can't be a truly creative person unless you have an identity of your own and something personal to contribute. That the greatest truths in art come not just from imagination but from real life, and thus it's important first of all to develop a personal life, but also to use what you live and what you learn when creating art. Emotions are the tool of raw creation!

We might extrapolate that in past lifetimes she was too practical and too buttoned down. She didn't know how to let go or how to ride the wave of her own emotions. Maybe she was a worker bee who toiled away in a boring, practical field just to make a living when her soul yearned to play an instrument, to be on stage as a dancer, or to do something else, but a need for security prevented it. With her Saturn in Capricorn she could have had success and money but ultimately discovered how little they meant to her since she had to sacrifice so much to get them. Perhaps she was a lawyer who wanted to be an actress and so on but lacked the talent to do so yet nevertheless tossed aside her lucrative career and ended her life impoverished. Or maybe she clung to the career and felt that her life had been wasted. It's all about security and what she truly values — what defines security in her mind and heart, and how can she get it. In this lifetime she has the same need for security, but also is learning to let go a little and open up to creative impulses. Another message is that you can find security and make a living while doing what you love, but you need to get in touch with your own emotions and understand what desires motivate you.

The energies in this chart are quite blurred. There is always a reason for that. If someone has to come in with a Neptune-Sun square there is always a purpose. In this case it is to show that sometimes things are clearest when they are most blurry. That is always the case with emotions. Feelings often make no sense at all, but they're usually right, whether or not logic can uphold them. We all have to learn to trust our hearts, and that's what she's doing in this lifetime. She is learning to do what's truly best for her — once she understands what that genuinely is.

This next example is a sweetheart of a guy. A kinder person you can't find anywhere, yet he has severe relationship problems and bad luck with women.

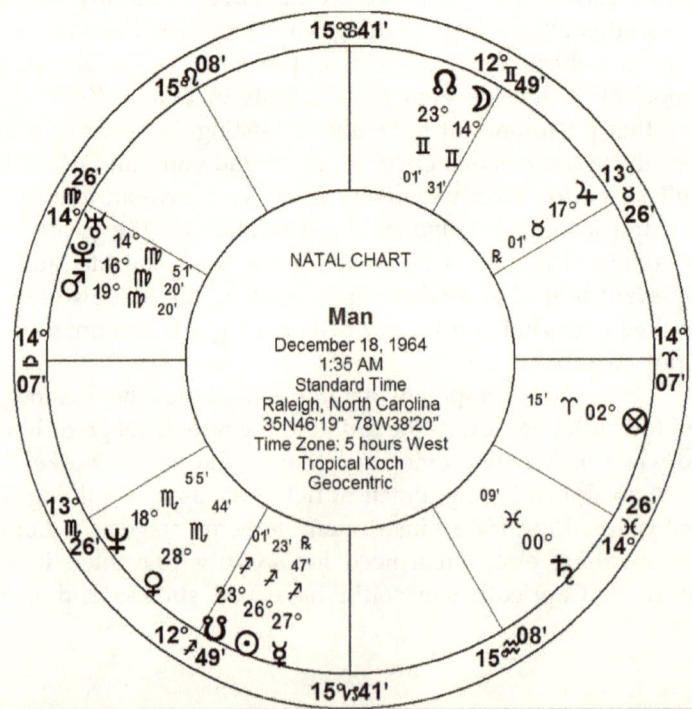

With Sun in Sagittarius conjunct Mercury in the third house of communication, he's a good teacher and enjoys talking to people. The Sun receives a sextile from Saturn, indicating responsibility, stability, and personal discipline.

Mars is a bit debilitated in the twelfth house, and here it tends to function behind the scenes with little accolades. There is a tight conjunction involving Pluto—dynamism and power, and Uranus, giving lightning reflexes, and a desire to be independent and do as he chooses. This cluster of energy is very potent. It could indicate someone quite mercenary, selfish, or even dangerous, but he has channeled it into a martial arts expertise. A trine from Jupiter adds optimism and buoyancy. And a sextile from Neptune adds rhythm, musical ability, and a little spirituality. He wants to use his power for the greater good and to make the world a better place.

Although it's a bit wide at the Uranus point, because of the tightness of the conjunction, we have to say that the whole cluster squares the Sun-Mercury conjunction. This is very intense yang energy. This man walks into a room and people notice him and he seems to have a strong masculine presence.

The Moon is in Gemini, not a terribly emotional placement, and in the ninth house. Often people who have ninth house Moons move far from home and make a new life with people who are quite different from those who qualify as family. Taken together, these elements downplay the emotional intensity.

The Moon is square the Mars-Pluto-Uranus cluster and that amps up the level of emotionality, but not necessarily in a good way. The Mars square bestows deeper emotions, but a tendency to quarrel and to have some digestive upsets. The Pluto square can be rather domineering to say the least, but also increases his need for control and makes the martial arts emotionally satisfying. The Uranus square demands space and freedom from attachment.

In a man's chart, the Moon describes the women he seeks, and in this case we might make the point that the women who are attracted into his life are assertive, passionate, and independent. Another way to say this is that they're bossy, domineering, unreliable, yet manipulative. All of these things have proven to be true.

It's interesting to note that although the Mars cluster squares the Sun and the Moon, those two planets are too widely placed to be in genuine opposition. But if they're both square, should we consider it a T-Square by default? This is always a debate worth considering. Often I will do this because of the way energy radiates, and often something that touches two separate elements will provide a bridge for energy to connect. If we do conclude there is a T-Square, the energy will funnel out through the Mars cluster. That would tend to describe a man who takes refuge (twelfth house) in his masculine pursuits and independence (Mars etc), and who holds other people (Moon) at arm's length, particularly when relationships (Moon) tend to block his day to day life (Sun).

Venus is placed in the passionate sign Scorpio, but lies in the decidedly unemotional second house. Venus is another indicator of the way a man reaches out for feminine companionship, and in this case he's often lost money because of the women in his life. Although Neptune is in the same sign, we'd really have to say it's too wide to be a conjunction. The only significant aspect to Venus here is the square from Saturn in the fifth house. This is difficult. It makes it hard from him to get the love he needs.

Saturn in the fifth is no fun. Saturn is all about work and life lessons and who wants to apply that energy to their love life? Nobody! It also sometimes indicates problems with children, but as he has not yet married, he has no children to consider. The real problem here is that Saturn places limits on his love life — it's hard for him to meet women or to get a romance off the ground, and these problems are not only described by the fifth house Saturn placement, but they're intensified by the square to Venus.

One of the nicer elements in this chart is the Neptune-Jupiter opposition in two and eight. Normally we would say any opposition creates problems, but Neptune and Jupiter work well together. Neptune we would expect to sap his financial strength, but actually Neptune in two often brings great wealth, and that would be increased by Jupiter. He isn't wealthy but he earns good money and feels successful.

His yang elements are strong — perhaps too strong, while the yin elements are downplayed or debilitated. The question is why — and the answer is Karmic. With a horoscope like this we can assume that in other lifetimes he had love, but didn't appreciate it enough. Perhaps he went hunting and left his wife alone for long periods of time, or focused on his own needs but never on hers. Perhaps he was abusive and didn't see the damage he had done. He was all yang and no yin.

In this lifetime, he yearns for more yin involvement but can't get it. Women push him away or take advantage of him. You might say it's a case of the shoe being on the other foot. He is learning that he can be a real man, but that's not enough. Being macho is nice but it's not enough to coddle his heart, and in this lifetime, he is experiencing the yearning for yin energies. As time passes and he lives through various entanglements, he sees again and again how nice it would be to have a woman who appreciates him as much as he does her. But he doesn't find it. Yearning serves its purpose although it's not a happy one. It builds a Karmic sense of appreciation for women and those yin energies. Then in another lifetime he can go one step further and can find someone who gives him a bit more. One way to help that energy along would be to do something selfless in this lifetime. He could adopt a child and give love or volunteer as a big brother, once again giving love and nurturing. It's very useful to be willing to give selflessly with Saturn in five.

It's quite interesting to picture the sorts of lives someone might have lived based on a horoscope. With a little imagination it's possible to come up with a number of scenarios that are very close to accurate. But it's also important to remember to be very careful if you're doing this for someone else. Don't just say "you had such and such a past life," because it will sound very real to the person and can affect them strongly. Say that they could have lived a scenario like this example or that so they realize you're not describing precise events. You can see Karmic patterns very well with astrology but not the precise details and there's no point in scaring someone into thinking they were Jack the Ripper—or Mother Theresa when in fact they probably were not. As always when doing a reading, use caution and good judgment when other people's sensibilities and feelings are involved.

Nancy Frederick is an internationally acclaimed astrologer who has been consistently in print for over twenty years. If you read astrology magazines, you've read Nancy! She has published thousands of articles in all the national astrology magazines. Nancy contributes frequently to Dell *Horoscope* Magazine, with a bimonthly column, many articles, features like the Yearbook, Purse Books and Love Sign Guides. As the founding editor of *ASTRO SIGNS*, she conceptualized the popular mini-magazine, designed its format, and wrote much of its contents for many years. She also wrote most of the contents of *Astrology Your Daily Horoscope* for fifteen years.

She is the author of six books combining various aspects of metaphysics with romance. They are: *Love and Sex Under the Stars*, Dell, 1989 and a new version for 2014; *Tarot: Love is in the Cards*; *The Lover's Dream*; *Palmistry: All Lines Lead to Love*; *Love Games: Psychic Paths to Love*, Lynx Books, 1988

Nancy is certified by many astrology organizations, and has taught astrology privately in New York and Los Angeles, has lectured in New York and taught through the Learning Annex in Los Angeles as well as at conferences sponsored by the AFA.

In addition to being an astrologer, she is a master of the Tarot and uses the cards in her counseling work. Nancy has done much research over many years into other aspects of metaphysics. A spiritualist, she worked for some years with a trance medium, talking directly to spirit and getting information about Karma, reincarnation, and technical astrological details.

Ms. Frederick spends much of her time counseling a large international clientele. She's also the author of six popular novels. Visit www.nancyfrederick.com to contact her.

www.ingramcontent.com/pod-product-compliance
Lightning Source LLC
Chambersburg PA
CBHW031942080426
42735CB00007B/236